THE CAMBRIDGE COM
BRITISH FICTION SI

This *Companion* offers a compelling engagen
end of the Second World War to the present day. Since 1945, British literature
has served to mirror profound social, geopolitical, and environmental change.
Written by a host of leading scholars, this volume explores the myriad cultural
movements and literary genres that have affected the development of postwar
British fiction, showing how writers have given voice to matters of racial,
regional, and sexual identity. Covering subjects from immigration and ecology
to science and globalism, this *Companion* draws on the latest critical innovations
to provide insights into the traditions shaping the literary landscape of modern
Britain, thus making it an essential resource for students and specialists alike.

David James is Reader in Modern and Contemporary Literature at Queen Mary,
University of London. Author of *Contemporary British Fiction* and *the Artistry
of Space* (2008) and *Modernist Futures* (2012), his collaborative volumes on
late-twentieth- and twenty-first-century narrative include *The Legacies of
Modernism* (2012), *Fiction since 2000: Postmillennial Commitments* (2012),
and *Andrea Levy: Contemporary Critical Perspectives* (2014). For Columbia
University Press, he co-edits the book series *Literature Now.*

A complete list of books in the series is at the back of this book.

BRITISH FICTION SINCE 1945

THE CAMBRIDGE
COMPANION TO
BRITISH FICTION
SINCE 1945

Edited by

DAVID JAMES
Queen Mary, University of London

CAMBRIDGE
UNIVERSITY PRESS

CAMBRIDGE
UNIVERSITY PRESS

32 Avenue of the Americas, New York, NY 10013-2473, USA

Cambridge University Press is part of the University of Cambridge.

It furthers the University's mission by disseminating knowledge in the pursuit of
education, learning, and research at the highest international levels of excellence.

www.cambridge.org
Information on this title: www.cambridge.org/9781107562714

First published 2015

Printed in the United Kingdom by Clays, St Ives plc

A catalog record for this publication is available from the British Library.

Library of Congress Cataloging in Publication Data
The Cambridge companion to British fiction since 1945 / edited by David James.
pages cm. – (Cambridge companions to literature)
Includes bibliographical references and index.
ISBN 978-1-107-04023-6 (hardback) – ISBN 978-1-107-56271-4 (paperback)
1. English fiction – 20th century – History and criticism. 2. English fiction –
21st century – History and criticism. I. James, David, 1979– editor.
PR881.C35 2015
823'.91409–dc23 2015016111

ISBN 978-1-107-04023-6 Hardback
ISBN 978-1-107-56271-4 Paperback

CONTENTS

CONTENTS

CONTRIBUTORS

KIRSTI BOHATA is Senior Lecturer in English at Swansea University. She is the author of *Postcolonialism Revisited: Writing Wales in English* (2004), co-editor of *Stranger Within the Gates: Selected Stories* (2008), and guest editor of a 2010 double issue of the *International Journal of Humanities and Arts Computing*. Her interdisciplinary work also spans the digital humanities and disability studies.

PETER BOXALL is Professor of English at the University of Sussex. His recent books include *Since Beckett: Contemporary Writing in the Wake of Modernism* (2009) and *Twenty-First-Century Fiction: A Critical Introduction* (2013). A co-editor of *The Oxford History of the Novel in English, Volume VII: British and Irish Fiction since 1940* (2015), he currently edits the journal *Textual Practice*.

JOSEPH BROOKER is Reader in Modern Literature at Birkbeck, University of London, where he is Director of the Centre for Contemporary Literature. He is the author of *Joyce's Critics* (2004), *Flann O'Brien* (2005), and *Literature of the 1980s* (2010), and he has acted as editor or co-editor of special issues of the *Journal of Law and Society*, *New Formations*, *Textual Practice*, and *Critical Quarterly*.

SARAH BROPHY is Professor of English and Cultural Studies at McMaster University. Her research addresses embodiment, race, gender, and sexuality in contemporary visual culture and literature. She is the author of *Witnessing AIDS: Writing Testimony and the Work of Mourning* (2004) and co-editor with Janice Hladki of *Embodied Politics in Visual Autobiography* (2014). Her work has appeared in *Journal of Literary and Cultural Disability Studies*, *Review of Education, Pedagogy and Cultural Studies*, *Interventions*, *Contemporary Women's Writing*, *Literature and Medicine*, and *PMLA*.

DAVID GOLDIE is Senior Lecturer in English in the School of Humanities at the University of Strathclyde. He has written extensively on Scottish twentieth-century literature, from essays in *The Oxford History of the Novel in English* (2011) and *The Cambridge Companion to Scottish Literature* (2012) to articles in the *International Journal of Scottish Literature*, the *Review of Scottish Culture*, and the *London Review of Books*. He is the co-editor, with Gerard Carruthers and Alastair Renfrew, of *Beyond Scotland: New Contexts for Twentieth-Century Scottish Literature* (2004) and, with Roderick Watson, of *From the Line: Scottish War Poetry 1914–1945* (2014).

WEIHSIN GUI is Associate Professor of English at the University of California, Riverside. He is the author of *National Consciousness and Literary Cosmopolitics: Postcolonial Literature in a Global Moment* (2013) and editor of an essay anthology on the Singaporean poet Arthur Yap, entitled *Common Lines and City Spaces* (2014). His essays have appeared in *Journal of Postcolonial Writing, Journal of Commonwealth Literature, LIT: Literature Interpretation Theory*, and *Pacific Coast Philology*.

MATTHEW HART is Assistant Professor of English and Comparative Literature at Columbia University. He is the author of *Nations of Nothing But Poetry* (2010) and has published articles and chapters in venues such as *ALH, The Cambridge Companion to the Twentieth-Century English Novel, Contemporary Literature, MFS*, and *The Oxford History of the Novel*. He is co-editor, with Jim Hansen, of *Contemporary Literature and the State* (2008), a special issue of *Contemporary Literature*, of which he is also an associate editor. With David James and Rebecca L. Walkowitz, he is the founding co-editor of the *Literature Now* book series, published by Columbia University Press.

DOMINIC HEAD is Professor of English at the University of Nottingham. His previous publications include *The Modernist Short Story* (1992), *The Cambridge Introduction to Modern British Fiction* (2002), *The State of the Novel* (2008), and, as editor, *The Cambridge Guide to Literature in English* (third edn., 2006). He has also published monographs on Nadine Gordimer, J.M. Coetzee, and Ian McEwan. He is currently finishing *Modernity and the Rural English Novel* and editing *The Cambridge History of the English Short Story* (both forthcoming with Cambridge University Press).

KASIM HUSAIN is a PhD candidate in English and cultural studies at McMaster University in Hamilton, Canada. His dissertation, entitled 'Race, Religion and the Cultural Politics of Neoliberalism in the Contemporary British Novel', articulates a method of reading the history of neoliberalism in the United Kingdom in relation to migration narratives and second-generation *bildungsroman*. His research has appeared in *Postcolonial Text, South Asian History and Culture*, and Chandrima Chakraborty, ed., *Mapping South Asian Masculinities* (2015).

JULIA JORDAN is Lecturer in Post-1945 Literature in the Department of English Language and Literature at University College London. Author of *Chance and the Modern British Novel* (2010), she has edited *B. S. Johnson and Postwar Literature* (2014) in addition to an anthology of Johnson's writing, *Well Done*

God! (2013). Her work on twentieth-century avant-garde and experimental writing has appeared in *Textual Practice, Critique,* and *Modern Language Review*. She is currently working on a book about accidents in contemporary fiction.

MICHAEL LEMAHIEU is Associate Professor of English and director of the Pearce Centre for Professional Communication at Clemson University. He is the author of *Fictions of Fact and Value: The Erasure of Logical Positivism in American Literature, 1945–1975* (2013) and co-editor of the journal *Contemporary Literature*.

NICKY MARSH is Professor of English at the University of Southampton. Author of *Money, Speculation and Finance in Contemporary British Fiction* (2007) and *Democracy in Contemporary US Women's Poetry* (2007), she is also co-editor of *Literature and Globalization* (2010) and *Show Me the Money: The Image of Finance, 1700 to the Present* (2014).

EMMA PARKER is Reader in Postwar and Contemporary Literature at the University of Leicester. She is the author of *Kate Atkinson's* Behind the Scenes at the Museum: *A Reader's Guide* (2002), editor of *Contemporary British Women Writers* (2004), and co-editor of the journal *Contemporary Women's Writing*. She is currently co-editing, with Mary Eagleton, *The Palgrave History of British Women's Writing, 1970–Present,* and she is a founding member of the Contemporary Women's Writing Association (www.the-cwwa.org).

AARTHI VADDE is Assistant Professor of English and International Comparative Studies at Duke University. She specializes in twentieth- and twenty-first-century Anglophone literature and globalization studies. Her essays on contemporary literature, transnational modernism, postcolonialism, and environmentalism have appeared in such venues as *Novel, Comparative Literature, Public Books, Modern Fiction Studies,* and *Ariel*. She is currently completing a book entitled *Chimeras of Form,* which charts the aesthetic innovations of modernist writing in relation to colonial and contemporary philosophies of internationalism.

DANIEL WESTON is Lecturer in Twentieth-Century English Literature at the University of Hull. His research focuses on literary representations of landscape, place, and environment, with particular emphasis on contemporary poetry, fiction, and non-fiction. Integrating textual analysis and cultural geography, his latest work considers ecology and literary form. His articles have appeared in *Cultural Geographies, Journal of D. H. Lawrence Studies, Textual Practice, Contemporary Literature,* and *C21 Literature*.

ACKNOWLEDGEMENTS

In preparing this *Companion* I've had the good fortune of working with outstanding contributors who have brought to their topics critical insight and flair. They have managed to do justice to the necessarily pedagogical aspects of a volume of this kind, while nonetheless opening up new and urgent areas of exploration by drawing on some of the field's latest scholarly developments. Striking that balance is no mean feat, but it's a task that my authors here have embraced with great energy and commitment. I thank Ray Ryan for inviting me in the first place to conceive this volume for the Cambridge list, and for encouraging me to take some risks with it, too. His generous advice in the early stages has been matched only by his generous patience in the later ones. Also at the Press, Caitlin Gallagher has been the epitome of efficiency and reassurance, especially as this manuscript neared submission. The Press's scrupulous copy-editing and production teams have, as ever, been a pleasure to work with. A final debt of gratitude is owed to the Victoria Miro Gallery, and to Idris Khan for permitting us to use his captivating work.

CHRONOLOGY

1945   Henry Green, *Loving*; George Orwell, *Animal Farm*;
Christopher Isherwood, *The Berlin Stories*
Soviet Red Army liberates Auschwitz and Birkenau camps in
January. VE-Day on 8 May. Atomic bombing of Hiroshima
on 6 August and of Nagasaki on 9 August. August revolution
in Vietnam. Clement Attlee's Labour Party wins election over
Winston Churchill's Conservatives.

1946   Green, *Back*; Somerset Maugham, *Then and Now*
Winston Churchill delivers the 'Iron Curtain' speech at
Westminster College, Fulton, Missouri. United States con-
ducts atomic weapons tests at Bikini Atoll in the Pacific.

1947   Malcolm Lowry, *Under the Volcano*
Nationalisation of British coal mining. Cold War commences.
Truman Doctrine of containment implemented.

1948   Sylvia Townsend Warner, *The Corner That Held Them*

1949   Elizabeth Bowen, *The Heat of the Day*; Orwell, *Nineteen
Eighty-Four*
NATO formed. British Mandate of Palestine terminated.
Israeli declaration of independence.

1950   William Cooper, *Scenes from Provincial Life*; Rose Macaulay,
The World My Wilderness; Angus Wilson, *Such Darling
Dodos*
People's Republic of China recognised by Britain. Outbreak of
Korean War.

1951   Graham Greene, *The End of the Affair*; Anthony Powell, *A
Question of Upbringing*
Churchill returns as PM.

1952   H. E. Bates, *Love for Lydia*; Evelyn Waugh, *Men at Arms*; Wilson, *Hemlock and After*
        Britain becomes a nuclear state after detonating an atomic weapon in Operation Hurricane at Montebello Islands test site, Australia.

1953   Agatha Christie, *A Pocket Full of Rye*
        The double helix structure of DNA discovered by Cambridge University's James Watson and Francis Crick.

1954   Kingsley Amis, *Lucky Jim*; William Golding, *Lord of the Flies*; George Lamming, *The Emigrants*; Iris Murdoch, *Under the Net*
        Food rations end in Britain. Vietnam War begins.

1955   Nigel Dennis, *Cards of Identity*
        Conservatives win election under Sir Anthony Eden

1956   Sam Selvon, *The Lonely Londoners*; Wilson, *Anglo-Saxon Attitudes*

1957   John Braine, *Room at the Top*; Colin MacInnes, *City of Spades*
        Founding of the European Economic Community.

1958   Bates, *The Darling Buds of May*; Alan Sillitoe, *Saturday Night and Sunday Morning*

1959   Alexander Cordell, *Rape of the Fair Country*; Sillitoe, *The Loneliness of the Long-Distance Runner*; Keith Waterhouse, *Billy Liar*
        New Cuban government formed under Fidel Castro. Britain grants independence to Cyprus. Annual 'Commonwealth Day' replaces 'Empire Day'. Conservatives win under Harold Macmillan.

1960   Lynne Reid Banks, *The L-Shaped Room*; Stan Bartow, *A Kind of Loving*; Olivia Manning, *The Great Fortune*; David Storey, *This Sporting Life*; Raymond Williams, *Border Country*
        'Wind of Change' speech delivered by PM Harold Macmillan.

1961   Sid Chaplin, *The Day of the Sardine*; Muriel Spark, *The Prime of Miss Jean Brodie*
        United States ceases diplomatic relations with Cuba. Building of the Berlin Wall commences.

1962   Anthony Burgess, *A Clockwork Orange*; Doris Lessing, *The Golden Notebook*
        Burundi and Rwanda become independent. Cuban Missile Crisis.

1963   Margaret Drabble, *A Summer Bird-Cage*; Nell Dunn, *Up the Junction*; B. S. Johnson, *Travelling People*; Alexander Trocchi, *Cain's Book*
        Charles de Gaulle rejects the United Kingdom's entrance into the European Economic Community. Martin Luther King Jr. delivers 'I Have a Dream' speech in Washington, DC. John F. Kennedy assassinated.

1964   Raymond Williams, *Second Generation*; Wilson, *Late Call*
        U.S. President Lyndon Johnson institutes Civil Rights Act. Harold Wilson's Labour Party wins general election.

1965   Drabble, *The Millstone*
        UK Race Relations Act introduced.

1966   Jean Rhys, *Wide Sargasso Sea*
        Britain suspends trade relations with Rhodesia.

1967   Angela Carter, *The Magic Toyshop*
        Abortion Act, legalising termination. UK Sexual Offences Act, decriminalising homosexuality.

1968   Bowen, *Eva Trout*; Barry Hines, *A Kestrel for a Knave*; Powell, *The Military Philosophers*
        Martin Luther King Jr. assassinated in Memphis, TN. Student protests and mass strikes in Paris against the de Gaulle administration in May.

1969   John Fowles, *The French Lieutenant's Woman*; B. S. Johnson, *The Unfortunates*; Bernice Rubens, *The Elected Member*
        UK Divorce Reform Act.

1970   Muriel Spark, *The Driver's Seat*; J. G. Farrell, *Troubles*
        Labour lose election to Conservative Party led by Edward Heath. Equal Pay Act.

1971   Lessing, *Briefing for a Descent into Hell*; Johnson, *House Mother Normal*; V. S. Naipaul, *In a Free State*
        Immigration Bill, restricting the automatic right of Commonwealth citizens to remain in the UK. Founding of Greenpeace.

1972   Carter, *The Infernal Desire Machines of Doctor Hoffman*;
         Margaret Drabble, *The Needle's Eye*; John Berger, *G*
         Miners' strike. 'Bloody Sunday' in Northern Ireland.

1973   Martin Amis, *The Rachel Papers*; J. G. Ballard, *Crash*; J. G.
         Farrell, *The Siege of Krishnapur*
         Britain joins the European Economic Community. Yom
         Kippur War in October (Sinai and Golan Heights).

1974   Martin Amis, *Dead Babies*; Lessing, *The Memoirs of a
         Survivor*; Murdoch, *The Sacred & Profane Love Machine*
         Labour wins election under Harold Wilson.

1975   Ian McEwan, *First Love, Last Rites*; Salman Rushdie, *Grimus*;
         Selvon, *Moses Ascending*
         Margaret Thatcher becomes Tory leader. Sex Discrimination
         Bill.

1976   Storey, *Saville*
         UK Race Relations and Domestic Violence Acts. Notting Hill
         Riots.

1977   Carter, *The Passion of New Eve*; Drabble, *The Ice Age*

1978   McEwan, *The Cement Garden*; Fay Weldon, *Praxis*; Murdoch,
         The Sea, the Sea

1979   Carter, *The Bloody Chamber and Other Stories*; Naipaul,
         A Bend in the River; Penelope Fitzgerald, *Offshore*
         Thatcher's Conservative Party wins the general election, begin-
         ning four consecutive terms in government (ending 1997).

1980   William Golding, *Rites of Passage*; Graham Swift, *The
         Sweetshop Owner*; Julian Barnes, *Metroland*
         Ronald Regan becomes U.S. president.

1981   McEwan, *The Comfort of Strangers*; Rushdie, *Midnight's
         Children*; Swift, *Shuttlecock*

1982   Swift, *Learning to Swim and Other Stories*; Pat Barker, *Union
         Street*; Kazuo Ishiguro, *A Pale View of Hills*; Timothy Mo,
         Sour Sweet; John Wain, *Young Shoulders*
         The Falklands conflict.

1983   Michèle Roberts, *The Visitation*; Rushdie, *Shame*; Swift,
         Waterland

1984   Amis, *Money*; Barker, *Blow Your House Down*; Barnes, *Flaubert's Parrot*; Carter, *Nights at the Circus*; Anita Brookner, *Hotel du Lac*
            Miners' strike. Conservative Party Conference at Brighton bombed by the IRA.

1985   Jeanette Winterson, *Boating for Beginners*; Caryl Phillips, *The Final Passage*; Peter Ackroyd, *Hawksmoor*

1986   Ishiguro, *An Artist of the Floating World*; Jim Crace, *Continent*; Kingsley Amis, *The Old Devils*

1987   McEwan, *The Child in Time*; Penelope Lively, *Moon Tiger*; Drabble, *The Radiant Way*; Naipaul, *The Enigma of Arrival*
            Stock market crash. Conservatives led by Thatcher elected for a third term in government.

1988   Rushdie, *The Satanic Verses*; Alan Hollinghurst, *The Swimming Pool Library*; David Lodge, *Nice Work*; Bruce Chatwin, *Utz*; Swift, *Out of This World*
            National Curriculum introduced to UK schools by the Education Reform Act.

1989   Amis, *London Fields*; Barnes, *A History of the World in 10½ Chapters*; Ishiguro, *The Remains of the Day*; Winterson, *Sexing the Cherry*; James Kelman, *A Disaffection*; Rose Tremain, *Restoration*
            Dismantling of the Berlin Wall, closing the Cold War. Iran issues fatwa against Salman Rushdie.

1990   Hanif Kureishi, *The Buddha of Suburbia*; A. S. Byatt, *Possession*; Nicholas Mosley, *Hopeful Monsters*
            Unification of East and West Germany.

1991   Amis, *Time's Arrow*; Barker, *Regeneration*; Carter, *Wise Children*; Phillips, *Cambridge*; Ben Okri, *The Famished Road*; Iain Sinclair, *Downriver*
            Gulf War begins.

1992   McEwan, *Black Dogs*; Winterson, *Written on the Body*; Alasdair Gray, *Poor Things*; Swift, *Ever After*
            Conservative Party led by John Major wins general election.

1993   Barker, *The Eye in the Door*; Irvine Welsh, *Trainspotting*; Phillips, *Crossing the River*

1994   Jonathan Coe, *What a Carve Up!*; Romesh Guneskekera, *Reef*; Hollinghurst, *The Folding Star*; Kelman, *How Late It Was, How Late*; Rushdie, *East, West*
First women priests ordained by the Church of England.

1995   Amis, *The Information*; Barker, *The Ghost Road*; Nick Hornby, *High Fidelity*; Ishiguro, *The Unconsoled*; Rushdie, *The Moor's Last Sigh*

1996   Helen Fielding, *Bridget Jones's Diary*; Alex Garland, *The Beach*; Swift, *Last Orders*

1997   Amis, *Night Train*; Crace, *Quarantine*; McEwan, *Enduring Love*; Will Self, *Great Apes*; Sinclair, *Lights Out for the Territory*; Winterson, *Gut Symmetries*
Princess of Wales dies in a car accident in Paris with Dodi Fayed. Referendums held on Scottish and Welsh devolution. Labour government elected under Tony Blair's leadership. Hong Kong returned to China.

1998   Pat Barker, *Another World*; Nicola Barker, *Wide Open*; Justin Cartwright, *Leading the Cheers*; A. L. Kennedy, *Original Bliss*; Kureishi, *Intimacy*; McEwan, *Amsterdam*
Peace agreement reached in Northern Ireland.

1999   Crace, *Being Dead*; Glenn Patterson, *The International*; Rushdie, *The Ground Beneath Her Feet*; Tremain, *Music and Silence*

2000   Ishiguro, *When We Were Orphans*; David Mitchell, *Ghostwritten*; Zadie Smith, *White Teeth*
George W. Bush elected U.S. president. Vladimir Putin becomes Russian president.

2001   Barker, *Border Crossing*; McEwan, *Atonement*; Rushdie, *Fury*; Rachel Seifert, *The Dark Room*; Winterson, *The PowerBook*
Twin Towers in New York destroyed by coordinated terrorists attacks on September 11. Tony Blair's Labour government is re-elected.

2002   Jon McGregor, *If Nobody Speaks of Remarkable Things*; Zadie Smith, *The Autograph Man*; Sarah Waters, *Fingersmith*

2003   Monica Ali, *Brick Lane*; Amis, *Yellow Dog*; Pat Barker, *Double Vision*; Mark Haddon, *The Curious Incident of the*

Dog in the Night-Time; Patterson, *Number 5*; Phillips, *A Distant Shore*; Swift, *The Light of Day*
Second Gulf War (Iraq war) begins in March.

2004 Hollinghurst, *The Line of Beauty*; Kennedy, *Paradise*; Andrea Levy, *Small Island*; Lodge, *Author, Author*; Mitchell, *Cloud Atlas*
European Union expands to include Cyprus, the Czech Republic, Estonia, Hungary, Latvia, Lithuania, Malta, Poland, Slovakia, and Slovenia. Indian Ocean tsunami strikes on 26 December (following the Sumatra-Andaman earthquake) several coastal areas in Southeast Asia, killing more than 200,000 people.

2005 Maggie Gee, *My Cleaner*, Ishiguro, *Never Let Me Go*; Tom McCarthy, *Remainder* (Metronome Press edition); McEwan, *Saturday*; Phillips, *Dancing in the Dark*; Zadie Smith, *On Beauty*
Labour wins a third term in government under Tony Blair.

2006 Kiran Desai, *The Inheritance of Loss*; Mitchell, *Black Swan Green*; Self, *The Book of Dave*; Ali Smith, *The Accidental*; Waters, *The Night Watch*

2007 Pat Barker, *Life Class*; Kennedy, *Day*; Nicola Barker, *Darkmans*; Lessing, *The Cleft*; McGregor, *So Many Ways to Begin*; McEwan, *On Chesil Beach*
Bulgaria and Romania join the EU. Gordon Brown becomes PM and leads Labour until 2010. Global economy enters a downturn.

2008 Lessing, *Alfred & Emily*; Ross Raisin, *God's Own Country*

2009 Byatt, *The Children's Book*; Hilary Mantel, *Wolf Hall*; Phillips, *In the Falling Snow*
UK officially in recession for the first time since 1991. Barack Hussein Obama is inaugurated as U.S. president on 20 January, becoming the first African American to hold the position.

2010 Howard Jacobson, *The Finkler Question*; Levy, *The Long Song*; McCarthy, *C*; McGregor, *Even the Dogs*
General election results in hung parliament: Conservatives and Liberal Democrats form a coalition, with David Cameron as PM.

2011   Barnes, *The Sense of an Ending*; Hollinghurst, *The Stranger's Child*
Thousands march in London in protest against government budget cuts. DUP and Sinn Féin win majority of seats in Northern Ireland Assembly election. Scottish National Party wins overall majority in Scottish Parliamentary election. Welsh Labour Party wins half of the Welsh Assembly seats. In early August, riots spread across London, Birmingham, Bristol, and Manchester.

2012   Mantel, *Bring Up the Bodies*; McEwan, *Sweet Tooth*; McGregor, *This Isn't the Sort of Thing that Happens to Someone Like You*; Self, *Umbrella*; Zadie Smith, *NW*
Queen Elizabeth II celebrates Diamond Jubilee. London hosts Olympic Games in July and August. Obama re-elected U.S. president.

2013   Kate Atkinson, *Life after Life*; Iain Banks, *The Quarry*; Jim Crace, *Harvest*
House of Lords approves same-sex marriage bill.

2014   Jacobson, *J*; McEwan, *The Children Act*; Mitchell, *The Bone Clocks*; Self, *Shark*; Ali Smith, *How to Be Both*
Ebola virus epidemic breaks out across West Africa. Israel launches 'Operation Protective Edge' in Gaza, costing the lives of 66 Israeli military personnel and killing 1,462 Palestinian civilians (according to UN figures), including 495 children and 253 women. National referendum on Scottish independence: with a turnout of 84.5 per cent, Scotland votes 'No' (55.3 per cent to 44.7 per cent).

2015   Sarah Hall, *The Wolf Border*; Ishiguro, *The Buried Giant*; McCarthy, *Satin Island*; Andrew O'Hagan, *The Illuminations*; Phillips, *The Lost Child*
Church of England appoints Rev. Libby Lane as Britain's first woman Bishop. Tributes are paid in London in January to the victims of the *Charlie Hebdo* terrorist attacks in Paris. Defying all predictions, the Conservatives win May general election and David Cameron forms a majority government. In a historic landslide victory, the Scottish National Party led by Nicola Sturgeon wins 56 out of 59 seats in Scotland.

DAVID JAMES

Introduction: Critical Constructions of British Fiction since 1945

Overlapping generations of writers with diverse ambitions, backgrounds, and commitments have ensured that British fiction since the Second World War evades neat portraits of affiliation or progression, in mode as well as in matter. Classifications become hard to justify, because of the multiple ways in which late twentieth- and twenty-first-century writers have imaginatively responded to the era's changing social realities, and because '[c]reativity itself', as British-Guyanese writer Fred D'Aguiar observes, 'cannot be contained for long in any fashion or vice-hold which the process of naming and compartmentalizing seeks to promote'.[1] Moreover, the very construction of this field faces one obvious logistical consideration: the ever-expanding end-dates for 'post-1945' as a periodising rubric make comprehensive accounts of so many decades of cultural transformation seem increasingly unviable. Still, undaunted, this *Companion* provides its own atlas of an era whose unwieldy temporality and perpetually moving horizon do nothing to discredit its usefulness in framing some of the most significant developments in British fiction.

Although it does not pretend to grant an exhaustive coverage, this collection does intend to offer distinctive commentaries, drawing on some of the field's latest areas of critical interest. In what follows, chapters range from surveys of writers working within particular national and regional traditions to readings that pursue fiction's responses to financial upheaval, that trace the impact of new technologies on the literary rendition of perception and embodiment, that chart the novel's engagement with conditions of globalisation, and that situate formal innovations within transnational parameters. By embracing the challenge of creating a stylistically attentive, historically attuned and pedagogically valuable roadmap of literary fiction since mid-century, this *Companion* utilises a broad lexicon of critical concepts and procedures that the study of postwar British writing now deserves.

In the 1960s and 1970s, such critical vocabularies often circulated around the fortunes of the novel as a cultural form. Debates centred on how writers were extending or repudiating modernism's legacy of formal experimentation, whether they followed the aesthetic and political trajectories of social realism's postwar renaissance, and how they navigated the impulses of an emergent postmodernism towards self-referentiality and textual play. For some critics, the direction was clear: the novel had reached a watershed moment in wake of modernism, such that writers in the 1950s 'participated in the rejection of experimental forms', as Rubin Rabinovitz asserted, 'and a return to a more traditional style'.[2] Undoubtedly, this was a time when the 'social novel' rose to prominence thanks to emerging figures such as Alan Sillitoe, Kingsley Amis, and John Braine, among others. In characterising the period, Raymond Williams detected a 'return to older forms, and to specifically English forms, especially by comparison with the most widely discussed work of the 1920s and 1930s, which was largely experimental in form and cosmopolitan in spirit'.[3] Today, scholars are revising this portrait of the early postwar years as a phase of retrogression and provincialisation. Not only do we now appreciate how such writers as Sillitoe or Barry Hines were hardly straightforward 'realists', combining as they do episodes of psychological interiority that catalysed innovations in imagery, syntax, and narrative perspective. We can also realign the national coordinates of 'British fiction' to include its postcolonial agents of change. Immigrant writers including Sam Selvon and George Lamming capitalised on the global reception and institutionalisation of modernist principles. By extending the project of aesthetic experimentalism for an arena of metropolitan intellectuals, they entered and perpetuated a sphere of artistic prestige, as Peter Kalliney has shown, despite the formidable racial disenfranchisements they were likely to face in daily life.[4] Their fictions of migration and taxing assimilation are a testament to how vibrant and differentiated fiction's development was in the immediate years following the War, in contrast to received opinions about its social realist orientation. Such is the evidence, if we ever needed it, of the way the forms and purposes of postwar narrative remain resistant to schematic categorisation.

Nonetheless, bifurcations of realism and experimentation die hard in criticism on this period. While Malcolm Bradbury reminds us that 'realism can be a form of radical experimentalism' just as 'experimental novels are concerned with exploring and discovering, if not directly depicting, a reality',[5] the distinction has persisted because of the novel's propensity to be apprehended as a chiefly referential medium. Thanks to this long-standing 'humanist reading of the novel', writes Andrzej Gasiorek, 'as primarily realist and essentially liberal', critics have 'tended to pit realism against experimentalism, conceiving them as opposites rather than as writing practices that stand in a complex, mutually interanimating relation to one another'.[6] These divisions provoked an 'oscillation', as Bradbury termed it, 'between two views of the novel, one as a report on history and the social and moral world, the other of it as a self-conscious and self-discovering fiction'.[7] One of the most influential versions of this split vision came from Iris Murdoch, whose 1961 essay 'Against Dryness' portrayed postwar novelists confronted by forking tendencies: either writers were wedded to a 'journalistic' mode of realism or else they remained seduced by a self-absorbed and consoling 'crystalline' aesthetic, a hangover from high modernism.[8] Less severe though equally reliant on an image of binary options, David Lodge also saw fiction in 1969 standing before a set of 'crossroads' where realist imperatives intersected the more adventurous path to formal innovation. Here, the stakes of fiction's survival were located in the writer's capacity – informed by postmodernism's positive and enabling influence – to incorporate some awareness of the constructive possibilities of self-reflexive representation, instead of 'continuing serenely along the road of fictional realism'.[9]

Even amid this rhetoric of compromises and crossing paths, critical prognoses of fiction's wellbeing at the time could also sound decidedly upbeat. Evaluating the 'situation of the novel' in 1970, Bernard Bergonzi was largely optimistic, suggesting that '[i]n the arena where novels are produced, publicized, reviewed and, presumably, read, there is every indication that the form is in a state of high vitality'.[10] Indeed, whatever despondency there was could be found less in the writing than in the criticism practiced upon it, highlighting what Bergonzi called 'a paradox in the fact that despite the commitment of novelists to the power and authority of the fictional form, critics have for a long time been predicting the end of the novel, in tones ranging from cool indifference to apocalyptic gloom'.[11] It would be heartening to imagine that more than forty years later this paradox might now be resolved or rebuked. But some of our most inventive writers today are perpetuating the doomsaying: 'The literary novel as an art work and a narrative art form central to our culture is indeed dying before our eyes'. So declared Will Self, using the occasion of his 2014 Richard Hillary memorial lecture at Oxford to offer not only a desolate forecast of the novel's fate in a digital age, but also a waspish characterisation of commentators who spend time working on it: 'Literary critics – themselves a dying breed, a cause for considerable schadenfreude on the part of novelists – make all sorts of mistakes, but some of the most egregious ones result from an inability to think outside of the papery prison within which they conduct their lives' work'.[12] Self appears unwilling to acknowledge the wealth of scholarship that has felt no need to declare the death of printed books in order to analyse how literary creativity reacts to digital contexts or how narrative genres operate within and adapt to contemporary media ecologies.[13] Beyond the academy, there's a sense here too that the fiction-reading public is not given its due. Because

general readers, as Self implies, are now drawn more readily to their tablets
rather than to the printed word, they are no longer on par with 'the kind of
psyche implicit in the production and consumption of serious novels (which
are what, after all, serious artists produce)', a sensibility that 'depends on a
medium that has inbuilt privacy'.[14] Lured away from the page by portable
devices and forever short for time, contemporary readers are left in this
scenario with an appetite merely for 'the naïve and uncritical realism', as
Tom McCarthy denounces it, 'dominating contemporary middlebrow fiction'. This population of potential novel-readers are emblematic, in Self's
words, of the 'current resistance of a lot of the literate public to difficulty in
the form'.[15] Arguments of this type about the waning of educated readers'
desire for literary (read: *difficult*) fiction tacitly bemoan a lost age for literature's apparent supremacy, when avid audiences supposedly had a greater
aptitude for tackling the 'serious' novel without distraction. Beneath the
despondent surface of such verdicts on the state of fiction flows an undercurrent of nostalgia that's as speculative as it is sullen.

Diagnoses of the novel's postwar journey into obsolescence or middlebrow
naivety after the audacious monuments of early twentieth-century modernism soon sound empirically insubstantial and needlessly polemical, once we
understand in more culturally plural terms what fiction-reading has actually
contributed to ordinary lives – irrespective of the diversions nowadays of
digital communication and entertainment – together with the varieties of
affective work it continues to carry out.[16] Correlations between the state of
fiction and the state of reading can also become (as in Self's case) conspicuously selective in an age of world literature, when they rest on conjectures
about the inclinations of primarily Anglo-American audiences. Furthermore,
they are far from unprecedented, echoing commentators in the past who
have had similar axes to grind. In the early 1990s, D. J. Taylor, for instance,
began his own barbed account of the novel in postwar Britain by warning
that '[s]ooner or later … anyone seriously interested in modern fiction will
be forced to confront an enquiry which is more or less unanswerable: why
devote so much attention to an art-form which nearly everybody admits is in
a wretched state, and in which large numbers of intelligent people have lost
interest?'[17] Among those people who are 'intelligent' and 'seriously interested
in modern fiction' we could surely include the readers of this *Companion*,
who – by virtue of their willingness to dedicate rather more attention to
challenging fiction than perhaps critics like Taylor and Self presume – ensure
that the study and discussion of postwar writing expands precisely in ways
that question generalising assumptions about the state British fiction is in.
Since vigorous 'debate about the novel', as Doris Lessing reflected in 1971,
'has been going on since the novel was born', the very continuance of such

debates today says more about fiction's endurance than its enervation.[18] That '[c]ultural contest enacts itself through our subjectivities', in Alan Sinfield's phrase, suggests that fiction remains a dexterous and adaptable art form most suited to express our subjecthood.[19] As the following chapters attest, fiction is far from moribund with plenty of work left to do in refracting and intensifying our vision of cultures and subjects, past and present.

When fiction's importance as an agent in and commentator on cultural contest alters over time, so does the very vocabulary we use to recognise and describe its efficacy. One purpose of this collection is therefore to afford readers access to the latest insights from distinguished scholars who are working in a field that is advancing in methodologically exciting directions. Of course, whether in the number of writers it covers or in the range of approaches it deploys, no companion could hope to be exhaustive for such an abundant period as this: a period that witnessed both the advent and decline of a welfare state; the consequent polarisation of left and right governments; the expansion of a global economy in which Britain played a smaller part in comparison to the authority it formerly wielded over its now-contracted and dissolving empire; and the move through the 1980s into an era of aggressive privatisation, where commercial deregulation initiated an ethos of competitive free-market internationalism that correlated with the rise of entrepreneurial individualism. It has been, of course, a period of extended, traumatic, and controversial confrontation, too: the thirty-year Troubles in Northern Ireland; the Argentine invasion of the Falkland Islands in 1982; and the coalition combats in the Persian Gulf beginning in the early 1990s and resurging in the Bush-orchestrated 'War on Terror' from 2001, whose initiatives, supported by Tony Blair, included the highly contentious invasion of Iraq in 2003. To trace the full spectrum of fictional responses to these domestic and geopolitical sea changes would be an encyclopaedic exercise – due, indeed, as much to the fictions themselves as to the histories they narrate. 'Random, eclectic, in many cases blatantly hostile to the traditions it supplanted', notes Talyor, 'the great corpus of post-war writing in this country owes much of its randomness and eclecticism to the variety of social factors to which it has been subjected'.[20] Among the most fraught and historically extensive of those factors have been the political, territorial, and religious conflicts in Northern Ireland, the consequences of which for poetry and fiction can be more thoroughly explored elsewhere in scholarship devoted to this particular context.[21]

Accordingly, the goal of this book is to offer readers not so much a definitive survey of each and every sector of fiction published in the United Kingdom, but rather to demonstrate approaches inspired by current domains of critical interest that have opened up new interpretive opportunities. Divided into three parts, the book begins with a series of essays that move from regionalism to migration, provincialism to globalisation, giving attention to writers who capture issues of nationhood and identity that have been 'denied conventional forms of social and political self-expression', as David Goldie argues, by their 'prevailing constitutional situation' (Chapter 3). What contributions to this section also make clear is that to invoke the nation as a critical optic for modern fiction is not to turn away from but in fact to shed light on the wider ramifications of decolonalisation. As James Procter contends, examining the 'regional' work of Pat Barker and David Peace, 'debates on empire and its aftermath have tended to flicker between metropolitan centre and postcolonial periphery while paying scant attention to the internal margins of provincial Englishness'.[22] Turning to immigration across the period, Aarthi Vadde considers modes of 'British fiction centred on the experience of exclusion', as migrant writers dramatize 'conflicts over the meaning of national traditions' and reflect 'upon the significance of collective identity in a multiracial, international society' (Chapter 4).

Part II connects cultural, ontological, and environmental concerns with elements of literary technique, as contributors historically track different registers of queer and feminist writing, new modalities of 'nature writing', and the novel's depiction of scientific and technological advancement. Finally, Part III is devoted more explicitly to questions of form. Here chapters address the generic renovations and transformations that have emerged among the afterlives of modernism and the multifaceted formations of postmodernism, as writers from B. S. Johnson and Christine Brooke-Rose in the 1970s (Chapter 9) to David Mitchell and Hilary Mantel in the 2000s re-envision the futures of novelistic experimentation and reanimate fiction's incorporation of history (Chapters 10 and 13). Listening in to contemporary literature's dialogues with the nuances of postmodern thought, this section follows British writing across a period when some of its most virtuosic practitioners, as Joseph Brooker notes, paradoxically 'speak so authoritatively about the loss of epistemological authority' (Chapter 10). Loss of a more economic kind makes a striking appearance, as well, when Nicky Marsh brings the story of fiction's engagement with cultural crisis right up to date in her account of the British thriller as a genre peculiarly suited to the temper and tumult of global finance (Chapter 12).

By no means all-encompassing, then, these three sections nevertheless showcase alternative ways of conceptualising postwar British fiction as a field. Some areas of focus are all the more valuable for being recuperative: in Chapters 1 and 7, for instance, Dominic Head and Daniel Weston bring back into view localised treatments of regional environments, reassessing the vibrancy of often-overlooked rural narratives of place, habitation, and ecological consciousness. Elsewhere, the critical impetus is one of expansion rather than recovery, as Weihsin Gui 'measures how fiction's play of references and allusions patterns and shapes the worlds it inhabits and imagines', elucidating as he does the forms British fiction assumes to chronicle the contiguities and cross-currents of transnationalism (Chapter 14). Complementing this consideration of the novel's response to what Gui has called the 'sweeping force field of narratives of cultural and economic globalization',[23] Aarthi Vadde and Matthew Hart likewise move beyond a national paradigm to reassess the critical geography of British fiction through globalism: both as a lived experience and as a style of thought. These new frames entail not only an analysis of writers' transnational reception through translation, but also our awareness that the novel's 'global circulation', as Rebecca L. Walkowitz argues, has 'shaped its strategies and forms of appearance'.[24] As well as material texts, circulation of course includes people and communities, commitments and desires – all of which reconstitute social imaginaries and extend horizons of artistic possibility. In this sense, new conditions for social collectivity, racial interaction, and cosmopolitan accommodation amount to more than mere backdrops for those writers concerned with ethnicity and belonging; rather, the 'political and social processes of immigration shape the whole literary system, the relationships among all the works in a literary culture, and not simply the part of that system that involves books generated by immigrant populations'.[25]

Given the scale and implication of these systemic transformations over the second half of the twentieth-century and into the twenty-first, one might reasonably wonder whether the very notion of 'British fiction' is sustainable at all. Perhaps the label is best seen as a critical convenience rather than a point of lengthy contention, a placeholder rather than an imposition, enabling us to make certain practical decisions about selection and organisation. Either way, this *Companion* reveals that there are more interesting and urgent debates circulating today than those concerned about the legitimacy of national denominations. After the Scottish referendum on independence in 2014, devolution may seem imminent in years to come, making the epithet 'British' sound all the more vexed. But then again, that would be a rather presentist assumption: fiction in Britain acquired an extraterritorial disposition and cosmopolitan purview long before political question marks appeared over the constitutional integrity of the United Kingdom. Approaching a form that often 'rejoices in mongrelization', in Salman Rushdie's memorable phrase,[26] critics have been alert for some time to the challenges late twentieth-century writing has posed to settled categories and frameworks. Bradbury, for one, admitted that 'it seems no longer easy to fix on some distinctive contemporary movement or tendency, or treat contemporary writers with a firm critical finality'.[27] In part, his hunch still obtains today, as classifications of modes and movements alike – however historically precise and narratologically robust – give us only partial answers to the question of why some fictions either endure as touchstones for the postwar period or remain so prescient of later cultural moments.

One of the purposes of this *Companion*, though, is to demonstrate how certain collective tendencies can nonetheless be discerned across this aesthetically hybrid and temporally protracted literary scene: tendencies that tell us something fruitful about the development of novelistic technique; about the way present modes relate to past movements; and about how we can group seemingly unconnected writers together via common social, environmental, economic, or philosophical preoccupations without homogenising their aims or compromising our grasp of their work's formal particularities. In short, this volume invites its readers to welcome what is a 'perennial problem with literary history', in Dominic Head's words, the problem being that criticism often 'emphasizes change, drawing chronological lines in the sand that may be preliminary signposts', thereby 'requiring complication and enrichment, so that the way the history is manufactured is constantly under review'.[28] That each new generation of readers will shift the criteria for this review is a prospect as invigorating as it is inevitable. With that shift, of course, our critical language will evolve, too, a process the authors here engage with and energise as they rearticulate the story of British fiction since 1945.

NOTES

1 Fred D'Aguiar, 'Against Black British Literature', in *Tibisiri: Caribbean Writers and Critics*, ed. Maggie Butcher (Sydney: Dangeroo Press, 1988), p. 109.
2 Rubin Rabinovitz, *The Reaction Against Experiment in the English Novel, 1950–1960* (New York: Columbia University Press, 1967), p. 5.
3 Raymond Williams, quoted in Rabinovitz, pp. 9–10.
4 See Peter Kalliney, *Commonwealth of Letters: British Literary Culture and the Emergence of Postcolonial Aesthetics* (New York: Oxford University Press, 2013), chapter 1: 'Modernist Networks and Late Colonial Intellectuals'.
5 Bradbury, 'Introduction to the 1990 Edition', *The Novel Today: Contemporary Writers on Modern Fiction* (London: Fontana, 1990), p. 10.
6 Andrzej Gasiorek, *Post-War British Fiction: Realism and After* (London: Arnold, 1995), p. 17. Similarly, Dominic Head concludes his account of postwar fiction by viewing it as far more stylistically polyphonic than arguments distinguishing realism from experimentation would suggest, urging us to trace 'different brands of formal hybridity, where "innovation" can embrace tradition, and where the reworking of realism can be just as insightful as its rejection'. *The Cambridge Introduction to Modern British, 1950–2000* (Cambridge: Cambridge University Press, 2002), p. 259.

7   Bradbury, 'Introduction', *The Novel Today*, p. 10.
8   Iris Murdoch, 'Against Dryness: A Polemical Sketch', *Encounter* (January 1961), pp. 16–20. For a discussion of the pertinence and implications of Murdoch's term for twenty-first-century fiction, see David James's 'A Renaissance for the Crystalline Novel?' *Contemporary Literature* 53.4 (Winter 2012): 845–74; and, for a consideration of the wider influence of Murdoch's fiction and philosophy, Mark Luprecht, ed., *Iris Murdoch Connected* (Knoxville: University of Tennessee Press, 2014).
9   David Lodge, 'The Novelist at the Crossroads', *The Novelist at the Crossroads and Other Essays on Fiction and Criticism* (London: Routledge, 1971), p. 22.
10 Bernard Bergonzi, *The Situation of the Novel* (London: Macmillan, 1970), p. 12.
11 Ibid., p. 13.
12 Will Self, 'The Novel is Dead (This Time it's for Real)', Richard Hillary Memorial Lecture, 6 May 2014. Retrieved from http://www.theguardian.com/books/2014/may/02/will-self-novel-dead-literary-fiction. Accessed 15 December 2014.
13 See Jessica Pressman, *Digital Modernism: Making it New in New Media* (New York: Oxford University Press, 2014); and Naomi S. Baron, 'Redefining Reading: The Impact of Digital Communication Media', *PMLA* 128.1 (2013): 193–200. For an encyclopedic handbook of approaches to reading multimedia forms, the virtual codex, and cybertextualities, see *A Companion to Digital Literary Studies*, eds. Ray Siemens and Susan Schreibman (Oxford: Blackwell, 2013). For an exploration of the utility of computational analysis for tracing patterns of change in literary culture across time, see Matthew L. Jockers, *Macroanalysis: Digital Methods and Literary History* (Urbana: University of Illinois Press, 2013).
14 Self, 'The Novel is Dead (This Time it's for Real)'.
15 Tom McCarthy, 'Writing Machines', *London Review of Books*, 18 December 2014, p. 21. Self, 'The Novel is Dead (This Time it's for Real)'.
16 See Timothy Aubry, *Reading as Therapy: What Contemporary Fiction Does for Middle-Class Americans* (Iowa City: University of Iowa Press, 2011), a study of the collective effects of empathic experience for nonprofessional readers of fiction. Analysing collaborative contexts for evaluation – Amazon reviews, the Oprah Winfrey book club – Aubry argues that shared emotional responses 'promote forms of recognition, identification, and sympathy among strangers living without the support of stable local communities' (205).
17 D. J. Taylor, *After the War: The Novel and English Society Since 1945* (London: Chatto & Windus, 1993), pp. xiv–xv.
18 Doris Lessing, 'Preface to *The Golden Notebook*' (1971), in *A Small Personal Voice: Essays, Reviews, Interviews*, ed. Paul Schlueter (London: Flamingo, 1994), p. 36.
19 Alan Sinfield, *Literature, Politics and Culture in Postwar Britain* (Oxford: Blackwell, 1989), p. 4.
20 Taylor, *After the War*, p. xx.
21 See Neal Alexander, 'The Carceral City and the City of Refuge: Belfast Fiction and Urban Form,' *Canadian Journal of Irish Studies* 33.2 (2007): pp. 28–37, and also his 'Remembering to Forget: Northern Irish Fiction after the Troubles', in *Irish Literature since 1990: Diverse Voices*, eds. Scott Brewster and Michael Parker (Manchester: Manchester University Press, 2009), pp. 272–83. Also: Elmer

Kennedy-Andrews, 'The Novel and the Northern Troubles', in *The Cambridge Companion to the Irish Novel*, ed. John Wilson Foster (Cambridge: Cambridge University Press, 2006), pp. 238–58; Liam O'Dowd, 'Republicanism, Nationalism, and Unionism: Changing Contexts, Cultures, and Ideologies', in *The Cambridge Companion to Modern Irish Culture*, eds. Joe Cleary and Claire Connolly (Cambridge: Cambridge University Press, 2005), pp. 78–95; O'Dowd, 'New Unionism, British Nationalism and the Prospects for a Negotiated Settlement in Northern Ireland', in *Rethinking Northern Ireland: Culture, Ideology and Colonialism*, ed. David Miller (London: Longman, 1998), pp. 70–93; and Aaron Kelly, 'Introduction: The Troubles with the Peace Process: Contemporary Northern Irish Culture', *Irish Review* 40.40–41 (2009): pp. 1–17.

22 James Procter, 'The Return of the Native: Pat Barker, David Peace and the Regional Novel after Empire,' in *End of Empire and the English Novel since 1945*, eds. Rachael Gilmour and Bill Schwarz (Manchester: Manchester University Press, 2011), p. 203.

23 Weihsin Gui, *National Consciousness and Literary Cosmopolitics: Postcolonial Literature in a Global Moment* (Columbus: Ohio State University Press, 2013), p. 2.

24 Rebecca L. Walkowitz, 'The Location of Literature: The Transnational Book and the Migrant Writer', *Contemporary Literature* 47.4 (Winter 2006), p. 527. See also Walkowitz's development of this argument in 'Theory of World Literature Now', her introduction to *Born Translated: The Contemporary Novel in an Age of World Literature* (New York: Columbia University Press, 2015), pp. 1–48.

25 Ibid., p. 533.

26 Salman Rushdie, 'In Good Faith', *Imaginary Homelands: Essays and Criticism 1981–1991* (London: Penguin, 1992), p. 394.

27 Bradbury, 'Introduction', *The Novel Today*, p. 12.

28 Dominic Head, 'H. E. Bates, Regionalism and Late Modernism', in *The Legacies of Modernism: Historicising Postwar and Contemporary Fiction*, ed. David James (Cambridge: Cambridge University Press, 2012), p. 41.

PART I

Reformations of National Identity

I

DOMINIC HEAD

Mapping Rural and Regional Identities

The idea of the region as a specific locale, characterised by particular activities, and producing identifiable identities, was a staple inspiration for the British novelist before World War II. Although the regional and provincial novel has waned in importance since then, especially in England, occasional important novels in this tradition have appeared in which one of the central themes of modernity – the tension between the country and the city – has inspired inventive treatments. This chapter is concerned with the periodic aesthetic revival of an apparently dying tradition, a mode of writing that has a more significant bearing on continuing cultural preoccupations – and perceptions of Englishness – than is usually recognised.

It should be acknowledged that it is possible to make a case for the continuing growth of the regional novel if the definition of the 'regional' includes urban fiction.[1] We can then see particular moments of regional resurgence, as, for example, in the novels of David Storey and Alan Sillitoe from the end of the 1950s, where the depiction of northern working-class experience took the urban provincial novel in new directions. One might also include London novels such as Monica Ali's *Brick Lane* (2003) or Zadie Smith's *White Teeth* (2000) in this expanded definition of the regional, novels in which questions of ethnicity and tradition intersect in the appropriation of particular metropolitan locales. However, both in the work of the gritty northern realists, and in the moment of multicultural fiction, there are larger national questions that have been the focus of critical attention. Storey's *This Sporting Life* (1960), for example, encapsulates a moment of generational class change and social mobility, as does Sillitoe's *Saturday Night and Sunday Morning* (1958), with an emphasis on the claustrophobia of working-class experience. *White Teeth* frames a moment of multicultural possibility, which seems optimistic in the wake of the political consequences of 9/11: as with Sillitoe and Storey and Ali, the contemporaneous resonance of the novel is not entirely dependent on the regional element. This chapter takes as its focus those novels in which regional/provincial settings cannot so easily be detached from their literary effects, and this is usually the case when the rural is combined with the regional.

The heyday of the rural English novel is to be found before World War II. One reason for this is the simple question of social relevance: changes to agricultural practice and a move away from family farming, together with the development of conurbation and the disappearance of the self-contained village or market town, have consigned the stage of the rural regional novel to the past. While this is indisputable, and certainly explains the comparatively low incidence of serious rural fiction since World War II, it is also true that significant novels engaging with rural themes continue to be written, although the 'regional' element has become increasingly less prominent. Moreover, if the circumstances of traditional rural life are disappearing – and thereby also the immediate inspiration for the rural novelist – this can imply an oversimplified connection between social change and literary response. That connection is certainly significant, but it can also mask the extent to which rural writing can be an ideational engagement with a discursive tradition, and, by virtue of that, an oblique rather than a direct engagement with the contemporary.

The other key social change since 1950, which has dramatically altered perceptions of rural writing, is the end of the Empire and the rapid development of multicultural Britain. This has two interrelated problems for our current appreciation of the depiction of rural space: first, the rural is a site of ethnic exclusivity (although it is a mistake to assume the rural is always a site of privilege at the same time); and second, the historical preservation of rural estates was often dependent on colonial exploitation. These difficulties are prominent in some challenging novels by black British writers that demonstrate very clearly how literary convention and social reality can be brought together in complex ways.

Before considering some of these challenging works – novels by David Dabydeen, Caryl Phillips, and V. S. Naipaul – it is worth considering how the problem of exclusivity has been registered by a writer who has continued the rural tradition in, perhaps, a more committed manner. I am thinking of Adam Thorpe, whose extraordinary novel *Ulverton* (1992) invites us to think about how the formal conventions of the novel in the twentieth century have come to distance writers from the successful evocation of place. Thorpe writes the history of a place – a village in South-West England – over an extended period of history (1650–1988), and achieves this by flouting the usual novelistic emphasis on character. The novel comprises twelve different episodes, each written in a different style, so that the most obvious narrative continuity is supplied by the village of Ulverton itself.

As a novel, of course, *Ulverton* must also concern itself with the human drama, and this is done by placing individual plights in relation to well-known historical events (the moment of Cromwell's Irish campaigns supplies the setting to the novel's framing episode; World War I is the context for its most memorable scene of social interaction), and also by providing historical echoes of characters long dead, even if the recollections are faulty or unjust. This dynamic produces one of the novel's central effects, the simultaneous celebration and distrust of local history.

Thorpe's rich ambivalence in relation to the village community embraces the anti-nationalistic convictions of the local, one of the recurring political themes of rural regional fiction. The tension between the novelist's powerful rendering of poignant moments in the lives of imagined individuals and the impersonal indifference of typical historical tendencies to overwrite the past is partly a demonstration of the power of fiction. But it is also a demonstration of the uncertainty and indeterminacy of living in a small community, and by virtue of that, a warning against the certitude of belonging. This idea is conveyed more starkly in Thorpe's later novel *Pieces of Light* (1998), a return to Ulverton, in which Thorpe makes the idea of belonging in this place, this English village, the central problem. Hugh Arkwright lodges in the large Ulverton house belonging to his aunt and uncle, with an ancient wood in the grounds of the house which Hugh's Uncle Edward believes to be a remnant of the forest that once covered all of England. Indeed, he hopes that this 'wildwood' will reclaim the land, and there is a suggestion that he has been storing nerve gas to facilitate this process. The green fascism of Uncle Edward, who also associates with Nazi sympathizers, is a stark reminder of the dangers of exclusivity and the pursuit of origins in relation to place.

As I have intimated, one reason for the rarity of fresh treatments of rural regional fiction is the rapidly changing social composition of England, especially since the 1948 'Windrush' generation, which dates the emergence of a new form of English multiculturalism. A consequence of this has been a fresh element to contribute to urban rather than rural culture, since the rural is usually perceived as a site of privilege and ethnic exclusivity. This is an idea that was explored by several notable black British writers in the second half of the twentieth century. James Proctor has written an influential account of how rural experience is constructed along ethnic lines. The general problem he identifies is 'the continuity between the black population and the city' and its corollary: the 'discontinuity between the black subject and the country'.[2] There is a resonance here with one of the strands in Caryl Phillips's *A Distant Shore* (2003), a novel that encapsulates the sense of insularity and exclusivity that haunts depictions of village England, yet which also demonstrates how that insularity is self-defeating, out of kilter with social change in general. Solomon (formerly Gabriel), the African migrant fleeing the horrors of internecine war, is murdered by racist thugs. He has a white counterpart, however, in Dorothy, the retired white English schoolteacher who is living a different kind of exile, having been forced to retire early in disgrace. Her mental instability, though occasioned by a series of traumatic personal experiences, has also an emblematic significance: she has the propensity, following the lead of others, to divide the world into sheep and goats, as when she seems to adopt the pub landlord's estimation of local youths as 'louts' and 'hooligans', or when she recounts her mother's prejudice against 'gypsies', a prejudice that dictates her own fear.[3]

Dorothy is an emblem of ethnic self-destructiveness. Her father's attitudes in particular – his Euroscepticism (p. 27), his racism (p. 42) – are at one with the rejection Dorothy experiences as a newcomer to the village of Weston, symbolically isolated in the satellite new development of Stoneleigh. Yet there is also a local geopolitical point, here: the logic of suburban development will eventually erode the logic of discrete village identity. The larger geopolitical point is the sense in which A Distant Shore, as Stephen Clingman has it, maps 'the transnational in the national', albeit 'mainly in negative form'.[4] Yet, while such an enterprise may have a cathartic effect in its implications – narrow nationalistic racism is rendered irrelevant in the face of the inevitability of global migrancy – this does not apply readily to the novel's treatment of place. Dorothy may be the embodiment of a self-destructive tendency, a symptom that can be addressed. However, the depiction of the English village seems irredeemable: it is a space in limbo, unable to encourage more efficacious cosmopolitan tendencies.[5]

David Dabydeen's *Disappearance* (1993) fashions a powerful fusion of literary history, ethnicity, and belonging. It is narrated by a Guyanese engineer, whose craft – learned from an Englishman called Fenwick – is in building sea defences. The novel concerns his arrival and sojourn in the village of Dunsmere to help defend a stretch of coastline near Hastings that is being rapidly eroded. The idea of the subaltern's ambiguous mission in the colonial motherland is prominent, and the symbolism of crumbling post-imperial England is pointed throughout the novel. At the heart of Dabydeen's novel is the relationship between the protagonist and his widowed landlady, Janet Rutherford, who once spent time teaching in an African village, taking it upon herself to undermine the mythology of English pastoral, as her part in the process of political enlightenment and liberation: 'England is more than maidens dancing around maypoles, which is the kind of image we gave the African while our men were pilfering their treasury'.[6] Mrs Rutherford's hope was to have infused her African pupils with the desire to make the voyage to England, and to stake their claim through an informed understanding of the 'mythic power of the garden' (p. 72). But it is a rarefied, intellectual project, a role prevented by brute economics and the poverty foisted upon immigrants, which makes the rural unattainable.

The narrator, however, though highly sceptical about the pastoral route to decolonisation, finally seems to be in a position to fulfil the role that Mrs Rutherford has envisaged, but fails to perform the function of the 'devil in the garden' (p. 159). This restraint is partly determined by his training as an engineer, and the colonial legacy that defines him to an extent. Yet he is also restrained by his 'peculiar and deviant love' for Mrs Rutherford. Having failed to wreak the havoc she desires, he explains, meekly, 'I came to protect your house and to protect you' (p. 159). His sense of imprisonment is captured by the finished sea wall, 'an awesome deformity', which becomes another obvious symbol – in a novel of exaggerated symbolism – of the narrator's identity (p. 177). There is also a sense, however, that Dabydeen's outsider comes to a vantage point of authoritative judgement by the book's close, able to understand one of the fundamental contradictions in rural experience: the potential disparity between the perception of stable English rurality, and the transformations enshrined in the landscape as a consequence of human occupations.

Like Phillips's *A Distant Shore*, *Disappearance* rehearses the inhospitability of rural England to the outsider. Both novels stand in stark contrast to what is probably the most significant novel in England since 1950 concerning ethnicity and rural England: V. S. Naipaul's *The Enigma of Arrival* (1987). Naipaul's novel is a highly original work, and it is easy to see why works such as *Disappearance* and *A Distant Shore* seem to be written in response to it, because Naipaul provocatively bridges the usual gulf between migrant writing and rural literature. Indeed, the exploration of the connection between landscape and migrant identity is at the heart of *The Enigma of Arrival*, a connection that is also a self-exploration for Naipaul.

It is important to realize that Naipaul is not blind to questions of power and ideology. He is acutely aware of the significance of colonialism on the formation of his identity, and makes the investigation of this a studiedly literary matter, with the 'Naipaul' figure emerging as the repository of colonial cultural ideology. The more complex aspect of his quest is the degree of recuperation he engages in, salvaging aspects of the ideology of English identity – the ideology from which he has, partly, established his intellectual credentials – in order to build a new sense of self. The working-through of this contradiction is what gives the book its depth and richness: the literal journey, from Trinidad to rural England, an intriguing instance of postcolonial migration, is enfolded into the conventional structure of the autobiographical novel, the quest for maturity, and the discovery of the materials from which the writer will fashion his work. This is Naipaul's attempt to insert himself into the canon of English literature, but also to enrich and extend the canon, in a familiar pattern of postcolonial revisionism.

If Dabydeen's *Disappearance* is a riposte to Naipaul's novel, it is the outsider status of his narrator that enables him to anatomize the English, and to reveal the connection between the exercise of colonial power and the fantasy of the English garden of tranquillity. He is tainted by his subalternity, but is able to return to Guyana with no discernible loss of self. That kind of dispassionate scrutiny of the imperial legacy is not appropriate for *The Enigma of Arrival*, because 'Naipaul' is not an outsider in the same way. Indeed, the book concerns itself with a kind of negative ideational 'homecoming': the experiences which enable 'Naipaul' to recognize false versions of rural England produce a form of self-negation, too, such that his personal investment in the conventions of rural writing is greater than it is for the authors of those conventions.

This obliges us to temper our judgement of the novel's ambivalent treatment of the rural tradition. It is easy to see a contradiction between the exposure of the false version of England and the writer's desire to keep faith with it. But this paradox also suggests an alternative form of agency, a form of self-discovery through appropriation. The figure of the writer in the landscape, withdrawn, contemplative, is actually the ideal site of agency for the way this transitional postcolonial work is conceived.

Kazuo Ishiguro's *The Remains of the Day* (1989) is another novel in which the immediate political context can obscure the subtlety of its engagement with the tradition of writing about English places. Indeed, an 'orthodox' reading of Ishiguro's novel has emerged, in which the novel's treatment of place is seen to challenge 'the myth of an Arcadian England', with the express purpose of attacking the political uses of nostalgia in the Thatcher era.[7] While this is an intelligent reading of the novel in context, it can have the effect of displacing the central narrative device of Stevens's trip to the West Country as a journey of enlightenment, a journey that invites reflections on the travelogue, and perceptions of place, in ways that are not straightforward.

The problem of place in Ishiguro's novel, and its reception, is complicated by the famous and resonant passage in which Stevens reflects on his vision of 'the rolling English countryside' at the end of his first day's motoring. It is here that he makes the equation between the 'greatness' of 'the English landscape at its finest', the 'greatness' of Britain, and the qualities that make a 'great' butler. The 'sense of restraint' that Stevens associates with the English landscape – and which he suggests is superior to the 'unseemly demonstrativeness' of an African or American landscape – is thus linked, for the reader, with the oppression masked by Stevens's conception of 'professionalism' in service, the 'dignity', which is really obeisance to a dominant ideology. The novel makes clear, through its chain of associations – including the imperial resonances of domestic service, and the Nazi sympathies of Lord Darlington – that Stevens's ideological reading of the English landscape is one aspect of a faded imperial past (and its human costs), in this novel set in 1956, the year of the Suez crisis.[8]

A related issue is the way in which Stevens's journey is mediated by the guidebook in the library of Darlington Hall, one of a seven-volume series entitled *The Wonder of England*, by Jane Symons. This is a fictionalized version of the genre of guidebooks and travel books about Britain, a genre which proliferated in the interwar era, and which is often said to have played a seminal role in the construction of a certain kind of national identity, based on a celebration of rural southern England.[9] There is a sense in which Ishiguro's novel serves to support this standard version of the role of the guidebook in constructing Englishness. The references to Symons's work emphasize the conventional objects of attention for the interwar guide to England: her praise of Salisbury Cathedral sets the limits for what Stevens sees (p. 27), and, diligently pursuing her recommendations, he plans a 'circuitous' route to Salisbury, in order 'to savour to the full the many splendours of the English countryside' (p. 67). However, it is the emerging disjunction between the personal significance of the journey and the anodyne voice of Symons as a guide that is a key part of Stevens's journey. This is most apparent in the concluding scene at Weymouth where his devastating scene of self-knowledge is fully at odds with her superficial prose – she considers Weymouth 'a town that can keep the visitor entertained for many days on end' (p. 231). This is the only time that Stevens quotes her directly, a fact that serves to separate her account from his internal musings, now governed by momentous truths about his life.

It is true that there is a very clear strand of ideological thinking about place and Englishness in the novel, which links the pre-war and postwar settings in relation to national identity, and which contributes strongly to our sense of Stevens as an anachronism. However, while these associations are very much part of the novel's achievements, they can invite a too-dismissive reading of Stevens's encounters with place. There is also another very familiar narrative trope, which is, arguably, the most important structural feature of the novel, and which makes the journey very much the focus: the convention of the figure in the landscape, encountered by the traveller in ways that can prove decisive or transformative. This is a staple feature of the picaresque novel, but there may also be echoes here of the Wordsworthian encounter.[10] It is also a staple feature of some of the English guidebooks that Ishiguro is often taken to be satirizing in an uncomplicated way. The obvious example is H. V. Morton's *In Search of England* (1927), a 'motor-car journey round England' that is usually seen as the landmark text in this emerging genre, and which is structured as a series of illuminating encounters with strangers.[11]

It is important to remember that the rolling landscape Stevens associates with the greatness of Britain, and which might seem to evoke (for example) Morton's 'rounded contour of the West country', is made iconic only through his deluded engagement with it, at this early stage in his journey of personal growth.[12] The series of encounters traces a process of gradual enlightenment. The final scene occurs in Weymouth, where Stevens spends two nights following his heartbreaking encounter with Miss Kenton/Mrs Benn, and where he finally confronts the truth about his life. This occurs at that most liminal of spaces, the seaside pier (at Weymouth), where his breakdown is elicited by another stranger. Stevens is confronted with a future self-image in the lonely retired butler who engages him in conversation and brings forth his revelation: he realizes that he has given up his life for the service of a misguided man, who was at least able to make his own mistakes (p. 243). It is the series of encounters in the West Country that determine the epiphany of Stevens's inward journey. Deploying some of the devices of the travel narrative, Ishiguro presents the English journey as one of discovery, so that by the end of the novel we realize the absurdity of the untravelled Stevens pronouncing on the greatness of the English landscape, in his ignorance of people and place.

Another landmark novel of the 1980s, and one which is often read closely through the lens of its Thatcherite context, is Graham Swift's *Waterland* (1983). This is also a significant regional novel, however, and its credentials in this area give it a resonance beyond its immediate context. After his early novels, Swift makes use of his 'native' setting of suburban south London, producing a complex form of autobiographical spatial poetics, apparently quite distinct from Swift's early work, in which, as David James points out, Swift 'resisted the creative appropriation of autobiographical settings', allowing himself to be 'drawn to evocative places with which he was personally unfamiliar'.[13] *Waterland* follows this principle of evoking an imagined territory, an aspect of the book that can seem unlikely to readers impressed by the narrative power of a book so dependent on its Fenland setting: 'After the success of *Waterland*, Swift surprised (and disappointed) many by denying that he had grown up in the East Anglian Fens'.[14] I want to consider the implications of this 'surprise', the expectation that *Waterland* – the most prominent English rural regional novel of the late twentieth century – must surely have been inspired by personal investment in place.

An interest in the actual landscape is not, however, a pronounced element in academic readings of Swift's novel, a de-emphasis that seems to be justified by Swift's more 'theoretical' interest in what his setting denotes. Indeed, academic critics have focused on the problem of history in *Waterland*, especially in the light of Linda Hutcheon's still powerful and persuasive appropriation of the novel as an exemplary instance of postmodernist poetics, and it is this emphasis that has made the novel seem very much part of its intellectual context. Hutcheon's characterization of *Waterland* as 'historiographic metafiction' pinpoints the postmodern anxiety in Swift's novel about narrating with authority – as a historian or a novelist – and Swift's decision to treat this irresolvable dilemma self-consciously, as his central theme.[15]

There is certainly a postmodern impulse in the motif of silt, which stands in opposition to 'history itself, the Grand Narrative, the filler of vacuums, the dispeller of fears in the dark', and embodies an alternative understanding of human endeavour.[16] This 'process of human siltation – of land reclamation', 'a slow and arduous process', is made to stand in opposition to 'your revolutions, your turning-points, your grand metamorphoses of history' (p. 8). Through this opposition the novel invites a metaphorical understanding of silt and the process of siltation, an analogue for a mundane, unheroic conception of human endeavour and industry, and for modernity, which also 'obstructs as it builds; unmakes as it makes' (p. 10).

At the same time, however, *Waterland* insists on the particularity of the Fenland landscape as a place dominated by the problem of drainage and the control of silt, so that the metaphorical association of the perpetual process of managing land is ultimately disappointed, since it cannot be dissociated from its literal origin. The opposition in the novel can then be figured as the opposition between local and national/international history. More accurately, the opposition is between locatable, regional experience on the one hand, and intangible textbook headline history on the other. The most obvious rhetorical trope in the novel, in fact, is the juxtaposition of the local with the national/international: Thomas Atkinson's achievements in draining land along the Leem are recorded in 'the year of Trafalgar' (p. 60); his maltings at Kessling are completed in the year of Waterloo (p. 61); World War II rages while Freddie Parr drowns in the 'Fenland backwater' (p. 24); and so on. The point of these oppositions serves to distinguish between that which is close to lived experience and that which is abstract, distanced from it. It is this disjuncture that prompts Tom Crick to jettison the history curriculum, and to supplant it with his own story. The French Revolution (confined to a topic) is a function of the history curriculum, whereas the industry of Crick's ancestors have a much more palpable effect, creating (from water) 'a land ... which would one day yield fifteen tons of potatoes or nineteen sacks of wheat per acre', and which would also provide a home for Crick (p. 14). This emphasis on tangible experiences – agriculture, food, home – set against the abstractions of revolution, insists on the local and regional element of vital experience.

If *Waterland* can be seen as a rare exploration of the viability of rural regionalism, in *Wish You Were Here* (2011) Swift offers a more thorough-going engagement with the motifs of the twentieth-century rural tradition, but one with no regional purchase. However, a central effect of the novel is to demonstrate (and lament) the loss of the regional. Indeed, Swift's novel puts a contemporary crisis of farming into an international political context, so that the collapse of a family farm in Devon, a casualty of the BSE crisis, is also associated with other catastrophes: the later cattle burnings of the foot-and-mouth crisis, but also the burning towers of the World Trade Center on 9/11.

Swift can seem to telegraph his meaning in this novel. However, if the book is read in relation to the rural tradition, the apparent clumsiness is ameliorated, because some of the patterning is derived from motifs famil-iar to the rural tradition, consciously 'overworked' in a self-reflexive enter-prise: the son leaving the farm for war; the catastrophic fire; the hallowed place; and so on. In the context of a new form of global crisis that displaces regional self-consciousness, Swift's exaggeration of those plot features asso-ciated with rural regional writing show a range of fictional strategies emptied of their richness in the face of an implacable and homogenising historical moment. Yet the ironic echoes serve the purpose of crystallizing aspects of the current agricultural crisis, implying nostalgia for a rural ideal: sustain-able activity, productive of community, and invulnerable to international events. This productive nostalgia offsets the apocalyptic narrative of the novel, in which modernity, in the form of intensive farming methods and international warfare, threaten the very basis of human subsistence. It also musters a complex literary celebration of the rural by evoking the haunted nostalgia of interwar rural fiction.

This conscious juxtaposition of the contemporary with a past literary-historical moment, in order to illuminate the present, is an inter-esting formal paradox: a managed anachronism serves the purpose of a more precise explication. Something similar occurs in Jim Crace's *Harvest* (2013), a complex and powerful work that insists on historical continuity in its deliberation on the struggle for subsistence. Paradoxically, it is the narrative's very lack of historical specificity – its apparent 'timelessness', a recurring feature of Crace's oeuvre – that forges the historical chain. What we do know for certain is that the action takes place at a particular moment during the several centuries of enclosure, and concerns the introduction of sheep onto common fields, and the breaking up of a small rural settlement. It is a complex elegy for pre-industrial rurality and for the communal values potentially inherent in a way of life now locked into the past. Crace relies on a popular perception about the power shift signalled by enclosure, the shift from people to profit, to underpin the book's moral structure.

The village in *Harvest* is no rural idyll, however. The novel opens with the arrival of three strangers, who claim a homestead on common ground, through the custom of laying a hearth and lighting a fire.[17] These newcomers are soon made scapegoats, wrongly accused of starting a fire at the manor house, and a strong element of the book concerns the insularity of an enclosed community, suspicious of outsiders. To this extent it is a fable about racism and migrancy. But the rural imagination remains prominent. The final meaningful act undertaken by narrator Walter Thirsk is to plough a return furrow in a field earmarked for enclosure, as a political gesture. Together with the surviving male interloper he sets about the task, saving the task of sowing a bag of wheat seed for himself. The passage conveys the satisfaction and the skill of ploughing, a form of set piece that is familiar in rural writing; but here it is overlaid by the anxiety of change, together with the consciousness that the act alone is symbolic. Yet, for Thirsk, there is exhilaration in this final defiant act of ploughing: 'I'm thrilled in some strange way ... the earth abides, the land endures, the soil will persevere for ever and a day. Its smell is pungent and high-seasoned. This is happiness' (p. 233). Crace's achievement here is simultaneously to poeticize and politicise a conventional and prosaic rural activity, adopting the perspective of the (defamiliarised) urban reader.

This chapter has been concerned with the surprising endurance of rural fiction, a paradox encapsulated in J. L. Carr's short novel *A Month in the Country*, first published in 1980, but finished in 1978. From a literary-historical perspective, Carr's novel seems to epitomise a phase of traditional novel writing swept aside (in estimations of its importance) by the wave of fictional experimentation associated with the 'post-consensus' era, especially following the election of Margaret Thatcher to power in 1979.[18] A closer inspection, however, reveals a compelling treatment of ethnicity and identity that is genuinely contemporary.

Superficially, *A Month in the Country* – on the face of it, a rural English reverie, set in 1920 – seems to evoke an uncomplicated nostalgic view of England, its drama of love and loss projected onto a snapshot of interwar England gone forever. In this respect it appears to echo a dominant literary theme of the era in which it is set, a tone set by the officer class returning from the First World War 'determined to preserve the rural England they'd known', epitomised by the traditional English village.[19] The respective commissions of war survivors Tom Birkin and Moon in Oxgodby – Birkin's to uncover a fourteenth-century Church mural; Moon's to find a grave from the same era – are focused on English village tradition, with the Christian church at its heart. The legacy of the late Miss Adelaide Hebron, which funds both commissions, has also a sense of dynastic closure (she is a spinster) and assertion about it: it is an ancestor of hers, the excommunicated Piers Hebron, whose grave Moon has been employed to find. Yet there is a contrary movement which discredits the appearance of English tradition, a theme conveyed quite directly through the symbolic activities of art restoration and archaeology: that which Birkin and Moon uncover explodes the notion of continuity and tradition apparently contained in Miss Hebron's legacy.

In some respects Carr anticipates Svetlana Boym's critique of 'restorative nostalgia', a pursuit of 'truth' associated with 'national and nationalist revivals'.[20] Ultimately, Birkin is in awe at the 'breathtaking' achievement of the revealed work (p. 46). In particular, he is astonished by the portrayal of one damned individual, with 'a crescent shaped scar on his brow', an individual who is so particularised as to suggest a portrait. Moon makes the connection between the falling man in the mural and the excommunicated Piers Hebron, whose grave he eventually excavates to reveal a crescent pendant on a chain, which indicates that Miss Hebron's ancestor – so Moon speculates – converted to Islam 'to save his skin', having been 'caught in some expedition' (p. 79).[21]

Art and politics, already yoked together in Miss Hebron's commission, intersect in the contemporary moment, just as they had in the fourteenth century. The depiction of the outcast Piers Hebron, and his burial site outside the church wall, underscore the in-built failure of nostalgia, conceived as the desire for a return to a spiritual home. The apparent desire of Miss Hebron, to leave a legacy that will enhance the glory of the village church, and her family's place in its history is thoroughly undermined by the discovery of her ancestor's apostasy, which compromises the symbolic role of the church as the Christian heart of a traditional English village community.

The experience of reading the novel, however, produces a less thematic or politicised response, for this is a highly evocative book about a distant summer replete with possibilities. When Moon plans to present the grave of Piers Hebron for public perusal without the crescent, in order to 'leave him with his reputation no worse than it was before' (p. 80), there is a desire for concealment that will preserve the status quo. The reader is being asked to collude with this tampering of archaeological evidence, which preserves an idea of traditional village England.

In a larger sense, this is precisely the tension that orders the reading experience of the book: the evocation of nostalgia as an aesthetic experience creates the idea of a lost world of possibility. This paradox is conveyed by the human drama culminating in Birkin's lost chance to embrace the beautiful Alice Keach: he is paralysed by his desire and cannot respond to her (p. 81). Yet the aesthetic perfection of the book depends upon the lost moment, frozen in time. Indeed, Birkin's whole experience at Oxgodby must remain 'in memory' as 'a sealed room furnished by the past, airless, still, ink long dry on a put-down pen' (p. 85). In the closing paragraphs, the novel's own aesthetic paradox is associated with Elgar, Housman, and the artistic rendering of the English landscape. That which eludes Housman, and the individual heritage tourist who follows in his footsteps, is the feeling of being genuinely at one with place, of capturing an English place without the simple nostalgic sense that the 'moment' has passed.

A more complex and self-conscious nostalgia, the production of which is Carr's notable contribution to English fiction, is what makes this novel so important as an enactment of how the rural idyll continues to haunt our collective consciousness. By virtue of its multivalent treatment of place and cultural memory, *A Month in the Country* is perhaps the most satisfying example of the trend examined in this essay: that rich and increasingly paradoxical remapping of rural and regional identity.

This chapter has suggested that, as the circumstances of rural existence continued to change dramatically after 1945, rural fiction became more concerned with *ideas* about the countryside – rather than with the verisimilitudinous depiction of a settled rural existence – thus extending a literary tradition into a new era of debate about the relationship between country and city. This has resulted in sometimes-surprising allusions to, or deployments of, rural conventions in mainstream fiction. For example, novels such as Ishiguro's *The Remains of the Day* and Swift's *Waterland*, more usually read in the context of Thatcherism and postmodernism, have a stronger connection with the rural tradition than is immediately apparent. Yet the novels considered here also show how familiar postwar literary themes, concerning questions of ethnicity, identity, community, and exclusivity, can also be framed through a fresh treatment of rural conventions. This is a literary legacy that is too often overlooked, revealing as it does a complex nostalgia for the past bound up with an anxiety about the future.

NOTES

1 See, for example, K. D. M. Snell, 'The Regional Novel: Themes for Interdisciplinary Research', in *The Regional Novel in Britain and Ireland, 1800–1990*, ed. K. D. M. Snell (Cambridge: Cambridge University Press, 1998), pp. 1–53.

2 James Proctor, *Dwelling Places: Postwar Black British Writing* (Manchester: Manchester University Press, 2003), pp. 169, 174.

3 Caryl Phillips, *A Distant Shore* (London: Secker and Warburg, 2003), pp. 7–9, 65–6. Hereafter cited parenthetically.

4 Stephen Clingman, *The Grammar of Identity: Transnational Fiction and the Nature of the Boundary* (Oxford: Oxford University Press, 2009), p. 94.

5 For a more detailed discussion of the novel in relation to cosmopolitanism, see Alan McCluskey, 'Contemporary Cosmopolitan Literature: Ethics, Materiality and the Role of Empathy', unpublished doctoral dissertation, University of Nottingham, August 2014.

6 David Dabydeen, *Disappearance* (London: Vintage, 1999), pp. 70–1. Hereafter cited parenthetically.

7 Christine Berberich, 'This Green and Pleasant Land: Cultural Constructions of Englishness', in *Landscape and Englishness*, eds. Robert Burden and Stephan Kohl (Amsterdam: Rodopi, 2006), pp. 218–19.

8 Kazuo Ishiguro, *The Remains of the Day* (London: Faber & Faber, 1989), pp. 28–9. Subsequent page references are to this edition.

9 As Ben Knights observes, '"Mrs Symons" volumes are unknown to the British Library catalogue'. For Knights, 'the English travelogue was ... fuelled by an exponential rise in car ownership' in the interwar period ('In Search of England: Travelogue and Nation Between the Wars', in *Landscape and Englishness*, pp. 166, 169).

10 Where there is an element of a moral test or personal transformation in a meeting on the road, there are inevitably Biblical resonances (such as the parable of the Good Samaritan, or the Conversion of Paul, on the road to Damascus, as described in the Acts of the Apostles).

11 H. V. Morton, *In Search of England* (London: Methuen, 1929), p. viii.

12 Ibid., p. 179. In a contrasting view to my reading of Stevens's description, Berberich locates the landscape more precisely, as 'the area around Salisbury', which, with 'the ancient, revered sites of Amesbury and Stonehenge has, of old, been hailed as a ... quintessentially *English* place'. The argument here is that Ishiguro makes 'Stevens' landscape description' hit a 'sensitive nerve with his *English* readership' ('This Green and Pleasant Land', p. 219).

13 David James, 'Quotidian Mnemonics: Graham Swift and the Rhetoric of Remembrance', *Critique: Studies in Contemporary Fiction* 50.2 (2009), pp. 131–2.

14 Ibid., p. 132.

15 Linda Hutcheon, *A Poetics of Postmodernism: History, Theory, Fiction* (London: Routledge, 1988), p. 15.

16 Graham Swift, *Waterland* (London: Picador, 1984), p. 53. Hereafter cited parenthetically.

17 Jim Crace, *Harvest* (London: Picador, 2013), p. 1. Hereafter cited parenthetically.

18 I shall quote from the Penguin Modern Classics edition, introduced by Penelope Fitzgerald (London: Penguin, 2000). Carr signs off his novel with the place and date of completion: 'Stocken, Presteigne/September, 1978' (p. 85).

19 Valentine Cunningham, *British Writers of the Thirties* (Oxford: Oxford University Press, 1988), p. 229.

20 In particular, Carr's treatment of the mural anticipates Boym's discussion of the restoration of Michaelangelo's frescoes in the Sistine Chapel, sceptical of the restorers' desire to remove all the cracks and scars in Michaelangelo's work, most notably the crack between the outstretched fingers of God and Adam. Svetlana Boym, *The Future of Nostalgia* (New York: Basic Books, 2001), pp. 45, 41.

21 Rosemarie McGerr argues that some of the historical assumptions made in the novel are questionable – for example, Moon's immediate conclusion about Piers Hebron's heresy – and contribute to a sense of indeterminacy about historical construction. This argument seems to speak more to her reading of Pat O'Connor's film version of the novel, however: the novel's thematic pattern relies on our acceptance of the characters' historical interpretations. ('"It's not all that easy to find your way back to the Middle Ages": Reading the Past in *A Month in the Country*', *Criticism*, 47.3 [2005], pp. 353–86.)

2

KIRSTI BOHATA

Welsh Fiction

Modern Welsh writing in English entered the early decades of the twentieth century with two distinctive traditions, which, although internally diverse, can be broadly categorised as rural and industrial writing. This binary division may be further refined into the tripartite division of the country favoured by Raymond Williams, when he acknowledged 'the deep differences between industrial South Wales, [a primarily] rural North and West Wales, and the very specific border country from which I myself come.' Writing a few years before the first devolution referendum in 1979, however, Williams also saw some possibility of union:

> We don't get past [these differences] by inventing a pseudo-historical or romantic Welshness; indeed that would only divide us further. We get past it by looking and working for unity in the definition and development of a modern Wales, in which the really powerful impulses – to discover an effective modern community and to take control of our own energies and resources – can be practically worked through.[1]

Such differences (as much linguistic and cultural as regional) would in part lead to the 'no' vote in the devolution referendum of 1979. But what we can see in the novels published from 1945 to successful devolution in 1997 and beyond is that Anglophone literature has been an important site for the interrogation of history and community, experimenting with form and content to grapple with complexity and difference. And in post-devolution writing, novelists give voice to a whole range of 'new' Welsh identities.

It is difficult to understand postwar writing without a glance back to the 1930s, formative years for several key authors. During the interwar years a highly developed working-class literature emerged from the industrial valleys: realist, socialist, internationalist, and angry. But by 1939, the industrial novel was already changing, and the publication of Richard Llewellyn's *How Green Was My Valley* (1939) marked a turn away from realism. Meanwhile in Welsh-speaking Wales, disregard of Welsh culture and history by the

British political establishment led to the politicisation of a Welsh-speaking intelligentsia. These new cultural nationalists undertook a revision of Welsh history and also direct action against the British state, which was perceived as a colonising power. Indeed, the unfinished business of the 1930s lay behind many of the English-language novels published in the late 1940s. Even as they sought a way forward into a postwar world, many novelists oriented themselves to the past, understanding the present in light of recent, pre-war history.

A case in point is *The Little Kingdom* (1946), the first novel of Emyr Humphreys, a writer who, over the next half-century, came to be widely recognised as the most significant English-language novelist of twentieth-century Wales. *The Little Kingdom* is a direct response to the burning of the Penyberth bombing school on the Lleyn peninsula in 1936.² Penyberth was originally a medieval farmhouse 'that occupied a significant place in the history of Welsh literary culture'.³ It was demolished in the face of Wales-wide opposition to make way for a Ministry of Defence training facility. In protest it was set ablaze by three prominent Welshmen, and from the dock Saunders Lewis, the founder and leader of Plaid Genedlaethol Cymru [National Party of Wales], made a speech 'which remains a classic statement on a culture's right to safeguard its existence.' Emyr Humphreys was galvanised by Penyberth and he came to understand contemporary Wales and its 'colonial' history of subservience to an English hegemony in light of that conflagration.⁴

In brief, *The Little Kingdom* is about the efforts of a small group of activists to protest and eventually burn down an aerodrome being built in North-East Wales. We are briefly introduced to the condescending government agent: 'And this was Wales. These young people were talking Welsh he supposed. Might be a foreign country; bad cooking, bad language, bad train service, and bad business'.⁵ But the central nationalist organisation is equally dismissive because the incursion is not in the traditional heartland of the west, but an already culturally compromised east. *The Little Kingdom* was written during the Second World War (Humphreys was a conscientious objector working for Save the Children) and what this novel is most concerned with is the charismatic danger and megalomania of the messianic young nationalist antihero, Owen Richards. Owen's rhetoric – 'our will to exist', the 'survival of the fittest, survival only of those who have the unbroken will to survive' – inevitably recalls fascist Europe and Hitler in particular, who was still undefeated at the time of composition (pp. 87–88).

In form, *The Little Kingdom* adopts elements of realism, using small-town Welsh society to depict a range of representative (generally corrupt and ineffectual) characters. But the novel is clearly influenced by modernist techniques, particularly sudden, disorientating shifts of perspective and free indirect discourse. The presentation without authorial judgement of multiple perspectives would become key to Humphreys novels, although in this first novel interior monologues dominate to expose Owen's megalomania. Humphreys's interest in compelling yet troubling national(ist) leader figures was enduring. In *A Man's Estate* (1954), Hannah's messianic fantasies and the 'fanatical, chauvinistic and paranoid' nationalism of her mother, Mrs Elis, recall 'the swaggering thirties nationalism of Germany, Italy and Spain'.[6] The dubious charisma of Owen would resurface in a moderated, more nuanced form, in *A Toy Epic* (1958); the attractive yet untrustworthy Michael is the only character with the energy and drive to face the future, a vitality derived directly from his allegiance to a hitherto rejected Welsh culture. Amy Parry, another compelling figure who flirts with both nationalism and socialism, is the central character of the 'Land of the Living' series (1971–1991) – seven novels which anatomise the history and divisions of twentieth-century Wales. There is no doubt in Humphreys's substantial oeuvre of his allegiance to a Welsh-speaking Wales, a cultural and national entity which he regards as being in danger of obliteration. Internally self-defeating, it is seen as under perpetual threat from a politically dominant Anglophone power from without. Yet Humphreys's willingness *as a novelist* to present an ambivalent, sometimes ironic, picture of nationalism and Welsh culture, even as he is personally committed to both, is a recurring feature in his work. In *The Little Kingdom* he has Owen quote Montaigne: '"We are, I know not how, double in ourselves, so that what we believe we disbelieve, and cannot rid ourselves of what we condemn"' (p. 155).

If Humphreys set many of his novels in an earlier period he saw as crucial to the understanding of postwar Wales, so, too, did writers from the different milieu of socialist, industrial South Wales. Gwyn Thomas began his writing career with some bitterly satirical works representing the mass unemployment in his contemporary Rhondda in the 1930s. Characterised by his grim wit and a satirical, ironic, sometimes surreal humour, Thomas's novels and shorter fictions are searing critiques of the economic, cultural, and aesthetic desolation of Rhondda: 'Among us the standard of living had for long been so low that people tripped over it and took their time about getting up again'.[7] By the end of the war, Thomas was experimenting with form. Allegory underpins farce in *The Alone to the Alone* (1947), while Stephen Knight draws attention to the resistant, 'carnivalised' humour in *The World Cannot Hear You* (1954), a 'forgotten masterpiece of Welsh writing in English'.[8] Like many of the earlier industrial novelists of the 1930s, Thomas emphasised community solidarity amongst his 'voters'. But in 1949, in the wake of a Labour landslide and nationalisation of the mines and perhaps less certain of this class unity, he turned to the past. His epic yet unconventional historical novel, *All Things Betray Thee* (1949), is set in the 1830s of the Merthyr Rising and Chartism. The novel was an attempt to understand the myth of the emergence of a proletarian consciousness. It exceeds the bounds of realism, while reworking the generic conventions of historical fiction, in its attempt to represent the epic significance of the industrialisation of Wales and the struggle to become a self-aware and politically radical working class. Merging actual historical events – the Merthyr Uprising of 1831 and the Chartist march on Newport in 1839 – it 'echo[es] a contemporary sensibility about the enormity of loss', infusing the 1830s with something of the disappointments of the 1930s Depression years.[9] Glyn Jones, a contemporary of Thomas, applauded its 'complete newness of style and attitude';[10] and Raymond Williams regarded it as 'the most important novel in the whole phase',[11] praising its allegorical mode: 'the events, though vividly described, are in effect themes for what is the real movement of the novel: a pattern, a composition, of voices in which what is being said is both of and beyond its time'.[12] Contentiously, Thomas used anglicised nomenclature, which Raymond Williams saw as a 'deliberate distanc[ing]' technique and Stephen Knight as capitulation to a London publisher and a 'compromise with the tastes of the colonizing [English] reader'.[13]

By the mid-twentieth century, the vibrant and initially radical nonconformist culture of the nineteenth century was in sharp decline. Thomas had little time for the Chapels, and in *All Things Betray Thee*, as elsewhere in his fiction, nonconformity is satirised as one of the oppressive institutions of the new industrial town of Moonlea (Merthyr). Alongside the great house and the County Gaol, stands 'the big new Greystone chapel in which Mr Bowen kept hell on a gilt leash'.[14] This image of the chapel as self-serving, conservative, and in thrall to money and social status is indebted to Caradoc Evans's 1915 satire on nonconformity, *My People*, which is further evidence of how Thomas overlays one period of history upon another. Even those more sympathetic and understanding of Welsh nonconformity, such as Emyr Humphreys in his major novel *Outside the House of Baal* (1965), have to acknowledge that this major cultural, spiritual, and latterly political force which dominated Welsh-speaking and early industrial Wales alike during the nineteenth century was now a spent force, even as he invites the reader to understand its worth.

Outside the House of Baal, published a few years after Saunders Lewis's dire warning about the state of the language, is an attempt by Humphreys to 'calibrate the changes that had drastically refashioned Welsh society during the first sixty years' of the twentieth century.[15] The narrative moves between a day in the life of an aged Calvinistic Methodist minister, J. T., and his sister-in-law, Kate, and lengthier sections which tell the story of their long lives, wider family connections and conflicts. The spare style of this novel (and others) is consciously modelled on the economy of Welsh, the language his characters notionally speak; moreover, this dignified English overcomes any sense of barrier between Welsh-language society and the English-speaking reader. The historical vision and the assessment of noncon-formity is complex and Humphreys carefully structures the novel so as to present the characters, and particularly the minister J. T., 'in a double focus that complicates judgement' and preserves a 'rich ambivalence of tone'.[16] By having J. T. visit the southern coalfield in his youth, Humphreys also brings the two dominant cultures of Wales – here represented by the socialist worker and the nonconformist minister – literally into conversation. Allowing 'each of these two regional cultures to reflect on the other',[17] Humphreys pro-duces a dialectic which foregrounds contradiction rather resolving it. In his 'elaboration of contrasts' and by remaining silent on key experiences of the characters, Humphreys invites the reader to construct their own meanings and, crucially, M. Wynn Thomas argues, 'they are also made to reflect on the terms of their own preference'.[18] Humphreys addresses the crucial question of historical amnesia and fracture in what he sees as 'a society under siege from hostile historical forces'.[19] The overall prognosis is bleak. His own son sees J. T. as 'a spiritual Red Indian living in a language reservation'.[20] By the end of the novel the minister seems increasingly displaced and lacking direc-tion, as suggested by the closing line of the book: 'Got to have the address or we won't know where to go'.[21] The speaker is Kate, who is setting out on a visit, but her comment's symbolic resonance is clear.

The question of future direction also troubles Glyn Jones in *The Valley, The City, The Village* (1956), a novel that, as the title suggests, portrays proletarian, rural, and urban Wales, in an attempt to move beyond the rural/industrial divide. Trystan, a troubled artist, finds some sustenance in his native industrial valley and a refuge in the rural village, and Jones iden-tifies the importance of nonconformist culture to both. Importantly, he sees in nonconformist traditions a reverence and respect for words and stories, if not for the experimental literature Jones was himself developing. The city, on the other hand, is disorientating and lacking in anchorages. Here Welsh society fragments along the lines of the English class system: the proletariat become a debased underclass, while the middle-class 'adopts a conspicuously Anglicized lifestyle, or else ... turns to a nationalist politics based on the fetishization of Welsh-language culture'.[22] For a writer inter-ested in literary experimentation, the urban alienation of modernist writing might have seemed an obvious choice. And yet Jones found it an unsuit-able form for writing about community. Ultimately, he would develop a deliberately hybrid form of Welsh modernism that binds the modern and ancient, drawing on European and Welsh traditions[23] – in particular, the role of the *cyfarwydd,* or storyteller, in Welsh culture.

Humphreys in *Outside the House of Baal* and Jones in *The Valley, The City, The Village* are both, in their different ways, marking the passing of a more collective or communitarian identity and the rise of individualism. And the lone individual – in this case, a boy on the cusp of adolescence – is at the heart of Jones's masterpiece, *The Island of Apples* (1965). A quasi-magic realist plot merges with a close account of the declining industrial landscape as two boys, at least one of them not imaginary, roam the town and hinterland of Ystrad (Merthyr Tydfil). Dewi Davies meets his friend and hero, Karl Anthony, when he is washed up by the river in a scene 'reminiscent of medieval romance' (and both Karl Anthony's initials and the title of the novel suggest King Arthur and Afallon or Avalon).[24] At the end of the novel, the enigmatic Karl disappears in another flood on a boat named *Tir Na n'Og* after the Celtic 'Land of Youth'. Dewi's emerging erotic identity pivots on his fascination with the beautiful, exotic, mysterious Karl. In one scene, Dewi grips Karl's knife under his pillow, listening to the sound of the river. He is unable to sleep 'after the excitement of listening to Karl' telling stories about his distant homeland:

> And I kept on thinking about Karl himself, about his thin silver earrings, and his golden-brown face, and his pale eyebrows, very thick and straight, but made of fine silvery hair, pure white against the sunburn of his skin. And about him crossing the ravine in the darkness on the girders of the bridge, and the wild river rushing along two hundred feet below him. Every time I was going to drop off to sleep I would be with him, and feel myself falling.[25]

Aside from the superabundant river associated with Karl, the homoerotic charge is often sublimated into the excitement of unlikely feats of climbing on and up the derelict industrial landscape.[26] Indeed, homoerotic displacement or sublimation, particularly around the figure of the working-class male body, is a recurring theme in Glyn Jones's writing.[27] Karl bears some resemblance to the shamanic adolescent, Gladstone, in *Make Room for the Jester* (1964) by Stead Jones. Gladstone is a queer, aloof and compelling leader of a gang of boys who roam the decaying streets of a north Wales town. He disappears at the end of the novel, into a possibly mythic realm of exotic travel and exploration.

The move away from realism, first in Gwyn Thomas and then in Glyn Jones, though artistically important, was not universal. As Daniel G. Williams argues, Raymond Williams's *Border Country* (1960) marked a return and a commitment to realism. But not a return to the realism of the industrial novels of the 1930s, rather, the development of a new appropriate mode of realism in which the individual could be represented as thoroughly embedded in modern community, thus allowing the community's relationship to wider structures both past and present to be explored. *Border Country* melds a detached third-person narrative with the voices and experiences of the communities it portrays – specifically the working-class village of Glynmawr, based on Pandy where Williams grew up. It shares with several of the novels already discussed a concern with revisiting history in order to understand the present, much of the novel being set in the past at the time of the 1926 general strike. The strike is experienced via Harry, a railway signalman and the father of the protagonist, Matthew Price. The larger questions of the novel are about exile and return, about the relationship of Matthew, a Glynmawr boy turned English academic, with his father and by extension his village, his class and his Welshness. As Daniel Williams points out, *Border Country* works 'against the grain of both the naturalist novel of objective surfaces and the modernist novel of inner subjectivity', such that the 'goal was to create a balance between these two modes'.[28]

Another development of the industrial novel came with the arrival of a major female voice. Menna Gallie's two industrial novels adapt the traditions of coalfields writing. Her first novel, *Strike for a Kingdom* (1959), looks back to the General Strike and subsequent miners' strike of 1926. It includes some trenchant, characteristically humorous, scenes in which themes of unemployment, masculinity, disability, and one's identity within the community are discussed. *Strike for a Kingdom* uses an innovative detective plot in which a mine manager is found murdered, thus, '[a]t a stroke Gallie restructured industrial conflict through the apparatus of a genre that was noted for being led by women writers'.[29] Her second industrial novel, *The Small Mine* (1962), is set in the present of National Coal Board (NCB)-run mines and an increasingly individualistic and consumerist culture. It begins, unusually, underground. The description of Joe Jenkins, on his knees at the coal face, is markedly erotic, noting his 'slender, muscled, strident young thighs ... his face was black, beautified, dramatized by the coal... the licked inner bottom lip wetly red, sensual, male'.[30] Joe takes up a job in a 'small mine' – one not controlled by the NCB – against the wishes of his father who sees it as 'doing the dirty on nationalisation' although his doting mother is nostalgically gratified to see her son come home 'in his dirt', 'just like old times' – there being no pithead baths at the small mine.[31] In both novels, Gallie privileges the normally occluded worlds of women and children, providing a glimpse of the informal networks of support, news bearing, and domestic work alongside the more familiar politics of the miners.

By the late 1960s and early 1970s, the decline of the one-time globally powerful coal industry of South Wales was glaringly apparent. Nationalisation had not lived up to its promises and the failures of the NCB were tragically symbolised by the Aberfan disaster of 1966, when an improperly managed coal tip buried a school in tons of coal slurry, killing 144 children and adults, while a culpable NCB (and Labour Government) tried to evade responsibility. Less dramatic but nonetheless evident was the fragmentation of solidarity in favour of an emerging individualist consumerism, already alluded to in *The Small Mine*. Ron Berry and Alun Richards, in their different ways, portray this new world of cars and televisions, of increasing detachment from an older working-class history. In *Flame and Slag* (1968), and other novels such as the influential *So Long Hector Bebb* (1970), Ron Berry created a vivid portrait of this new South Wales, insecure but powerfully alive, in part through a vivid use of the idiomatic English of the valleys and a pugnacious wit. *Flame and Slag* is particularly interesting for the way it marks a deep fracture between contemporary Coal Board working culture and the earlier solidarity of the 1920s and 1930s. The novel moves back and forth between contemporary Wales and a journal recounting the sinking of the main pit. Ironically, the notebooks have been recovered from a house engulfed in a disaster that closely recalls Aberfan in which the ailing, silicotic diarist is crushed to death.

There is some recognition in Berry's writing of the existence of a residual Welsh-language history and culture in the Rhondda: for instance, he includes untranslated Welsh sentences in *Flame and Slag*, although these words are generally spoken by women and linked with age, madness, or babies. But it is presented as a language being cheerfully consigned to the past. In the fiction of Alun Richards, there is outright hostility to the rise of Welsh-language cultural nationalism during the 1960s and 1970s, and he shares with Berry a sense of its irrelevance to the situation in the coalfields. *Flame and Slag* satirises Welsh-language nationalist intellectuals as ineffectual and feminine in a South Wales still clinging to its masculine, working-class traditions even as the world of the miners is being (literally) demolished around them by the NCB. The white collar and 'white fingered' managers are

> childlessly married to Aberystwyth University girls, young *Plaid Cymru* wives who canvassed Daren at local elections, enthusiastically futile ... on Daren's hundred per cent Labour borough council, utterly futile against a die-hard nucleus of Communist voters who abused the two Nationalist as if they were degenerate debs.

The two 'B.A.'s are duly 'educated' by a 'cidery conclave of primitive Socialists'.[32]

In Richards's *Home to an Empty House* (1974) the language is simply an immaterial fad, easily trumped by materialism: 'I said, "I don't speak Welsh." Bilingualism is all the rage now, everywhere except where money or commerce is concerned.' As the language falls victim to 'money' and 'commerce' so, too, does class politics: 'I wasn't interested in class either, it's as dated as TB', although this last statement is undermined by the fact that the speaker's husband *does* have TB.[33] If Berry and Richards are dismissive of the cultural nationalism and wider sense of Wales addressed by Emyr Humphreys in *Outside the House of Baal* and other novels, they nevertheless epitomise a distinctive Welsh literary voice that would be developed by later writers. In *Home to an Empty House*, much of the novel is mediated through a female consciousness, anticipating Christopher Meredith's important female voice and perspective in two post-industrial novels *Shifts* (1988) and *Sidereal Time* (1998). In Berry's novels, there is a concern with the body and disability, often connected with industry and landscape but also representing wider social and political relations, which anticipates the concerns of writers (and literary critics) of post-devolution fiction. At the time of the first devolution referendum in 1979, Welsh fiction in English – notwithstanding the efforts of some writers – could be characterised as broadly reflecting two different versions of Wales. One, a nation sustained by its closeness to a Welsh-language heritage itself in crisis. The other grappling with the slow decline of industry and rise of individualism, while regarding itself primarily as a resolutely Anglophone *region* of Britain, even as it was distinctively Welsh in character.

Literary responses to the resounding 'no' vote were mixed. Robert Watson in *Rumours of Fulfilment* (1982) and Paul Ferris in *A Distant Country* (1983) – both authors arguably semi-detached from Wales – are directly concerned with the recent referendum. Ferris's condescending novel presents Wales as an inward-looking, moribund nation. Watson's is a more nuanced and ambivalent plot in which two sisters negotiate their relationship with nation via their husbands and lovers, one choosing to marry within Wales (and facing some limiting consequences), the other choosing an English lover and an uncertain but potentially liberating future: the novel ends with her setting fire to her father's Welsh cottage.[34]

Emyr Humphreys's eloquent response to the disappointment of the referendum was to publish *The Taliesin Tradition* (1983). In the face of political failure in the past, the nation, he argued, had been sustained by its writers. And during the 1980s, the question of the survival of the nation was an urgent one. In his short novel *Jones* (1984), Humphreys examined the question of loyalty and exile through an unsympathetic figure who can be read as an allegory of the nation. Born inauspiciously at the deathly hour of four o'clock in the morning on a dark and rainy autumn morning, Goronwy Jones has left his native farm ('to get away from the sound of his father's voice'[35]) and deserted his Welsh speaking first love for London and state of permanent emotional limbo. He has lived a rootless existence, collecting art and moving in cosmopolitan circles, but is now debauched, prematurely aged, and isolated in one of a series of impersonal London flats. The novel is full of images of death, extinction, and futility. At the centre of these is Jones's stunted development and his inability to take responsibilities (at home in Wales) that would lead to maturity and fulfilment.

Fear of death and disintegration drives the protagonist of Mary Jones's *Resistance* (1985). Ann has been diagnosed with a rare cancer of the mouth, which might at any moment cause her jaw to implode. Seeking temporary refuge in a rural hotel somewhere in mid-Wales, she becomes disorientated because both location and the hotel itself are full of unsettling signs she cannot interpret. As a monoglot English speaker her illness in some ways represents the dire state of the Welsh language. Her lack of Welsh is 'a tumour – a painful presence, threatening you' (i.e. Welsh speakers).[36] During her stay, she nevertheless develops a relationship with Aled, a charismatic, enigmatic nationalist. He ultimately kills himself with his own bomb, destroying the farmhouse that forms part of the hotel; the gaping hole in the roof mirrors the void in Ann's jaw and initiates her terrified flight back to the city. M. Wynn Thomas rightly argues that '*Resistance* is a significant novel because it successfully dramatizes the peculiar mixture of fascination and anxiety with which the majority culture and language-group regards the incomprehensible minority culture and language-group in Wales.'[37] However, in this complex novel the symbolic imagery may be read in contradictory ways. Certainly the most hopeful moments are in the dialectic diagnoses and tentative connections made between Ann and Aled.[38]

Sickness and potential recuperation are recurring themes in Welsh writing in English in this period. In a novel about a steel works scheduled for closure, *Shifts* (1988), Christopher Meredith likens the workers hoping for short-term contracts to patients in a doctor's surgery, hoping for a prescription. This novel also marks a conscious shift in the terms of debate, from political divisions between an old Labour South and a possibly exclusionary cultural nationalism in the north and west to an attempt to see Wales whole. Meredith, who himself learned Welsh as an adult, reconnects the post-industrial south with its longer Welsh history. A soon-to-be redundant steelworker – flabby, short-sighted, and sexually inept – tries to trace his community's roots to the first iron works. Like Ann in *Resistance*, Keith has, without even realising it, been living in a landscape he can only partially decipher. Delving into

the past, he comes up against the barrier of language. But as he begins to
decipher and understand Welsh words, he begins to move from blank incom-
prehension to tentative acts of recovery. From the opening chapter, Keith has
carried a piece of blank paper in his pocket; the first word he writes down
is transcribed from the wall of his closing strip mill – *Arweinwyr* [leader], a
word he doesn't understand but will learn.[39] But as Tony Bianchi remarks, the
scene is also disconcerting since 'the novel projects no context for turning that
knowledge into practice'.[40]

Meredith's second novel, *Griffri* (1991), builds similar bridges between
his corner of South-East Wales and the Welsh-speaking Wales of the cultural
nationalists, which at times had sought to disown the 'bastardised' South.
Set in twelfth-century Gwynllwg (Gwent), amongst bards and princes, during the time of the Anglo-Norman conquest of this region, it portrays the
hybridisation of the region as the Welsh adopt elements of Norman dress
and military tactics. Yet at the same time, by transferring the central issues
of Anglicisation, change, and internal fracture to this region and period, it
places borderland Gwent at the metaphorical centre of 'authentic' Wales. Of
course, in a postmodernist historical novel, the very question of authenticity
is sceptically questioned. The central figure, Griffri, is a poet, 'the keeper of
memory', whose patrons are the princes of Gwynllwg. In a novel about the
unreliability not only of history but of art and literature (the appropriation
of stories to suit powerful patrons is a recurring theme), Griffri never really
understands the slippery politics and machinations that drive the wider plot,
and he ends by failing to recognise his aged mother, and confessing: 'I'm not
sure if I'm *us* any more'.[41]

The questionable status of 'us', and the associated experience of fractured
identity, has interested those of 'hyphenated' allegiances in Wales, including
the Welsh-Jewish writer Dannie Abse. A poet, novelist, and practising doctor
who grew up in Cardiff, lived in London, and spent a large amount of time
in Ogmore – where his holiday home was put at the disposal of a major new
national publisher in the 1980s – Abse always cultivated multiple perspectives and identities. Exile and duality is a recurring theme in his fiction and
memoirs, the borders between which were highly permeable, resulting in
a series of uncanny echoes across his prose works. In a highly intertextual
novel, *The Strange Case of Dr Simmons and Dr Glas* (2002), Abse portrays the émigré Jewish community of North London (and a scattering of
diasporic Welsh) through the delusional and psychologically fractured character of Dr Simmons. Simmons is hypersensitive to any attempt to 'pass',
and inclined to see 'mental dislocation' wherever he looks; the implication
is that his stunted and warped psyche is at least in part caused by his own
questionable identity.[42]

Dannie Abse and Bernice Rubens tend to be linked in surveys of British Jewish writing by their Welshness.[43] Jasmine Donahaye sees them as similarly uninterested in 'the value of Welsh cultural particularity and Welsh political and national … consciousness'. But the similarities between their writing and also in their approaches to Wales are rather slight. Abse, particularly in his later fiction, finds connections between Welsh, Jewish, and 'exiled' identities, while Rubens tends to introduce 'Welsh national identification and national aspirations' as 'the target of satire or mockery' in novels such as *Yesterday in the Back Lane* (1995).[44] In her epic novel *Brothers* (1983), one section of which tells the story of a Jewish family escaping from Tsarist Russia to the Welsh coalfields, Wales is a place of refuge and some welcome, repeating a long-standing stereotype of Wales as particularly sympathetic to Jews, indeed, even seeing the Welsh as 'part of the lost tribes of Israel'.[45] Rubens, it has been remarked, is hard to fit into the broader categories of Welsh writing in English.[46] But her engagement with disability, quasi-incestuous sexualities, the relationship between history and the individual, and indeed her interest in the misfit and social outsider, invites a discussion that references such important recurring themes in Welsh writing in English. Her darkly comic novel, set in 'one-eyed' (small-town) Porthcawl, *I Sent a Letter to My Love* (1975), about the frustrations of a sister caring for her disabled brother and their subsequent quasi-incestuous romance by letter, is a case in point.[47]

Exile and inter-cultural connections are themes explored in detail by a number of post-devolution writers. *Mr Schnitzel* (2000) by Stephen Knight examines Austrian-Welsh heritage and history in a formally accomplished novel that transposes elements of Welsh culture into a fantastical Austrian setting, including that quintessential concept of *hiraeth* (longing for home), while also exploring the amputated sense of dislocation experienced by a European immigrant in Wales. The Second World War provides a retrospective frame for other novels such as Stevie Davies's *The Element of Water* (2001). Owen Sheers's *Resistance* (2007), and Peter Ho Davies's *Welsh Girl* (2007), explore themes of cultural displacement by way of two reimagined histories of the War. In *Welsh Girl*, despite Germany being the official enemy, it is the English who come out badly, as land-appropriating rapists, while between the exploited Welsh girl and the German prisoners of war there is some sympathetic connection. In *Resistance*, the English are absent as are the local Welshmen who have disappeared into the hills, supposedly to take action against the invading German army. In their absence, a deep if ambivalent connection is established between the displaced German officers and the women left isolated in a valley that has become their whole world. Wales, as a subjugated country, is repeatedly shown in these novels as the location of humanistic values that transcend the grubby motives of war. Another aspect of the Second World War is treated in *A Bridge Over the River* (2008) by Johannes Gramich. Welsh minority experiences allow the narrator to understand complex identifications of the German linguistic and ethnic minority in Czechoslovakia during the Third Reich, including the fate of those displaced peoples expelled from Czechosolovakia after the war as 'Germans'. More recently still, Francesca Rhydderch's *The Rice Paper Diaries* (2013) expands this transnational imaginary, moving between Wales and occupied Hong Kong.

Political devolution in 1997 marked a watershed for novels exploring the intersections of national, gender, sexual, linguistic, and class identities from a multitude of locations and perspectives. A frequent motif in these novels is a 'return' to Wales, often to lay ghosts of the past to rest, such as Tristan Hughes's deft gothic tragedy *Revenant* (2008) and Erica Wooff's fantastical lesbian novel *Mud Puppy* (2002). Wooff's queer narrative playfully appropriates the iconography of '[p]icture postcard' Wales to create a much more fluid and dynamic performance of national identity, which begins and ends with the shifting, seething fertility of estuarine mud in Newport. The connection between lesbianism and a gender-queer, rebellious Welshness is evident throughout the twentieth century, including in novels by Rhys Davies such as *The Black Venus* (1944) and *The Ram with Red Horns* (1996), and it comes to the fore in post-devolution fiction such as Stevie Davies's historical novel *Impassioned Clay* (1999) and Fflur Dafydd's *Twenty Thousand Saints* (2008). A gay Welsh-speaking identity has also been put on the map by the work of John Sam Jones, most recently in his autobiographical novel *Crawling Through Thorns* (2008).

Mixed-race identities are the focus of Charlotte Williams's memoir-cum-novel *Sugar and Slate* (2002), while Trezza Azzopardi set her first novel, *Hiding Place* (2000), in Cardiff's 'Tiger Bay', among the Maltese community who run cafes, betting rings, and prostitution rackets in a still-vibrant marine quarter. In an understated yet devastating trauma narrative, the adult Dolores returns to the now semi-derelict streets where she grew up and gradually probes the dark corners of an abused childhood in which her superstitious Maltese father regards her and her burned stump of a hand as a curse. Another post-industrial landscape of violence, sexual abuse, and narcotic nihilism appeared in the same year in Rachel Trezise's raw but powerful autobiographical first novel, *In and Out of the Goldfish Bowl* (2000). In Naill Griffiths's *Sheepshagger* (2001), a boy is sexually abused in the rural uplands around Aberystwyth, a gothic site of brutal nature and even more brutalising violence. Place is intrinsic to the portrayal of bodily and psychic vulnerability and entrapment in all three novels. Azzopardi's Cardiff slum house 'is empty now: one top window is boarded up, the other gapes; a smash of black glass juts from the frame like a broken bone',[48] while in Trezise's Rhondda everyday objects are soaked with the evidence of violence, as in the 'blood-stained, once-lemon sheets' a raped child hides in a cluttered toy draw.[49] Griffiths extends the hinterland of Aberystwyth into an allegory of Wales as a damaged, colonized country, where tourists buy up cottages and farms for holiday homes, figuratively and literally raping the indigenous people and culture.

It may seem a paradox of post-devolution writing that the exuberance and confidence of a prolific new wave of writers is in part marked by trauma fiction. Another notable theme is the prominence of physically mutilated and disabled figures. Disability is not a new topic in Welsh literature, as a cursory study of coalfields literature from Gwyn Thomas and Ron Berry will show. Earlier in the period, disability was often used to represent class relations and the exploitation of workers by the capitalist machine. In more recent fiction, representations of disability and psychological or bodily mutilation may be linked not only to the effort to make visible marginalised groups in post-devolution Wales, but also read in more symbolic terms. Postcolonial critics and disability scholars have noted the way in which the disabled body has been used to represent other subjugated groups struggling to overcome the legacy of colonialism.[50] Alongside the child with the burned hand in *The Hiding Place* and a range of physically or mentally disabled characters in Griffiths's novels – *Sheepshagger, Stump, Runt* (2006) – there are many other examples of disabled characters: the narrator with a callipered leg in Desmond Barry's novel *A Bloody Good Friday* (2002) set in Merthyr the town that is 'top of Britain's sick list';[51] the deaf grandfather doubled with the culturally mute young wife in Sheenagh Pugh's *Folk Music* (1999); the wheelchair-using Jason who fights for a typically laddish lifestyle in Richard Evans's *Entertainment* (2000); and the disabled young men and their carers in Lewis Davies's *My Piece of Happiness* (2000). Several of these stories represent characters transcending physical difficulty, but more often there is an affirmation of difference, privileging the perspective of the 'not normal'. Most important, and the text that most obviously connects physical disability to Welshness, is Lloyd Jones's remarkable novel *Mr Vogel* (2004). As one character remarks in a self-conscious reflection on the narrative: the 'pervasive interest in cripples ... [is] related to [the Welsh] state of peripheral resistance'.[52] *Mr Vogel* and its sequel *Mr Cassini* (2006) are also examples of the burgeoning genre of psychogeography, both fictional and non-fictional, of which Ian Sinclair's *Landor's Tower* (2001) is probably the best known. In Lloyd Jones's novel, his narrator (and his quasi-mythical characters) is on a quest across Wales – undertaking a 1,000-mile walk around the edge of the country, while the 'sequel' *Mr Cassini* involves traversing the centre. The very land and history is constituted in the novel by the process of walking, with the landscape and some odd companions providing an imaginative catalyst for the narrator.

This chapter began with identifying the presence of at least two major strands of Welsh writing in English in the twentieth century, which although occasionally touching, represent the broadly distinct and even mutually hostile 'cultures' of a Wales that is fractured along political, topographical, linguistic, and cultural lines. Much has been made of the fiction of the divide between the rural north and west (sometimes associated with the agrarian nationalism espoused by Saunders Lewis) and the industrial south (proletarian, internationalist, anglicised). But this is of course an oversimplification, as the work of Glyn Jones in the 1960s shows. And even those writers who were dismissive of cultural nationalism, such as Ron Berry and Alun Richards, are from today's post-devolution perspective rightly regarded as distinctively Welsh and central to the canon of Welsh writing in English. If the 'no' vote of 1979 marked a low point in the view of many Welsh writers, the 1980s continued to produce major novels; and since the establishment of the Welsh Assembly in 1999, there has been a renaissance of multivocal Anglophone fiction. In political terms, a sometimes exclusionary nationalism has given way to a broader civic nationalist vision of Wales, one that promotes the Welsh language while also embracing English-language traditions. Some Welsh-language writers are even publishing in English, marking a new departure in language and cultural politics. Catrin Dafydd's *Random Deaths and Custard* (2007) and sequel *Radom Births and Love Hearts* (2015) are about the contradictions of Welsh-medium education and bilingualism in south Wales; Fflur Dafydd's *Twenty Thousand Saints* (2008) is an English-language rewriting of a Welsh-language novel about the fallout of the failed 1979 referendum. It is not that Wales is speaking with a single voice, or that there is widespread unity and agreement – that argument would fall into the trap of a falsely simplified national identity about which Raymond Williams (as we saw at the outset) was rightly critical. Rather, it is the case that writers, publishers, and readers now have the confidence and the will to explore both painful and enabling differences, thereby engaging with multiple, complex versions of Wales and its relationship with the world.

NOTES

1 Raymond Williams, 'Are We Becoming More Divided?', in *Who Speaks for Wales: Nation, Culture Identity*, ed. Daniel Williams (Cardiff: University of Wales Press, 2003), p. 189.

2 During the 1930s and early 1940s the Ministry of Defence requisitioned several military ranges on sites of Welsh cultural, literary or linguistic significance. None is more iconic than Penyberth. Other sites included Mynydd Epynt, a military range to this day, and the Preseli mountains, a proposal successfully resisted in a campaign led by nonconformist ministers, pacifists and poets.

3 M. Wynn Thomas, 'Emyr Humphreys: Regional Novelist?', in *The Regional Novel in Britain and Ireland 1800–1990*, ed. K. D. M. Snell (Cambridge: Cambridge University Press, 1998), p. 205.

4 Ibid., pp. 205, 206.

5 Emyr Humphreys, *The Little Kingdom* (London: Eyre and Spottiswoode, 1946), p. 41. Hereafter cited parenthetically.

6 M. Wynn Thomas, 'A Huge Assembling of Unease: Readings in *A Man's Estate*', in *Mapping the Territory: Critical Approaches to Welsh Fiction in English*, ed. Katie Gramich (Cardigan: Parthian, 2010), pp. 188, 191–2.

7 Gwyn Thomas, *The Dark Philosophers* (Cardigan: Parthian, 2006), p. 104.

8 Stephen Knight, *One Hundred Years of Fiction: Writing Wales in English* (Cardiff: University of Wales Press, 2004), pp. 108–9.

9 Dai Smith, *Aneurin Bevan and the World of South Wales* (Cardiff: University of Wales Press, 1993), pp. 273, 121.

10 Glyn Jones, *The Dragon Has Two Tongues: Essays on Anglo-Welsh Writers and Writing* new edn. ed. Tony Brown (Cardiff: University of Wales Press, 2001), p. 106.

11 Raymond Williams, 'Working-class, Proletarian, Socialist: Problems in some Welsh novels', in *The Socialist Novel in Britain: Towards the Recovery of a Tradition*, ed. H Gustav Klaus (Brighton: St Martin's Press, 1982), p. 118.

12 Raymond Williams, '*All Things Betray Thee*: An Introduction', in *Who Speaks for Wales: Nation, Culture Identity*, ed. Daniel Williams (Cardiff: University of Wales Press, 2003), p. 160.

13 Williams, 'The Welsh Industrial Novel', in *Who Speaks for Wales*, p. 109. Knight, *One Hundred Years of Fiction*, p. 106.

14 Gwyn Thomas *All Things Betray Thee* (Cardigan: Parthian, 2011), p. 24.

15 M. Wynn Thomas, '*Outside the House of Baal*: The Evolution of a Major Novel', in *Seeing Wales Whole: Essays on the Literature of Wales*, ed. Sam Adams (Cardiff: University of Wales Press, 1998), p. 121. Saunders Lewis's speech 'Tynged yr Iaith' [The fate of the language] was broadcast in 1962 and predicted the demise of the language by the end of the twentieth century, without radical action.

16 Ibid., p. 132.

17 Thomas, 'Emyr Humphreys', p. 211.

18 Thomas, '*Outside the House of Baal*', pp. 127, 139.

19 Emyr Humphreys, cited in Thomas, 'Outside the House of Baal', p. 141.

20 Emyr Humphreys, *Outside the House of Baal* (London: Eyre & Spottiswoode, 1988), p. 421.

21 Humphreys, *Outside the House of Baal*, p. 454.

22 M. Wynn Thomas, *Corresponding Cultures and the Two Literatures of Wales* (Cardiff: University of Wales Press, 1999), p. 105.

23 See Laura Wainwright, '"The Huge Upright Europe-Reflecting Mirror": The European Dimension in the Early Short Stories and Poems of Glyn Jones', in *Almanac – A Yearbook of Welsh Writing in English: Critical Essays* Vol. 12. (2007/08), pp. 55–88.

24 Knight, *One Hundred Years of Fiction*, p. 122
25 Glyn Jones, *The Island of Apples* (Cardiff: University of Wales Press, 2011), p. 126.
26 Daniel G. Williams discussed this in an unpublished paper, 'National and Sexual Independence in Glyn Jones's *The Island of Apples*', at the In/Dependent Wales conference, Gregynog, Newton, April 2014.
27 See Tony Brown, 'Glyn Jones and the Uncanny', in *Almanac – A Yearbook of Welsh Writing in English: Critical Essays* 12 (2007/08), pp. 89–114.
28 Daniel G. Williams, 'Writing Against the Grain: Raymond Williams's *Border Country* and the Defence of Realism', in *Mapping the Territory: Critical Approaches to Welsh Fiction in English*, ed. Katie Gramich (Cardigan: Parthian, 2010), pp. 225–6.
29 Stephen Knight, '"The Uncertainties and Hesitations that were the Truth": Welsh Industrial Fictions by Women', in *British Industrial Fictions*, eds. H. Gustav Klaus and Stephen Knight (Cardiff: University of Wales Press, 2000), p. 168.
30 Menna Gallie, *The Small Mine* (Dinas Powys: Honno, 2000), p. 1.
31 Ibid., p. 42.
32 Ron Berry, *Flame and Slag* (Cardigan: Parthian, 2012), p. 59.
33 Alun Richards, *Home to an Empty House* (Cardigan: Parthian, 2006), pp. 105, 106.
34 On the implications of endogamy for devolution narratives, see Lynne Pearce, 'Devolutionary Desires', in *De-Centring Sexualities: Politics and Representations Beyond the Metropolis*, eds. Richard Phillips, Diane Watt, and David Shuttleton (London: Routledge, 2000), pp. 241–57.
35 Emyr Humphreys, *Jones* (London: Dent, 1984), p. 25.
36 Mary Jones, *Resistance* (Belfast: Blackstaff, 1985), p. 89.
37 Thomas, *Corresponding Cultures*, pp. 160–1.
38 Kirsti Bohata, '"Unhomely Moments": Reading and Writing the Nation in Welsh Female Gothic', in *The Female Gothic: New Directions*, eds. Diana Wallace and Andrew Smith (Basingstoke: Palgrave, 2009), pp. 180–95.
39 Christopher Meredith, *Shifts* (Bridgend: Seren, 1997), p. 212.
40 Tony Bianchi, 'Aztecs in Troedrhiwgwair: Recent Fictions in Wales', in *Peripheral Visions: Images of Nationhood in Contemporary British Fiction*, ed. Ian A. Bell (Cardiff: University of Wales Press, 1995), p. 44–76.
41 Christopher Meredith, *Griffri* (Bridgend: Seren, 1991), pp. 9, 158.
42 Dannie Abse, *The Strange Case of Dr Simmonds & Dr Glas* (London: Robson, 2002), p. 23.
43 Bryan Cheyette, 'Imagined Communities: Contemporary Jewish Writing in Great Britain', in *Contemporary Jewish Writing in Europe: A Guide*, eds. Vivian Liska and Thomas Nolden (Bloomington: Indiana University Press, 2008), pp. 90–117.
44 Jasmine Donahaye, *Whose People? Wales, Israel, Palestine* (Cardiff: University of Wales Press, 2012), p. 143.
45 Bernice Rubens, *Brothers* (London: Abacus, 1984), p. 204.
46 Michelle Deininger, '"It was Forbidden, Strictly Forbidden": Contesting Taboo in Bernice Rubens' *I Sent a Letter to My Love*', in *Mapping the Territory: Critical Approaches to Welsh Fiction in English*, ed. Katie Gramich (Cardigan: Parthian, 2010), p. 289.

47 Bernice Rubens, *I Sent a Letter to My Love* (1975; Cardigan: Parthian, 2008), p. 38.

48 Trezza Azzopardi, *The Hiding Place* (London: Picador, 2000), p. 6.

49 Rachel Trezise, *In and Out of the Goldfish Bowl* (Cardigan: Parthian, 2000), p. 37.

50 See: Clare Barker, *Postcolonial Fiction and Disability: Exceptional Children, Metaphor and Materiality* (Palgrave: Macmillan, 2012); Ato Quayson, 'Looking Awry: Tropes of Disability in Postcolonial Writing', in *Relocating Postcolonialism*, eds. David Theo Goldberg and Ato Quayson (Oxford: Wiley-Blackwell, 2000), pp. 217–230; Ato Quayson, *Aesthetic Nervousness: Disability and the Crisis of Representation* (New York: Columbia University Press, 2007).

51 BBC, 'Wales Top of Britain's Sick List' 2 January 2007, retrieved from http://news.bbc.co.uk/1/hi/wales/6224925.stm, accessed 1 March 2015.

52 Lloyd Jones, *Mr Vogel* (Bridgend: Seren, 2004), p. 175.

3

DAVID GOLDIE

Scottish Fiction

Scottish fiction has been lauded in recent years for its formal and linguistic inventiveness, its diversity, and the sense it gives of an increasingly self-confident culture edging closer to a distinctive expression of national self-determination. This, though, is a relatively recent phenomenon: the result of only thirty years or so of experiment and development. For much of the second half of the twentieth century, in the years before the political and social changes brought about by the Thatcher governments' assault on the postwar settlement and the consequent destabilisation of the United Kingdom's constitutional arrangements, Scottish fiction, like Scottish culture more generally, was arguably much less ambitious, less focused, and less self-assured. Like a set of disconnected stories in search of a theme, Scottish fiction might be said to have suffered, in the years following 1945, a deep and disorientating crisis of confidence.

The Scottish Literary Renaissance movement that had gained prominence in the decade before the Second World War had brought with it an expansive sense of the possibilities open to a self-assured, assertive national literature. Although it had sometimes fallen far short of the political and aesthetic aspirations of its remarkable animateur, the poet Hugh MacDiarmid, the Renaissance had created the conditions for a literature confident in the lyrical and expressive power of Scots dialect and aware of its potential to grasp and bend the nation's sometimes intractable histories into shapes that asserted national distinctiveness and commonality of purpose. Novels such as Lewis Grassic Gibbon's *Scots Quair* trilogy (*Sunset Song* [1932], *Cloud Howe* [1933], and *Grey Granite* [1934]), Eric Linklater's *Magnus Merriman* (1934), George Blake's *The Shipbuilders* (1935), James Barke's *The Land of the Leal* (1939), and Neil Gunn's *The Silver Darlings* (1941) dwelt on issues of decline, particularly the decay of rural community and the debilitating effects of industrial growth followed by slump, but all were written out of a sense of the interconnectedness of the Scottish historical and cultural experience and were confident of their place in a emergent national culture.

Each might be described as a 'state of the nation' novel, and although none are particularly optimistic about that state, all take for granted the place of fiction in analysing and beginning the work of fixing it. Like the writers of the pre-independence Irish Revival, many Scottish writers considered themselves to be, if not quite unacknowledged legislators, at least powerful, vocal representatives of a nation denied conventional forms of social and political self-expression by its prevailing constitutional situation.

This aspirational quality of what has been called 'national epic' that characterised much pre-war writing was largely absent in the fiction that followed the war.[1] The writers who dominated the period wrote rarely about Scotland directly, and when they did they seemed more preoccupied with fragmentation rather than integration, with lives lived at a distance from a binding sense of national distinctiveness and purpose. One of the United Kindgom's most popular mid-century writers, for example, Alistair MacLean, chose to set all but one of his thrillers outside of his native Scotland, preferring to explore the dilemmas of national loyalty and homosocial relations in the wider British experiences of World War II and the Cold War. Muriel Spark similarly set only one novel in her native Scotland, *The Prime of Miss Jean Brodie* (1961) – a disarmingly humorous and slyly devastating assault on Scottish Presbyterian respectability – but for the most part played out her elaborate fictional games against African, English, European, and American backgrounds. There could be said to be little that is characteristically Scottish in her work, influenced as it is by contemporary European movements such as the *nouveau roman*, were it not for the fact that she was frequently aware in her writing that the circumstances of her formation were everywhere implicit in the alienated conditions of her fiction. Spark called the Edinburgh in which she grew up a 'place that I, a constitutional exile, am essentially exiled from.' She added, 'It was Edinburgh that bred within me the conditions of exiledom; and what have I been doing since then but moving from exile into exile?'[2] Growing up a racial Jew and a woman in a city that was the home of John Knox and the historic capital of a now stateless nation, Spark was primed in childhood to understand the effects of de-centredness and disconnection: a reassuring sense of familiarity co-existing with an uneasy feeling of not quite belonging that would give her fiction its characteristically uncanny charm, blending the familiar and homely with the unsettling and alien.

The alienated condition that Spark describes is one that was common also in the writing of those who chose to stay in Scotland and write about the country in their fiction. Much of the Scottish writing of the long postwar period is, as Liam McIlvanney has noted, dominated 'by the figure of the failed artist': characterised by a suspicion that Scotland is a nation actively hostile to the creative imagination and haunted by a sense that authentic culture happens elsewhere.[3] This is manifested most clearly in the number of works in the years following the war that set up the genre expectations of *Bildungsroman* and *Künstlerroman* only to frustrate them. Archie Hind's *The Dear Green Place* (1966) portrays an aspiring young writer crushed by his inability to reconcile the worlds of the east-end Glasgow slaughterhouse in which he works and the west-end literary salons that represent for him the tantalising outposts of global culture. Gordon Williams's *From Scenes Like These* (1968) signals its theme by taking its title from Robert Burns's 'The Cottar's Saturday Night': 'From scenes like these auld Scotia's grandeur springs/That makes her lov'd at home, rever'd abroad'. But the novel shows with a grim relish how inappropriate such ideas of grandeur, love, and reverence are to modern Scotland, illustrated by the brutalisation of its young hero Dunky Logan. Logan is an impressionable adolescent whose early idealism, fostered among other things by his youthful reading of Robert Louis Stevenson and John Dos Passos, is crushed and turned to self-loathing by his exposure to an adult world characterised by its cruel carelessness and violent misogyny. His attempts at self-improvement are ridiculed by family members resentful of education and intellectual ambition, who '*wanted* you to be as thick and dim as they were'. 'You started off trying to be different, trying not to turn out like all the others', Logan muses at the novel's end, but 'you ended up worse than them. You ended up knowing you were a disgrace, full of all the things you hated in other people'.[4]

This sense of the failure of sensibility and education in the face of a relentless, alienating industrial culture is found in a range of works, from J. F. Hendry's *Fernie Brae: A Scottish Childhood* (1947) to George Friel's *Mr Alfred MA* (1972), in which sensitive, educated individuals – in the case of these novels, a university student and a teacher – are defeated by what seem to them the unbridgeable schisms of a Scottish psyche divided along lines of class, religion, gender, and language. Their protagonists aspire to swim in the currents of European culture but find themselves foundering on the rocks of homegrown cynicism and ignorance, bereft of aesthetic confidence and a supportive national culture. A character insists to David Macrae, the Stephen-Dedalus-like hero of Hendry's *Fernie Brae*, that Scotland '"must recover a sense of nationhood ... like Ireland'. David replies '"I think we must first recover a sense of identity", before adding that, "until we know who we are, there's little use in finding out what we are"'.[5]

Joan Didion famously suggested that 'we tell ourselves stories in order to live'. The context in which she writes this, in *The White Album* (1979), is of a broken subculture, of a moment of social optimism and bold experiment fragmenting, in the California of the late 1960s, into a frightening social and personal instability. This, Didion informs us through both form and content, is a culture that has lost a meaningful sense of its own plot: a culture she can only understand through 'flash pictures in variable sequence, images with no "meaning" beyond their temporary arrangement', certain of which 'did not fit into any narrative I knew'.[6] Scotland, it hardly needs saying, is not California. But a similar sense of dislocation resulting from the failure of a minority culture can be seen in the Scottish writing of the long postwar period. The paradox of the works mentioned previously, among many others, is that while each is, like Didion's essay, an achieved, powerful work of literature in its own right, all posit the impossibility of a satisfactory Scottish narrative practice under prevailing conditions. The stories that many Scottish writers told themselves in the mid-century were of failure, decline, and paralysis: of a people who had become separated from their history, had lost confidence in their language, had been denatured and class-riven by a now failing industrialization, and who stood islanded from the currents of global culture. This sense of dislocation, of the failure to be able to tell ourselves convincing stories in order to live, was reinforced by influential critical commentaries, such as those of Cairns Craig, which have suggested that Scotland had become, by its atypical constitutional nature and its troubled cultural history, effectively 'unrelatable, un-narratable'.[7] As Craig's work has amply demonstrated, the problem facing many contemporary and near-contemporary Scottish writers is one of narration, and specifically of telling ourselves new stories to live by and thus assisting in the process of narrating a more self-confident nation into being. Of course, not all fiction produced and consumed in Scotland sees itself as 'national' in this way and so resists being read through this matrix – some notable Scottish fiction writers such as Spark, Allan Massie, Candia McWilliam, William Boyd, Ali Smith, and James Meek have either left Scottish issues at the margins of their work, to be traced by implication, or have ignored them entirely.

But what is often seen as a new wave of Scottish fiction writing, initiated by and developing from Alasdair Gray and James Kelman in the early 1980s, appears to have taken on the challenge identified by Craig and to be experimenting with new ways of narrating Scotland that are not as reductive and defeatist as the work of their predecessors and which chime more convincingly with the changes in class and gender relations, the attitudes towards traditional culture and the place of the Scots language, and the more self-confident Scottish political and cultural nationalism that has emerged since the failed devolution referendum of 1979 and which has culminated in the referendum on Scottish independence in 2014.

In the first instance, this aspiration was voiced by Gray in the motto 'work as if you live in the early days of a better nation', adapted from the Canadian writer Dennis Lee and used by Gray in several works, including the frontispiece to his *Unlikely Stories, Mostly* (1983). His landmark novel, *Lanark: a Life in Four Books* (1982), can be seen as the first serious attempt to imagine and narrate this better nation into being. In one way, *Lanark* is a conventional anti-*Künstlerroman* in the distinctive Scottish style associated with Hendry, Hind, and Friel, dealing, in two of its books, with the (plainly partially autobiographical) struggle and ultimate failure of a would-be artist, Duncan Thaw. Thaw shares the difficulties common to the heroes of these other works in attempting to plot a route to adulthood and aesthetic fulfillment through the flux and disintegrative forces generated by a polarised mid-century Scotland. He identifies, in addition, a particular impediment to artistic practice in what he sees as the cultural and topographical illegibility of the city, Glasgow, and the nation, Scotland, in which he grows up. Hendry had described 'the inarticulate map of the fighting city' that was Glasgow,[8] and Gray's Thaw amplifies this view, in positing an unarticulated city and nation awaiting an art that will allow its inhabitants to see themselves in their environment properly and whole, free of the cultural cringe that makes them believe that life there is not worthy of a confident artistic representation:

> 'Glasgow is a magnificent city,' said McAlpin. 'Why do we hardly ever notice that?' 'Because nobody imagines living here,' said Thaw. ... 'think of Florence, Paris, London, New York. Nobody visiting them for the first time is a stranger because he's already visited them in paintings, novels, history books and films. But if a city hasn't been used by an artist not even the inhabitants live there imaginatively. What is Glasgow to most of us? A house, the place we work, a football park or golf course, some pubs and connecting streets. That's all. No, I'm wrong, there's also the cinema and library. And when our imagination needs exercise we use these to visit London, Paris, Rome under the Caesars, the American West at the turn of the century, anywhere but here and now. Imaginatively Glasgow exists as a music-hall song and a few bad novels. That's all we've given to the world outside. It's all we've given to ourselves'.[9]

Lanark addresses and attempts to remedy this problem only indirectly. The two books that constitute the Thaw narrative are written for the most part in the manner of a realist novel and end in the frustration of Thaw's artistic aims and his suicide. It is in the other two books and in the structure of the novel (in which book three comes before books one, two, and four and the epilogue occurs four chapters before the end) that Gray makes the most serious attempt to rework the Scottish environment imaginatively, creating a phantasmagorical parallel world in which Glasgow is transformed into

Unthank, and Thaw into an analogous individual, the eponymous Lanark. Gray constructs an imaginative world reminiscent of Kafka in its atmosphere of brooding, irrational threat and of Borges or Calvino in its senses of fictional philosophical play and fabulation, exploiting metafictional and typographical tricks, self-drawn illustrations, and inventive elaborations such as an index of the work's real and imaginary plagiarisms. In theme the novel is apocalyptic, and offers little sense of social or political amelioration, but in form it is an eye-opening introduction to the rich possibilities of rehabilitating and re-inhabiting a familiar place by means of the imagination.

Gray may have been audacious in his hope of making life follow art, or at least allow itself be transformed by his art, but it is some measure of the success of his ideas in the political realm that his trademark phrase – 'work as if you live in the early days of a better nation' – was one of the quotations chosen to be inscribed into the Canongate Wall of the new Scottish parliament building, opened in 2004. The critical and popular success of *Lanark* and of Gray's subsequent novels and short stories might be said to have put Scotland back on the literary map, drawing wider British and global attention to a newly self-confident, experimental Scottish fiction, and it has also promoted a particular self-consciousness about narrative style and fabulation that has come to characterise much of the Scottish fiction of the late years of the twentieth and early twenty-first centuries.

Scottish fiction has long had a particular concern with fabulation especially in relation to the stability of texts and the reliability of narratives and their authors. These concerns are fundamental to classics of nineteenth-century Scottish fiction such as James Hogg's *The Private Memoirs and Confessions of a Justified Sinner* (1824) and Robert Louis Stevenson's *The Strange Case of Dr Jekyll and Mr Hyde* (1886), both of which spin out their outlandish tales from multiple viewpoints and narrative fragments. This concern can also be found in works such as J. M. Barrie's *Sentimental Tommy* (1896) and Neil Munro's *Gilian the Dreamer* (1899), which, in their portrayals of untrustworthy young writers in the making, encourage in readers a scepticism about those who would make a career of fiction. Muriel Spark for all her own experimental, fabulating tendencies is noticeably wary of writer figures in her novels, tending to show them as deserving of our deepest suspicions.[10]

But since Gray's *Lanark*, this sense of an ambivalent fascination, a mistrustful wonder with stories and those who feel compelled to tell them, has been expounded and examined more confidently by Scottish fiction writers, and, importantly, with much less of an assumption than was the case with their predecessors that the narratives they create are inimical to the Scottish contexts out of which they emerge. Gray himself extends this confident, if still ambivalent, fascination in the novels that followed *Lanark*. His *1982 Janine* (1984) is a work that demonstrates the power of story-telling in the vitality of its narrative and typographic inventions but which also interrogates, through the obvious character flaws of its narrator, Jock McLeish, the dubious compulsions that can underlie fabulation: McLeish's elaborate, richly detailed, and frequently pornographic fantasies revealing a mind on the way to complete breakdown. Gray explores similar ambiguities in *Poor Things* (1992), this time showing the ways in which a skilled use of narrative can both enthral and betray characters and readers: the novel's heroine, the indeterminate Bella Baxter/Dr Victoria McCandless, emerging in one account as a beguiling child-woman constructed physiologically by a Frankenstein-like surgeon and textually from fragmented gothic and romantic tropes by her husband, and in another as a confident self-authored feminist and social reformer.

Gray's depiction of Bella, in one of his illustrations, as 'Bella Caledonia' reinforces the impression given throughout the novel (and made frequently in Gray's other works) that the reader is being invited to draw political parallels, and in particular to read the work as a form of national allegory.[11] Viewed in this way, his experiments in narrative form can be seen as both a questioning of the conventional narratives that have shaped Scotland, and an attempt to create more compelling and complex stories according to which it can learn to live: just as Bella Baxter asserts a right to escape the narrative domination of the patriarchal influences that surround her and author her own counter-story, so, too, perhaps can Scotland free itself imaginatively from the forces that have objectified it in a simplifying, regressive Caledonianism.

One writer who has followed Gray's bold formal experimentation and applied it more or less directly to the politics of contemporary Scotland is Iain Banks. He is perhaps best known outside of Scotland for his science fiction, written under the name Iain M. Banks, and in particular for the Culture Series, from *Consider Phlebas* (1987) to *The Hydrogen Sonata* (2012). In these books and stories Banks constructs a benevolent extraterrestrial society, 'The Culture', which might be thought of as an extension into imaginative hyperspace of Gray's communitarian political idealism. The dilemmas of the Culture do not hinge around nationalism as such, as it is a notably heterogeneous society encompassing a range of artificial and natural species and a diversity of gender possibilities, but Banks can be said to follow Gray in the ambition of his project, revelling in the powerful ability of the literary mind to spin new worlds out of the stories it tells. Banks, like Gray, is less interested in the technology of future worlds typical of 'hard science fiction' than in their attendant ethical and political dilemmas and the opportunities they offer for liberal social reinvention and innovative wordplay (particularly in the ironic naming of state functions and apparatus). His more ostensibly reality-based novels, from *The Wasp Factory* (1984) on, frequently employ bold thematic and formal experiments: for example, in juxtaposing conflicting narrative styles in *Walking on Glass* (1985), overturning genre conventions with the hyperbolic violence of *Canal Dreams* (1989), and reworking the distinctive Scottish trope of the divided, antithetical self in *Complicity* (1993). His perhaps most accomplished novel, *The Bridge* (1986), draws self-consciously on Gray's *Lanark* and focuses on an iconic Scottish structure, the Forth Rail Bridge, which features in the background of Gray's Bella Caledonia illustration for *Poor Things*. *The Bridge* brings together elements often seen in Scottish fiction, particularly the representation of the divided self – in this case, the protagonist Alexander Lennox, comatose following a car crash, and his alter ego, John Orr, who finds himself negotiating a phantasmagorical world modelled on the Forth Bridge, with a further narrating presence in the id-like barbarian whose violent narration is, significantly, rendered phonetically in a broad Scots. The novel exploits a rich source of allusions and forking narrative paths, but, like Gray's *1982 Janine*, invites the reader to interrogate the compulsion to fabulate at the same time as she enjoys its effects: we are never wholly sure whether *The Bridge*'s embedded stories are a pleasurable exhibition of Lennox's mental complexity, a way of exercising his mind and telling stories in order to stop dying, or evasive strategies to stop him confronting, and waking up to, the pain of his relationship with the ambivalent Andrea Cramond and his hedonistic complicity with the Thatcherite economic revolution.

Similar questions are posed by Irvine Welsh's *Marabou Stork Nightmares* (1995), in which the narrative is split between the recollections of the comatose protagonist, Roy Strang, largely recounted in dialect Scots, and his fantasies of African adventure and exploration, told in Standard English. But in this book, which is marked by even more adventurous typographical experimentation than that found in Gray or Banks, it becomes increasingly clear that Strang's fabulations are a desperate attempt to obscure and escape a disturbing history of sexual abuse in which he has been first victim and then perpetrator – an abuse that has led to a failed suicide attempt and which will end in his murder at the hands of the woman he raped. Welsh's writing is less buoyantly nationalistic than Gray or Banks (a much-quoted rant in *Trainspotting* has his central character, Mark Renton, talk of Scotland as 'a country of failures', and Scots as 'the most wretched servile, miserable, pathetic trash that was ever shat intae creation'), but it shares with them an ambivalent fascination for spinning stories and for almost compulsive literary experiment, as if Scottish conditions demand a bolder, more radical and localised set of literary conventions than the inherited ones which posed so many problems for Hind, Hendry, and Friel.[12]

For writers like Welsh, and others – such as Jeff Torrington whose *Swing Hammer Swing!* (1992) gloriously recreates the surreal wit and verbal inventiveness of Glasgow's Gorbals in the 1960s, or Des Dillon, who in *Me and Ma Gal* (1995) captures the oddnesses and consolations of childhood friendship in the wastelands of industrial Lanarkshire – the use of narrative fragmentation, interior monologue, and typographic experiment have a socio-political purpose in creating a fictional form adequate to a complex representation of Scottish working-class life. For others, formal experiment has allowed a broader palette from which to work, an opportunity to expand Scottish fiction's range far beyond the masculinist 'Clydesideism' that had tended to dominate Scottish writing and cinema in the 1960s and 1970s.

Ali Smith's *Hotel World* (2001), *The Accidental* (2005), and *There But For The* (2011) experiment with multiple perspectives, typography, word games, and puns partly to challenge their bourgeois milieux and partly to illustrate the possibility of building unconventional networks of connection: embodying an intriguing paradox in the way they create a powerful sense of human sympathy out of fragmented, incompletely articulated experiences. Janice Galloway, similarly, experiments with fragmented narratives and the disposition of words on the page, as well as time and perspective shifting, in order to explore the anomie of travel and the frustrations and compensations of female homosociality in *Foreign Parts* (1994) and, in *The Trick is to Keep Breathing* (1989), to construct a disjointed and disturbing, but ultimately affirmative, depiction of bereavement, breakdown, and survival.

Similar experiments can be seen in recent unorthodox approaches to genre fiction, such as Frank Kuppner's idiosyncratic blend of crime fiction and personal reminiscence in *A Very Quiet Street* (1989) and *Something Very Like Murder* (1994) or Ken MacLeod's revisiting the issues of Covenanting and Scottish religious sectarianism in a science fiction crime context in *The Night Sessions* (2008). Andrew Crumey is one of the most innovative and engaging Scottish writers to emerge out of this context in the last twenty years. His speculative fiction has a strong European and global dimension, drawing on the influence of Borges, Calvino, and Milorad Pavić in its intricate, nested narratives, non-linearity, and ludic encyclopaedism – evident, for example, in *Pfitz* (1995) and *D'Alembert's Principle* (1996) – and writers such as David Foster Wallace and Richard Powers in its inventive intertwining of science with literary and musical culture – in novels such as *Music in a Foreign Language* (1994) and *The Secret Knowledge* (2013). And there is often a Scottish dimension to this: *Mobius Dick* (2004) applies the ideas of entanglement and the many-worlds interpretation of quantum physics to create an allohistorical Scotland, conquered by the Nazis in World War Two, later subject to socialist revolution, and now home to the plans of a sinister corporation to develop a worlds-creating and potentially world-ending quantum computer. Crumey continues this intriguing reworking of the long-standing Scottish preoccupation with themes of division and the divided self in *Sputnik Caledonia* (2008), a novel reminiscent of Gray's *Lanark* in the way it doubles its central character, Robbie Coyle, a Scottish boy fixated on space exploration, with Robert Coyle, trainee cosmonaut in a parallel British People's Republic, contrasting homegrown *Bildungsroman* with dystopian counterfactual history.

Crumey's concern with historical reinvention strikes a chord with much near contemporary Scottish writing – especially resonant because of Scotland's claim, through Sir Walter Scott, to be the home and experimental ground of modern historical fiction and because much of the rhetoric of modern Scottish nationalism concerns itself with the need to reclaim a distinctive Scottish history from Unionist hegemony. *Sputnik Caledonia* is allohistory but also family history, Robbie's aspirations being cultivated by his father's familial socialism, and there are many other recent Scottish novels which invite us to interpret a family, with its stifling hidden secrets and unfulfilled hopes, as a metaphor for modern Scotland – its troubled past a paralysing inhibition on present action. Such issues are implicit in Banks's *The Crow Road* (1992) and *The Steep Approach to Garbadale* (2007), and form a central part of Andrew O'Hagan's subtle exploration of the flawed patriarchal ideas underlying Scottish mid-century socialism and town planning in *Our Fathers* (1999). The idea of a flawed patrimony and its consequent damage runs all the way through Allan Massie's novels of postwar Europe, *A Question of Loyalties* (1989), *The Sins of the Father* (1991), and *Shadows of Empire* (1997) and can be found, too, in the literature of the Scottish diaspora – most notably in Alistair MacLeod's moving account in *No Great Mischief* (1999), of a damaged and damaging national and familial Scottish history in contemporary Canada. It is found, too, in one of the most innovative and formally interesting recent novels of Scottish family history, Kirsty Gunn's *The Big Music* (2012). Gunn's novel follows in the recent Scottish tradition exemplified by Gray, Banks, Galloway, and Crumey, of fragmented multi-layered, multi-perspective narrative, and is constituted as an 'archive' consisting of sometimes incomplete journal entries, manuscripts, and stories relating to the family of John Callum MacKay Sutherland, one of a line of great pipers of the Grey House in a remote strath in Sutherland. Its particular innovation is to structure the story in terms not of narrative, but in the manner of the piobaireachd, 'the classical compositional form of the

Highland bagpipe' that makes the Ceol Mor or Big Music which gives the book its name.[13] The book follows four 'movements', from the Urlar or opening theme through development and variation, to the Crunluath, or Crown, and its pendent Crunluath A Mach, which recapitulates the opening theme. In this case, the book ending with a repetition of its opening paragraph: the framing of the eighty-three-year old piper, John Callum, against a landscape benignly indifferent to him, to his family, and to his music, with its repetitive refrain '*I don't mind, I don't mind, I don't mind*': a refrain that plays both on nature's carelessness and – in a meaning derived from a particular use of the word 'mind' in Scots – its absence of memory for all those who have inhabited and left their mark on it.

In these novels the concern with history is both intimate and immediate, played out as it is in a domestic context, but it is also implicitly national and imperative, expressed as an urgent need to confront and comprehend our shared past in order to place it in an enabling perspective. The compulsions they manifest are epitomised in the rhetorical question advanced by a character in Massie's *Shadows of Empire*: 'How can we commit ourselves to the future if we cannot tell and confront the truth about our past?'[14] This question underlies much of the work of James Robertson, too, in a series of philosophically probing, formally-sophisticated novels that, in *The Fanatic* (2000) and *The Testament of Gideon Mack* (2006), explore the contemporary resonances of Scotland's troubled religious history, and in *And the Land Lay Still* (2010) and *The Professor of Truth* (2013), deal with the impacts of a more recent, near contemporary history – *And the Land Lay Still*, in particular collecting (its central character a photographer) the fragmentary snapshots of an occluded popular history of the last fifty years into a forensic display of Scottish identities and issues that matches in its scope and complexity the kind of national epic to which the writers of the Scottish Renaissance aspired. The aims of the kind of revaluative historical fiction Robertson practises are perhaps most clearly signalled in the epigraph (from Ben Okri) that opens *Joseph Knight* (2003): 'Nations and peoples are largely the stories they feed themselves. If they tell themselves stories that are lies, they will suffer the future consequences of those lies. If they tell themselves stories that face their own truths, they will free their histories for future flowerings'.[15] The awkward, unacknowledged truth that Robertson confronts in *Joseph Knight* is the Scottish engagement with, and enrichment from, slavery at the time of the nation's greatest cultural and intellectual flowering, the Scottish Enlightenment. To emphasise the ways in which slavery has been written out of the Scottish memory, Robertson constructs his narrative – in a modernist manner reminiscent of Virginia Woolf's *Jacob's Room* – out of fragments arranged around an absent centre. Joseph

Knight, an actual historical slave who successfully won his freedom through an action in the Scottish courts in 1778, is, for most of Robertson's narrative, represented only indirectly through his traces: in the memories and accounts of those who knew him during his slavery and his court case; in the fractured testimonies of those who came across him after his moment in the limelight; and, most symbolically, as a ghostly trace, imperfectly brushed out of the family portrait that hangs in the library of his former owner, John Wedderburn. For most of the novel Knight is an object, a source of interest only to those curious about his court case and afterlife as a free man, and in particular to an investigation agent Archibald Jamieson, hired by Wedderburn, through whom much of the novel is focalised. Knight only fully becomes a subject, discovered to us living and breathing, so to speak, when he is finally tracked down by Jamieson in the book's closing chapter. Here, for the first time, Knight is represented directly to the reader and his voice is heard in direct speech. He asks Jamieson, 'And whit is it ye want?', to which Jamieson replies, 'Naething, I want naething frae ye. I jist wanted tae see ye – and tae hear ye'.[16]

Jamieson might be said speaking on behalf of himself and the reader here, satisfying our mutual curiosity about Knight's mysterious disappearance but also allowing us the opportunity to redress a historical wrong – creating a narrative space in which a voice, long silenced and obscured, can now be heard directly. And the novel makes the most of this opportunity, giving us access for the first time directly to Knight's own views and opinions on the events focused on him that have become familiar to us through the accounts of others throughout the novel.

The other element worth remarking on, and something that might surprise the unprepared reader, is the fact that Knight's voice is, like Jameson's, a distinctively Scots one, employing a broad and conventionally unliterary vernacular. The novel is reminding us here not only of a historical fact that much of the discourse of the great Scottish Enlightenment was conducted in Scots (a reminder made forcefully throughout the book), but also that Scots is a wholly proper language for serious thought and for serious contemporary fiction. In other circumstances such an observation might seem unremarkable, but it is really only since the emergence of the work of James Kelman in the 1980s that the Scottish vernacular voice, and particularly the Scottish working-class voice, has been fully recognised and valorised as a contemporary literary form.

The issue of voice, and particularly that of the gulf separating the Standard English expected in educational and literary contexts from everyday spoken Scots, was one that both exercised and deterred many mid-twentieth-century writers. On the one hand were writers who expressed, or had their characters expressing, a mistrust of Scots as a language capable of communicating adequately a full range of feeling and thought. Mat Craig, the failed-writer protagonist of Hind's *The Dear Green Place*, puts this particularly forcefully, when he describes Scots, in a moment of frustration, as a 'self-protective, fobbing off language which was not made to range, or explore, or express: a language cast for sneers and abuse and aggression; a language cast out of a certain set of feelings – from poverties, dust, drunkenness, tenements, endurance, hard physical labour; a reductive, cowardly, timid, sniveling language cast out of jeers and violence and diffidence'.[17] For others, equally anxious about language issues, the problem lay rather in the sense that there was some crucial loss of affective power and cultural nuance in having, as literary and educational culture demanded, to translate from Scots vernacular into Standard English. At a basic level, this is sometimes expressed as the repression of a natural language by one that is contextually inappropriate and therefore inauthentic.

A classic example is found in Grassic Gibbon's *Sunset Song*, in which Chris Guthrie's education causes her to think of herself as two distinct beings, the 'English Chris' constructed by school and polite expectation and the natural, Scots-speaking 'Scottish Chris' of the fields and its folk – enforcing a type of self-division that has often been argued to be one of the abiding characteristics of Scottish fictional identity.[18] It is a case that Williams's Dunky Logan advances with adolescent simplicity and gusto: 'What sounds better – "gie your face a dicht wi' a clootie" or "give your face a wipe with a cloth"? One was Scottish and natural and the other was a lot of toffee-nosed English shite'.[19] Williams's way of putting this comes near, perhaps, to James Kelman's approach to language, both in its preference for the apparent authenticity of vernacular Scots and for the pleasure it takes in challenging literary politesse with self-consciously 'bad' language. Kelman has been both celebrated and ridiculed for his extensive use of aggressive profanities, and has certainly brought significant attention to what constitutes inappropriate language in the Scottish novel since his controversial winning of the Man Booker Prize in 1994 for *How Late it Was, How Late*. Kelman's considerable achievement in a range of novels and short stories, among them *Not Not While the Giro* (1983), *The Busconductor Hines* (1984), *A Chancer* (1985), *Greyhound for Breakfast* (1987), and *A Disaffection* (1989), has been to demonstrate the power of demotic Scots as a literary language – not just as a mechanism for direct speech, in the way it had tended to function previously, but as an appropriate language for narration and reflection.

Kelman has described how in his early experiences of reading, people from his background 'were confined to the margins, kept in their place, stuck in the dialogue. You only ever saw them or heard them. You never got into their mind. You did find them in the narrative but from the outside, never from the inside, always they were "the other"'.[20] His way of addressing this exclusion in his own fiction has been to collapse the hierarchical distinctions between an objectifying Standard English narration and the subjectivities of Scots-dialect direct speech, and employ instead a free indirect style in a dialect Scots orthography, a style that eschews the distinctions created by quotation marks and moves freely between narrator and character. Using this mode he has been able to explore a diversity of characters, from the feckless gambler Tammas in *A Chancer*, the alienated teacher Patrick Doyle in *A Disaffection*, to the alcoholic ex-convict Sammy Samuels in *How Late it Was, How Late* from their own perspective and in a way that defers authorial judgment on them.

A large number of the writers discussed in this chapter have benefitted from the example of Kelman's experimental freedom with dialect, among them Banks, Torrington, Welsh, and Roberson, as have many more significant and popular contemporary Scottish writers, such as Alan Warner and Christopher Brookmyre. Though these experiments in dialect, especially the urban dialects of Glasgow and Edinburgh, have sometimes encouraged the return of an aggressive, unempathetic masculinism, they have also broadened the vocal range of Scottish fiction, augmenting the other thematic and formal experiments of recent years discussed here – the historical revision, the challenges to patriarchal assumptions, and above all the bold approaches to fabulation and multi-layered narrative. If writers following Gray have opened up the imaginative possibilities for the telling of new stories for an emerging nation to live by, those who have followed Kelman have made it possible to tell the stories of that nation confidently in something like its own language.

NOTES

1 Douglas Gifford, Sarah Dunnigan, and Alan MacGillivray, eds., *Scottish Literature in English and Scots* (Edinburgh: Edinburgh University Press, 2002) p. 836.
2 Muriel Spark, 'What Images Return', in *Memoirs of a Modern Scotland*, ed. by Karl Miller (London: Faber and Faber, 1970), p. 151.
3 Liam McIlvanney, 'The Politics of Narrative in the Postwar Scottish Novel', in *On Modern British Fiction*, ed. Zachary Leader (Oxford: Oxford University Press, 2002), p. 182.
4 Gordon Williams, *From Scenes Like These* (London: Allison & Busby, 1980), pp. 222, 255.
5 J. F. Hendry, *Fernie Brae: A Scottish Childhood* (Edinburgh: Polygon, 1987), p. 166.
6 Joan Didion, *The White Album* (Harmondsworth: Penguin, 1981), pp. 11, 13.

7 Cairns Craig, *The Modern Scottish Novel: Nation and Narration* (Edinburgh: Edinburgh University Press, 1999), p. 21.
8 Hendry, *Fernie Brae*, p. 190.
9 Alasdair Gray, *Lanark: A Life in Four Books* (London: Granada, 1982), p. 243.
10 See David Goldie, 'Muriel Spark and the Problems of Biography', in *The Edinburgh Companion to Muriel Spark*, eds. Michael Gardiner and Willy Maley (Edinburgh: Edinburgh University Press, 2010), pp. 5–15.
11 Alasdair Gray, *Poor Things* (London: Bloomsbury, 1992), p. 45. See also Kirsten Stirling, *Bella Caledonia: Woman, Nation, Text* (Amsterdam: Rodopi, 2008), pp. 88–96.
12 Irvine Welsh, *Trainspotting* (London: Secker & Warburg, 1993), p. 94.
13 Kirsty Gunn, *The Big Music (Selected Papers)* (London: Faber and Faber, 2012), xi.
14 Allan Massie, *Shadows of Empire* (London: Vintage, 1998), pp. 302–3.
15 Ben Okri, *Birds of Heaven* (London: Phoenix, 1996), p. 21.
16 James Robertson, *Joseph Knight* (London: Fourth Estate, 2004), p. 361.
17 Archie Hind, *The Dear Green Place* (Edinburgh: Birlinn, 2001), p. 244–5.
18 The classic exposition is in G. Gregory Smith, *Scottish Literature: Character and Influence* (London: Macmillan, 1919), with its description of this divided nature as the 'Caledonian Antisysygy'.
19 Williams, *From Scenes Like These*, p. 23.
20 James Kelman, 'Elitism and English Literature, Speaking as a Writer', in *And the Judges Said …: Essays* (London: Secker & Warburg, 2002), p. 63.

4

AARTHI VADDE

Narratives of Migration, Immigration, and Interconnection

In 1948, a Labour-led government under Clement Atlee passed the British Nationality Act (BNA). This legislation created a new category, 'Citizen of the United Kingdom and Colonies', which conferred citizenship rights on all Commonwealth subjects. The BNA was designed to retain some coherence over British identity at the very moment in which the Empire was disintegrating and the welfare state was consolidating; however, the legislation had unexpected consequences. During 1948 and 1962 (when Parliament passed The Commonwealth Immigrants Act to tighten immigration), approximately 500,000 Commonwealth citizens, most of them formerly colonial subjects of colour from the West Indies and Asia, arrived in the United Kingdom to live and work. This wave of migrants, often referred to as the Windrush Generation, tested the distinctions between citizen and subject, English and British, alien and native that were latent in immigration law and the United Kingdom at large.

Although immigrants have had a presence in the United Kingdom for centuries, the BNA produced a significant minority population for the first time: one with a complex emotional relationship to England. Colonial subject-citizens had been educated in English traditions and imagined they were coming home to the Motherland. Such migrants found their expectations dashed when they encountered hostility from native citizens and endured isolation upon entering the United Kingdom. Both ghettoised and required to assimilate, postwar migrants faced economic and cultural challenges, which gave birth to new kinds of British fiction centred on the experience of exclusion, conflicts over the meaning of national traditions, and reflection upon the significance of collective identity in a multiracial, international society. These themes structure several generations of British literary history: the Windrush generation, the black British generation, and the global network generation. Windrush writers such as Sam Selvon, George Lamming, and V. S. Naipaul were invariably immigrant writers, while their successors in the black British generation included both

61

migrants and their descendants born in the United Kingdom. Black British denoted a new and contentious category of minority identity for people of colour who considered the United Kingdom their primary homeland.

Of course, colonial subjects do not constitute the only constituency to enter the United Kingdom. Germans, Jews, and Poles, refugees in the aftermath of World War II, arrived in smaller numbers in the 1950s, as did East Asians in subsequent decades. The 1990s also saw increased immigration from Hong Kong in anticipation of the island's transfer from British to Chinese sovereignty in 1997. It is further important to note that British migration narratives are not unidirectional, solely authored by immigrants to the United Kingdom. Global network novels, authored by immigrants and natives alike, have emerged towards the end of the twentieth century and in the beginning of the twenty-first. They consider migration an ordinary feature of a globalized world, and assess both its desirable and destructive consequences. The latest generation of British fiction, global network novels build on the contributions of earlier immigrant and minority fictions as they situate British culture within contemporary contexts of transnational integration and cosmopolitan belonging.

The Windrush Generation: Anomie and Dislocation

The Windrush generation takes its name from the *Empire Windrush*, a German troop-ship commandeered by the British during the war, which arrived in Tilbury in 1948 carrying about 500 West Indian migrants. The majority of the England bound were male. They had been soldiers in the RAF; others were looking for jobs and educational opportunities. Significant writers of this era include Roger Mais and Andrew Salkey in addition to Lamming, Naipaul, and Selvon. These writers worked together at various times on the famed BBC radio show 'Caribbean Voices' to promote West Indian literature and culture. The radio show helped Windrush writers stay financially afloat in hard times, but the BBC also represented a microcosm of the metropolitan experience in which Caribbean writers found themselves broadcasting to audiences 'back home' in the islands, but denied the opportunity to address English audiences through the domestic service. Lamming called their annexation 'a perfect example of the colonial contract as it operated in the wholesale department of culture', yet he and his colleagues also exploited their institutional reserve to stage debates about the nature of West Indian writing.[1] Salkey recalled BBC gatherings as the occasions where 'I got to know people like V. S. Naipaul, George Lamming, Sam Selvon. We looked at each other's work, we all threatened to write *the* West Indian novel'.[2]

Such historical anecdotes establish a central feature of Windrush generation fiction: though composed, reviewed, and institutionalised within England, many of its authors conceived of it as West Indian. Indeed, the unified category 'West Indian' expressed a cultural nationalism that developed only out of the crucible of migration as black and brown islanders from across the Caribbean found themselves homogenised and racialized in opposition to a white English population. Two landmark novels of the era, Lamming's *The Emigrants* (1954) and Selvon's *The Lonely Londoners* (1956), capture the complexities of this mid-century phenomenon in which West Indian and minority British identity emerged side by side. *The Lonely Londoners* centres on Moses, a seasoned veteran of London life, who serves as a guide both to readers and newly arrived immigrants. As Moses initiates the young, naïve, and aptly nicknamed Galahad into the banalities of urban life – for example, taking of public transport and adjusting to the condensation of breath in cold weather – Selvon uses immigrant confusion to particularise English climate and customs. His scenes of estrangement frame West Indian adaptation to London not as social integration but as detached reflection upon exclusion. His protagonists adjust to their surroundings by learning that they cannot overcome discrimination on the bus, at the labour office, or in restaurants. They can, however, become more expert readers of English manners in these ordinary spaces.[3] Reading or interpretive skills emerge as survival skills in response to an everyday form of racism expressed through oblique slights and gentile snubs rather than direct slurs. Moses calls such treatment the 'Old Diplomacy', a wry phrase that contextualizes domestic tactics of exclusion within a tradition of imperial euphemism and condescension that he describes as peculiarly English.[4] His irony, however, cannot overcome the mounting sense of anomie, the sense of 'a great aimlessness, a great restless swaying movement that leaves you standing in the same spot' (p. 170), that comes from observing the fragile standing of West Indian migrants in London.

Lamming's novel *The Emigrants* shares this sensation, and builds anomie into its experimental literary form. Unlike Selvon, Lamming begins his novel in the Caribbean, tracing the journey of a group of emigrants from the islands to the English shore. The colony to metropole narrative might recall the country-to-city trajectory of the nineteenth century *Bildungsroman*, but diverges from it in two important ways. First, *The Emigrants* lacks a consistent protagonist, like Selvon's Moses, to mediate and explain disorientating experiences. Second, Lamming replaces the *Bildungsroman's* traditional plot of incorporation, in which an individual finds his or her place within society, with a deliberately desultory narrative designed to mirror the emigrants' collective loss of purpose and eventual dispersal into the streets of London. In this respect, the novel echoes a pre-Windrush migration novel by Jamaican writer Claude McKay entitled *Banjo: A Story without a Plot* (1929). Such 'plotless' fictions like Lamming's and McKay's were not unstructured, but paradoxically designed to stage the breakdown of their characters' motivations in the face of hostile metropolitan conditions. Episodic in form, they depicted lives adrift in a perpetual present. Such stories captured the historical displacement of black migrants in Europe, while also gesturing towards something far larger: the existential angst of black peoples who found themselves alienated from their African roots and unincorporated into European definitions of personhood and civilization. The plotless fiction's tone, part lament and part provocation, captured the disaffection of a black population that imagined itself, to paraphrase Paul Gilroy, as countercultural to modernity.[5] The stabilizing force of plot, a device that lends intention and meaning to the story's organization, gives way specifically in *The Emigrants* to a deliberate severing of causality between narrative segments, large temporal gaps in the story's exposition, and moments of misrecognition amongst the characters themselves. The promises of the classic *Bildungsroman* – marriage, family, steady employment – are absent from the Windrush novels of collective disillusionment.

Although not written during the 1950s, V. S. Naipaul's *The Enigma of Arrival* (1987) contains important recollections of the Windrush decade. Part novel, part memoir, it unfolds not in London, but in the countryside town of Wiltshire where the middle-aged Naipaul resides in a manor cottage on a slowly decaying English estate. *Enigma* with its country setting, self-reflective orientation, and realist narrative style could not be more different in tone and politics from Selvon's or Lamming's novels. Whereas their works amplify the discontinuities of migration and the fragmentation of urban life, Naipaul's minimize these alienating conditions by allowing English tradition to confer order upon the past. In *Enigma*, he deeply values the authority and continuity of tradition, and sanctifies the once-fine manor grounds upon which he resides. At the same time, he realises that his own colonial, racialized presence destroys the pastoral idyll into which he has thrust himself: 'Fifty years ago there would have been no room for me here on this estate'.[6] Naipaul's rueful narrative dwells on the ironies of the imperial history that brought him to England, first in 1950 as a scholarship student to Oxford, and later, in the 1980s, as an accomplished writer still compelled to compare his self-described provincial upbringing in the colonies with the mythical England of his childhood dreams. Naipaul's sense of belonging to England is inseparable from his sense of dislocation and even intrusion within it. His nostalgia for an idealised English past leads him to disaffiliate from other migrant writers and reconstruct himself as a solitary traveller. The melancholy which suffuses *Enigma*, though eloquent and sincere, shores up a reactionary strain of thinking within post-imperial Britain. Opponents to immigration and the social welfare state linked the Empire's contraction and the United Kingdom's increased racial diversity to the region's cultural devolution. Unable to countenance the possibility that immigrants such as himself might change English culture for the better, Naipaul conjures up a fantasy of a bygone world in order to insulate Englishness from England's history of imperial violence and its subsequent transformation by new immigrants.

The Black British Generation: Definition, Representation, Performance

The major writers of the Windrush generation used fiction to underline and define cultural identities. The black British generation contested them. In 1983, Salman Rushdie published an essay entitled 'Commonwealth Literature Does Not Exist', in which he rejected the aggregation of writers from around the former British Empire into a category known as 'Commonwealth'. Recall that the British Nationality Act established this category in the political sphere when it opened the borders of the United Kingdom legally, if not culturally, to immigrants dubbed Commonwealth citizens. Rushdie declared the category 'Commonwealth Literature' an 'exclusive ghetto', which much like the BNA, created a space for writers of colour within British fiction while denying them entry into the more sacred category of 'English literature'.[7] Rushdie called for abolishment of the Commonwealth category and the reinvention of English literature to denote all literature written in the English language rather than a more narrowly policed zone of national culture. It is fair to say that, if Commonwealth literature does not exist, then black British literature may not exist either and for similar reasons of aggregation, homogenisation, and ghettoisation. The 'black' in 'black British' has a complicated history. Unlike the United States, where black designates people of African descent, in Britain, 'black' could also informally refer to South Asians and other immigrants of non-European origin. An umbrella term for ethnic minority literature, 'black British' runs the risk of dividing minority culture away from majority culture and misrepresenting its place in the British tradition as a result. On the other hand, the category can be seen as affirmative of the irreducible cultural differences and unique creativities that exist within minority communities. The Caribbean Arts Movement, active in the late 1960s and 1970s, is one example of a grassroots collective that arose with the particular aim of fostering writers of colour and promoting oppositional politics through the creation of independent presses and bookstores. Members of this movement included writers Edward Kamau Braithwaite, Wilson Harris, and Linton Kwesi Johnson whose politics were often far more radical than Rushdie's (and in that regard prove his point about the folly of Commonwealth literature's misleading aggregations). It is thus important to deploy literary categories provisionally, paying attention to the distinctions they create but also being mindful of the motivations behind them and their consequences for how we conceive of British fiction. Novelists that fall under the category of black British, for example Naipaul, Rushdie, Buchi Emecheta, Beryl Gilroy, Kazuo Ishiguro, Hanif Kureishi, Andrea Levy, Timothy Mo, and Caryl Phillips, may have very little in common, indeed.

Paying attention to the politics of categorization is useful because it reflects major concerns of British fiction in the 1980s as issues of minority identity, multiculturalism, and entrenched institutional racism came to a head in the aftermath of the more separatist movements of the 1960s and 1970s. Minority writing contemplates the problem of representation with particular complexity, and often turns to motifs of performance to explore how the arts and media shape common conceptions of minority groups. Rushdie's *The Satanic Verses* features two actors as its protagonists, one, Gibreel Farishta, a Bollywood star in India and the other, Saladin Chamcha, a television actor in Great Britain. While Gibreel enjoys stardom and devotion in India, Saladin's success as the lead actor in *The Aliens Show* reinforces his anonymity. The show, punning on alien, employs a multiethnic cast to play space creatures whose monstrous bodies demand heavy prosthetics and makeup. The show erases immigrants' physical bodies under grotesquely comic ones that betray anxieties surrounding immigration as a form of invasion. By playing an absurd alien, Saladin contributes to domestic stereotypes of migrant populations as a homogenised horde while failing to make his own face more recognisable.

The Satanic Verses suggests that representations have the force of reality, and that part of the immigrant condition involves losing control over how one is perceived. When Saladin, unrecognized by police officers despite his celebrity, is mistaken for an undocumented migrant, he finds himself in a detention centre filled with other detainees whose bodies have developed animal parts. One prisoner explains the transformation as a by-product of language: 'They [the police] describe us. ... That's all. They have the power of description, and we succumb to the pictures they construct'.[8] Such an explanation contends that description is not just reflective of external reality but also a form of social construction. When backed by powerful institutions, such as the state, it has dramatic effects upon its targets. Rushdie turns to the fantastic as a strategy for literalising the detainees' dehumanisation. He presents them as tragic foils to the comic aliens on *The Alien Show*. In a nightmare vision of life imitating art, the novel draws a link between representational and practical violence, between media power and police force.

Kureishi's *The Buddha of Suburbia* joins Rushdie's novel in exploring the connection between artistic and media representations of minorities and dominant understandings of what constitutes British culture. However, he pursues the politics of representation from the point of view of a mixed-race actor named Karim who is trying to create a character to play. The son of an English mother and Indian father, Karim identifies as an 'Englishman, born and bred, almost'; however, the director of his acting troupe labels him 'black' and restricts him to playing characters from his 'own background'.[9] When Karim portrays his uncle in a monologue that includes a carefully rehearsed rendition of him 'raving in the street' (p. 179), a fellow actor criticises his portrayal for reinforcing negative stereotypes of minorities and suggests it constitutes a form of self-hatred. Circumscribed by his colleagues' competing notions of authenticity, Karim rebels against their assessments. So does Kureishi, who stages the dialogue to show that political correctness can promote discrimination in the process of attempting to rectify it. His novel identifies and dismantles the assumptions behind such correctness when Karim rejects two claims: first, that he is blind to the social conditioning that produces stereotypes; and second, that his story can be evaluated on the grounds of whether it affirms or denies dominant representations, 'white truth' (p. 181) as one character calls them. Like Rushdie's detainee, Karim understands the power and danger of description, and he identifies the demand for sanitized imagery as an insidious form of artistic imprisonment. *The Buddha of Suburbia* upholds the value of artistic autonomy, meaning that the artist's first responsibility is to the integrity of his or her art and not to the demands of his or her community. Only by serving a truth irreducible to relativism or ideology (white truth) can the ethnic artist fight the standards that oppress minority groups and deny them the same flexibility of expression as majority ones.

Kureishi's outlook on the relationship between artistic expression and the community at large complements that of Kobena Mercer, a well-known cultural critic. Mercer has argued that if art is understood as 'an accentuation of the expressive over the referential, or as an emphasis on the complexity rather than the homogeneity of black experiences in Britain, then what is at stake is not a categorical break with the past, but the embryonic articulation of something new which does not fit a pregiven category'.[10] In emphasizing the expressive over the referential, Mercer invests aesthetic production with the power to articulate ideas that do not already exist in the world and that certainly do not conform to a prefabricated category of what constitutes blackness or Britishness. Mercer's point can be viewed as anti-representational in this regard, both in a formal and political sense. He does not invest art with the purpose of describing society mimetically or taking sides in a debate, but rather with the capacity to change our patterns of perception about the world. That capacity is the 'something new' which makes fiction not just invented but inventive.

If we turn back to *The Satanic Verses*, we get a fine example of how the expressiveness of its form and style pushes back against the violent representations depicted through the plot. Gibreel, exhausted and frustrated after a trying day in London, decides he will take revenge on London. Invested with the divine powers of an angel, another example of Rushdie's signature use of the fantastic, he threatens to 'tropicalize' the city by making its climate and social habits resemble India's:

> Gibreel enumerated the benefits of the proposed metamorphosis of London into a tropical city: increased moral definition, institution of national siesta, development of vivid and expansive patterns of behavior among the populace, higher quality popular music, new birds in the trees (macaws, peacocks, cockatoos), new trees under the birds (coco-palms, tamarind, banyans with hanging beards). ... No more British reserve; hot-water bottles to be banished forever, replaced in the fetid night by the making of slow and odorous love. Emergence of new social values: friends to commence dropping in on one another without making appointments, closure of old folks' homes, emphasis on the extended family. Spicier food; the use of water as well as paper in English toilets; the joy of running fully dressed through the first rains of the monsoon.
>
> Disadvantages: cholera, typhoid, legionnaires' disease, cockroaches, dust, noise, culture of excess.
>
> Standing on the horizon, spreading his arms to fill the sky, Gibreel cried: 'Let it be'. (pp. 365–6)

The form of this passage is a catalogue: it enumerates the social, natural, biological, and behavioural qualities that separate English life from Indian life. Although Gibreel's theory of tropicalization implies a clear distinction between English and Indian cultures, the catalogue contradicts itself from beginning to end as the initial promise of 'increased moral definition' is undermined by a 'culture of excess'. To use Mercer's vocabulary of the referential and expressive, Gibreel's catalogue is less referential of real world differences between England and India than it is expressive of his cultural confusion and, consequently, his desire for clarity and familiarity. His compulsion to make lists within lists, to mix facts with opinions, to interject the trivial with the serious, undermines the catalogue's orderliness and the rational practise of list making. It also reflects the deliberate loquaciousness of Rushdie's style in which chatter, even to oneself, introduces inconsistencies in absolutist thought and overly narrow understandings of culture. The above passage suggests that the more we elaborate cultural differences, the more we might reveal about how interconnected cultures are. This point is made humorously by the language with which Gibreel casts his spell. 'Let it be' is a command that threatens to make London like India, but it is also the title of a classic pop song by the Beatles. Rushdie's pun is at once ridiculous and clever as it knots English references into the expression of Gibreel's most intense antagonism against London. It reflects the tone of many of Rushdie's novels, which refuse to treat serious issues of xenophobia, alienation, and pain somberly. Their fantasy and humour introduce new strategies for understanding migrant and minority conditions without succumbing to the pieties and constrictions of responsible representation.

The black British generation teaches us that neither peoples nor fictions can ever be fully controlled by the categories which represent them. However, such individuality does not mean that definitional quandaries regarding ethnicity or nationality are unimportant. Such quandaries are a major theme of Kureishi's and Rushdie's works and they arise again in the fictions of Kazuo Ishiguro. While his first novel *A Pale View of the Hills* (1982) addressed the experience of a Japanese immigrant in England, his third novel *The Remains of the Day* (1989) stands out for applying the tropes of immigrant fiction – cultural dissonance, displacement, adaptation, and an ethnographic eye – to a novel that revolves around a native of England and an icon of Englishness: a butler. Ishiguro's protagonist is Stevens, the head butler in a grand old country house recently purchased by a wealthy American. The new owner's desire for 'the real thing', an authentically English butler in an authentically English home, points to the commodification of England in the aftermath of imperial decline.[11] More precisely, the demand for authenticity implies that the landlord's definition of Englishness is very narrow indeed – a position which Stevens himself shares when he compares the greatness of Britain to the greatness of butlers. Stevens's professional pride is, in part, a reflection of his national pride and his desire to keep English traditions alive even after the historical circumstances of Great Britain have changed. Ishiguro shows through Stevens's unreliable narration that such a preservation mission demands an elaborate and unsustainable performance yoked to definitions of greatness that constrict as much as they comfort:

> [Great butlers] wear their professionalism as a decent gentleman will wear his suit: he will not let ruffians or circumstance tear it off him in the public gaze; he will discard it when, and only when, he wills to do so, and this will invariably be when he is entirely alone ... when you think of a great butler, he is bound, almost by definition, to be an Englishman. (p. 43)

To be impervious to 'circumstance' is to be impervious to change, and furthermore, to pair circumstance with 'ruffians' implies that it belongs to the sphere of violence rather than progress. Stevens's sartorial language ('wears his professionalism') reveals him to be participating in an elaborate, if unconscious, performance of Englishness. His professionalism is a form of self-invention that, over the years, transforms a set of duties into a suit that never comes off: a second skin. Ishiguro's fine-grained attention to diction and syntax creates a character who no longer knows how to separate performance from natural behaviour. His speech ticks, forgotten affectations, and other ongoing patterns of display produce a complex understanding of the ways in which chosen affiliations to an idealised England come to look like inherited characteristics of Englishness. The giddiness of Rushdie's prose differs markedly from the seemingly staid voices of Kazuo Ishiguro's novels. Yet, both writers share a migrant theory of identity, which imagines the definition and representation of collectivities as more deeply indebted to performance practices than to any innate differences among races and nationalities.

The Global Network Generation: Locality and Interconnection

Fiction from the Windrush generation and the black British generation explored the limits and possibilities of displacement and cultural mixture from within the legacy of the British Empire and multiracial England. Windrush writers described feeling cut off from the centre of the world before going to England, their moment of arrival thereby portrayed as one of fear, desire, and expectation. Black British writers, though also interested in arrival, attended more to the enigmas and dissatisfactions of long-term residence in a nation that never quite treated members of minority groups as full citizens. Fiction in this context has thematically retained elements of Britain's imperial mythos; but its concerns have also recentred on ordinary spaces indelibly marked by diverse populations. The global network generation, which came of age in the 1990s and 2000s, presents the next and latest stage in British fiction on the topic of migration, immigration, and interconnection. Global network fiction distinguishes itself from its predecessors by decentralising Britain as subject and target. W. G. Sebald's *The Emigrants* (1996), Caryl Phillips's *A Distant Shore* (2003), Hari Kunzru's *Transmission* (2004), and Kiran Desai's *The Inheritance of Loss* (2006) are novels with multinational settings that emphasise the connections across countries rather than the multiculturalism of a single one. They pay special attention to how world systems of labour, commerce, and nationality condition networks of migration, and invariably go beyond British colonialism in their accounts. *The Emigrants* focuses on German refugees (of Jewish and non-Jewish descent) in the wake of World War II, while *A*

Distant Shore follows the journey of an African refugee who enters England illegally after escaping a civil war in his unnamed home nation. Both Sebald and Phillips turn away from urban London and the bucolic countryside to situate historically working-class regions of Northern England – an economically depressed Manchester for Sebald and the mining village of Weston for Phillips – within wider transnational geographies. Sebald's narrator connects Manchester, 'the birthplace of industrialization' to the Polish city of Lodz, 'once known as *polski Manczester*' and the site of the infamous Litzmannstadt ghetto during the war.[12] The narrator suggests that the specificities of one locale lend insight into another as he contemplates the harrowing demands of the Nazi labour camps from within the industrial modernity that Manchester exemplified in the nineteenth century. Sebald does not conflate Manchester and Litzmannstadt, of course, but he does show how Nazi ideologues adopted and perverted an English narrative of civilisation and efficiency in their organization and propagandistic representation of the Jewish ghettoes. In turn, Phillips's protagonist Solomon in *A Distant Shore* escapes civil war only to find himself the victim of 'blood and soil' nationality rhetoric amongst English thugs. An example of what Rebecca Walkowitz calls 'comparison literature',[13] the novel evaluates ethnocentrism and sectarian violence as features of both Solomon's home and adopted nations. By collating narratives of a possible genocide in Africa and a hate crime in England, its form invites readers to compare violence at several scales and to reflect metafictionally upon the ethics of such an enlarged vision.

Global network novels devise international frameworks in order to show points of contact between countries and regions often separated from one another by reputation, ideology, or economics (for example, a 'developed' Europe versus an 'underdeveloped' Africa). They complicate what can sometimes seem like a facile slogan of globalization: we are all interconnected. Globalization refers to the processes – economic, cultural, and legal – which open up the flow of ideas, goods, peoples, and services across national borders. The result of these processes is the increased interdependence of countries, which can have positive and negative effects. Positive effects include easier access to more cultural diversity for more people. Negative effects include increased international inequality and the potential for cultural imperialism, meaning that the cultural influence of more powerful nations threatens the existence of local cultures in less powerful ones. Desai and Kunzru depict the dark side of a globalized economy, respectively using the conventions of tragedy and comedy to do so. In *The Inheritance of Loss*, set mainly across a Himalayan Indian town named Kalimpong and New York City, Desai juxtaposes the story of an older Indian generation's patterns of migration to England with a younger generation's patterns of migration to the United States. Biju, representative of the younger generation, works in a kitchen where he joins the shadow classes of the global economy. Invisible and exploited because of his undocumented status, Biju nonetheless faces the brutal economic calculus that he can earn more in New York than in Kalimpong. The transition of global power from Britain to the United States does not alleviate or significantly alter the problem of poverty or the disillusionment of migration. Such is an inheritance that, Desai suggests, cannot be overcome.

Kunzru's *Transmission* tells an equally bleak tale of migration, but in a more light-hearted way. He focuses on a middle-class software engineer, Arjun, who migrates from one 'industrial fairyland' to another when he leaves Noida (North Okhla Industrial Development Area) in northern India for Silicon Valley in the western United States.[14] Arjun's university credentials make him an ideal candidate for international recruitment firms, and his career in information technology is emblematic of India's economic boom in the 1990s and 2000s. Kunzru intertwines Arjun's narrative with several other seemingly successful characters': Guy, a wealthy English businessman attempting to keep his company afloat and Leela, a lonely young Bollywood star filming in Scotland. Through the course of the novel, Arjun is laid off and, in an act of desperation, unleashes a computer virus called 'Leela' (in the image of his beloved Bollywood star) that wreaks global chaos and subjects Guy in particular to terrible losses. The three main characters never physically meet, but that lack of direct interaction is part of Kunzru's point. Virtual connections – film images, viruses, and financial transactions – exert more influence on people's lives than any face-to-face conduct in his novel. In *Transmission*, the globalized condition of interconnection is subject to the extremes of corporate optimism and state paranoia when Arjun's virus is misinterpreted by governments and media as a deliberate act of cyber-terrorism. Polarities of optimism and pessimism, excitement and hysteria distract from the more ordinary and insidious labour practises of transnational corporations, which helped to create the new class of educated yet disposable migrant workers to which Arjun belongs. Kunzru connects this overlooked, yet prevalent new form of insecurity characteristic of the 'precariat' class to overexposed, yet rare terror threats such as those of cyber-apocalypse.[15] The 'Leela' computer virus in *Transmission* is a twenty-first-century metaphor for the intensified paranoia that comes with increasing interconnection. It also adds a new media layer to the old social problem of xenophobia portrayed so forcefully in migration narratives.

The global network generation encompasses, more than previous generations, writers who migrated away from Britain alongside writers who migrated to it or through it on their way to settling in other places. Peter Ho Davies, Hilary Mantel, David Mitchell, David Peace, and Zadie Smith are writers born in the United Kingdom who live or have spent significant time residing in other countries (Davies and Smith in the United States; Mantel in Botswana and Saudi Arabia; Mitchell and Peace in Japan). Peace has discussed the sense of 'apartness'[16] that comes with living in Tokyo while composing *The Red Riding Quartet* (1999–2002), set in his hometown of Yorkshire, and *GB84* (2004), a novel about the landmark 1984–1985 miners' strike whose defeat signalled a major victory for Margaret Thatcher and the Conservative party. Peace's Yorkshire novels are based on a combination of careful historical research and personal memory, and what distinguishes them from other global network fictions are their singular setting and carefully constructed sense of place. Yet, Peace's desire to reassemble an accurate account of the past includes the conviction that localities like Yorkshire achieve their specificity through interconnection. Peace is interested in the social and economic conditions of Great Britain – local, national, and international – that shape Yorkshire's collective character, particularly its sense of internal colonization by the rest of England. The *Quartet*, in particular, strives to understand why a terrible rash of murders by a real-life criminal called the 'Yorkshire Ripper' could only have happened in Yorkshire, yet Peace readily acknowledges that attention to and identification with 'The Troubles' in Northern Ireland, a violently disputed internal colony of Britain, constituted a vital part of Yorkshire's collective identity in the 1970s–1980s.[17]

Smith's *NW* (2012) is another contemporary British novel that redefines locality in the wake of migration and globalization. Titled after the postal code for Northwest London, the novel follows the separate lives of four friends who once grew up together on a council estate (a public housing project). The residents of the estate include natives of the United Kingdom, older and more recent immigrants from Africa, Asia, and Eastern Europe, and second-generation migrants (children born in the United Kingdom.). What unites them all in the parlance of the novel is their status as 'local'.[18] To be a local in Smith's novels means to be part of a place that was co-created and whose imagination is still an unfinished project. It is less about nativist insularity than it is about civic care and the storehouse of shared memories that come from living together despite having little in common. Smith's desire to divide locality from homogeneity explains her novel's title. A postal code is a state designation not a national one, and the initials NW connect Smith's multicultural estate to no particular ethnos unlike, say, Thomas Hardy's Wessex, which alludes to a particularly Anglo-Saxon England. Smith's accomplishment in *NW* is to derive communal feeling from a demos, a group of people who do not share the

AARTHI VADDE

same ancestral roots but who make up the common populace of the estate and, in microcosm, the British state. This is not to say that Smith's novel transforms a poor neighbourhood into an urban pastoral, but rather that her novelistic project, begun with *White Teeth* (2000), makes migration and the communities that it grounds look casual and ordinary.

Many critics have compared Smith to Rushdie because of their comic tone and experiments with idiom.[19] Yet, this comparison overlooks a fundamental difference in attitude. Whereas Rushdie renders migration and multiculturalism a fantastic experience in virtuosic language, Smith's narrative voice suggests it is a fact of life best captured in the arch dissection of demotic speech: 'Living the dream. It was the year people began to say "living the dream," sometimes sincerely but usually ironically' (p. 301). As Smith's protagonist Keisha (who renames herself Natalie) reflects on her success in this short quotation, we realize that she is contemplating several interrelated dreams associated with migration; economic prosperity, upward mobility, and social assimilation. She is also contemplating their costs as entry into the upper middle class takes Keisha/Natalie away from the local intimacies of NW. Smith's novel joins an established tradition of British migrant fiction in reflecting upon immigrant dreams of success and their various modes of disillusionment. However, her take on the global network novel shows that a migrant or minority member can also be a local whose connections span multiple continents. Transnational solidarities are a crucial aspect of Smith's and Peace's novels just as transnational competition is a crucial feature of Kunzru's and Desai's. Global network novels distinguish themselves by analysing interconnection rather than simply praising or denigrating it. They are at the vanguard of British fiction in the twenty-first century.

NOTES

1 George Lamming, *The Pleasure of Exile* (Ann Arbor: University of Michigan Press, 1992), p. 67.
2 Andrew Salkey, interview with the BBC. Quoted in Philip Nanton, 'What Does Mr. Swanzy Want? Shaping or Reflecting? An Assessment of Henry Swanzy's Contribution to the Development of Caribbean Literature', *Kunapipi: Journal of Postcolonial Writing*, 20.1 (1998), p. 17.
3 Jed Esty has argued that Windrush fiction's ethnographic eye placed a crucial role in capturing British imperial culture in the act of 'becoming minor'. As the Empire contracted, the need for a specifically English national culture grew. Migrant writing, such as Selvon's, bears witness to its consolidation. See Jed Esty, *A Shrinking Island: Modernism and National Culture in England* (Princeton: Princeton University Press, 200), pp. 198–215.
4 Sam Selvon, *The Lonely Londoners* (New York: St. Martin's Press, 1956), p. 30. Hereafter cited parenthetically.

5 Paul Gilroy, *The Black Atlantic: Modernity and Double-Consciousness* (Cambridge, MA: Harvard University Press, 1993), pp. 1–41.
6 V. S. Naipaul, *The Enigma of Arrival* (New York: Vintage, 1987), p. 52.
7 Salman Rushdie, *Imaginary Homelands* (London: Penguin Books, 1991), p. 63.
8 Salman Rushdie, *The Satanic Verses* (New York: Random House, 1988), p. 174. Subsequent references are to this edition.
9 Hanif Kureishi, *The Buddha of Suburbia* (New York: Penguin, 1990), p. 170. Hereafter cited parenthetically.
10 Kobena Mercer, *Welcome to the Jungle: New Positions in Black Cultural Studies* (London: Routledge, 1994), p. 55.
11 Kazuo Ishiguro, *The Remains of the Day* (New York: Vintage, 1993), p. 124. Subsequent references are to this edition.
12 W. G. Sebald, *The Emigrants*, trans. Michael Hulse (New York: New Directions, 1996), pp. 192, 235–6.
13 Rebecca L. Walkowitz. 'The Location of Literature: The Transnational Book and the Migrant Writer', *Contemporary Literature*, 47.4 (2006), p. 536. See, also, Walkowitz's 'For Translation: Virginia Woolf, J. M. Coetzee, and Transnational Comparison', in *The Legacies of Modernism: Historicising Postwar and Contemporary Fiction*, ed. David James (Cambridge: Cambridge University Press, 2012), pp. 243–63.
14 Hari Kunzru, *Transmission* (New York: Penguin, 2004), p. 13.
15 For an extended analysis of the precariat as an emergent social class, see Guy Standing, *The Precariat: The New Dangerous Class* (London: Bloomsbury, 2011).
16 David Peace, Interview with Matthew Hart, *Contemporary Literature*, 47.4 (2006), p. 553.
17 Ibid., pp. 561–3.
18 Zadie Smith, *NW* (New York: Penguin, 2012), p. 6. Hereafter cited parenthetically.
19 See, for example, James Wood, 'Tell Me How Does it Feel?' *The Guardian*. Friday 5 October 2001. Retrieved from http://www.guardian.co.uk/books/2001/oct/06/fiction.

PART II

The Politics of Culture, Subjectivity, and the Environment

5

Re-Envisioning Feminist Fiction

Following the emergence of second-wave feminism in the 1960s, literature played a major role in the dissemination of the aims and ideals of the women's liberation movement. Feminist publishing houses founded in the 1970s and early 1980s such as Virago, The Women's Press, and Pandora carved out a space for women writers in an overwhelmingly male literary field, launching the careers of authors such as Michèle Roberts, Pat Barker, and Jeanette Winterson. Their debut novels, *A Piece of the Night* (1978), *Union Street* (1982), and *Oranges Are Not the Only Fruit* (1985) epitomise feminist fiction, both in their opposition to patriarchal culture and in their resistance to gender norms that affirm male dominance and female subordination. Although the women's liberation movement inspired a literary revolution, Gayle Greene laments the 'retreat' of feminist fiction towards the end of the 1980s.[1] The illusion of gender equality created by legal and social reform gave rise to post-feminism, reflected in fiction that recedes from the themes, concerns, and strategies characteristic of politically conscious texts of preceding decades.[2] However, feminist fiction has not expired but evolved in tandem with developments in feminist thought and the shifting conditions of women's lives. An examination of changing definitions of freedom, the diversification of feminist discourse, and the move beyond identity politics shows that literature that engages with the legacies of the women's liberation movement acquires new shapes in response to changing social, political, and literary landscapes. Nonetheless, feminist fiction continues to offer a radical critique of inequality as well as an empowering vision of alternative worlds.

Female Liberation and Post-Feminist Freedom

In novels published prior to the women's liberation movement, feminist concerns exist as an undercurrent. In contrast to Muriel Spark's 'cautious feminism', characteristic of women writers of her generation, quasi-feminist novels such as Lynne Reid Banks's *The L-Shaped Room* (1960), Doris Lessing's *The Golden Notebook* (1962), and Margaret Drabble's *The Millstone* (1965) feature heroines who pursue social and sexual independence.[3] Melanie, in Angela Carter's *The Magic Toyshop* (1967), refuses to be a living doll. Lessing's groundbreaking novel follows Anna Wulf and her friend Molly as they struggle towards liberation in a frame narrative titled *Free Women*. It focuses on the problem of identity and ascribes value to aspects of female experience previously overlooked or trivialised. Pursuing Virginia Woolf's aim to tell 'the truth about my own experiences as a body', Lessing includes the 'first Tampax in world literature'.[4] This project is extended by other writers: Barker's *Union Street* features backstreet abortion, and *Blow Your House Down* (1984) reveals the dangers of sex work; Roberts's *In the Red Kitchen* (1990) and Hilary Mantel's *Beyond Black* (2005) concern young girls sexually abused by male relatives. The main section of Lessing's narrative is interspersed with extracts from the four coloured notebooks in which Anna records different parts of her life. The split between private and public selves is reflected in the structure of the narrative, which switches between notebooks. Although Anna suffers mental breakdown, healing is achieved by integration of her various identities in the golden notebook. Putting art in the service of activism without sacrificing aesthetics to politics, the novel overturns narrative convention to construct 'new scripts for women's lives'.[5]

In the 1970s, writers directly influenced by second-wave feminism examine the sources of female oppression and protest women's status as 'the second sex' through the 'consciousness-raising' novel.[6] Fay Weldon's early work is populated by unhappy housewives trapped in narrow and mundane domestic roles that render them powerless and unimportant. In *Remember Me* (1976), 'Margot cooks the 5323rd dinner of her married life'; in *Praxis* (1978) women provide men with 'sex, comfort, company and secretarial services'.[7] Like Weldon, Roberts challenges patriarchal definitions of womanhood and femininity. Julie Fanchot, in *A Piece of the Night*, is a woman who seeks to please and appease as daughter, wife, and mother until her encounter with feminism prompts the question, 'Who am I?'[8] Julie embarks on a journey towards self-definition that transforms her from passive object into active subject. Twenty-one chapters mark her social and psychological growth or metaphorical 'coming-of-age'. Roberts adopts and adapts the *Bildungsroman*, or novel of development, in three ways: by inserting a woman into a genre that traditionally focuses on a man; through a fragmented narrative that switches between Julie's past and present; and by interweaving her 'voyage of discovery' with the story of a Victorian traveller, Amy Sickert (p. 110), signalling the novel's commitment to the historical progress of women as a group. In contrast to the plot of canonical novels, which invariably lead women to marriage or death, *A Piece of the Night* closes with the heroine facing a future replete with possibility, implicitly echoing Betty Friedan's question: 'Who knows what women can be when they are finally free to be themselves?'[9]

Carter's *The Passion of New Eve* (1977) and Weldon's *The Life and Loves of a She-Devil* (1983) reject domestic realism in favour of darkly comic fantasies that examine the social construction of femininity. In Carter's novel, the misogynist Evelyn is transformed into Eve by a group of radical feminists, forcing him to empathise with women. After the sex change, Eve undergoes social 'programming' illustrative of Simone de Beauvoir's dictum, 'one is not born, but rather becomes, a woman'.[10] Gleefully embracing bad-ness, Weldon's protagonist sets out to ruin the lives of her cheating husband and his mistress, Mary Fisher. When ugly, six-foot-two Ruth transforms her-self into a replica of her beautiful nemesis, she is literally and metaphor-ically reduced by having several inches surgically removed from her legs. However, Ruth's claim that 'I want to look up to men' satirises patriarchal definitions of desirable femininity that glamorise female subordination.[11] The postmodern narrative strategies employed by Weldon and Carter to disrupt the conventions of literature as well as gender point to a relationship between sexual and textual politics. However, as Rita Felski argues, realism is not necessarily a conservative genre that reflects ruling ideologies, and experimental writing is not always subversive.[12]

While feminist fiction of the 1970s and 1980s traces the struggle for wom-en's liberation, in the 1990s writers increasingly interrogate the meaning of freedom. Mantel's *An Experiment in Love* (1995) questions the value of edu-cation that turns women into men: 'little chappies with breasts'.[13] Set in the 1970s and 1980s, Weldon's *Big Women* (1997) is a satire about a feminist publishing company called Medusa (modelled on Virago). It presents the suc-cess of educated, middle-class women as feminism's triumph and – because of the restricted group of beneficiaries – its limitation. Helen Fielding's *Bridget Jones's Diary* (1996) queries the meaning of post-feminist freedom, anticipating concerns articulated in Angela McRobbie's *The Aftermath of Feminism* (2009). Bridget illustrates McRobbie's argument that since the 1990s the equation of liberation with economic independence and sexual freedom has produced a '*faux* feminism' and the illusion of equality whilst leaving patriarchy firmly in place.[14] The financial rewards of work that endow Bridget with the freedom to shop suggest that women's entry into the labour market supports capitalism rather than feminism. Further, Bridget confirms McRobbie's observation that women have only been allowed to advance on condition that they retain a sense of feminine vulnerability and sexual desirability.[15] Despite professional success, Bridget's search for 'Mr

Right' and allusions to Jane Austen's *Pride and Prejudice* (1813) indicate that she remains in thrall to romance and emotionally dependent on men for a sense of self-worth. By contrasting Bridget's progress in private and public realms, the novel underlines the importance of what Susan Stanford Friedman calls 'locational feminism', which acknowledges the contradictory subject positions women hold in different contexts and situations.[16] Fielding exposes the contradictions in Bridget's life by contrasting her words and deeds. She buys Susan Faludi's feminist bestseller *Backlash* but reads *Men are from Mars and Women Are from Venus*, a guide to romantic relationships that endorses essentialist gender stereotypes. Bridget's predilection for shopping, glamour, and romance appear to make her the poster girl for post-feminism, which sought to reclaim aspects of femininity repudiated by some second wavers as frivolous or disempowering. However, while Bridget resembles the heroines of chick lit, the genre Fielding's novel inspired, *Bridget Jones's Diary* is a cautionary tale about depoliticised 'free market' and 'one-dimensional' feminism concerned with little more than the economic advancement of individual women.[17]

Whereas Fielding satirises Bridget's girliness, Bella Bathurst's *Special* (2003) scrutinises the difficulties of being a girl in post-feminist culture. The novel's adolescent protagonists are all 'top girls': academic high achievers who aspire to be 'important people' leading 'significant lives'.[18] However, in a context where intellectualism is still implicitly associated with men, the girls' progress is impeded by the contradictory requirement to be both 'special' (clever), and 'normal' (feminine). Like Bridget Jones, Bathurst's teenage protagonists perform what McRobbie terms the 'post-feminist masquerade'. Caz is adept at the 'spectacle of excessive femininity' and 'disguise of womanliness adopted as a matter of personal choice'.[19] She 'is different in the presence of men. ... She laughed differently ... low and sweet and disturbingly suggestive' (p. 140). In contrast to the feisty, rebellious heroines of second-wave feminist fiction, the girls in *Special* internalise what Naomi Wolf calls 'the beauty myth', which demands that women adhere to increasingly impossible standards of feminine attractiveness.[20] In Weldon's *The Fat Woman's Joke* (1967), Esther refuses to slim simply to make herself aesthetically pleasing to men. Likewise, fourteen-stone Fevvers in Carter's *Nights at the Circus* (1984) and Dog Woman in Winterson's *Sexing the Cherry* (1989) are celebrations of female 'monstrosity'. However, just as Bridget Jones constantly counts calories so the girls in *Special* are ever anxious about their bodies. Even those who look like 'supermodels' worry they are fat (p. 258), and Hen is chronically anorexic. In the age of the designer vagina, super-skinny celebrities, and airbrushed media images, the woman warrior of second-wave feminism dissolves into the post-feminist woman worrier: Hen finds herself 'worrying about food, worrying about her clothes, worrying about the weather' (p. 172).

The rejection of feminism as 'boring political shit' leaves the girls unable to make sense of their misery (p. 110). At the same time, their claim to 'empowerment' is undercut by low self-esteem, insomnia, depression, and self-harm (p. 109). The novel also underscores the tragic consequences of the sexualisation of girlhood, linked to the widespread availability of pornography in mainstream culture and the commercialisation of female sexuality, issues that aroused increasing public alarm in the noughties. The thirteen-year-old protagonists wear 'naked clothing' (p. 136), and Vicky's allusion to the infamously flirtatious Wonderbra advertisement – 'Hel-*lo* boys' (p. 261) – indicates that their sexually precocious behaviour is shaped by hypersexual media images of women. For Hen, sex feels 'like something which she ought to want rather than actually did want' (p. 195), and Jules loses her virginity to a boy she has just met in the 'children's play area' behind a pub (p. 144), a painful and degrading experience. In contrast to the utopian optimism of second-wave feminist fiction, which typically stresses hope and new beginnings, *Special* ends bleakly: with Jules falling to her death, and Ali disappearing into the house of a man she barely knows. Overall, the novel offers a disturbing portrait of post-feminist culture in which girls who want to be moving 'onwards and upwards' are actually 'going nowhere' (pp. 27, 227).

Diversity and Inclusivity

While second-wave feminism focused on women's liberation, other struggles remained largely peripheral. In the 1990s, however, insights from postcolonial and queer discourse, coupled with changes wrought by globalisation and digitisation, shifted the critical terrain, creating what is sometimes referred to as third-wave feminism. Like the challenges posed to mainstream Western feminism by scholars such as Gayatri Chakravorty Spivak, Chandra Talpade Mohanty, and Hazel Carby, novels by black and Asian women contest the universalism and ethnocentrism of feminist fiction by foregrounding racial difference. As the protagonist of Ravinder Randhawa's *A Wicked Old Woman* (1987) notes: 'We're in different boats, on different seas. ... Women weren't women only'.[21] Joan Riley's *The Unbelonging* (1985) stresses the intersection of systems of oppression that place women in a position of 'double jeopardy' through Hyacinth, a girl who suffers racial discrimination and domestic violence.[22] By contesting established narratives about migration and diaspora that privilege male experience, like Sam Selvon's *The Lonely Londoners* (1956), postcolonial feminist fiction underscores the importance of a polyvocal coalitional politics that takes account of various facets of identity rather than gender or race alone.

The work of Meera Syal and Bernardine Evaristo represents a generational shift in postcolonial fiction. While women of Asian, African, and Caribbean descent experience the pain of exclusion, alienation, and discrimination highlighted in texts such as Buchi Emecheta's *Second Class Citizen* (1974), they also question and redefine gendered national identities and the racialised boundaries of Britain to produce a new sense of belonging. In Syal's *Anita and Me* (1996), Meena initially seeks acceptance though assimilation into the overwhelmingly white town of Tollington. She refuses to wear Indian clothes, longs for fish fingers, laughs at racist jokes, and wishes to shed her skin and be reborn 'pink and unrecognisable'.[23] However, after her grandmother visits from India, Meena embraces her cultural heritage. She rejects Anita, who reproduces England's colonial relations with India by assuming a position of dominance (reflected in the primacy of her name in the title), and purports to be Meena's friend whilst enjoying 'Paki bashing' (p. 277). Meena learns to reconceive difference as personally and socially enriching, and the novel celebrates hybridity, epitomised by her rendition of Punjabi songs in a Birmingham accent. The novel is also notable for its acknowledgement that identity is not just multiple, but contradictory. Meena's middle-class mother, Daljit, incurs racial hostility but snobbishly disdains her white working-class neighbours, illustrating that women occupy 'shifting positions in relation to each other and to different systems of power relations'.[24]

Evaristo's emphasis on hybridity is reflected in the transgression of formal boundaries in her novels in verse, *Lara* (1997) and *The Emperor's Babe* (2001), as well as in her novel with verse, *Soul Tourists* (2005). Set in Roman London, *The Emperor's Babe* centres on Zuleika, the wife of a Roman general who becomes the emperor's mistress. A postmodern pastiche of historical fiction and chick lit, the novel points to the liberating potential of identities no longer determined by cultural roots, as well as the struggle for freedom faced by women defined by their relationship to men. Zuleika's dream of becoming a mosaicist symbolises her culturally composite identity as the 'nubian' daughter of Sudanese refugees and a 'Londinio', but simultaneously bespeaks a desire for healing following the shattering sexual trauma of being married at eleven. The novel blends comedy and tragedy, destabilising the boundaries of genre as well as form. Combining contemporary jargon, Cockney rhyming slang, Scots dialect, Creole, and Latin, its linguistic virtuosity collapses the line between past and present as well as conveying the cultural plurality of 'Londinium'. Free verse reflects a desire for release from restraints and the novel rewrites tradition using couplets – typically employed in epic poetry about the heroic adventures of a man – to describe the everyday life of a woman.

More recently, feminist fiction has been enriched by the emergence of Muslim voices. Without overlooking culturally specific forms of oppression, Muslim women writers challenge the prevailing Western perception that Islam is intrinsically patriarchal. Leila Aboulela's *Minaret* (2005) and Monica Ali's *Brick Lane* (2003) resist stereotypes of Muslim women as weak and oppressed, a task that acquired additional significance in the wake of the Islamophobia arising from the terrorist attacks on the United States on 9/11 and in London on July 7, 2005, especially in a context where female oppression is used as justification for the 'War on Terror'. In *Brick Lane*, Nanzeen acquires a sense of agency as she adapts to life in London's East End, and the novel subverts the dominant narrative of diaspora by concluding with her husband's return to Bangladesh while she remains in Britain, an independent woman. Since, as Ann McClintock argues, nation is a patriarchal construct, novels with transnational female protagonists implicitly destabilise patriarchy by blurring national boundaries.[25] In Aboulela's *The Translator* (1999), translation is a metaphor for Sammar's movement back and forth between the cultures of Sudan and Scotland.

Whereas second-wave feminist fiction redefines 'woman', queer feminist fiction deconstructs identity categories. In tandem with Judith Butler's influential imperative to make 'gender trouble', queer characters defy the binary categories of identity and desire. Like *The Emperor's Babe*, in which male cross-dresser 'Venus the Penis' offers men 'the best of both',[26] Sarah Waters's *Tipping the Velvet* (1998) and *Affinity* (1999) undermine binary genders through transvestism. Such novels demonstrate Butler's assertion that identity is 'performative', a matter of 'doing' rather than 'being'.[27] In *Tipping the Velvet*, male-impersonator Kitty Butler presents herself on stage as 'West-End swell' but wears a suit 'rounded, vaguely, but unmistakably, at the bosom, the stomach, and the hips' to emphasize female body, making her look 'like a very pretty boy'.[28] The novel thus illustrates Marjorie Garber's contention that transvestism engenders not just a category crisis but a crisis of category itself.[29]

Jeanette Winterson celebrates multiple, fluid, and illegible genders throughout her career. *The Passion* (1987) accents gender and sexual ambiguity through its cross-dressing, bisexual heroine, Villanelle, a woman who defies patriarchal tradition by becoming a Venetian gondolier and possesses webbed feet, a feature (according to legend) of boat*men*. *Written on the Body* (1992) refuses to disclose the gender of its bisexual protagonist, implying the redundancy and irrelevance of identity categories. The uncertain gender of Ali/x in *The PowerBook* (2000) points to the emancipating potential of cyberspace, while *The Stone Gods* (2007) exploits the promise of the cyborg, a figure that, according to Donna Haraway, is post-gender.[30] Like Waters, Winterson highlights the convergence between feminist and queer politics by undermining the structures of hetero-patriarchy.

Ali Smith's *Girl Meets Boy* (2007) draws on Ovid's *Metamorphoses* to retell the story of Iphis and Ianthe in a contemporary context, but turns a tale about transsexuality into one about androgyny in order to affirm gender insubordination and same-sex desire. Robin 'had the swagger of a girl. She blushed like a boy. She had a girl's toughness. She had a boy's gentleness'.[31] Through Robin, in whom girl meets boy, Andrea discovers 'the grey area was a whole other spectrum of colours new to the eye' (p. 84). In contrast to second-wave lesbian feminism's wariness of butch/femme roles, boyish girls insist that 'masculinity does not belong to men'.[32] Ash in Smith's *Like* (1997); the 'Half boy, all girl' Brooke in Smith's *There but for The* (2011); Nancy Astley in Waters's *Tipping the Velvet*; and Kay Langrish in her later Blitz novel *The Night Watch* (2006) – all of these characters demonstrate the subversive effect of 'heterosexual constructs' replicated in 'non-heterosexual frames'.[33]

Smith's desire to elude categories and eschew boundaries is reflected both at the level of narrative perspective – switching as she does between third- and first-person narrator in the two halves of *Like* – and at the level of genre, as *Artful* (2012) and *Shire* (2013) dissolve established modes by fusing essay, fiction, and autobiography/biography. The jokes and puns that pervade her work subvert heterotextuality by highlighting the instability and plurality of meaning: 'Virtuoso, Brooke's father said. Virtue so-so, Brooke said' (*There but for The*, p. 293). Showing that there is no straightforward line of development in feminist fiction, Smith's linguistic and formal playfulness harks back to avant-garde novels such as Brigid Brophy's *In Transit* (1969) and Christine Brook-Rose's *Between* (1968), which engage in dizzying formal experiment to undo gender binaries. Further, Maureen Duffy – an important precursor to Winterson, Waters, and Smith – has always centralised queer feminist concerns. In *The Microcosm* (1966), the main narrative about the lives of a group of lesbians is intercut with an account of the eighteenth-century cross-dresser Charlotte Charke. In *Alchemy* (2010), too, the narrative oscillates between present and past: seventeenth-century Amyntas Boston is a cross-dressing alchemist who declares herself 'two in one', her 'father's daughter, and his only son.'[34]

Another area of change concerns motherhood. Weldon's early novels present maternity as a misfortune to be resisted or escaped. In *Puffball* (1980), Liffey feels repulsed by the puffball mushroom that resembles her pregnant belly. Debunking the myth of maternal instinct, the novel refutes the 'natural' identification of womanhood with motherhood: 'Let us seize the word, seize the day; lay N on its side and call our blind mistress Zature'.[35] In *The Passion of New Eve*, Carter satirises the glorification of motherhood by rendering Mother, with her multiple breasts, grotesque. Further, mothers are typically rejected by daughters who fear sharing their fate. Alternatively, mothers are despised as agents of patriarchy who condition girls to embody normative femininity. The theme of mother-daughter conflict recurs throughout Roberts's work, which traces a transformative shift from alienation to reconciliation. *Flesh and Blood* (1994), which is structured like a palindrome, tells seven stories in two halves, the first half related from the point of view of the daughter, the second half from the mother, which produces a different outcome. The two halves of the story mirror each other and, subverting the mother-daughter dichotomy, the daughter in the first story becomes a mother in the last. Kate Atkinson interweaves stories of mothers and daughters in *Behind the Scenes at the Museum* (1996). The narrative of Ruby Lennox is interspersed with a series of chapter-long 'footnotes' that relate the lives of her mother, grandmother, and great-grandmother. While Ruby's story foregrounds the pain of maternal deprivation, details of Bunty's life explain her lack of maternal nurturance and generate sympathy for a woman who has been pronounced a monster. The novel suggests that the myth of the perfect mother generates mother-daughter conflict, demonstrating how patriarchy frustrates a potentially empowering mother-daughter bond.

The mother's perspective comes more clearly into view in Helen Simpson's *Four Bare Legs in a Bed* (1990), a collection of stories that introduces the theme of maternal ambivalence that runs throughout her work. Rachel Cusk queries the joys of motherhood in *Arlington Park* (2006), a novel that exemplifies the 'instability' of home in neodomestic fiction.[36] Maggie Gee also reimagines home by examining racism and the exclusions required to create domestic security in *The White Family* (2002) and *My Cleaner* (2005). A new interest in the plight of mothers is accompanied by a new perspective on older women, reflecting concerns about an aging population and the redefinition of 'old age'. In contrast to novels about old women looking back on their lives, like Pat Barker's *The Century's Daughter* (1986), republished as *Liza's England* (1996), Doris Lessing's *Love, Again* (1996) concerns a sixty-five-year-old widow whose lust for life is accompanied by an implacable desire for considerably younger men.

If feminist fiction has embraced a wider range of female experience since the 1960s, it has also broadened its focus to encompass men. The title of Barker's *Regeneration* (1991), the first instalment of her trilogy about the traumatic effects of the First World War, points to the need for the regeneration of established models of manhood. Alongside the new critical assessment of masculinity initiated by scholars such as Michael Kimmel and R. W. Connell in the 1980s, Alasdair Gray's *1982, Janine* (1984) and Graham Swift's *Last Orders* (1996) depict men damaged or beleaguered by their adherence to the norms of masculinity. Men are the central subjects in Zadie Smith's *White Teeth* (2000), which examines masculinity, father-son relations and male friendship in a postcolonial context. These themes are reprised in Smith's *The Autograph Man* (2002), in which the effects of celebrity and consumer culture on manhood are epitomised by Alex-Ti Tandem's obsession with the actress Kitty Alexander and compulsion to kneel before a twenty-foot poster of Julia Roberts whilst neglecting his girlfriend of ten years. Alex's slacker masculinity (he avoids commitment, lacks motivation, takes too many drugs) exemplifies what Gary Cross calls the emergence of the 'man-boy', an effect of the commercialisation of youth culture and response to men's confusion over shifting gender roles.[37] Evaristo's *Mr Loverman* (2013) addresses the complexities of gay black masculinity, unsettling a binary model of male power and female powerlessness. Such texts demonstrate that women are not necessarily either the subject or author of feminist fiction.

Graham Rawle's formally ingenious graphic novel *Woman's World* (2005) suggests that the reconfiguration of gender norms is liberating for women and men alike. Set in the early 1960s, the narrative focuses on Roy, a heterosexual man who seeks to escape the stifling constraints of postwar masculinity through cross-dressing. His feminine alter ego, Norma, embodies the normative model of womanhood championed by magazines such as *Woman's World*. Norma's identity is shaped by features on fashion, beauty, and romance supportive of the cult of glamour and sophistication. Her humorous adoption of the language of advertisements also indicates the commodification of femininity integral to a developing consumer culture. Constructed from words, phrases, and images cut from women's magazines of the day, the novel foregrounds the discursive construction of gender, and the variety of fonts mirrors its celebration of gender diversity.

Beyond Gender

Recent feminist fiction moves beyond gender and the politics of representation to engage broader social and political concerns. However, texts that do not take female oppression as their central theme may still be inflected with a feminist impulse or consciousness. As Friedman argues, 'moving *beyond* gender does not mean forgetting it'.[38] The expanding horizons of feminist fiction are exemplified by Andrea Levy's shift from the *Bildungsroman* to historical fiction. Her first three novels – *Every Light in the House Burnin'* (1994), *Never Far From Nowhere* (1996), and *Fruit of the Lemon* (1999) – depict the struggle for self-realisation of young working-class black girls in Britain, whereas *Small Island* (2004) examines the experience and impact of the Windrush generation. By moving beyond individual experience and by switching between the narratives of the four central characters (Hortense, Queenie, Gilbert, and Bernard), the narrative underlines the connections between black and white subjects engendered by colonialism. Queenie's illegitimate mixed-race baby, adopted by Hortense and Gilbert at the novel's close, serves as a metaphor for the legacy of empire and Britain's postcolonial future.

Waters's lesbian novels also map 'an alternative historical landscape', one that recuperates non-normative social and sexual arrangements suppressed or elided in the 'traditional male-centred historical narrative'.[39] Rather than attempting to uncover the truth about subjects hidden from history, she imagines lesbian lives, conveying that history constructs rather than records the past. Although less ludic than Carter's *Nights at the Circus* and Winterson's *The Passion* and *Sexing the Cherry*, which employ historiographic metafiction and magic realism to challenge the authority and objectivity of history, Waters's work is just as postmodern. Exemplifying this, assumptions about historical progress are unsettled by disrupted chronology in *The Night Watch*, which moves backwards through three sections dated '1947', '1944', '1941'.

Another significant development in feminist fiction concerns the changing relationship between the personal and the political. If second-wave feminist fiction demonstrates that the personal is political by showing how intimate aspects of women's private lives are shaped by larger political structures, contemporary authors make the political personal by highlighting how current affairs impact on women and gender relations. This is not an entirely new strategy: Zoë Fairbairns's *Closing* (1987) examines the effect of Thatcherism on women and Mantel's *Eight Months on Ghazzah Street* (1988) focuses on a woman dealing with the consequences of Islamic fundamentalism inspired by neocolonialism. However, this strategy figures more prominently in *fin-de-siècle* and postmillennial fiction: Gee's *The Ice People* (1998) and *The Flood* (2004) concern climate change; late capitalism, consumer culture, and branding are examined in Ali Smith's *Girl Meets Boy*; environmental disaster features centrally in Winterson's *The Stone Gods* and Sarah Hall's *The Carhullan Army* (2007); Ali's *In the Kitchen* (2009) explores transnational sex trafficking in the context of globalisation; Evaristo's *Blonde Roots* (2009) and Levy's *The Long Song* (2010) portray slavery; Roberts's *Daughters of the House* (1992) and *Ignorance* (2012) address the impact and legacy of the Holocaust in France.

Ali Smith's *Hotel World* (2001) epitomises the exploration of contemporary issues from a feminist perspective. The novel suggests that globalisation, symbolised by the *Global Hotel* chain referenced in its title, intensifies inequality by contrasting the lives of five women connected to the hotel in different ways. By spotlighting poverty and social exclusion, the novel belies the myth that by the end of the twentieth century Britain had become a classless society, a myth endorsed by Tony Blair's 1998 pronouncement that 'we're all middle-class now'.⁴⁰ Zadie Smith's *NW* (2012) debunks myths of meritocracy, social mobility, and multiculturalism through the fates of Leah and Natalie (formerly Keisha), two friends who find themselves unable to fully escape the Willesden council estate where they grow up despite a university education. Like *NW*, Ali Smith's *The Accidental* (2005) and *There but for The* include a range of male and female characters, but (unlike the more pessimistic *NW*) grant a woman (Amber) or girl (Brooke) a pivotal role in challenging political complacency or social disengagement, thus positioning women as agents of change and arbiters of hopeful futurity. Likewise, Ursula in Atkinson's *Life After Life* (2014) uses her gift of rebirth to escape domestic violence, save the lives of those she loves, and alter the course of history by assassinating Hitler, assuming the role of hero traditionally reserved for men.

The changing character of feminist fiction is further underlined by women writers' relationship to literary tradition. Drawing on Adrienne Rich's concept of 're-vision', numerous second-wave feminists rewrite master narratives in order to challenge their purportedly universal perspective and expose underlying assumptions about gender: Carter's *The Bloody Chamber* (1979) reimagines classic fairy tales; Winterson's *Oranges are not the Only Fruit* rewrites books of the Bible; Roberts's *The Looking Glass* (2000) revises Flaubert's *Madame Bovary* (1856).⁴¹ However, more recent authors assert a counterpoint to women's writing and feminist fiction, too. A. L. Kennedy's 'perverse romances' debunk the illusions of love endorsed by chick lit, while a protagonist like alcoholic Hannah Luckraft in *Paradise* (2004) departs from a tradition of feminist fiction full of empowered women as well as from a Scottish literary tradition populated by hard-drinking men.⁴² In addition, while many women writers follow Woolf's injunction to 'think back through our mothers' by flagging their indebtedness to a distinctly female artistic tradition, others illustrate the possibility of drawing inspiration from literary forefathers.⁴³ A homage to E. M. Forster's *Howards End* (1910), Zadie Smith's *On Beauty* (2005) highlights a relationship with the male canon based on political and artistic alliance rather than opposition.

Smith's self-conscious use of Forster also exemplifies a postmillennial shift to post-postmodernism or metamodernism – a philosophy that blends aspects of modernism and postmodernism to privilege affect and engagement over irony and detachment.[44]

In *On Beauty*, feminist issues are explored through male and female characters and integrated into a wider critique of neo-liberalism. As suggested by its title, which alludes to Elaine Scarry's essay 'On Beauty and Being Just', the novel links the theme of physical attractiveness to broader issues of social justice. Set in the affluent university town of Wellington during the 'War on Terror', the action takes place against the backdrop of growing conservatism in post-9/11 America and queries the widespread view that social justice movements are redundant, reflected in the elision of the second half of Scarry's title. Despite the assertion of gender equality, misogyny is pervasive: 'It was in the *air* ... this hatred of women and their bodies – it seeped in with every draught in the house; people brought it home on their shoes, they breathed it in off their newspapers'.[45] The novel highlights the gap between rhetoric and reality by contrasting the words and deeds of the Belsey family. Zora, a bright young student, constantly worries 'about her looks' (p. 173) and, despite being a 'feminist' (p. 409), wears 'impossible heels' (p. 415) that leave her only able to 'take little pigeon-steps' (p. 409).

Like *Special*, *On Beauty* is concerned with the impact of pornography on female sexuality as well as the endurance of the beauty myth. In second-wave feminist fiction, sex often plays a central part in the protagonist's quest for freedom. The importance of female passion and pleasure is underlined by the title of Weldon's seventh novel: 'Praxis' is the protagonist's name but also means 'turning point' and 'orgasm'. However, *On Beauty* questions the equation of sexual liberation with female emancipation. Zora's classmate Vee is a 'phallic girl', a young woman who mimics men by adopting a casual attitude to recreational sex.[46] She renders herself a passive sexual object, sending her tutor sexually explicit photographs of her body – 'images of orifices and apertures that were simply awaiting him' (p. 380) – and mimics pornography's violent model of sex: she lies with 'her head pressed against the bed as if an invisible hand were restraining her with a plan to suffocation, her legs splayed, her shorts off' (p. 316). Pornography offers no space for female pleasure: Vee wails and quivers with 'preorgasmic passion' despite being 'completely dry' (p. 316). As this suggests, the transformation of the 'female eunuch' into the 'phallic girl' leaves young women far from free.[47]

Zora's father, Howard, is a 'radical art theorist' (p. 115), a professor who presents himself as a feminist and encourages his students to interrogate the relationship between politics and aesthetics. Yet Howard

EMMA PARKER

attempts to justify his affair with colleague Claire through recourse to gender essentialism: 'men – they respond to beauty' (p. 207). Mesmerised by Vee's 'incredible' good looks (p. 252), he also has sex with his student. Further, Howard claims to be a Marxist but disdains his white working-class roots. Howard's son, Levi, is equally unaware of his own blind spots. He is 'raised soft and open, with a liberal susceptibility to the pain of others' (p. 355), and becomes increasingly involved in political activism. Yet Levi demonstrates the normalisation of sexism that arises from the pornification of culture: he covers his bedroom walls with posters of 'big black girls in bikinis' (p. 426). Zora is not exempt from hypocrisy. Though she claims to champion the rights of the underprivileged, she declines to join a Haitian workers' campaign for higher wages, which she dismissively refers to as 'Some Haitian protest thing' (p. 376). Despite the characters' self-involvement and self-interest, the potential for transformation is epitomised by Howard's altered vision of beauty at the novel's close. When he and his wife make love, Howard squeezes Kiki's 'lovely fat ass' (p. 396), producing a shared 'starburst of pleasure and love and beauty' (p. 397).

The combination of continuities and change in feminist fiction defies a linear narrative of development. New forms of feminist fiction exist alongside old, illustrating that literature concerned with issues relating to gender and sexuality has proliferated throughout the postwar period. Fiction continues to be revitalised by feminism just as feminist politics continue to be enriched and renewed by fiction. Feminist narratives have evolved in conjunction with the changing conditions and political context of women's lives, but the postmillennial retrenchment of patriarchy confirms that pronouncements about the redundancy of feminism and decline of feminist fiction have been premature; its influence and relevance remain profound. Literature that engages with the legacies of the women's liberation movement affirms that feminism remains an unfinished revolution and continues to insist on the possibility and necessity of social change.

NOTES

1 Gayle Greene, *Changing the Story: Feminist Fiction and the Tradition* (Bloomington: Indiana University Press, 1992), p. 200.
2 For example, the Equal Pay Act (1970), Sex Discrimination Act (1975), Domestic Violence Act (1976).
3 Patricia Waugh, 'The Woman Writer and the Continuities of Feminism', in *A Concise Companion to Contemporary British Fiction*, ed. James F. English (Oxford: Blackwell, 2006), pp. 188–208, 192.

4 Virginia Woolf, 'Professions for Women' (1931), *Collected Essays*, vol. ii (London: Hogarth Press, 1966), p. 288; Rachel Blau DuPlessis, 'For the Etruscans', in *The New Feminist Criticism: Essays on Women, Literature, and Theory*, ed. Elaine Showalter (London: Virago, 1986), pp. 271–91, 279.

5 Maria Lauret, *Liberating Literature: Feminist Fiction in America* (London: Routledge, 1994), p. 97.

6 See Simone de Beauvoir, *The Second Sex* (London: Picador, 1988); Lisa Maria Hogeland, *Feminism and its Fictions* (Philadelphia: University of Pennsylvania Press, 1998).

7 Fay Weldon, *Remember Me* (London: Coronet, 1979), p. 55; *Praxis* (London: Coronet, 1980), p. 100.

8 Michèle Roberts, *A Piece of the Night* (London: The Women's Press, 1978), p. 75. Hereafter cited parenthetically.

9 Betty Friedan, *The Feminine Mystique* (London: Penguin, 1992), p. 331.

10 Angela Carter, *The Passion of New Eve* (London: Virago, 1982), 80; Beauvoir, *The Second Sex*, p. 295.

11 Fay Weldon, *The Life and Loves of a She-Devil* (London: Coronet, 1984), p. 174.

12 Rita Felski, *Beyond Feminist Aesthetics: Feminist Literature and Social Change* (London: Hutchinson Radius, 1989), pp. 157–8; 161.

13 Hilary Mantel, *An Experiment in Love* (London: Penguin, 1996), p. 164.

14 Angela McRobbie, *The Aftermath of Feminism: Gender, Culture and Social Change* (London: Sage, 2009), p. 24.

15 Ibid., p. 79.

16 Susan Stanford Friedman, *Mappings: Feminism and the Cultural Geographies of Encounter* (Princeton: Princeton University Press, 1998), p. 18.

17 Imelda Whelehan, *The Feminist Bestseller: From Sex and the Single Girl to Sex and the City* (Basingstoke: Palgrave Macmillan, 2005), p. 155; Nina Power, *One-Dimensional Woman* (Winchester: Zero Books, 2009), p. 69.

18 Bella Bathurst, *Special* (London: Picador, 2003), pp. 87, 181. Hereafter cited parenthetically.

19 McRobbie, *The Aftermath of Feminism*, p. 67.

20 Naomi Wolf, *The Beauty Myth: How Images of Beauty are Used Against Women* (London: Vintage, 1991).

21 Ravinder Randhawa, *A Wicked Old Woman* (London: The Women's Press, 1987), pp. 48–9.

22 Frances M. Beal, 'Double Jeopardy: To be Black and Female', *New Generation* 51 (1969), pp. 23–8.

23 Meera Syal, *Anita and Me* (London: Flamingo, 1997), p. 146. Hereafter cited parenthetically.

24 Friedman, *Mappings*, p. 28.

25 Ann McClintock, *Imperial Leather: Race, Gender, and Sexuality in the Colonial Contest* (London: Routledge, 1995), p. 353.

26 Bernardine Evaristo, *The Emperor's Babe* (London: Penguin 2002), pp. 147, 47.

27 Judith Butler, *Gender Trouble: Feminism and the Subversion of Identity* (London: Routledge, 1990), p. 25.

28 Sarah Waters, *Tipping the Velvet* (London: Virago, 1998), p. 13.

29 Marjorie Garber, *Vested Interests: Cross-Dressing and Cultural Anxiety* (London: Penguin, 1993), p. 32.
30 Donna J. Haraway, *Simians, Cyborgs, and Women: The Reinvention of Nature* (London: Free Association, 1991), p. 150.
31 Ali Smith, *Girl Meets Boy* (Edinburgh: Canongate, 2007), p. 84. Hereafter cited parenthetically.
32 Ali Smith, *There but for The* (London: Penguin, 2012), p. 5. Subsequent references are to this edition; Judith Halberstam, *Female Masculinity* (Durham: Duke University Press, 1998), p. 241.
33 Butler, *Gender Trouble*, p. 31.
34 Maureen Duffy, *Alchemy* (London: Harper Perennial, 2005), pp. 75; 320.
35 Fay Weldon, *Puffball* (London: Hodder and Stoughton, 1980), p. 118.
36 See Kristin J. Jacobson, *Neodomestic Fiction* (Columbus: Ohio State University Press, 2010), p. 2.
37 Gary Cross, *Men to Boys: The Making of Modern Immaturity* (New York: Columbia University Press, 2008), p. 2.
38 Friedman, *Mappings*, p. 18.
39 Sarah Waters, 'Wolfskins and Togas: Maude Meagher's *The Green Scamander* and the Lesbian Historical Novel', *Women: A Cultural Review*, 7.2 (1996), pp. 176–88, 176.
40 Owen Jones, *Chavs: The Demonization of the Working Class* (London: Verso, 2011), p. 139.
41 Adrienne Rich, 'When We Dead Awaken: Writing as Re-Vision', *On Lies, Secrets, and Silence: Selected Prose 1966–1978* (London: Virago, 1980), pp. 33–49.
42 Kaye Mitchell, *A. L. Kennedy* (Basingstoke: Palgrave Macmillan, 2008), p. 67.
43 Woolf, *A Room of One's Own and Three Guineas* (London: Penguin, 1993), p. 69.
44 See David James and Urmila Seshagiri, 'Metamodernism: Narratives of Revolution and Continuity', *PMLA*, 129.1 (January 2014): pp. 87–100. For an archive of debates in visual and popular culture about contemporary art after postmodernism, see the webzine *Notes on Metamodernism*: http://www.metamodernism.com/.
45 Zadie Smith, *On Beauty* (London: Penguin, 2005), p. 197. Hereafter cited parenthetically.
46 McRobbie, *The Aftermath of Feminism*, p. 83.
47 See Germaine Greer, *The Female Eunuch* (London: Paladin, 1971). Greer coined the term 'female eunuch' in protest at the desexualisation of women in the culture of her day.

6

SARAH BROPHY AND KASIM HUSAIN

Innovations in Queer Writing

The early twenty-first century seems to have opened up a new era of acceptance and freedom for queer life. Looking back at his own coming of age, sociologist Kenneth Plummer describes the legislative and social changes of the late 1960s as pivotal. To be 'born at the cusp of postmodern times, when intimacies were being refashioned and taking new forms' meant that as a gay man he could encounter 'the stories of others' and realize 'that it was not homosexuality that was the problem, but the unethical responses of the condemners, those full of loathing and hatred'. Instead, Plummer suggests, after the 1967 Sexual Offenses Act decriminalising homosexuality, a grounded, moral, connected, and transparent life becomes, finally, possible.[1] Forty years later, new legislation promises finally to close some of the gaps in citizenship status of LGBTQ subjects and communities in the United Kingdom, including: the 2001 revision to the age of consent for sex between men from eighteen to sixteen (corresponding for the first time with the age of consent for heterosexuals); 2004's Gender Recognition Act, which granted trans people the right to have their gender of choice legally documented and recognised; the Equality Act of 2010, which enshrines anti-discrimination on the basis of sexual orientation; and the Marriage (Same-Sex Couples) Act of 2014.

There is another history to tell here, however: one of persistent inequality and shifting accommodations that complicates a simple narrative of inclusion. As short story writer and anthologist Adam Mars-Jones noted in 1983, 'For the past fifteen years homosexual men in Britain have been accorded a lavish fraction of civil rights. Homosexuals are, intermittently, freer than ever before'.[2] If Mars-Jones is being sardonic, then he does not mean to be cute; the point is that the purported magnanimity of tolerance masks its conditional logic. This qualified promise was crystallised in the Thatcher Conservatives' targeting of queer subjects through Section 28 of the Local Government Act (1987–1988), which cut local authorities' budgets for sex-education materials by banning government funding of the 'promotion'

95

of homosexuality. As historian Anna Marie Smith explains, 'Pro-Section 28 rhetoric' created an opposition between 'the good homosexual' and the 'dangerous queer'.[3] The pairing means that queerness could be figured both as an implicit threat to Prime Minister Margaret Thatcher's well-known preference for a familial basis of social organization, and as an identity that can be accepted by conservatives so long as the performance of gender and sexual identity inclines towards the norm.[4] While Section 28 was finally struck down in 2003 after fifteen years of activist struggle, neoliberalism continues to bifurcate queer activists into radical elements and those segments more willing to assimilate. Despite the 2007 Equality Act, inclusion is far from guaranteed, as is illustrated both by proliferating stories of same-sex couples being turned away from bed and breakfasts and two gay men's removal from a Soho pub for kissing.[5] As these varied twenty-first century incidents demonstrate, queer belonging is still unresolved, still precarious, with multiple political edges.

Contemporary queer British fiction is deeply entangled in the processes of embourgeoisement and normalisation. In her 2012 book *The Gentrification of the Mind,* American lesbian writer and activist Sarah Schulman powerfully inveighs against queer acquiescence to neoliberal culture. Key to her argument is the insight that gentrification is not only a material process whereby urban centres are re-occupied by professionals and entrepreneurs who displace more diverse, lower-income communities; it also evacuates the mental and spiritual memories of heterogeneity and political struggle that characterised gay enclaves from the 1970s to the 1990s, themselves already a vexed product of the concentration of capital and creativity in urban centres.[6] Successfully commodified, literary fiction might not seem to provide the most promising archive for queer criticality and radical activism. But it is nonetheless a premise of this chapter that, in addition to being fundamentally shaped by literal and metaphorical gentrification, British queer fiction from the 1980s to the present is characterised by considerable critical reflection upon these processes.

Writing in the preface to his HIV/AIDS-themed short story collection *Monopolies of Loss* in 1992, Mars-Jones wonders whether 'the truly responsible thing to do now would be to write sexy nostalgic fiction set in the period before the epidemic, safeguarding if only in fantasy the endangered gains of gay liberation'.[7] Some writers, as we shall see, endeavour to combine historical pleasure with some critique of its tendency to 'safeguard' imagined middle-class queer gains. Mars-Jones's own short fiction, however, determinedly set in the present, courts subtle and devastating ironies. It insists that the losses of the 1980s and 1990s were caught up in opportunities to claim property, assert influence, and cultivate niches that afforded some degree of social inclusion. In Mars-Jones's story 'A Small Spade', Bernard embarks on a weekend escape with his increasingly fragile HIV-positive lover, Neil, at a twee, gay-owned Brighton hotel teasingly called Rogues. On arrival, he reflects 'not for the first time [...], but much to his reassurance, gay life promised the depraved and delivered the cosy' (p. 79). But Brighton's all-encompassing, uncanny ease ultimately fails them. While the lovers have enacted a moratorium on forms of intimacy that might transmit the virus to Bernard, a visit to the most innocuous and genteel vegetarian café brings the small trauma of a splinter in Neil's hand, precipitating their own (much more than others') panic over containing his blood (p. 100). Anxiety that hard-won material and emotional security is on the verge of unravelling courses throughout the collected stories: the more Mars-Jones's characters try to control and make good on their (anticipated) losses, the closer they come to unsettling truths and, paradoxically, to ethically dubious action. In the volume's concluding story, 'The Changes of Those Terrible Years', the narrator inherits from a wealthy dying man whom he has befriended 'a large wedding-cake house' in Pimlico, and the sale of that friend's valuable modern art collection permits the conversion of the building's flats into a private hospice (pp. 233, 246). However, when the narrator has exhausted his persona as a man of charity (and televised exemplar of private health care's necessity), he imagines that the house itself wants him to benefit from selling in a hot real estate market (pp. 248–50). That this insight into the narrator's fragmented motivations becomes available only on a recursive reading of the story suggests the extent to which Mars-Jones's fiction engages presciently with the gentrification of both dwelling spaces and imagination twenty years before Schulman's clarion call to resist it.[8]

In 1983, Mars-Jones reflected critically on the transition that Plummer characterises as opening decisively onto freedom and integrity: 'The result has not been an explosion of unleashed sensibility and the instant integration of the minority (perhaps only Leo Abse, MP, expected these things); it takes people a while to get over the shock of decriminalization. The result has been an assortment of improvised moralities combining in various proportions reaction against, and imitation of, heterosexual precedents'.[9] The years between 1967 and 1983 were, Mars-Jones suggests, shaped more by mimicry of continuing heterosexual privilege than by an unleashing of *jouissance*. Interpreting the implications of this critique of emergent homonormativity for the politics of queer literature, Robert Caserio argues that contemporary queer fiction by British writers is perhaps above all a 'market niche'.[10] Despite the sense in which Section 28 foreclosed on the public sphere 'at the very moment of a gay and lesbian bid for it', argues Caserio, this literature's increasingly broad readership suggests a 'queer capture of public imagination', making it a significant 'transitional public institution'.[11] Our account of contemporary British queer fiction puts pressure on Caserio's argument that contemporary queer fiction is largely about 'compensatory thematics' offset by degrees of 'self-scrutiny' and rather more weight on his reflection that 'nevertheless, gay fiction's flights of fancy, however hopeful of surmounting real prejudice, keep close touch with what everyday life cannot overcome'.[12] Affect is, by turns, aspirational, guilty, tender, triumphant, and anxious in British queer fiction since the 1980s. What motivates that (sometimes vertiginous) incoherence is a twofold commitment: to limning everyday desire, pain, social inclusion/exclusion; and to reflecting on the troubling question of who gets to have a life (or an afterlife) and, if they do, on what social and generic terms.

Cover Stories: Queer Fiction and/as 'Life' Writing

If, as Philippe Lejeune has argued, 'what defines autobiography is above all a contract sealed by the proper name', then perhaps no contemporary writer has a stronger grasp of the 'deep signature' of autobiography than Jeanette Winterson.[13] Or, as Winterson's 2011 memoir *Why Be Happy When You Could Be Normal?* suggests, it might be more accurate to say that the autobiographical pact has its teeth in her: 'Part fact part fiction is what life is. And it is always a cover story. I wrote my way out'.[14] Winterson's memoir recounts what has been, since the 1985 publication of her autobiographical fiction, *Oranges Are Not the Only Fruit*, her famous story of being adopted by a working-class Pentecostal family in the northern town of Accrington, who raised her on fear and fabulous interpretations of the Old Testament.[15] *Why Be Happy?* offers a meta-narrative of *Oranges*' creation and significance. Winterson's contentious relationship with her adoptive parents emerges as both a function of her gender (they had expected to adopt a boy, Paul, instead of her) and her sexuality (they kick her out of the house when they discover her lesbianism) (pp. 201–2). The author's remembered confrontation, in fact, her final conversation, with her indomitable adoptive mother, Mrs W, resonates from one phone box to another: 'She tells me that my success is from the Devil, keeper of the wrong crib. She confronts me with the fact that I have used my own name in the novel – if it is a story, why is the main character called Jeanette?' (pp. 4–5). For Mrs W, the autobiographical signature 'Jeanette' is the sign not of authenticity, but of its converse: evil willfully working to sow seeds of difference and obstruction that undermine Mrs W's precarious hold on respectability, happiness, and narrative control.

Literary success (critical acclaim, adaptation for the BBC) is posited as confirming the inauthenticity of the adoptive kin relation. For Winterson, it is also the source of her claims to an autonomous life; her name will become a trademarked entity associated with inalienable genius, despite her well-known investment in courting the play of the 'unnameable'.[16]

Winterson is not alone in her long-standing preoccupation with leveraging life narrative genres. Many of her contemporaries also route ethical and political questions through novels that reference autobiography or biography. For instance, in *Trumpet: A Novel* (1998), Jackie Kay explores the contestation of musician Joss Moody's identity after his death. While Joss's widow, Millie, cleaves to her memories of life with the man she knew as Joss, tabloid biographer Sophie Stones exploits their adopted son Colman's anxiety about his own and his father's identities following his discovery that medical officers have noted the deceased Joss's sex as female 'in bold unequivocal red'.[17] Referentiality is a hallmark of queer fiction, and such vexation about genre raises questions about the terms by which lives are imagined, narrated, and valued. In reworking the life narrative of white American jazz pianist Billy Tipton, who was revealed to his family and the world after his death to have been born a girl, Kay's *Trumpet* offers a portrait, refracted through multiple narrators, of black Scottish trumpeter Joss Moody. Significantly, the novel provides less a sweeping queer historiography than a focus on the specific affective responses to violent attempts to redefine the meaning of Joss's life after the postmortem revelation of his sex to the public. The book's chapter titles – ranging from 'House and Home', 'People', and 'Interview Exclusive' to 'Cover Story' – reference and serve to counter a tabloid imagination that wants to capitalise on sensationalist renderings of difference. Gathering together multiple perspectives in this ironizing framework, *Trumpet* generates insight into the commingling of fiction and non-fiction and especially into the transgender subject's power of self-naming and others' support or undermining of that principle. As Irene Rose points out, this is a novel of 'incessant name-changing'. The self-re-invention of Josephine Moore as Joss Moody is an everyday and a jazz-world register of desire that puts pressure on 'symbolic inscription', and the fact that Joss's kin take the surname 'Moody' (replacing the Scots-inflected Millicent MacFarlane and William Dunsmore with Millie Moody and Colman Moody) moves this desire's implications beyond individual identity and into the realm of the transmissable: of genealogy.[18] At first Colman is consumed by betrayal and vengeance, but as he grieves his father's death, he comes to question journalist Sophie Stones's mission to expose, correct, and profit on Joss's life after his death: 'Imagine this photograph of his father as a little girl in a book with sinister captions. His father keeps coming back to him. He won't stop it. He won't let him alone. Coorie in, coorie in, he says, and tucks him into bed' (p. 256).

In this intensifying jazz-inflected riff, the crooning of Scots dialect remembered from the child Colman's bedtime is re-coded as an insistent call from the past to the present, addressed to the son and asking him to take on the role of holding and nurturing his father's stories – and, through those actions, allowing Joss Moody safely to rest. In the narrative's concluding epistolary evocation of the 'bits and pieces' of Joss's childhood, Joss's father's African-Scottish diasporic history resurfaces in the form of a letter and archive bequeathed to Colman (p. 276). This sequence conjures 'revenants without referents', in John McLeod's phrase, opening up 'the imagining of selves that have never fully existed – lives which have not been permitted to happen or become real'.[19] In Kay's work, then, we can discern a commitment to writing genealogies that prioritise what Sara Ahmed theorizes as 'wonky' lines: the phenomenon of making the world itself come into view aslant, as bodies fail to adhere to normative grids of intelligibility or to heteronormative kinship formations as the developmental basis of 'mature' adulthood.[20]

Kinship Beyond Queer Liberalism

As Ahmed suggests, the family 'orients' or directs culturally mandated paths to the good life along heteronormative and cis-normative lines. Dwelling long enough with difficulty and incoherence might make it possible to begin 'trac[ing] the lines for a different genealogy, one that would embrace the failure to inherit the family line as the condition of possibility for another way of dwelling in the world' and to resist inheriting one's own 'disappearance'.[21] Alan Hollinghurst's The Stranger's Child (2011) brings dilemmas of inheritance into view through its dramatisation of competing accounts of the life of a fictional World War I-era poet, Cecil Valance. At the seventieth birthday party of Cecil's sister-in-law Daphne Jacobs, the aspiring Valance scholar Peter Rowe observes, '"Mm, I was just thinking ... that if this Bill goes through next week it could open the way for a lot more frankness"', earning a cautious reply from a Sawle clearly keen to conceal their youthful affair for a while longer: '"Oh, Leo Abse's Bill, you mean", said Sawle, in an abstracted tone, and perhaps to avoid the charged phrase "Sexual Offences"'.[22]

This scene indexes the ongoing trajectory of legislative measures – here the then-proposed decriminalisation of homosexuality – that both police and sanction certain homosexual intimacies (and not others), thus altering the terrain of possibility for queer intimacies without necessarily querying the terms on which inclusion is being offered. But queer British writing, we want to argue, often complicates the potential presentism and utopianism of an official story of progress towards an inclusive society. Even though his brother Dudley ultimately goes on to garner critical acclaim as a memoirist long after Cecil's death in battle, it is Cecil who lives on positively in the family memory: 'C[ecil] was his parents' favourite, and Dud resented this, he was always making trouble', George remembers to Cecil's biographer, Paul Bryant (p. 352). What is more, through the mask of 'Two Acres', a critically scorned populist wartime paean to English tradition – secretly a love poem from Cecil to Daphne's brother George, which is disguised by its being written in her autograph book, and then by the chaste correspondence Cecil carried out with Daphne prior to dying in the trenches – Hollinghurst not only asserts a subversive queer presence within the Edwardian aristocratic and literary establishment; he also undercuts the normative character of patriotic ideals of heterosexual romantic love, inheritance, and the pastoral itself. Indeed, the novel problematizes the presumptuous method of inquiry of Cecil's biographer, Paul Bryant, which leads him to err in the details of his exposé of Cecil and George's affair. In this echo of Kay's critique of Joss Moody's exploitative biographer Sophie Stones, *The Stranger's Child* reinforces *Trumpet's* implicit caution that simply writing queer bodies into British cultural history is not sufficient to deconstruct the exclusionary premises of nationalist mythology altogether. To posit an alternate historiography of twentieth-century kinship as compensating for the exclusions of the predominant heteronormative account would be to participate in the promulgation of what David L. Eng calls queer liberalism, which 'marks a particular confluence of political and economic conditions that form the basis of liberal inclusion, rights, and recognitions for particular gay and lesbian ... citizen-subjects willing and able to comply with its normative mandates'.[23]

While Hollinghurst's oeuvre concentrates on the accommodations with the normative that gay men have attempted to win and to make, contemporary transgender-themed fiction set in the British Isles presents means of imagining kinship formations otherwise. In view of Judith Butler's figuration, in *Gender Trouble* (1990), of the trans subject as paradigmatic of gender's performativity and thus fundamentally non-identical with sex, it is perhaps unsurprising that prominent narratives such as Neil Jordan's *The Crying Game* (1992) and Patrick McCabe's *Breakfast on Pluto* (1998) take the predicaments of trans characters in a largely trans-phobic society as symbolic of how a broader social struggle (the Troubles in Northern Ireland, in both cases) exacerbates constraints on identity more generally, whether one is trans or cis, Catholic or Protestant.[24] McCabe's first-person narrator, Patrick 'Pussy' Braden, composes his memories from the vantage point of an in-patient treatment centre after a breakdown. The narration shuttles between first and third person, highlighting the entanglement of fantasy, resistance, and oppression. Pussy's confessional mode is partly compelled by a contentious relationship to the journaling that has been assigned as therapy: 'Was it any wonder I fed him a load of lies?'[25] However, these narrative associations between transgender subjects, fictionalisation, and resistance have political complications. For a cis author to depict a trans protagonist as a flagrant and unrepentant liar, as McCabe's portrait of Pussy Braden does, is to risk purchasing narrative self-reflexivity at the expense of subject status for the protagonist. Kay's *Trumpet* does something more nuanced, suggests J. Jack Halberstam, as it 'quietly sidesteps the equation between passing and lying, and instead investigates the particularity of desire', registering the priority of 'transsexual self-authorization'. However, Halberstam also reminds us that 'the transsexual has been used in queer theory as a symbol for the formulation of a subjectivity that actually threatens transsexual claims'.[26] The relationship between feminism, queer theory, and transgender studies is not always or necessarily fraught, but the latter emerged in part out of fundamental disagreements with the former critical movements. Consider how the ontological status accorded 'woman' by standpoint feminist scholarship de-legitimates trans experience, as in Janice Raymond's explicit location of transsexuality as 'a fabrication of a patriarchal medical system'.[27] As much as the insights of theory and of fiction can work to disentangle the conjoined understanding of gender and sex that underlies transphobic accounts like Raymond's, these representational modes do not always live up to their post-structuralist promises.

In *Feeling Backward*, Heather Love reads 'the association of homosexuality with loss, melancholia, and failure' against the grain of how 'such links ... [are] deployed against gays and lesbians so regularly'.[28] To this end, Love constellates queer modernist texts such as Radclyffe Hall's *The Well of Loneliness* (1928) that embrace these commonly derogated attributes, assembling them into an archive that eludes the normative imperatives shaping social and sexual futures. Sarah Waters's *The Night Watch* (2006), in its depiction of London during and immediately after the Second World War, tarries conspicuously with the backward. The novel proceeds retrospectively, beginning in 1947 before turning the clock back to wartime in sections set in 1944 and 1942. This structure frees Waters from the constraints linear chronology can place on characterisation in fiction, by refusing the assumption that psychological development deepens as a plot unfolds into a better future. The novel's reversed sequencing turns what could otherwise seem somewhat well-worn figurations of queerness on their heads. If the narrative temporality were linear, a character like the wartime ambulance attendant Kay Langrish might easily be regarded as thwarted, continuing to wear her uniform long after Armistice Day as she clings to the memory of purpose and belonging that the Blitz had granted her. So, too, could Duncan Pearce's narrative of incarceration as a war resister at Wormwood Scrubs (together with his subsequent social exclusion) risk being overdetermined by the moment of his adolescent lover Alec's fantasy of double suicide going awry. Whereas Kay's upper-class origins make her suitable for the role of romantic rescuer – as Kay's former lover Julia implies when she comments, '"Kay's such a heroine, though, isn't she? ... Kay's such a brick"' – working-class Duncan remains confined by the intersection between hegemonic masculinity and social disadvantage even after the end of his prison sentence.[29] Bereft of the status and financial capital to get ahead and to choose where he finds intimacy, Duncan assents willingly to the manipulative charity of living with his doting former guard, Mr. Mundy. An alternative domesticity but hardly an idealized one, this arrangement has the virtue of being codified, even as it remains obscure and unsettling in the eyes of Duncan's sister Viv and his former cellmate, the upper-class conscientious objector Fraser. As Fraser observes to Viv, 'It seems an odd sort of life ... for a boy like Duncan. He's not even a boy any more, is he? And yet it's impossible to think of him as anything else. ... I think he's made himself be stuck, as a way of – of punishing himself, for all that happened, years ago, all that he did and didn't do. ... I think Mr Mundy is taking very good care to keep him stuck' (p. 119). In narrating queer lives during and post–World War II, Waters's historical fiction eschews a portrait of the period's altered social norms as providing relief from heteronormative domination. Retreading historical ground from 1947 back through to the Blitz, *The Night Watch* traces the everyday vagaries of queer survival through peacetime and wartime. In so doing, she indicates that those temporary remediations that the war did afford queer life in mid-century Britain risk being submerged by nationalist historiography's haste to read the Second World War's ending as an unmitigated political triumph.

In Between Crisis and the Everyday: A Queer Good Life?

Looking backwards doesn't just 'queer' historiography; it also anticipates some of the ways in which the postwar consensus continued to fail queer subjects. The question then becomes: how else can we address the vicissitudes brought on by the atomisation characteristic of the late twentieth century? To put it another way, we want to consider here how queer British writing approaches what Lauren Berlant calls 'crisis ordinariness', by which she accounts for the ever-receding possibility of actually attaining our motivating fantasies.[30] The ubiquitous dissonance between ambition and realisation becomes an index of the cruelty involved in continuing to be optimistic about the good life's attainability. The 1980s, as portrayed in the work of Winterson and Hollinghurst, appeared to suggest that coming out and making good were less mutually exclusive than ever before. In her memoir, Winterson captures the appeal of Thatcher's Conservative Party for an aspiring working-class Northern lesbian writer:

> I had already left home. I was already working evenings and weekends to get through school. I had no safety net.
> I had no respect for family life. I had no home. I had rage and courage.
> I was smart. I was emotionally disconnected. I didn't understand gender politics. I was the ideal prototype for the Reagan/Thatcher revolution. (*Why Be Happy?*, p. 134)

As a challenge to the reigning postwar consensus that regarded the welfare state as a social good, Thatcherism drew support from many like Winterson that might in hindsight look unlikely.[31] The resonance of Thatcher's background – 'she knew the price of a loaf of bread. ... If a grocer's daughter could be prime minister, then a girl like me could write a book' – might well have implied that the entrepreneurial individualism of her party's campaign could herald more opportunities for others with reasons similar to Winterson's for mistrusting the outgoing socio-political order.[32]

As Winterson acknowledges, however, Tory campaign promises proved less egalitarian in practice (*Why Be Happy?* p. 140). Thatcher's premiership dramatically intensified social inequality, which in part explains the way in which material success became both a more widely admissible aspiration and frequently flaunted accomplishment. In a reflection that at once broaches and deflects the discomfiting question of her own status as beneficiary of this regime, Winterson – sitting in an upmarket Manchester basement bar wearing an 'Armani suit' and 'spray tan', displaying all the accoutrements of a television appearance – imagines her heterosexual double: 'if I hadn't found books ... I'd have gone into property and made a fortune. I'd have had a boob job by now, and be on my second or third husband, and live in a ranch-style house with a Range Rover on the gravel' (pp. 208–9).

In his 2004 novel *The Line of Beauty*, Hollinghurst captures these transformations in Britain's social strata from the perspective of an ostensible outsider, as the novel centres on the figure Nick Guest cuts during his time lodging in the West London house of Conservative MP Gerald Fedden and his family. Gay identity and lower-middle-class roots in provincial Barwick are less important as attributes that ultimately disbar Nick from belonging with the Fedden family than as lenses with which to reflect on the 1980s elite. As Hollinghurst puts it to one reviewer, Nick is 'someone who is not just looking on in horror, but is actually susceptible to the glamour of it all'.[33] Indeed, Nick idealises the Fedden family and the moneyed circle into which they provide him an entry. The novel portrays the 1980s as an era in which knowledge of all forms becomes capital. This occurs in cultural terms: Nick's supposed indispensability partly lies in his role of interpreting architectural and domestic heirlooms, which the Feddens possess in great quantity without much understanding. But in carnal terms, too, Nick follows an aspirational (and exoticizing) sexual trajectory: from trysts with the Portuguese banquet server Tristão to his first boyfriend, Leo, a black British council worker, before finally fixating on Wani, scion of the Lebanese Ouradi family of supermarket millionaires. Wani's resources allow Nick to produce *Ogee*, a limited-edition coffee table magazine that lasts one issue, and a shelved adaptation of Henry James' *The Spoils of Poynton* for the screen. These spectacular attempts and failures make Nick an apt personi-fication of the Thatcherite individual. He possesses both a reckless appetite for upward mobility and enough social judgement to recognise and to try to cash in on the changing cultural scene.

Recognition is itself a key fulcrum on which the novel's complex engage-ment with the increasingly difficult terrain for queer political struggle turns. In order to maintain his place in the Fedden's luxurious milieu (their well-appointed townhouse is in Kensington, their summer retreat in the Dordogne), Nick scrupulously avoids affiliation with queer identity until his climactic public outing. Meanwhile, Leo, who as the most politicised queer character in the novel is conspicuously also racialized, dies of AIDS, as his sister, Rosemary, relates posthumously to Nick, who has long since turned away from the friendship. The 'cover stories' we wrote of earlier retain some advantages, evidently, and the capacity to maintain them is a function of privilege. Nick's presence in a well connected, affluent MP's home remains politically symptomatic irrespective of his avowed liberal politics, or lack thereof. Ultimately, even his fleeing the Fedden's home amid Tory fixer Barry Groom's homophobic curses – 'stupid little pansy' and 'little cocksucker' – is less escape or refusal than a final confirmation of Nick's utility as a scape-goat.[34] On the doorstep, he faces the assembled Rupert Murdoch media, who are only too eager to sell the supposed scandal of Nick's affair with Wani under Gerald Fedden's nose so as to downplay the Tory minister's own lately revealed election-time dalliances in a hotel with one of his campaign workers. The sequence of social ironies by which the once-indispensable houseguest becomes disposable are foreshadowed in dreams of Nick's boarding a 'great heterosexual express' train when he first joins the family

SARAH BROPHY AND KASIM HUSAIN

circle in 1983 (pp. 23, 58–9). By the 1987 section of the narrative, Nick's earlier presentiments that his foothold in the Fedden's world is precarious come alarmingly true, as it becomes apparent that his continuing desire to be one with this power bloc effectively shores up Tory familial, political, and economic interests.[35]

The degree to which the queer good life inclines towards conformity with the norm, despite the undertow of everyday narcissism, shame, and guilt, is further exemplified in the curious afterlife of Omar Ali, the protagonist of Stephen Frears and Hanif Kureishi's 1985 film *My Beautiful Laundrette*. Much like *Laundrette*'s then-unprecedented mainstream cinematic depiction of interracial queer desire continues to earn critical approbation for presciently diagnosing nascent homonormativity,[36] Kureishi mines the film to revive Omar for his 2008 novel *Something to Tell You*, which centres on Jamal, a mixed-race wild child of late-twentieth-century London, confronting the material comforts and new insecurities of middle age. Whereas the film charted Omar's social climbing against the odds of class, race, and sexuality, seeking ultimately to reconcile with his former National Front-supporting skinhead lover Johnny and running his renovated laundrette together, Omar in his postmillennial iteration embodies a different zeitgeist: 'It was ironic to think how Omar meshed with his times. His commendable antiracism had made him into the ideal committeeman. Now, as an Asian, gay millionaire with an interest in a football club, he was perfect leadership material'.[37]

Kureishi deftly turns a former narrative subject into an object; being gay and Pakistani no longer provides a narrative-defining quandary, as Omar now plays a secondary role as a guest at that most typical of elite British rituals, the country weekend, always a site of social and sexual intrigue. Whereas the Ouradis, flush with new money in Hollinghurst's 1980s, are merely tolerated at Conservative functions as donors, concealing their son's sex life by hiring a stand-in fiancée (*The Line of Beauty*, pp. 185–8), *Something to Tell You* is written amid a New Labour ascendancy that saw Tony Blair build on Thatcherism's individualist market-oriented legacy; the hereditary privilege that allowed the country's establishment political class to visit bigoted indignities on the nouveaux riches has become both tenuous and counterproductive. Through Omar's reappearance as an icon of neoliberal success, Kureishi renders the queerness of the contemporary queer good life effectively banal.

What is tantalizing and politically revealing about such narratives is that they diagnose the shrinking grounds in Britain for heretofore life-sustaining fantasies, through their emphasis on optimism against the odds. Is Omar's queer liberal success worth the cost of gentrifying the working-class community of his upbringing? Is there any cause to hope that collective dreams might disrupt and reorient those that determine the atomising trajectories of Nick, Wani, and Leo? Considered through a critical perspective that highlights the sustained attention in this body of fiction to gentrification and the corollary drift away from activist citizenship in favour of promises of private gain, inclusion, and a measure of security, the fictions we have discussed redound upon the continuing urgency of Judith Butler's problematization of the pursuit of recognition under the sign of queerness:

> If the term 'queer' is to be a site of collective contestation ... it will have to remain that which is, in the present, never fully owned, but always and only redeployed, twisted, queered from a prior usage and in the direction of urgent and expanding political purposes, and perhaps also yielded in favour of terms that do that political work more effectively.[38]

Unevenly cognisant, yet conscious nonetheless, of sexual freedom since 1967 as conditional, wavering, and politically contradictory, contemporary queer fiction attempts to engage in the set of critical actions that Butler is circumspectly willing to hope for here. Fiction, especially in its autobiographically and historiographically inflected modes, twists, ironizes, and sometimes excoriates the terms with which queer life is narrated and valued – making 'the gentrification of the mind' a critical question rather than a conclusion.

NOTES

1 Kenneth Plummer, *Intimate Citizenship: Private Decisions and Public Dialogues* (Montreal: McGill-Queen's University Press, 2003), p. 116.
2 Adam Mars-Jones, 'Gay Fiction and the Reading Public', in *Mae West is Dead: Recent Lesbian and Gay Fiction*, ed. Mars-Jones (London and Boston: Faber, 1983), p. 13.
3 Anna Marie Smith, *New Right Discourse on Race and Sexuality in Britain, 1968–1990* (Cambridge: Cambridge University Press, 1994), pp. 226–7.
4 In Margaret Thatcher's words, 'Who is society? There is no such thing! There are individual men and women and there are families'. See 'Interview for *Woman's Own* ('No Such Thing as Society')', *Margaret Thatcher Foundation*, 23 September 1987, retrieved from http://www.margaretthatcher.org/document/106689.
5 Owen Bowcott, 'Gay Couple Wins Discrimination Case Against Christian Hoteliers', *Guardian*, 18 January 2011, retrieved from http://www.theguardian.com/world/2011/jan/18/gay-couple-win-case-hoteliers, and Adam Gabbatt; 'Gay Couple Claim They Were Ejected from a Soho Pub for Kissing', *Guardian*, 15 April 2011, retrieved from http://www.theguardian.com/world/2011/apr/14/gay-claim-ejected-pub-kissing. As Engin Isin has suggested, the organization of a several-hundred-strong kiss-in protest in response to the ejection of Jonathan Williams and James Bull from the John Snow pub in Soho can be read as a coalitional, activist politics of contemporary citizenship (*Citizens Without Frontiers*

[London: Bloomsbury, 2012], p. 156). Broaden the context a little more, however, and there is disturbing evidence of complicity amongst queer activism, urban development agendas, and neofascist groups in East London. See Decolonizing Sexualities Network, 'From Gay Pride to White Pride: Why Marching on East London is Racist', 15 March 2011, retrieved from http://www.decolonizingsexualities.org/decolonize-queer/.

6 Sarah Schulman, *The Gentrification of the Mind: Witness to a Lost Imagination* (Berkeley: University of California Press, 2012), pp. 14–15.
7 Adam Mars-Jones, *Monopolies of Loss* (London: Faber, 1992), p. 2. Hereafter cited parenthetically.
8 Caserio, Robert. 'Queer Fiction: The Ambiguous Emergence of a Genre', in *A Concise Companion to Contemporary British Fiction*, ed. James F. English (Oxford: Blackwell, 2006), pp. 209–28. Here, Caserio offers an account of queer liberation's 'ambiguous' and 'uneven progress' up to the year 2006 (p. 223), along with a comprehensive reading of Mars-Jones's contributions, including his novel *The Waters of Thirst* (London: Faber, 1994).
9 Mars-Jones, 'Gay Fiction and the Reading Public', p. 13.
10 Caserio, 'Queer Fiction', p. 211.
11 Ibid., pp. 211, 222, 220.
12 Ibid., pp. 219, 214, 220.
13 Phillipe Lejeune. 'The Autobiographical Pact', trans. Katherine Leary, in *On Autobiography*, ed. John Paul Eakin (Minneapolis: University of Minnesota Press, 1989), p. 19.
14 Jeanette Winterson, *Why Be Happy When You Could Be Normal?* (London: Vintage, 2012), p. 6. Hereafter cited parenthetically.
15 Jeanette Winterson, *Oranges Are Not the Only Fruit* (London and New York: Pandora Press, 1985).
16 Miguel Mota, 'What's in a Name? The Case of jeanettewinterson.com', *Twentieth-Century Literature* 50.2 (2004), p. 202. While Sarah Schulman points to English lesbian writers' success as a hopeful counterpoint to the disappearance of political queer content from American literary production (*The Gentrification of the Mind*, pp. 151–2), we suggest that the example of Winterson is rather more contradictory. As Mota observes of Winterson's assertion of legal control over the domain name jeanettewinterson.com, 'One could hardly imagine a more emphatic –indeed Thatcherite – assertion of autonomous individualism' ('What's in a Name?', pp. 196–7).
17 Jackie Kay, *Trumpet: A Novel* (London: Vintage, 1998), pp. 112–13. Hereafter cited parenthetically.
18 Irene Rose, 'Heralding New Possibilities: Female Masculinity in Jackie Kay's *Trumpet*', in *Posting the Male: Masculinities in Post-War and Contemporary British Literature*, eds. Daniel Lea and Berthold Schoene (Amsterdam and New York: Rodopi, 2003), pp. 144–6.
19 John McLeod, 'Business Unbegun: Spectral Subjectivities in the Work of Jackie Kay and Pauline Melville', in *Postcolonial Ghosts/Fantômes Post-Coloniaux*, ed. Judith Misrahi-Barak (Montpellier: Presses Universitaires de la Méditerranée, 2009), pp. 193, 182.
20 Sara Ahmed, *Queer Phenomenology: Orientations, Objects, Others* (Durham: Duke University Press, 2006), pp. 66, 172–4.

21 Ibid., p. 178.

22 Alan Hollinghurst, *The Stranger's Child* (London: Picador, 2011), p. 248. Hereafter cited parenthetically.

23 David L. Eng, *The Feeling of Kinship: Queer Liberalism and the Racialization of Intimacy* (Durham: Duke University Press, 2010), p. 24.

24 Neil Jordan (dir.), *The Crying Game* (Palace Pictures/Channel Four, 1992).

25 Patrick McCabe, *Breakfast on Pluto* (London: Picador, 1998), pp. 2, 95.

26 J. Jack Halberstam, *In a Queer Time and Place: Transgender Bodies, Subcultural Lives* (New York: New York University Press, 2005), pp. 52, 59, 64. On the politics of trans representations, see also Rita Felski, 'Fin de siecle, Fin de sexe: Transsexuality, Postmodernism, and the Death of History', *New Literary History* 27.2 (1996): 337–49; and Jay Prosser, *Second Skins: The Body Narratives of Transsexuality* (New York: Columbia University Press, 1998).

27 Sally Hines, 'Recognising Diversity? The Gender Recognition Act and Transgender Citizenship', in *Transgender Identities: Towards a Social Analysis of Gender Diversity*, eds. Sally Hines and Tam Sanger (New York: Routledge, 2010), p. 90.

28 Heather Love, *Feeling Backward: Loss and the Politics of Queer History* (Cambridge, MA: Harvard University Press, 2009), pp. 6–7.

29 Sarah Waters, *The Night Watch* (London: Virago, 2006), p. 212. Hereafter cited parenthetically.

30 Lauren Berlant, *Cruel Optimism* (Durham: Duke University Press, 2011), p. 10.

31 For more on the broad composition of the coalition that facilitated Thatcherite hegemony, see Stuart Hall's *The Hard Road to Renewal: Thatcherism and the Crisis of the Left* (London: Verso, 1988), especially 'The Great Moving Right Show', pp. 39–56.

32 Winterson, *Why Be Happy?*, p. 138.

33 Hollinghurst quoted in Tim Adams, 'A Classic of Our Times', *Observer*, 11 April 2004, retrieved from http://www.theguardian.com/books/2004/apr/11/fiction .alanhollinghurst.

34 Hollinghurst, *The Line of Beauty* (London: Bloomsbury, 2004), p. 413. Hereafter cited parenthetically.

35 For more on the politics of history, home, and risk in *The Line of Beauty*, see Sarah Brophy, 'Queer Histories and Postcolonial Intimacies in Alan Hollinghurst's *The Line of Beauty*', in *The End of Empire and the English Novel since 1945*, eds. Rachael Gilmour and Bill Schwarz (Manchester: Manchester University Press, 2011), pp. 184–201; and Nicky Marsh, 'Desire and Disease in the Speculative Economy: A Critique of the Language of Crisis', *Journal of Cultural Economy* 4.3 (2011), pp. 301–14.

36 Stephen Frears (dir.) and Hanif Kureishi (writ.), *My Beautiful Laundrette*. (MGM, 2003). See Gairola, Rahul A. 'Capitalist Houses, Queer Homes: National Belonging and Transgressive Erotics in *My Beautiful Laundrette*', *South Asian Popular Culture* 7.1 (2009), pp. 37–54.

37 Hanif Kureishi, *Something to Tell You* (London: Faber and Faber, 2008), pp. 174–5.

38 Judith Butler, 'Critically Queer', *GLQ: A Journal of Lesbian and Gay Studies*, 1.1 (November 1993), p. 19.

7

DANIEL WESTON

Nature Writing and the Environmental Imagination

This chapter opens with two soundings. The first. Shortly after his novel *Scenes from Early Life* won the 2013 Ondaatje Prize, the Royal Society for Literature's award for a work of fiction, non-fiction, or poetry evoking the spirit of place, Philip Hensher endorsed the prevailing current understanding of the novel's relation to environment: 'Of course, a narrative can't be just about a spirit of place; that is a subject for the lyric poem. A novel has to place the psychologies of individuals in a delicate relationship with the world that formed them.'[1] Like others before him, Hensher sees the novel, the literary form perhaps dedicated more than others to human narratives, employing place and environment (no matter how highly wrought or seemingly influential) as setting for psychological drama. This chapter aims to explore the complexity of this 'delicate relationship' as it has played out in postwar fiction attentive to place, and in place writing in other supposedly non-fictional mediums that increasingly draw on novelistic discursive procedures across the same period. In short, it aims to complicate the generic distinctions that have been thought to characterise the relationship between literature, place, and environment.

The second. 'Writing Britain: Wastelands to Wonderlands' was the title of the British Library's 2012 summer exhibition devoted to literary depictions of a nation's landscapes, scheduled as a showpiece for the Cultural Olympiad running concurrently with the London games of that year. The exhibition's extensive displays of manuscripts testified to the extent and range of literary landscapes – the fertility of the environmental imagination – from the medieval period to the present, to the array of texts centrally concerned with place, and to the way in which landscapes pervade and condition writers' ideas even where they are not the primary focus. Landscape, the exhibition implicitly claimed, is a repository of history: places offer ways of telling stories about those who live or travel there, and as such they possess narrative potential for writers to exploit. Structured thematically to draw links across periods, the exhibition also served as a timely reminder of the central importance of textual traditions in formulating and affecting the ways place is experienced and represented.

If 'Writing Britain' demonstrated the contemporary currency of environment in literature, it also flagged up the lack of anything approximating the 'nature novel' after 1945. The pastoral idyll of contemplative rural retreat and ecological harmony is evident in the writing of Britain from the earliest English literature (and further back, a familiar trope from Virgil onwards) but does not feature in the postwar novel. Consequently, fiction from this period did not feature as prominently in the exhibition as poetry and non-fiction prose. Postwar fiction that was included complicated the very idea of the nature novel. This process undoubtedly began before 1945 with Hardy and Lawrence, but the implications of their novels have been more thoroughly investigated and absorbed by postwar authors. Ideas of landscape, place, and nature have also been developed and conceptualised anew in this period in response to unprecedented environmental and ecological change and growing awareness that human activity has brought about the 'anthropocene' epoch. However, the apparent death of the nature novel does not preclude a chapter on nature writing in a volume such as this. Rather, its inclusion is important in two respects. Firstly, the postwar period has witnessed an atomised diversification of the environmental imagination after the demise of the traditional nature novel. Where a rigid genre has fallen away, a diffuse but more pervasive influence can now be felt in a wide variety of novels. Secondly, the period has also seen a marked increase in the deployment of novelistic techniques of representation in apparently non-fictional renderings of nature writing, and vice versa. As a result, this chapter re-examines this generic divide.

The idea of the 'environmental imagination' is one that emerges from ecocritical quarters. It comes from the title of Lawrence Buell's investigation of the 'American environmental imagination', primarily within the generic designation of 'literary non-fiction'.[2] The decision to adopt this focus, Buell explains, results from the fact that 'environmental nonfiction' conforms most readily to the criteria that he sets out for an 'environmental text'.[3] Whilst these criteria have become a widely used benchmark, their usefulness in relation to fiction has also become a matter of debate. The most important of the points Buell elaborates for an 'environmentally oriented work' is that 'the non-human environment is present not merely as a framing device but as a presence that begins to suggest that human history is implicated in natural history.'[4] Dominic Head has expressed some scepticism with regard to the apparent stringency of this point if applied to fiction: 'One can think of very few novels in which this principle is sustained throughout, and the logic of this requirement may contradict the novel's role as a social medium.'[5]

Amongst those few that have attempted this reorientation are Raymond Williams's unfinished *People of the Black Mountains* trilogy in which place rather than character provides the unifying factor for a series of narratives spanning prehistory to the present day. Adam Thorpe's *Ulverton* (1992) employs a similar structural principle, narrating various episodes in the lives of the eponymous village's inhabitants from the seventeenth century onwards. However, the links that are forged are temporal as often as spatial, situating individual lives in the context of social rather than environmental history. Thorpe's subsequent texts have also played out the historical connections and narratives invested in place. Whilst postwar fiction has, then, seen experiments in support of an ecocentric principle, Head argues that 'it is hard to conceive of the novel as a genre reinventing itself in this way'.[6] As a result, 'narrative fiction would seem to be peculiarly resistant to the operations of ecocriticism'.[7] Indeed, Head's misgivings are undoubtedly well grounded in relation to deep ecologists' call for the displacement of anthropocentrism and installation of environmental orientation in its place as *the* governing principle of the novel.[8] The basis of the novel in human narratives and interactions is incommensurate with this wholesale change.

However, it is possible to read Buell differently. Buell follows the statement of requirements for an environmental text immediately with the proviso that 'by these criteria, few works fail to qualify at least marginally, but few qualify unequivocally and consistently'.[9] There is, in fact, no call in Buell's construction for these principles to be 'sustained throughout', but rather that a text 'begins to suggest' the implication of human history in natural history. Indeed, the point is one of establishing dialogue between human and environmental narratives rather than of displacing one type with the other. If Buell's criteria are in this respect less 'deep green' than has been thought, they might also be more useful in discussions of the novel than has been hitherto acknowledged. This chapter argues that postwar novels and nature writing have both contributed to a burgeoning awareness of the entanglement of human and environmental narratives. It takes issue with the assumption that making room for the latter must necessarily be at the cost of the former but shows how two-way dialogues have registered in a range of texts.[10]

As previously noted, the postwar period has witnessed an increased formal traffic between formerly distinct genres of writing, with implications for the environmental imagination. David Shields has recently argued that contemporary artists across a whole range of media – though most working with text – are 'breaking larger and larger chunks of "reality" into their work', thus 'blurring (to the point of invisibility) any distinction between fiction and non-fiction'. Concomitantly, and increasingly often, '"nonfiction" material is ordered, shaped, and imagined as "fiction"'.[11] In relation to the present discussion, this broad trend has manifested as a tendency to include consideration of an impinging environmental reality into fictional worlds on the one hand, and a deployment of novelistic techniques to write environment in a narrative medium on the other. These features in novels and in nature writing have increased exponentially in recent years, not least in the so called 'new nature writing'. However, I will argue here that a distinct trajectory can also be mapped over the whole of the postwar period under consideration. If the new nature writing is distinctive, it is as a rediscovery of trends emanating in earlier phases of the postwar era.

Before beginning the survey proper, it is necessary to take note of two important texts that set the scene for rejuvenation after 1945. The first is Stella Gibbons's *Cold Comfort Farm* (1932). The absence of a postwar traditional nature novel in 'Writing Britain' is at least in part the result of this deconstruction in parody of the calcified generic stereotypes and plots of the rural novel – the 'novel of agricultural life', as Gibbons terms it – familiar from that earlier period. The novel brings to bear the rational urbanity of the town to depictions of country living in the form of Flora Poste who, orphaned at nineteen, goes from London to stay with her relatives the Starkadders at the eponymous farm. In the mock-dedicatory letter to Anthony Pookworthy, a 'master-craftsman' of the genre, Gibbons lays out the targets of her parody: the stylistic tendency to overwrite, and thematic tendency to combine a kind of environmental determinism with extended pathetic fallacy. Trained as a journalist, 'learning to say exactly what I meant in short sentences', she must modify her style for this genre 'to write as though I were not quite sure what I meant but was jolly well going to say something all the same in sentences as long as possible'.[12] She hopes to imitate Pookworthy's own books, which are 'records of intense spiritual struggles, staged in the wild setting of mere, berg or fen'. 'Your characters are ageless and elemental beings,' she mock-eulogises, 'tossed like straws on the seas of passion. You paint Nature at her rawest, in man and landscapes' (p. 6). These two features combine in her own pastiche: 'From the stubborn interwoven strata of his sub-conscious, thought seeped up into his dim conscious; not as an integral part of that consciousness, but more as an impalpable emanation, a crepuscular addition, from the unsleeping life in the restless trees and fields surrounding him'. (p. 45)

The remnants of Darwinism in the post-Hardy, sub-Lawrentian rural novel of the interwar years comes under fire when subjected to Flora's urban sensibilities. Gibbons attacks the unthinking conflation of human consciousness and primaeval setting in passages such as this, clearing some of the dead wood attached to literary depictions of nature. Neither could the effective separation of the urban and the rural be maintained: if the nature novel had effectively been killed off, whatever stepped into its place would have to conceive of nature within a wider network of concerns (social, environmental, conceptual, and aesthetic). Published in 1932, its immediate effect was the apparent cessation in serious treatments of the subject, though certainly not its popular abatement. After the war, the very impossibility of the nature novel in this vein led to a rethinking of human interactions with environment, and especially rural environments. This rethinking necessarily involved a consideration of aesthetic and generic concerns alongside the changed sense of the relationship that scientists and ecologists were beginning to uncover and disseminate.

The second important text to which I allude focused the new urgency of modern ecological concern and presented it to a wide audience: Rachel Carson's *Silent Spring* (1962). Though concerned primarily with the American environment, the book's influence was widespread and profound. For Timothy Clark, 'Carson's detailed polemic about the evils of mass pesticide and herbicide use was the landmark book from which the modern environmental movement is often dated'.[13] The important implication of Carson's particular focus is the recognition of humans' activity as a significant force – often a detrimental one – in ecology (the relation of living things to their environment). Carson's polemic thus signifies a paradigm shift in the consideration of human and environment. The text not only provides the motivation to rethink this relationship but also opens with an example of the means for doing so taken up subsequently in various forms. *Silent Spring* is largely a scientific book (if for a popular audience), but its opening chapter, 'A Fable for Tomorrow', is a kind of creative non-fiction, or even a fiction. The title of the book imagines a future catastrophe that might ensue from industrial farming techniques – the absence of birds and therefore of birdsong – that then plays out in the opening fable, which undermines inherited ideas of the pastoral. 'There was once a town in the heart of America where all life seemed to live in harmony with its surroundings', it begins, with a formulaic, fairy-tale-like construction. Man's place in this idyllic ecology is at this stage unproblematic. The subsequent unexplained deaths amongst beast and then man are conceived initially as 'a strange blight', 'some evil spell', or 'mysterious maladies', only for the ignorance of causes to be revealed: 'No witchcraft, no enemy action had silenced the rebirth of new life in this stricken world. The people had done it to themselves'.[14] The fable dramatises the failure of a certain way of depicting nature in light of new ecological findings and demands an alternative. It plays not only on the pastoral but also redeploys cold-war apocalyptic imagery pervading American (and British) culture at that time.

The pervasive and diffuse influence of *Silent Spring* is supplemented by a more specific legacy in fiction imagining a future environmental catastrophe. This narrative tendency is most apparent in a North American tradition, most recently encompassing texts such as Cormac McCarthy's *The Road* (2006) and Margaret Atwood's trilogy of apocalyptic novels: *Oryx and Crake* (2003), *The Year of the Flood* (2009), and *MaddAddam* (2013). A smaller number of British novelists have also produced work in this area. J. G. Ballard's novels from the 1960s onwards have combined technological and social dystopia with environmental breakdown. Critical reception has often gravitated towards the former but the different components are not easily divisible. For Ballard, ecological and communal breakdown go hand in hand. In the same year as Carson's *Silent Spring*, Ballard's *The Drowned World* (1962) envisages polar icecaps melted by solar radiation, with European and North American cities submerged. *The Burning World* (1964) sees industrial waste disrupt precipitation cycles resulting in water shortage. Both texts predate but speak to the increasing focus on climate change as the most important environmental issue in recent years. More recently, Will Self's *The Book of Dave* (2006) has followed Ballard in imagining social life in a future London after catastrophic flooding.

Speculative fiction of this kind is only the narrowest definition of Carson's influence. At the other end of the spectrum, in the broadest sense, the joint legacies of Carson's and Gibbons's decoupling of ecological reality and narrative form frees writers to investigate new interactions between the two. This takes place in relation to a variety of environments: rural, urban, and somewhere in-between. Where Gibbons demolishes rural environmental determinism, Jonathan Raban's writing has more recently posited the malleability of modern urban identity. A wide-ranging travel writer and novelist, Raban has considered many environments, but it is his urban texts that have proved most influential in postwar fiction. *Soft City* (1974) goes against the grain of prevalent trends in the 1970s and in some senses precedes the conceptual revisions of subsequent decades up to the present. The alienation that the city engenders, the most familiar trope of its literary representation from at least Dickens onwards, presents, for Raban, opportunity and freedom. At moments of alienation, 'the city goes soft; it awaits the imprint of an identity. For better or worse, it invites you to remake it, to consolidate it into a shape you can live in. You, too. Decide who you are, and the city will again assume a fixed form around you.' This 'soft city of illusion' is 'as real, maybe more real', than its material counterpart.[15] This is a narrative understanding of self and place, and Raban's book thus aims 'to investigate the plot, and its implications for the nature of character, of the modern city' (p. 10).

Raban's thinking bears the mark of the period's literary theory in its sense of the urban environment. In the city, selfhood and place are matters of semiotics: 'You become a walking legible code, to be read, and as often misinterpreted, by strangers'; 'people often have to live by reading the signs and surfaces of their environment and interpreting them in terms of private, near-magical codes' (pp. 51, 184). Just as reading the city is recast, so is writing it, with implications that play out in numerous urban fictions since. Often, a city locale 'does not lend itself to narrative' but 'needs a patchwork quilt of intrusions, guesses and observations to get anywhere near its truth' (p. 238). It is with a reflection on the attendant difficulties that *Soft City* closes:

> Writing a book one pretends to an omniscience and a command of logic which the experience of living in a city continuously contradicts. The truest city is the most private, and autobiography is the kind of writing which is least likely to muddy the city with the small untruths of seeming to know and deduce much more about its life than is really possible. (pp. 282–3)

Whilst novelists have not, by definition, followed Raban's turn to autobiography wholesale, the period since *Soft City* has witnessed numerous and various narratological innovations in response to the problems that this text crystallises, and many of these experiments have pressed against the borders of the novel genre.

The examples of Iain Sinclair and Peter Ackroyd capture some of this variety. The trajectory of Iain Sinclair's career has been from avant-garde poetry in the 1970s, through a fiction-writing phase in the 1980s and 1990s, towards topographical non-fiction from the late 1990s onwards (though all three genres have bled into one another). Autobiography permeates Sinclair's London fictions, but they are also overwhelmingly influenced by that environment's energies – London's forgotten histories are revenant throughout these texts. *White Chappell, Scarlet Tracings* (1987) concerns itself with a present-day narrative of antiquarian book dealers scavenging for numinous texts, but also encompasses a historical fiction concerning the Whitechapel murders of the 1880s, with the late-nineteenth-century atmosphere pervading the later time period, too. The text is autobiographical in the simplest sense that the first-person narrative of book dealing records a London milieu and a trade that Sinclair was involved in, but also in the idiosyncratic selection of arcane, unofficial histories of the city that it orchestrates. The same features can be found in *Downriver* (1991). This text is a 'grimoire of rivers and railways', a politicised book of spells to dispel the malevolent influence of Margaret Thatcher's government over the east

London districts with which it is concerned.[16] Again, narrated in the first person by a semi-fictionalised character named Sinclair, the text is an autobiographical and eccentric series of wanderings amongst the forgotten histories of overlooked places. It is, as its subtitle states, 'a narrative in twelve tales' – fractured yet coherent. Each section focuses on a particular area of the city and the whole is thus topographically arranged. In Sinclair's fictions, as in his later, supposedly non-fictional texts, the environment's histories are plural and interminable, belying any omniscient and authoritative narratorial perspective. Sinclair's most recent writing has drawn attention to the grey area between genres that all of his texts have in fact inhabited. *Hackney, That Rose-Red Empire* (2009) is 'a documentary fiction; where it needs to be true, it is'[17]; meanwhile, in *Ghost Milk* (2011), his response to the landscapes created for the London Olympics, Sinclair reflects that he has 'never been that good at recognizing the division between fiction and reality'.[18]

Likewise, Peter Ackroyd's city texts blur fact and fiction, as well as engaging in historical slippage. Alongside his biographical writing focused on London personages (some of which is creative in scope), Ackroyd's fiction writing – particularly a long run of London novels from *The Great Fire of London* (1982) to *The Lambs of London* (2004) – also gravitates to retelling the lives of historical figures and recreating the London in which they lived. Many of these texts also envisage the overhang of historical events in the present. *Hawksmoor* (1985), for example, is a dual narrative in which occult practices associated with early eighteenth-century architects rebuilding London's churches after the great fire seem to weigh heavily on the investigation of a series of present-day murders at the same sites. Though the technique here is similar to that employed by Sinclair, the tone is very different. For Ackroyd, human agency is diminished by the energies that reside in the environment – particular places witness the repetition of certain events over time – in opposition to Raban's notion of the city's liberating alienation. Thus, as it is described in *The Clerkenwell Tales* (2003), characters' voices are often subsumed in or as 'the cry of the city itself'.[19] Ackroyd's sense of the dominating urban environment is most apparent in *London: The Biography* (2000), shifting power away from inhabitants and towards the Leviathan-like city itself: 'We must regard it [London] as a human shape with its own laws of life and growth'. The city's biographer bows down to its 'monstrous form' in stating explicitly that his text is partial and certainly not exhaustive.[20] Though biographical and novelistic tropes are invoked in this kind of environmental history, the results are a long way distant from those Raban envisaged. They may be closer to Buell's notion of the environmental imagination.

Other writers have taken up different approaches to the complexities of the urban environment. If the city's historical reverberation has been important, so, too, has its resonance as the site of ordinary life in postwar fiction's return to the quotidian. *White Teeth* (2000), Zadie Smith's acclaimed first novel, shuttles between and links numerous narrative threads and London lives of unremarkable people, recalling the narrative strategies of Dickens' metropolitan novels but differing from them in refusing tidy endings. Here, narrative closure is modulated against a sustained tension that refuses to dissolve the individual voices of its numerous protagonists into an urban cacophony. Rather, the contingency of the city is allowed to register. Jon McGregor's city novels have also focused on ordinary lives. *If Nobody Speaks of Remarkable Things* (2002) is documentary in tone, focusing on the interwoven lives of unnamed inhabitants of a street in an unnamed northern city, but also stylistically adventurous, employing complex free indirect discourse to drop into characters' perspectives. The shifting viewpoint best embodies the song of the city, McGregor writes, because 'the song sings the loudest when you pick out each note'.[21] The commitment to recovering overlooked voices in the metropolis (Smith) and in the provincial city (McGregor) is also comparable to the same aspiration in Scottish urban novels by James Kelman and Irvine Welsh, whose works represent figures on the margins.

If Raban's revisions to narratives of the city preceded (or even precipitated) a new sense of that environment, then the 1970s also witnessed the beginnings of a changed way of viewing and representing the rural and the natural. Richard Mabey's writing then and since has been crucial to this shift in two respects: it offered a revisionary account of what nature is and where it might be found, and it questioned the suitability of various narrative forms for best capturing this revised sense of nature. Though Mabey works with natural-history traditions, his writing tends towards more personal than scientific reflection and forges innovations that have been taken up in fictional discourses, as well as imparting the benefits of the latter to non-fictional genres. *The Unofficial Countryside* (1973) is the first in a series of Mabey's texts to question the place of nature: 'Looking for wildlife we turn automatically towards the official countryside, towards the great set pieces of forest and moor. If the truth is told, the needs of the natural world are more prosaic than this. A crack in the pavement is all that a plant needs to put down roots'.[22] With a change in focus and scale, the unofficial countryside – 'covering everything from a planned suburban playground to the accidentally green corner of a city-centre parking lot' – might provide an equally rich sampling of nature (p. 14). The shift is away from an aesthetic that brackets nature off from everyday life and towards one that 'confront[s] the modernised countryside' and assesses the relationship between the natural and the man-made (p. 23). Due to the kind of land-scapes that he visits, Mabey is concerned with locales that bear the marks of human intervention – canals, working and redundant quarries, car dumps – and with 'their wild inhabitants' (p. 14). The new sites that Mabey envisages and that many (fiction and non-fiction) writers have more recently followed him to are the marginal, the liminal, the edgeland.[23] The recognition of the braiding of the domestic and the wild that occurs in these places is one of the most important features of the postwar environmental imagination in a wide variety of texts.

A fictional analogue for this gravitation to edgelands can be seen in the turn towards recording suburbia. Novels of this environment dramatise the revision of first impressions of this supposedly banal locale, often by way of initially unfavourable comparison. Thus, in Julian Barnes's *Metroland* (1980), residents of the west London rim (the same terrain that Mabey con-siders) 'lived there because it was an area easy to get out of'. The novel's narrator, in his youth, finds 'independent existence could only be achieved by strict deconditioning' from suburbia's deadening influence, but later learns to find observing the details of life lived there 'relevant, fulfilling, sensibility-sharpening'.[24] This acceptance is written as accommodation rather than capitulation. Hanif Kureishi's *The Buddha of Suburbia* (1990) follows a similar revisionary pattern. It is narrated by a protagonist who initially feels himself to be 'condemned ... to a dreary suburb of London', conceiving of it as 'a leaving place' and yearning for the city, but later learns to see 'what flourished in the cracks' and appreciate the nuance beyond this dichotomy.[25] These texts, then, exemplify the process of rethinking the sub-urbs not as non-places devoid of history and vitality but instead as particular expressions of postwar social changes and their interface with environment.

For Mabey, change in location also necessitates a formal revision. He had originally intended to write *The Unofficial Countryside* 'as a travelogue' tra-cing journeys around London's perimeter, believing the account of walking to be 'a neat device for weaving ... thoughts and observations into a narra-tive'. However, 'a programmed hike like this ... made the whole enterprise feel too much like an old country walk'. Instead, 'it was a change in focus that was needed, a new perspective on the everyday' (pp. 21, 24, 26). The form that the text takes as a result is one that resists the teleological pull of the quest narrative and is, instead, episodic in structure. The same attentive-ness to narrative formations and deformations is the abiding characteristic of Mabey's work since, and (alongside the scoping out of edgelands) its mostly widely felt legacy. *Beechcombings* (2007) contests anthropocentrism in suggesting that 'the entire history of our relationships with trees could be seen as [a] kind of debate. We argue them into forms that suit us, they respond with tortuous narratives of their own'.[26] More recently still, *Turned Out Nice Again* (2013) investigates 'that ceaseless, nagging narrative we British have about the weather', finding it to be both 'an incontestable feature of the physical world' and 'a creature of our imaginations'.[27]

The recognition of hybrid human/natural environments and the narrative self-reflexivity that are exemplified here have come to be seen as one of the defining features of the 'new nature writing' of recent years.[28] Of the non-fictional writers who have been grouped together under this sobriquet, Robert Macfarlane's texts are amongst the most novelistic in narrative construction. Macfarlane's new formulations of nature writing employ hybrid, generically ambiguous literary forms. His advocacy of a shift 'from wildness as a state of land to wildness as a state of mind' suggests a testimonial approach that is evident in his evocative texts: *Mountains of the Mind* (2003), *The Wild Places* (2007), and *The Old Ways* (2012).[29] Each is characterised by a narrative arc tracing a trajectory away from one mode of conceiving of place's meaning and towards another. They reproduce this change in the structure and form of the text, employing novelistic techniques of deferral and revelation. Thus, the first half of *The Wild Places* records journeys to the far-flung north and west of Britain and Ireland before the second half returns to the south and east – 'the undiscovered country of the nearby' – to find wildness in the midst of human settlement.[30] *Mountains of the Mind* and *The Old Ways* embody comparable movements. The notion of 'wild' shifts from landscape untouched by human intervention towards one in which human and non-human influences enter into complex, fluid interactions. Wild places are no longer seen as spaces without history, but conversely as sites in which histories remain traceable. That these findings are presented as such by Macfarlane's ever-present narratorial 'I' leads Jos Smith to find that '*The Wild Places* is modelled on the form of *bildungsroman*'.[31]

Other writers of nature and place have taken issue with this approach and the anthropocentrism that seems to underwrite it. In particular, Kathleen Jamie has reproved testimonial approaches and their unexamined relation to a tradition that reduces 'the variety of our engagement' with environment.[32] Her own prose texts, *Findings* (2005) and *Sightlines* (2012), are less akin to the novel in structure. They are more like short story sequences or (unsurprisingly, given Jamie's other, primary literary output) collections of poems. They comprise discrete essays that chime synchronically with one another rather than telling a diachronic story as Macfarlane's work tends to do. Notwithstanding these differences, the pervasive influence of creative literary forms is one of the defining features of new nature writing. Most follow Macfarlane in drawing on the novel's formal arrangement. Even those who, like Jamie, do not, nonetheless write in dialogue with this dominant literary form of the postwar period.

If new nature writing employs novelistic discourse, its practitioners are aware that to do so is not quite new. The use of the techniques of fiction in place writing spans the postwar period. A number of contemporary writers in this field are consciously engaged in recovering key texts from the traditions in which they work, and in assembling a nature writing canon in light of the popularity that the genre is currently experiencing. Three texts for which Macfarlane has written forewords to reissues exemplify the generic hybridity of this writing prior to its recent rejuvenation: Jacquetta Hawkes's *A Land* (1951), J. A. Baker's *The Peregrine* (1967), and Nan Shepherd's *The Living Mountain* (1977).

Jacquetta Hawkes trained as an archaeologist and geologist, and it is with these disciplines that *A Land* engages, though in an extremely idiosyncratic manner. The text's aim is 'to tell the story of the creation of what is at present known as Britain'.[33] This wording already hints at the historical contingency of this very designation when it is viewed from the geological perspective of deep time. This is only one of two themes Hawkes identifies, though the other is intimately bound to it: there are many forms that the narrative of Britain might take and any of them 'would be in some sense creations of the storyteller's mind, and for this reason the counterpoint to the theme of the creation of the land shall be the growth of consciousness, its gradual concentration and intensification within the human skull' (p. 11). If this self-reflexive awareness of the unavoidable shaping hand of narrative preludes contemporary nature writing, it also seems novelistic – akin to a certain kind of postmodern metafiction. However, *A Land* is not punctuated with a disarming commentary related to consciousness surrounding a main narrative charting Britain's geological history. Rather, it is an unclassifiable text that shuttles between the two, often performing them in tandem. It sutures the two together by recourse to Hawkes's personal experiences and memories: her own biography is not bracketed off from the growth of consciousness with which she is concerned. This kind of shift between seemingly incommensurate scales is entirely characteristic of the whole text.

Whether agency lies with the land or the consciousness that tells its story is (by design) never entirely pinned down in this narrative. A kind of geological determinism appears to operate at points – 'By the end of the Palaeozoic era the possibility of Wordsworth was assured' – whereby landform formulates literary form (pp. 67–68). This might seem similar to the power that Ackroyd's London holds over its inhabitants, but there is more mutuality here. Hayden Lorimer has described Hawkes's text as a 'geo-physical vision of distributed agency', an attempt to 'write a memoir *for* the earth'.

As 'experimental earth writing, with a twist of domesticated psychodrama', *A Land* exemplifies 'the ways that subjectivities take expression through a relationship with landscape' but differs from other such examples in relating 'the project of self-understanding' to geology rather than topography.[34] In this, the text embodies the kind of dialogue that Buell's sense of the environmental imagination designates, and, crucially, it exploits the pliancy of the novel's narrative form to do so.

Where Hawkes's text is expansive in scope and inclusive in method, Baker's *The Peregrine* is more precisely managed. Published five years after *Silent Spring*, and focused on a bird of prey that suffered greatly through the accumulation of pesticides up the food chain, the text is elegiac in tone and its narrator near monomaniacal in focusing on a single species, or, more specifically still, on two pairs of peregrine falcons over the course of a winter in their East Anglian hunting ground. Following the raptor and describing in repetitive, minute detail its daily routine of waking, hunting, and feeding without plot progression, the text is akin to modernist structural experimentation rather than traditional narrative panorama. The same might be said for its descriptive aesthetic. Though the landscape that the bird inhabits is a familiar one – these intensively farmed and populated Essex fenlands are well within the orbit of London – it is one that is constantly made strange by a process of defamiliarisation. The rhythms of the text, focused almost exclusively on the bird and without establishing details, are accompanied by a shifting perspective that often approximates the bird's-eye view, and by an almost incantatory tone: 'The peregrine lives in a pouring-away world of no attachment, a world of wakes and tilting, of sinking planes of land and water. We who are anchored and earthbound cannot envisage this freedom of the eye'. Attempting to overcome this limitation, the text assumes the perspective by which the peregrine 'sees and remembers patterns that we do not know exist'. Adopting the well-established novelistic pose of a compelling protagonist's story narrated from the sidelines by a first-person onlooker-narrator, *The Peregrine* also begins to break down this distinction by folding the two together. The diary of a single winter is the form taken up in order to 'preserve a unity, binding together the bird, the watcher, and the place that holds them both'.[35] This aim informs the innovative perspectival register. The environment provides the grounds for an imaginative foray beyond the anthropocentric. Paradoxically, the necessity for this endeavour springs from the separation of man from nature through environmental damage that Rachel Carson's work drew attention to immediately prior to Baker's text.

By different means again, Nan Shepherd's *The Living Mountain* joins Hawkes's and Baker's texts in looking beyond human perspectives on environment. Shepherd's text combines elements of the other two. If the interpenetration of mountain and mind is the text's subject (akin to Hawkes's interplay of land and consciousness, though the scale here is regional rather than national), then the structural device deployed is similar to Baker's. Narrated in the first person but focused on the Cairngorm Mountains, the text suggests that the range as a whole is the 'living' mountain of the title, and each chapter details parts of this landform-protagonist. Topographical features are treated not as distinct in themselves but as the 'elementals' that comprise its character. The narrative formulates an ecology in progressing from ground and land, through elements (chapters devoted to water, frost and snow, air and light), plant life, animals, and then man. Later chapters tend towards 'the senses' and finally 'being' as a gradual revelation of the means by which the earlier description of the elements that make up the living mountain have been recognised. This is not, though, a drift towards anthropocentrism. Shepherd is careful to emphasise the relinquishing of self-required, the 'quiescence' needed for intimate dwelling. Neither does the text project consciousness: 'I do not ascribe sentience to the mountain'. Rather, 'consciousness interacts with the mountain-forms', and what results is 'matter impregnated with mind'.[36] Shepherd's writing, then, along with Hawkes's and Baker's, prefigures new nature writing in utilising novelistic modes to describe nature *and* human engagements with nature.

Some of the questions treated in these 'non-fictional' nature writing texts have also informed a number of more unequivocally fictional depictions of rural environments. Graham Swift's *Waterland* (1983) shares with these texts an awareness of the dangers attendant to too easy a sense of settled rural dwelling and the supposed stability of the country in opposition to the city's contingency. The text concerns the remembrances of Tom Crick, a history teacher who grew up on the Fens, the flatlands of eastern England, his family history there, and the place's longer natural and social history. Like Hawkes, Swift is concerned with the construction of these narratives of place, and the text's postmodern mechanisms draw attention to the disparity between (capital 'h') History and storytelling. The text establishes early on that 'the chief fact about the Fens is that they are reclaimed land, land that was once water, and which, even today is not quite solid', subject to siltation and thus susceptible to flooding, hence the paradoxical conflation of water and land in the text's title. However, this 'equivocal operation of silt' does not serve only as a topographical metaphor for a primary concern with the ambivalence of history.[37] Rather, the Cricks's lives and the tragic events the text describes are the result of living in this environment. So, too, are the broader trends of the region's social history and, to some extent, the prevailing characteristics of those who live there. Though concerned with human history, environment plays a determining role in this text.

More recently, Swift has again deployed a family saga to focus the changing fortunes of a region: *Wish You Were Here* (2011) is narrated by Jack Luxton and charts the fortunes of his family on their Devon dairy farm through the afflictions of BSE and then foot-and-mouth crises. Like *Waterland*, this text is at pains to demonstrate that the local, rural environment is determined by a broader network of outside forces – the Iraq war plays a large part in the family tragedy that the text reports. Likewise, the changing character of the area results from the national economy with the Luxtons, like many who can no longer make a living from the land, selling their farmhouse as a second home for the family of a London banker. Thus, although 'north Devon was off the beaten track' and 'getting away from it all' becomes a refrain, the text comes to the awareness that 'nowhere was really immune, even quiet green places in the depths of the country'; indeed, they, too, 'might be involved in some latent war, with a larger, unlocal malaise of insecurity'.[38] Similarly, Ross Raisin's *God's Own Country* (2008) is concerned with the decline of the farming community as ownership of the countryside – literally and culturally – shifts to incoming (or just visiting, second-home owning) urbanites and suburbanites. Again, tragedy plays out of this shift. Tim Pears's *Landed* (2010) charts the same process. In these recent texts, writers play off the characteristics that Gibbons lampooned in *Cold Comfort Farm* – a rural population beset by fate and written about in a pervading tone of misery – but they do so knowingly, and they move away from the codification of the rural world as retreat, the antithesis of the city and cosmopolitan life (its culture and its corruption). Rather, now the two are part of a network, inextricable. If Raymond Williams's seminal *The Country and the City* (1973) critiqued literature's disavowal of the relationship between these two environments, then the contemporary rural novel, like contemporary nature writing, responds to the implicit demand to depict the links between the two.

Such writers often focus on contemporary disenchantments of the natural world and the lives of those who live in its midst. Jim Crace's fictions have drawn attention to the same process operating in different historical periods. As such, they offer a fitting place to conclude this chapter. Crace's run of novels have emphasised moments in history that have seen changes in land use and the altered relation between human and environment that has ensued from the dawn of the bronze age in *The Gift of Stones* (1988) to the enclosure acts in *Harvest* (2013). Crace can be grouped with Swift and Raisin as interested in the material and socioeconomic determinants of place rather than the forces of abstract or neo-Darwinian nature, but he differs from those two in that his fictional worlds are not direct renderings of real places (Raisin's North York Moors, Swift's fens and Devon farms). Rather, his fictional worlds are paired down and without specific historical and geographical referents. The postwar novel has witnessed the recuperation of these environmental histories and the human histories that are bound up in them. It has sought to deploy the resources of fictionality to reflect on the construction of these narratives. Looking back over this survey, the novel might seem the most (rather than least) likely candidate to house the environmental imagination, and this might account for just how extensive the non-fictional borrowings from fictional technique have become.

NOTES

1 Philip Hensher, 'Space, the final frontier', *Guardian Review*, 18th May 2013, p. 15. Specialists in poetry might quibble with Hensher's sense of the *lyric* poem.
2 Lawrence Buell, *The Environmental Imagination: Thoreau, Nature Writing, and the Formation of American Culture* (Cambridge, MA: Belknap Press, 1995), p. 2.
3 Ibid., p. 8.
4 Ibid., p. 7.
5 Dominic Head, 'The (Im)Possibility of Ecocriticism', in *Writing the Environment: Ecocriticism and Literature*, eds. Richard Kerridge and Neil Sammells (London: Zed Books, 1998), p. 37.
6 Ibid., p. 37.
7 Ibid., p. 32.
8 On the distinction between 'environmentalists' and 'deep ecologists', see Jonathan Bate, *The Song of the Earth* (London: Picador, 2000), pp. 36–7.
9 Buell, *The Environmental Imagination*, p. 8.
10 Broader, less insistent conceptions of ecocriticism are akin to this way of thinking. Greg Garrard, for example, has noted that 'the widest definition of the subject of ecocriticism is the study of the relationship of the human and the non-human'. Greg Garrard, *Ecocriticism* (Abingdon: Routledge, 2004), p. 5.
11 David Shields, *Reality Hunger: A Manifesto* (London: Hamish Hamilton, 2010), pp. 3, 5, 14.
12 Stella Gibbons, *Cold Comfort Farm* (London: Penguin, 2006), pp. 5–6. Hereafter cited parenthetically.
13 Timothy Clark, *The Cambridge Introduction to Literature and the Environment* (Cambridge: Cambridge University Press, 2011), p. 77.
14 Rachel Carson, *Silent Spring* (London: Penguin, 2000), pp. 21–2.
15 Jonathan Raban, *Soft City* (London: Picador, 2008), p. 2. Hereafter cited parenthetically.
16 Iain Sinclair, *Downriver (Or, The Vessels of Wrath); A Narrative in Twelve Tales* (London: Penguin, 2004), p. 531.
17 Iain Sinclair, *Hackney, That Rose-Red Empire* (2009; London: Penguin, 2010), p. 579.

18 Iain Sinclair, *Ghost Milk: Calling Time on the Grand Project* (London: Hamish Hamilton, 2011), p. 138.

19 Peter Ackroyd, *The Clerkenwell Tales* (London: Vintage, 2004), p. 120.

20 Peter Ackroyd, *London: The Biography* (London: Vintage, 2001), p. 2.

21 Jon McGregor, *If Nobody Speaks of Remarkable Things* (2002; London: Bloomsbury, 2003), p. 1.

22 Richard Mabey, *The Unofficial Countryside* (London, Sphere Books, 1978), p. 12. Hereafter cited parenthetically.

23 Mabey notes elsewhere that the ecological term for such a place is an 'ecotone': 'a zone where one habitat merges with another, creating something with a character more than the sum of its parts' (*A Good Parcel of English Soil* (London: Penguin, 2013), pp. 7–8).

24 Julian Barnes, *Metroland* (London: Vintage, 2009), pp. 34, 41, 61.

25 Hanif Kureishi, *The Buddha of Suburbia* (London: Faber, 2009), pp. 23, 117, 238.

26 Richard Mabey, *Beechcombings: The Narratives of Trees* (London: Vintage, 2008), p. 26. Note the plural and ambiguous assignment of agency in the text's subtitle.

27 Richard Mabey, *Turned Out Nice Again: On Living With the Weather* (London: Profile Books, 2013), pp. 6, 75.

28 This now-prevalent grouping emerged out of a 2008 issue of *Granta* with the same title: Jason Cowley, ed., *Granta 102: The New Nature Writing* (Summer 2008).

29 Robert Macfarlane, 'Foreword', in *A Wilder Vein*, ed. Linda Cracknell (Ullapool: Two Ravens Press, 2009), p. vii.

30 Robert Macfarlane, *The Wild Places* (London: Granta, 2007), p. 225.

31 Jos Smith, 'An Archipelagic Literature: Re-Framing "The New Nature Writing"', *Green Letters: Studies in Ecocriticism*, 17.1 (2013), pp. 5–15, p. 7.

32 Kathleen Jamie, 'A Lone Enraptured Male', *London Review of Books*, 6 May 2008, p. 26.

33 Jacquetta Hawkes, *A Land* (London: Cresset Press, 1951), p. 10. Hereafter cited parenthetically.

34 Hayden Lorimer, 'Memoirs for the Earth: Jacquetta Hawkes's Literary Experiments in Deep Time', *Cultural Geographies*, 19 (2012), pp. 90, 101.

35 J. A. Baker, *The Peregrine* (New York: New York Review of Books, 2005), pp. 35, 14.

36 Nan Shepherd, *The Living Mountain* (Edinburgh: Canongate, 2011), pp. 90–91, 102.

37 Graham Swift, *Waterland* (London: Picador, 1992), pp. 8, 9.

38 Graham Swift, *Wish You Were Here* (London: Vintage, 2011), pp. 312–13.

8

PETER BOXALL

Science, Technology, and the Posthuman

It is one of the peculiar contradictions of modernity that the technology that extends the reach of the human, that helps humans to master their environment, also works to weaken the human itself as a category. As Hal Foster has put it, technology is a 'demonic supplement', at once 'a "magnificent" extension of the body' and a '"troubled" constriction of it'.[1] This is a contradiction that reaches a kind of intensity at the beginning of the period under consideration here. Take, for example, Bertolt Brecht's play *Life of Galileo* (first performed in 1943). Galileo's (supposed) invention of the telescope allows humankind to reach far into space, to cast their influence way beyond the immediate parameters of the body. As a result, Galileo says in Brecht's play, the 'movements of the heavens have become more comprehensible', and 'the battle for a measurable heaven has been won'.[2] But the problem that lies at the heart of *Life of Galileo* is that, in gaining a deeper understanding of the universe, humankind forsakes their centrality to it. The church cannot allow Galileo to disseminate his new knowledge of the movement of the planets, because in doing so he would expose the fact that the earth is not at the centre of the universe, and that, in turn, the universe is not constructed in accordance with human reason. To win the battle to measure our environment is to reveal that 'the earth is a planet and not the centre of the universe', that 'the entire universe isn't turning around our tiny little earth' (p. 53). The desire for knowledge and control of the environment, which science and technology allow us to satisfy, leads, by a peculiar dialectic, to the loss of such mastery. The current environmental crisis that threatens our planet is perhaps only a logical conclusion to such a process. The technology that has allowed humankind to control the planet has also made it inhospitable to humans, and to all other species, so if we are to understand our environment now, as Richard Powers puts it in his short story 'The Seventh Event', we have to think 'beyond the gauge of the human'.[3] The history of the human has led us to a situation in which the human itself can only be contemplated from elsewhere, from some posthuman perspective.

So, to think about science and technology in relation to the human is to recognise that technology has a kind of posthuman logic built into it – a logic which arises in part from the philosophical fragility of the category of the human itself. However powerful the human has been as an ideological and political force throughout the history of modernity – despite the centrality of our investment in the human to everything that has been done in art and science – it has always rested on a kind of fudge, a kind of category error. As Augustine famously puts it in *City of God*, the human is a 'kind of mean between beasts and angels', an approximate category which shares something with both the divine and the animal, without belonging properly to either.[4] As such, as Hugo von Kleist has famously demonstrated in his essay 'On the Marionette Theatre', the human encounters itself in a continual play between the material and the spiritual, between the dumb self-presence of matter, and the divine self-presence of spirit. In working in this way between two states, neither of which it can properly attain, the human, Kleist argues, remains peculiarly at odds with itself, lacking in the simple unity with self that is the province both of pure matter and pure spirit. Inanimate matter – even the matter from which we craft artificial human parts, such as those which make up the moving parts of a puppet, or those of a prosthetic limb – can achieve a grace that fleshy human parts cannot reach. He knows of people, the speaker in Kleist's essay declares, who have 'been unfortunate enough to lose their own limbs', and who wear 'artificial legs made by English craftsmen'. These people dance on their artificial legs, he says, and can 'perform and execute' their movements 'with a certainty and ease and grace which just astound the thoughtful observer'.[5] The prosthetic attachment to a human body knows a kind of self-containment that no human body could, as the human body is always caught between self and knowledge of self, always barred from that dwelling within oneself that, for Kleist's speaker, belongs only to spirit and material, to gods and puppets. 'Where grace is concerned', he writes, 'it is impossible for man to come anywhere near a puppet. Only a god can equal inanimate matter in this respect' (p. 16).

The thinker who has given perhaps the sharpest and most influential expression to this contradiction at the heart of the human, and of the human engagement with technology, is Sigmund Freud. In his 1930 work *Civilization and its Discontents*, Freud offers a picture of the human as a vulnerable, naked thing, as a 'poore inch', a 'feeble animal organism'. The human is an inadequate thing, which knows, as matter does not, as the animal does not, as the god does not, its own inadequacy. The development of civilisation, in Freud's account, is an attempt to overcome this basic generic inadequacy – to harness the power of technology in order to make humans secure in their environment, as gods and puppets already are. Tools allow the human to extend itself into its environment, to amplify that poor 'inch of nature', so that 'with every tool man is perfecting his organs', or 'is removing the limits to their functioning'.[6] As Brecht's Galileo deploys the telescope to extend the range of human seeing, Freud suggests that the development of tools across the history of civilisation has allowed us to extend every human motor and sensory function:

> Motor power places gigantic forces at his disposal, which, like his muscles, he can employ in any direction; thanks to ships and aircraft neither water nor air can hinder his movements; by means of spectacles he corrects defects in the lens of his own eye; by means of the telescope he sees into the far distance; and by means of the microscope he overcomes the limits of visibility set by the structure of his retina. In the photographic camera he has created an instrument which retains the fleeting visual impressions, just as a gramophone disc retains the equally fleeting auditory ones. … With the help of the telephone he can hear at distances which would be respected as unattainable even in a fairy tale. Writing was in its origin the voice of an absent person; and the dwelling house was a substitute for the mother's womb, the first lodging, for which in all likelihood man still longs, and in which he was safe and felt at ease.

All of these forms of extension – these 'things that, by his science and technology, man has brought about on this earth' – allow the human to exert a kind of control, in both time and space.[7] The capacity to move in space produced by the ship and the motor car has a corollary in the capacity to see and hear at a distance granted by the telephone and the telescope, and the forms of archiving, storing, recording, offered first by writing, and then by photography and sound recording, act as extensions of memory, stretching ourselves backwards into the past, and forwards into the future. These forms of technology, Freud suggests, allow us in some ways to move beyond that stranded condition that Kleist outlines in his essay on the 'Marionette Theatre'. Science and technology make humans god like. But the central argument in *Civilization and its Discontents* is that this extension does not overcome the peculiar inadequacy that is native to the human, but exacerbates it; or, more interestingly, exacerbates and overcomes this inadequacy at the same time. The more humanity armours itself against its infirmity, the more infirm it becomes, the less adequate to itself. The more it relies on technological supplement to aid its extension into the world, the less it is able to achieve that peculiar, graceful harmony with its own being that Kleist finds in puppets and in gods. 'Man', Freud writes, 'has, as it were, become a kind of prosthetic God. When he puts on all his auxillary organs he is truly magnificent; but those organs have not grown onto him and they still give him much trouble at times'.[8] In the strange gap that Freud sees here

between the organic and the inorganic – the junction between the human
body and its prosthetic entry into the word – one can see the contradiction
between extension and constriction that Foster sees as native to the development of human technology. The more our tools shape the environment,
the more flimsy our own presence as human controlling agent becomes.
Think of Ripley controlling the robotic forklift in the closing scenes of the
film *Aliens* (1986): technology amplifies the human only to the extent that
it dwarfs it.

Any discussion of the connections between science, technology, and the
posthuman in the postwar British novel has, at the outset, to attend to these
contradictions in the relations between technology and the human. The
development of the novel in the period is arguably characterised by the lapsing of the human as the dominant figure for civilised life, and the emergence
of a posthuman rhetoric and aesthetic, which shares much with the other
postal compounds that shape cultural life in the later decades of the century – such as postmodernism, poststructuralism, postcolonialism, and so
on. In what follows I will trace successive waves in this emergence of a posthuman structure of feeling at work in the British fiction of the postwar. But
even as this posthuman logic comes to expression, in tandem with developments in the technological production of the culture, it is important to recognise that the forces that shape this emergence are already in place much
earlier, and are in fact integral to the way that the human itself as a category
has always recognised itself. Hal Foster argues that the modernist aesthetics that developed over the first half of the century turned around what he
calls the 'double logic' of the prosthetic – that the 'machinic imagery of high
modernism' that one can find in Wyndham Lewis and Filippo Marinetti is
produced by a historically defined consciousness of the prostheticised posthuman body that has always been grafted on to the natural body, since
humans were first able to use tools.[9] The modernist politics of the machine,
Foster writes, are circumscribed by the response one takes to the technologies that enhance and adumbrate the body. Modernism is shaped by the
tension between the 'utopias of the body extended, even subsumed in new
technologies', and the 'dystopias of the body reduced, even dismembered
by them'. As the technologies that arm and extend the human enter into a
period of rapid development with the advent of twentieth-century modernity, the modernist imagination has either to '*resist* technology in the name
of a natural body or *accelerate* it in the search of a postnatural body on
the other side'.[10] The tension between the natural and the artificial that
has shaped the history of the human undergoes an intensification with the
development of twentieth-century speed and industrial power, and the new
forms of violence and conflict that such speed and power allowed. This

tension, Foster argues, is a determining force in the history of modernism. It is also this tension, this splitting between a residual, natural human and a technologically produced posthuman, that determines the production of the aesthetic imagination at the beginning of the period, in the wake of high modernism, and of the Second World War.

George Orwell's 1949 work *Nineteen Eighty-Four* is possibly the novel that sets the tone for this postwar sensibility most influentially. This is a novel that is possessed, at its heart, by a vision of a mechanised, posthuman state, a state in which the forms of interiority and autonomy that are the foundations of human being have been banished. The now-mythical story of Winston Smith's battle against the tyrannical powers of the Anglo-American state (named Oceania) turns tightly around the relationship between the natural and the postnatural body. The telescreens that oversee all activities in Oceania produce a scenario in which privacy is banished, and with the enforced loss of privacy, the state also abolishes the experience of private ownership of the individual body. The novel displays an indifference to and an estrangement from the body that remains even now peculiarly shocking. Winston has a varicose ulcer on his leg that itches him throughout the novel, and this irritant is the mark of a wide gulf between public body and private mind, a kind of radical disassociation that signifies the disintegration of the human compound. The leg ulcerates because of poor circulation, as if the body is not properly connected, not properly wired in to Winston's sense of himself. When Winston discovers a body part lying in the road after one of the routine bomb attacks that are unleashed on the city – he finds a 'human hand severed at the wrist', 'so completely whitened as to resemble a plaster cast' – he shows the same kind of indifference to the amputated limb as he does to his own ulcerated flesh, simply 'kick[ing] the thing into the gutter'.[11] But against this dawning sense of the body as disposable public property – as the numb material upon which the state exercises its bio-power – the novel sets up a kind of rear-guard action, an attempt to recover a natural, 'human' body from the posthuman, postnatural conditions determined by an emergent global capitalism. The novel begins, of course, when Winston decides to rebel against the tyranny of the state by writing a diary, and in doing so he calls to that earlier conception of privacy, of the private ownership of the self, body, and mind that the Party has so effectively banished. The living room in Winston's flat is arranged accidentally in such a way that Winston is able to set up a writing desk in an alcove that cannot be overseen by the telescreen. 'For some reason', the narrator says,

> the telescreen in the living room was in an unusual position. Instead of being placed, as was normal, in the end wall, where it could command the whole

room, it was in the longer wall, opposite the window. To one side of it there was a shallow alcove in which Winston was now sitting. ... By sitting in the alcove, and keeping well back, Winston was able to remain outside the range of the telescreen. (p. 7)

It is this accidental architectural anomaly that suggests to Winston the idea of writing the diary. Without this fold in the surveilled space of the state, Winston would not have expressed dissent, any more than any of the other apparently unconscious inhabitants of Oceania. But from this chance possibility of withdrawal, Winston builds an entirely new relationship with his body, salvaging a properly human consciousness from the mechanised being that is produced by the Party. From the possibility of privacy inside his room, Winston finds a way of articulating the experience of privacy inside his own mind – the sense that he has sovereignty over the 'few cubic centimeters inside [his] skull' (p. 29), and that as a result he is able to think and reflect as an autonomous individual agent. From this recognition, and from the *articulation* of this recognition, Winston stages a modest rebellion against the state, and the sign of this rebellion is the gradual reassertion of his ownership over his own body, his body as natural and whole as opposed to estranged and prosthetic. The ulcer on his leg acts as a kind of litmus, indicating Winston's greater integration, the freer circulation of his blood. As he and Julia, Winston's co-conspirator, set up a little house where they can be freely alone together – a rather mocking mirror image of 1940s domesticity – Winston finds that his ulcer starts to heal. Meeting Julia repeatedly during the course of June, Winston notes that 'his varicose ulcer had subsided leaving only a brown stain on the skin above his ankle' (p. 157). As Winston finds a way of living securely within the 'few cubic centimeters inside his skull', so his body comes back under his ownership, his skin becoming once more the tightly sealed border of the self.

If *Nineteen Eighty-Four* is in part the story of this assertion of Foster's 'natural body' against the postnatural bodies administered by the tyrannical state, however, the lasting legacy of Orwell's novel is the failure of such an assertion. *Nineteen Eighty-Four* is, above all, a despairing work, a 'dystopia of the body reduced, even dismembered' by the technological apparatuses of the state that are bent on disaggregating the human, on undermining the procedures that allow for secure tenancy within the body, and within the cubic centimetres inside the skull. The most prescient stroke in an astonishingly prescient novel is Orwell's recognition that the development of new technologies for the surveillance and reproduction of the culture would conspire with shifts in the intellectual, political, and economic climate, to radically erode the basis upon which our conception of the free democratic subject was founded. The telescreens infiltrate all private space, and the 'speakwrite' machines in the 'ministry of truth' allow the state to manipulate all historical archives, and with this double manipulation of reality comes a failure of rationality, a failure of the philosophical protocols that had enabled us to produce accurate pictures of collective life, in which private, autonomous individuals shared a common public sphere. O'Brien, the state intellectual who 're-educates' Winston, gives him lectures on the new, posthuman epistemology as he tortures him, and these lectures resemble crude prototypes of thought forms that were still to come in 1948, thought forms that we have come to associate not only with posthumanism, but with postmodernism, poststructuralism, and the other political and epistemological manifestations of the 'post'. For Winston, the experience of living inside one's own body relies on our capacity to make independently verifiable statements about a common world. The Party, he thinks, 'told you to reject the evidence of your eyes and ears. It was their final, most essential command' (p. 84). The attempt to manipulate reality relies on the Party's ability to undermine our capacity to deploy reason and common sense to frame our occupation of the world, our ability to look at the world with our eyes, to listen with our ears. Resistance thus takes the form of an insistence on the truth of reason, and the reality of the world that we can register with our senses, and that we can measure and record with accuracy and fidelity. 'Freedom', Winston thinks, is the 'freedom to say that two plus two makes four. If that is granted, all else follows' (p. 84). But the story of *Nineteen Eighty-Four* is the story of the failure of such statements, and the disappearance of the individual freedoms that were based upon them. Winston thinks that the mind and the body can be 'kept alive', by 'passing on the secret doctrine that two plus two make four' (p. 230); this is how to 'pass on from body to body the vitality which the Party did not share and could not kill' (p. 229). But the revelation of *Nineteen Eighty-Four* is that, under the conditions produced by contemporary technology, as well as by contemporary politics and economics, such fundamental truths, and such intrinsic vitality, no longer obtain. As O'Brien says to Winston, with a Baudrillardian grin, 'Men are infinitely malleable' (p. 282); reality is not immanent in the world, but created by the most powerful observer. The power of O'Brien's proto-postmodern denial of reality, as much as the pain of torture, overcomes Winston's faith in the link between reality and our perception of it. O'Brien persuades him easily that 'two and two could have been three as easily as five, if that was what was needed' (p. 271), and with this submission to O'Brien's logic, Winston gives up both his faith in the human, and his recovered sense of ownership of the 'natural body'. Under torture, his body becomes once again utterly alien to him – 'its actual appearance', he says, 'was frightening, and not merely the fact that he knew it to be himself'. His 'varicose ulcer was an inflamed mass with flakes of skin peeling off it', and O'Brien forces him to look at this rotting, emaciated body, and to acknowledge that the human itself, in this vision of wastage, shrinkage, and decrepitude, has expired. 'Look at that disgusting rotting sore on your leg', O'Brien says. 'You are rotting away. ... You are falling to pieces. What are you? A bag of filth. Now turn round and look into that mirror again. Do you see that thing facing you? That is the last man. If you are human, that is humanity'(p. 285).

Orwell's depiction of the last man – which recurs in the title of Francis Fukuyama's famous vision of posthistory and posthumanity, *The End of History and the Last Man* (1992) – is a particularly despairing one, a vision coloured by a lifetime of political disillusion. But it remains exemplary of a kind of structure of feeling that dominates the British novel from the mid to late 1940s to the early 1970s. This period saw the development of a particular kind of prose realism – shaped by writers such as Patrick Hamilton, James Hanley, Muriel Spark, Ann Quin, Graham Greene, Henry Green, Elizabeth Taylor, and others. Interest has grown recently in this group, as Julia Jordan attests later in this volume (see Chapter 11). An aesthetic that often seemed to epitomise lacklustre kitchen-sink realism is now being considered as far more experimental, and far more delicate in its address to reality than was previously acknowledged. This, I think, is certainly true, and the work of Ann Quin and Elizabeth Taylor will be given a much more prominent position in future histories of the novel than they were accorded in twentieth-century accounts of literary fiction. But it is the case that the examinations of realism conducted by these writers – from the 'click' in the head experienced by the pathological George Harvey Bone in Hamilton's novel *Hangover Square* (1941) to the strange emptiness of the protagonist of Taylor's *Angel* (1957) to the odd fluctuations in the realist aesthetic registered by Muriel Spark in the wake of the 1973 oil crisis in *The Takeover* – are shaped by the recognition of a kind of lapsing of the human, for which there seemed little remedy. The experiments in realism undertaken by this generation of writers were conducted in the spirit of that scepticism exercised by O'Brien: the sense that the foundations upon which the human had rested had been eroded, combined with a sense that there is no new measure, no revolutionary epistemology available with which to repoint or reconstruct the alienated subject.

This experience, this period of a mutedly experimental realism, comes to an end with the emergence of a second wave in this development of the posthumanist postwar novel – a wave that begins with the emergence of a new generation of writers in the early 1970s. The first stirrings of this new aesthetic might be traced to the appearance of two works, very different from each other, that were both published in 1970, although both were written over the later 1960s. Both the works I am thinking of – Samuel Beckett's *The Lost Ones*, and J. G. Ballard's *The Atrocity Exhibition* – respond to the same perception, that the production of a global public sphere, which is mediated and surveilled, as Beckett's narrator puts it, down to 'the least particle of ambient air',[12] has produced a situation in which we have been finally expelled from our own bodies, in which the very possibility of interiority has given way before an administered and mechanised world state. Here, in both Beckett's and Ballard's works, Winston's residual sense that the few cubic centimetres inside the skull might come under the sovereignty of the autonomous self has been completely annulled. In Beckett's extraordinary text, the technologies that have led to global seeing, to global interaction, have also led to a kind of empty, robotic automatism, in which 'searchers' (the 'Lost Ones' of the title) move in compulsive patterns around the inside of a cylinder, obeying a set of precise rules for the carriage and deportment of the body, which seem to have no definable purpose. The searchers climb up and down ladders, explore 'niches or alcoves' (p. 203) sunk into the brilliantly lit wall of the cylinder, gaze into the eyes of other searchers, looking for something, some missing principle, perhaps, that might animate life in the cylinder. They are looking, one is led to speculate, for that quality that Winston seeks to preserve from the denuding gaze of the Thought Police, as his wasted, suppurating body is stripped bare by O'Brien, what he calls that 'something in the universe – I don't know, some spirit, some principle – that you [O'Brien] will never overcome' (p. 282). But if that principle for Winston is humanity itself, some particular means of inhabiting our flesh, ordaining it with reason, love, compassion, Beckett's text is a machine designed to expel any such residual faith in the capacity of the human to negotiate between the competing demands of matter and spirit, of Augustine's beasts and angels. The searchers are not looking for recognition by another person, they are not looking for love or for shared feeling. 'Man and wife', the peculiarly affectless narrator declares, 'are strangers two paces apart to mention only this most intimate of bonds' (p. 213). The searchers are not looking for another person with whom they might communicate; and neither are they looking for themselves, for some confirmation of a human interiority that is proof against the relentless exposure that life in the cylinder entails. Unlike Winston, whose famished gaze is so often turned inward, the narrator declares that, in the cylinder, 'none looks within himself where none can be' (p. 211). The inside, in this vision of total mediation, is as empty as the outside; the 'inner world', as Judith Butler puts it, 'no longer designates a topos'.[13] *The Lost Ones* marks the moment, glimpsed in preview in *Nineteen Eighty-Four*, when the coming together of globalisation and surveillance technology turns the human inside out, ejecting us into a totalising space of automation.

It is just as Beckett is reaching this moment of posthuman expulsion, quite late in his career, that J. G. Ballard publishes *The Atrocity Exhibition* – a work that marks, along with his 1973 *Crash*, a coming together of the posthuman body with the mediatised image among the technologies of late modernity. As Beckett enacts the failure of interiority as a function of the globalisation of the visible, so Ballard sees, in *The Atrocity Exhibition*, that what Guy Debord calls in 1967 the 'society of the spectacle' has summoned us all to a kind of visibility that has totally transformed the topography and geometry of the body. Ballard's work – so experimental and innovative that it remains difficult to classify – offers an extraordinarily naked depiction of a mode of being that has been released from the paradigms of enlightenment rationalism, and that is driven by a kind of psychosexual eroticism that calls to an entirely different rhetoric and protocol of embodiment. The landscape is an intense blend of a bland suburban architecture – concrete overpasses overhung by enormous billboards, interspersed with office blocks, plazas, and carparks – with an exploded, displaced body, which is magnified, distorted, and plastered onto the mediated, photographic surface. Here, the bland and deadened has become the charged, the erotic, as, in William Burrough's phrase, the 'line between inner and outer landscapes is breaking down'.[14] The overpass becomes as erotically charged as the inner thigh, dashboard and gearstick merge with the language and symbolism of pornography. And as the fractured external world becomes overcharged with the animus of interiority, the electric current of the unconscious, we see exactly that splitting open of the self that is experienced by the searchers in Beckett's *The Lost Ones*. As the searchers find that they cannot live inside the self, so the displaced, evacuated characters in *The Atrocity Exhibition* find, from the outset, that the body cannot hold them, that it continually splits open to release them into some rerouted outside. The 'protagonist' Travis, also called by a host of other names beginning with 'T', finds that his very face, the surface which brings mind into contact with world, is fractured, unbound. 'For some reason', the narrator says, 'the planes of his face failed to intersect, as if their true resolution took place in some as yet invisible dimension, or required elements other than those provided by his own character and musculature' (p. 2). The human is not inside, but projected onto the outside, in magnified images of facial parts and genitalia plastered on giant billboards hung over plazas and underpasses. Karen Novotny, one of the recurring figures, finds her 'fractured smile spread across the windshield' of a car; Talbot, one of the 'T' characters, finds 'his own face mediated from the billboard beside the car park' (pp. 35–36); 'Dr Nathan', 'limping along a drainage culvert', finds himself 'peering' at the 'huge face' of Elizabeth Taylor, 'painted on the sloping walls of the blockhouse', magnified to such a degree that 'the wall on his right, the size of a tennis court' contained little more than the right eye and cheekbone' (p. 13).

In both Beckett's and Ballard's works of 1970, then, we find this same cracking open of the self, this same failure of interiority, as the search for spirit finds itself directed not inwards but outwards. But if Beckett and Ballard are responding collectively to a new relation between the global public sphere and the lapsing of the human, the direction taken by this response is perhaps very different, almost diametrically opposed. Beckett's automata seemed to be an afterimage of those imagined earlier by Wyndham Lewis, under the sign of a machinic modernism; this is the final yielding of the human to an affectless, mechanised antihumanism. Against this pale after-image of modernism, Ballard's work offers something entirely different, a new way of conceiving being that might take us past the impasse of disaggregated humanism, towards a different kind of psychosexual geography, one shaped by a posthuman verve and eroticism that is difficult to detect in Beckett's wound-down machines. Both Beckett's and Ballard's pictures of globally mediated spaces contain niches and alcoves, those folds in the revealed system that are perhaps the leftovers of that alcove in which Winston sits to write his diary. But if those niches in Beckett are peculiarly stunted, offering no apparent 'way out' of the cylinder, nowhere to escape from the brightness that falls from the air, the impetus of Ballard's global imagination is towards the discovery of new faultlines, new fractures and limit boundaries that open to unseen dimensions and strange, unthought geometries. Where Hal Foster suggests that the modernist imagination seeks a form of 'acceleration' that takes us towards a 'postnatural body on the other side', then Ballardian speed, power, and information flow takes us past a far horizon, into that other side that has not yet been properly thought or seen. The geography of *The Atrocity Exhibition*, like that of Beckett's *Lost Ones*, can appear sealed, a global system that has revealed its interior, in which nothing remains latent or withdrawn or unseen. Beckett's hermetic cylinder makes a kind of appearance in *The Atrocity Exhibition*, in what the narrator calls the 'impossible room' – 'a perfect cube', whose 'walls and ceiling were formed by what seemed to be a series of cinema screens' (p. 44). We are entirely enclosed within a perfectly mediated system in Ballard. Yet this very completion, the experience of the global totality of the image, leads to a peculiar ejection into an outside, an odd 'intersection of planes', where a new, impossible angle opens up between war and ceiling, an odd niche or alcove in the smooth surface of the visible. As the culture industry mediates the world, turning it into a Warholian replica of itself, the erotic drives released by the image open new contours, push out to a new reality, a new organisation of the inside and the outside. 'Planes intersect', Dr Nathan says. 'On one level, the tragedies of Cape Kennedy and Vietnam serialized on billboards. ... On another level, the immediate personal environment, the volumes of space enclosed by your opposing hands ... the angle between these walls. On a third level, the inner world of the psyche'. Where these planes intersect, where the geometry of interiority meets with the architecture of the built environment, and with the mass production of the spectacle, there, Dr Nathan says, 'images are born, some kind of reality begins to assert itself' (p. 72).

It is this assertion of a new reality – a new kind of posthuman accommodation of personal space and built space, framed by the speed and violence of the image – that opens onto a new wave in the production of the posthuman. What Ballard makes possible in 1970 is the expression of a new relation with the image, recognising that the image is not the reflection of a pre-existing life world but that life world itself. As Burroughs puts it, 'The human image' in *The Atrocity Exhibition* 'explodes into rocks and stones and trees' (p. viii). The human is turned inside out, merging with the inorganic, the material. But in doing so, in exploding the human image, Ballard suggests that we are fashioned out of the images we make. 'Since people are made of image', Burroughs writes, 'this is literally an explosive book' (p. viii). And it is precisely this recognition, this discovery of a new geography of desire, of possibility, of rerouted being, carried in the surface of the image, that determines the passage of posthuman thinking across the remaining decades of the century. Under his peculiar, pornographic, sometimes misanthropic and misogynistic optic, what Ballard makes possible is the reorganisation of relations between subject and world through the manipulation of the image, of the performed and mediated spaces in which we encounter ourselves and each other.

The explosion of literary possibility that is unleashed in the British novel in the last quarter of the century follows, to a significant degree, from this reorganisation of being, this encounter with a newly decentred form of consciousness. Where Orwell's Winston seeks to keep the human compound intact, to maintain a rationalist relationship between interiority and the natural body, in the face of political and technological forces that are threatening to abolish it, Ballard lets the whole apparatus of human rationality come asunder, and in so doing releases us into new geometries of thought. And the passage of the novel in the decades that follow makes of this decentering of the human, this exploding of a sense of the interiority of the consciousness, an entirely new posthuman aesthetics and politics. Writers such as Angela Carter and Jeanette Winterson discover in the posthuman spectacular body the possibility of a new kind of feminist or postfeminist politics.

The expression of the human has doubled, through most of the history of civilisation, as a defence of a patriarchal status quo, and a naturalisation of unequal distributions of wealth and power. In the sudden freedom that the disaggregation of such structures affords, these writers produce forms of unregulated being, forms of thinking and writing in which gender is freed from the restrictions of embodiment, and in which we discover new capacities for self-fashioning. From Carter's *The Passion of New Eve* (1977), in which the body is fashioned from its cinematic representation, to Winterson's *Written on the Body* (1993), in which the narrator opens a peculiar space between genders, to the experiments in electronic identity in Winterson's *The Power Book* (2000), the British novel has discovered the possibility of a new feminist politics in the junction between posthumanism, spectacular mediation, and the production of a technological as opposed to a natural public sphere. If the innovative realists between the 1940s and the 1970s were circumscribed by a form of humanism that lived on after its conditions of possibility had expired, the next generation of writers – Salman Rushdie, Julian Barnes, and Kazuo Ishiguro as well as Carter and Winterson – freed themselves from such circumscription by thinking their way past the limits of the human itself. Where the human has always found itself in a difficult relationship with its prosthetic extension as techne (where such extension has both enlarged the human and constricted it), writers in the 1980s and 1990s discover a freedom from such restrictions by dispensing with the human as a category altogether. If being is made out of its extension as image, as electronic code, as machine or clone, then there is no longer any tension between some notion of proper natural being and such being as it is brought into the media sphere. By recognising that 'people are made of image', we allow for a kind of free interchange between interior and exterior landscapes that has been denied us throughout our histories. Indeed, it is perhaps such denial – the policing and blocking of interchanges between the inside and outside of being – that has constituted the human; the sense of liberation that late-twentieth-century posthumanism brought with it arose from the perception that this denial was finally being overcome.

If the second wave of posthuman thinking that I am identifying here was characterised by this sense of possibility, this sense that the experience of being dissolves into the manufactured image, I think it is nonetheless possible to detect a third wave in the development of a posthuman aesthetic, emerging only now, in the first decades of the twenty-first century. This new wave is closely bound up with the realisation that environmental disaster is the greatest threat facing our planet, and the connected realisation that the political sphere, in which human and posthuman interaction takes place, has a connection to a material environment, one which cannot be simply dissolved, which cannot be reduced to the condition of specularity, or to an effect of discourse. The perception that we are somehow fashioned out of our own representations, liberating though it seems, has made it difficult to produce a critical sense of our own relation with our environment. As such, a recent generation of writers, philosophers, ethicists, and environmentalists are trying to develop a way of understanding how the material environment intersects with discursive forms, without simply reviving older political forms, or reverting to prior models of human being. British novelists such as Ali Smith, David Mitchell, Zadie Smith, and Tom McCarthy are seeking, in various modes, to produce a way of seeing that might allow us to understand how new forms of technological being might relate to a material reality, a reality that does not come to us in terms of humanist models – that does not obey the protocols of Winston's 'two plus two equals four' – but which nevertheless requires us to apprehend it.

The dissolution of the human compound, this generation of writers might suggest, has freed us into the domain of the image. As Tom McCarthy's extraordinary novel *Remainder* (2006) demonstrates, however, this has left as a 'remainder' a kind of materiality that underlies being, which *is* being, but which does not easily find expression within our mediated circuits of representation. The protagonist of McCarthy's novel is famously estranged from his environment when he is struck down by what he can only call 'technology'. 'About the accident', the narrator says in the opening paragraph of the novel, 'I can say very little. Almost nothing. It involved something falling from the sky. Technology. Parts, bits. That's it, really'.[15] He receives a huge sum of money as compensation for this forgotten trauma, which he invests in 'telecommunications and technology' (p. 45) – as if he can sense a terrible conspiracy between information technology and the circuitry of the global economy. The investment of electronic money in the very technology that alienated him from himself, of course, does not help him to find his way back into the world, but rather pushes him further and further into neurosis. He becomes obsessed with the performance of what he calls 're-enactments', in which he invents forms of empty, repetitive, Ballardian representation that have no purchase on the real, that cannot quite capture the fullness of an original experience that comes to him in the evacuated form of déjà vu. His attempts to recover the experience of authentic being are continually undone by what he calls 'surplus matter', by a kind of materiality that is everywhere around him, but which cannot make its way into his representations and re-enactments of the world.

McCarthy's novel – which has become iconic for this new wave of British writers seeking to give expression to a contemporary posthumanism – suggests, with an absolutely singular kind of insistence, that the forms we have in which to enact our relations with the world cannot accommodate this matter, cannot account for the 'remainder' that is not captured in language, in the image. But if *Remainder* is caught in a kind of neurosis that emerges from this failure, at its heart is a vision of a new kind of writing that might give expression to a kind of posthuman materialism, a kind of writing that might be equal to the challenge of describing our transformed relations with the world, without reverting to exploded conceptions of the sovereign human. At the heart of McCarthy's novel there is a vision of a kind of accommodation with self that is as complete as that which is achieved by puppets and prosthetics in Kleist's essay on the marionette theatre. In the midst of his re-enactments, when the protagonist of *Remainder* is trying desperately to match the world that exists in his faulty memory with the material world around him, he occasionally experiences that sublime kind of balance that Kleist sees in the dance of the puppet. Puppets, Kleist's narrator says, are 'for all practical purposes weightless. They are not afflicted with the inertia of matter, the property most resistance to dance. The force which raises them into the air is greater than the one which draws them to the ground' (p. 16). As McCarthy's re-enactor moves into the heart of his own dance with matter, it is precisely this kind of weightlessness that he experiences. 'For a few seconds', he says, 'I felt weightless – or at least differently weighted: light but dense at the same time. My body seemed to glide fluently and effortlessly through the atmosphere around it – gracefully, slowly, like a dancer through water' (p. 135). McCarthy's narrative doesn't mean to suggest, of course, that this accommodation between being and matter is possible for us now. *Remainder* is precisely the story of this unavailability. But what such posthuman novels of the current century imply is that for us to understand the possibilities of posthuman life under the conditions produced by contemporary information technology we have to find a new accommodation with matter – the accommodation that Kleist had already envisaged in 1810, when the human was still the most powerful construct on the planet.

NOTES

1 Hal Foster, 'Prosthetic Gods', *Modernism/Modernity* 4.2 (1997), p. 5.
2 Bretolt Brecht, *Life of Galileo*, trans. John Willett (London: Methuen, 1986), p. 108. Hereafter cited parenthetically.
3 Richard Powers, 'The Seventh Event', in *Granta* 90 (2005), p. 59.
4 Augustine, *The City of God Against the Pagans*, trans. David S. Wiesen, (London: William Heinemann, 1968), vol. iii, p. 203.

5 Heinrich von Kleist, 'On the Marionette Theatre', in Idris Parry, *Hand to Mouth and Other Essays* (Manchester: Carcanet, 1981), p. 15. Hereafter cited parenthetically.

6 Sigmund Freud, *Civilization and its Discontents*, trans. Joan Riviere (London: Hogarth Press, 1982), pp. 28, 27.

7 Ibid., p. 27–28.

8 Ibid., p. 29.

9 Foster, 'Prosthetic Gods', p. 7.

10 Ibid., pp. 4–5, p. 5.

11 George Orwell, *Nineteen Eighty-Four* (London: Penguin, 1989), p. 88. Hereafter cited parenthetically.

12 Samuel Beckett, *The Lost Ones*, in *The Complete Short Prose, 1929–1989*, ed. S. E. Gontarski (New York: Grove Press, 1995), p. 215. Hereafter cited parenthetically.

13 Judith Butler, *Gender Trouble: Feminism and the Subversion of Identity* (New York: Routledge, 2006), p. 171.

14 William Burroughs, 'Preface', in J.G. Ballard, *The Atrocity Exhibition* (London: Harper, 2006), p. vii. Hereafter cited parenthetically.

15 Tom McCarthy, *Remainder* (London: Alma, 2011), p. 5. Hereafter cited parenthetically.

PART III

Recalibrations of Form and Genre

9

JULIA JORDAN

Late Modernism and the Avant-Garde Renaissance

Fiction after Modernism

'There are not many of us, and in the English way we do not form a "school"'. So wrote B. S. Johnson in 1967, defining himself and a small group of other writers (Christine Brooke-Rose, Alan Burns, Maureen Duffy, Rayner Heppenstall, and Ann Quin, in this instance) against the prevailing literary culture of the 1960s. The unpublished piece, entitled 'Experimental British Fiction', is remarkable for its fundamental contradictions. Johnson writes of a 'we', and yet explicitly refuses the collectivisation this might entail: 'we do not form a school'. He continues in similarly contradictory style to declare that his 'we', despite his chosen title for the piece, 'object to being called "experimental"'. This term is dismissed not for its imprecision, but 'because of the pejorative sense the term bears for most English critics': this group, or non-group, of writers swim against the tide of critical opinion, but nevertheless do not wish to be subject to any negative critical appraisal. Their relationship to modernism is also paradoxical: while they 'regard the novel as an evolving form in which there is no point whatsoever in doing something that has been done before', their 'greatest debt is owed to James Joyce, of course'.[1]

This last puzzling contradiction discloses an anxiety that is deeply historical. To be an experimental writer after modernism is to inherit something defined by its resistance to tradition; the group must be continually engaged in trying to repeat unrepeatability without, of course, repeating it: 'It is not a question of influence, of writing like Joyce: it is a matter of accepting that for practical purposes where Joyce left off is a starting point' (p. 2). They will succeed in keeping the legacy of modernism alive by rejecting anything that stands for modernism, by 'evolving' the 'form' away from its key tenets; they will absolve their debt to Joyce only by paying him the very Joycean compliment of sacrilege and subversion. Similar tensions can be felt throughout late modernism, signalling a legacy of complex negotiations between itself and its predecessors. Late modernism as a term implies being past the main event; irrelevant; at an angle; it implies difference, but, perhaps, *not yet*. Lecia Rosenthal has detected in late modernism a proleptic anxiety that derives from its putative lateness. 'As much as modernism may want to move forward', she writes, 'it never escapes the anxiety that drives the search', identifying this anxiety as spatial: 'The fear that the space of the new ... has been overtaken and exhausted, saturated by the accumulated residue of so many non-alternatives'.[2] In addition to this 'aesthetics of lateness' that continues into the 1960s, I read in many of the writers surveyed here an urge towards displacement and an appeal to nothingness. In the slippage between truth and representation, and a heightened sense of the ethical questions that inhere in the idea of authorial control, we can see the aspects of late modernism that have continuity with the (even later) avant-garde generation. In his anxious movement between self-effacement and self-conscious inheritance, Johnson and his 'we' display characteristically late-modernist traits. And yet, as a generation they were also responding to new artistic impetuses from the continent and America, to the dissolution of Empire and the migration of colonial subjects to England. As products of the postwar political settlement, their inheritance was not just modernism but the cultural and political conditions of late modernism itself.

This essay will consider how the doubling movement that this consciousness entails – back to modernism, and ceaselessly forward – contributes to the avant-garde renaissance that flourished in the 1960s and early 1970s. Exploring whether there is a case for a degree of coherence or collectivisation (one defined in part by the group's very resistance to it), I will position a generation defined by its straining at the boundaries of literary categorisation. This straining is detectable in the return to and transformation of modernist concerns into a preoccupation with truth, along with an attraction to images of negation, displacement, and the inadequacy of articulating knowledge through language. In this sense, experimentalists of the 1960s were influenced particularly by Samuel Beckett. For Beckett, the question of truth had become one of epistemological impotence, a whittling down of the aspects of the material world that it is possible to know: 'What I want is the straws, flotsam, etc., names, dates, births and deaths, because that is all I can know.'[3] In the 1940s and 1950s, late-modernist writers such as Henry Green had experienced their literary position as one of constricted or limited space, of having nothing left, or of being constituted in the aftermath of consuming modernist greed: 'There's no one to follow [Joyce and Kafka]. They're like cats which have licked the plate clean. You've got to dream up another dish if you're to be a writer'.[4] Beckett contrasts authorial and epistemological mastery with negation, marking the late modern as a 'whole zone of being' previously set aside 'as something unusable', a zone defined by 'impotence, ignorance'.[5] The writers that I am interested in here blur and remake this zone in their own image, inhabiting already-conquered territory while sim-ultaneously refusing to lament the supposedly lost vitality of modernism. Instead, requisitioning non-linear and fragmented forms of narration, they resist mourning their marginalised status, and instead actively attempt to repair their ability to represent the 'truth' of experience with mimetic fidelity.

Novels at the Crossroads and up the Cul-de-Sac

In a relatively short space of time the idea that the novel somehow 'died' in Britain for a while following modernism has gone from being a mat-ter of consensus to a position that lacks any compelling critical advocacy. In David Lodge's famous 1969 essay 'The Novelist at the Crossroads', he wrote that 'it is something of a commonplace of recent literary history, for instance, that the "modern" experimental novel, represented diversely by Joyce, Virginia Woolf and D.H. Lawrence, which threatened to break up the stable synthesis of the realistic novel, was repudiated by two subsequent generations of English novelists'.[6] Nevertheless, the 1950s had seen a critical backlash directed at formal innovation from a literary mainstream that was unquestionably biased towards realism; from the virulently anti-modernist C. P. Snow and Kingsley Amis to John Wain, whose dismissal of experimen-tal literature as 'motivated by faddishness or the irritable search for new gimmicks' was typical.[7]

Lodge suggests that characterisations of 'an incorrigibly insular England defending an obsolete realism against the life-giving invasions of fabulation' are an 'oversimplification' (p. 90). Nevertheless, his language hints at the 'othering' of experiment that took place, positioning it as a foreign, contin-ental, and somewhat suspicious affectation, rather than a type of writing that has its own set of traditions and its own continuities with the past. While advocating an acceptance of 'aesthetic pluralism',[8] Lodge makes clear that realism and the novel are inseparable: 'It is difficult to conceive of there being a conflict of interests between the novel and realism' (p. 85). Ultimately, for him, it is the 'self-defeating banality or self-indulgent excess' of experimentalism that remains potentially disruptive to realism's ability to do the work of synthesis between different novelistic modes.[9] Early in his career, Ian McEwan followed in this tradition in a complacent critique of what he saw as the sterility of this period of experimental fiction: 'The for-mal experimentation of the late sixties and early seventies came to nothing largely because the stuff was inaccessible and too often unrewarding – no pleasure in the text. And there can surely be no more mileage to be had from demonstrating yet again through self-enclosed "fictions" that reality is words and words are lies.' As an alternative, McEwan proposes that 'experimentation in its broadest and most viable sense should have less to do with formal factors like busting up your syntax and scrambling your page order, and more to do with content – the representation of states of mind and the society that forms them'.[10] Yet this definition of 'viable' experimentation stretches it to the point of becoming meaningless – only a caricatured version of experimental fiction would not in some way represent 'states of mind and the society which forms them'. Indeed, B. S. Johnson explicitly rejects this idea of experiment of content rather than form: 'It is both conceited and ignorant to believe that we (or anyone else) can have anything new to say about humanity', instead straining to 'say whatever it is we choose to say in a *new manner*' ('Experimental', p. 1).[11]

In a 1965 lecture Johnson characterised the realist novel as the literary equivalent to a house built in 'daub-and-wattle' in the face of the existence of the literary equivalent of 'ferro-concrete techniques'.[12] Johnson's feelings were widely replicated. In his 1964 introduction to Ann Quin's *Berg*, Giles Gordon wrote that the English novel had been 'languishing in self-satisfied gentility for quite some years'.[13] Influences from the continent were crucial to the emerging sense that there were alternatives to this unsatisfactory status quo. John Calder, who along with Marion Boyars published American and European fiction as well as Beckett, was hugely important to Giles Gordon and those like him, as Gordon wrote in his introduction: by introducing 'Beckett, Burroughs, Creeley, Duras, Claude Mauriac, Henry Miller, Pinget, Robbe-Grillet, Sarraute, and the important Scottish novelist Alexander Trocchi. We felt fiction mattered again'.[14] As Thomas Davis has noted, the mass migrations from the West Indies to England also contributed to experimental writing: 'Unlike the Angry Young Men, Caribbean writers reanimated features of modernism'. In fact, 'the experimental qualities of works such as [Samuel] Selvon's *The Lonely Londoners* and [George] Lamming's *The Emigrants* immediately installed these writers at the fore of a renewed modernism'.[15]

In 1975, Gordon published *Beyond the Words: Eleven Writers in Search of a New Fiction*, an anthology of writing whose express purpose was to enter into dialogue with Johnson's categorisation of writers from his 1973 collection *Aren't You Rather Young to be Writing Your Memoirs?* Johnson had listed eighteen writers who he believed were writing 'as though it mattered, as though they meant it',[16] although by the time Gordon's anthology was published two of them, Johnson and Ann Quin, had committed suicide. In his introduction to the collection Gordon suggests it should be read as an 'antidote' to Karl Miller's landmark *Writing in England Today* (1968). This latter collection, according to Gordon, 'omitted any writer whose abilities and inclinations were remotely divorced from the, so called, realistic'. He resented the parochialism and anti-intellectualism of the 'working class vernacular posing as social realism' of the Angry Young Men and other figures of the fifties: Kingsley Amis, Alan Sillitoe, John Wain, and John Osborne. Gordon asks, 'Where has "being realistic" got the present decade? Where has "social realism" got this century?'[17]

The sense of coming after the main event, both of the Second World War and of modernism, continued to be strongly felt into the 1960s and early 1970s, and consequently, a literary culture emerged that continually returned to images of negation and annihilation. Just as Tyrus Miller describes late-modernist writing in terms of 'each work tend[ing] toward formal singularity, as if the author had hit a dead end and had to begin again',[18] and Lodge imagines writers hesitating at a crossroads between realism and fabulation, so the metaphor of the dead end or cul-de-sac recurs in prognoses about postwar experimentalism. Alan Burns describes how he eventually reached 'a dead end. Particularly in *Babel*, but also in *Dreamamerika!* ... I had driven myself into a certain corner'.[19] For innovators in the 1960s, notions of possible or probable failure and continual marginalisation mingled with British society's generalised uncertainty.

There are, clearly, a number of problems with the bluntness of the binary division between experimentalism and realism, even though it evidently resonated for this group of writers. One such danger is of over-polarisation: literary experimentation did not die out after modernism to return triumphant in the 1960s; many 'realist' writers, or those not generally included amongst the various lists of experimenters, are deeply engaged in expanding the definition of realism in various ways. Many writers at mid-century, in the first wave of experimental late modernism, such as Samuel Beckett, Ivy Compton-Burnett, Lawrence Durrell, and Henry Green, are short-changed by both generic labels, and many later explicitly 'experimental' writers of the postwar era similarly resist easy categorisation: Rayner Heppenstall, Anthony Burgess, and Iris Murdoch all have a foot in both camps, and might just as easily be categorised in entirely different ways altogether. Moreover, definitions of realism and experimentalism are themselves so shifting and multifarious that any clear distinction between the two is impossible, and most late-twentieth-century novelists write in both modes. Andrzej Gasiorek has argued this case compellingly, suggesting that the distinction between realism and experimentation that was so important to modernism has no bearing on the postwar period: any blunt opposition between the two is flawed, he suggests, because it 'construes realism as a set of narrative techniques, and experimentalism as their subversion'.[20] He advances a case against the assumption that avant-garde writing is inherently radical, which would presuppose realism as a conservative monoculture rather than a flexible and heterogeneous grouping of different modes of representation. As such, Gasiorek points to writers who synthesise narrative innovation with realist techniques, and writes that the *'nouveaux romans* of Christine Brooke-Rose, the Dada-inspired collages of Alan Burns, and the metafictions of B.S. Johnson offer increasingly rarefied versions of the earlier shock tactics, thereby revealing they are the fag-end of a decaying tradition'.[21]

The contested term 'experimental' – rejected by some writers, used as a pejorative epithet by others – is unavoidably imbued with the possibility of failure.[22] The experimental work might make the discovery, in its metamorphosis from expected to unexpected, that its new-found difference is unwelcome or unworkable. B. S. Johnson would often say that his work is not experimental for precisely this reason: his failed experiments don't make it out 'there' (to a reading public), they remain in his room. To dismiss these figures as problematically modernist, or as thereby politically quiescent, is to continue a critical tradition of denigrating experimental novelists – one which is anticipated in the very task postwar avant-gardists set themselves. In this respect, the recent expansion in scholarship on late modernism sets us a challenge: to see literary development around mid-century not through the lens of an anxiety of lateness, or as a fag end, a space that has been used up, or indeed even as a rejection of realism per se, but instead as a set of responses to a genuinely felt crisis of representation that followed modernism and the Second World War.

Truth and Representation: Experimental Realism

It was therefore the experimentalists' very desire to extend and reanimate realism in the wider sense that was at stake; they were unified not by a rejection of realism's precepts, but by an attempt to force mimetic narrative modes to become freshly responsive to the 'truth'. In 1981, summing up the postwar literary scene in Britain, Charles Sugnet wrote, 'The whole public has been conned (or has conned itself) into accepting as fixed, "natural", and "real" an order of things which is a human artefact'.[23] Maggie Ross wrote that 'perhaps we've absorbed mechanization and its depersonalizing influences, and are ready to revert to an earlier, more durable aesthetic. The move is towards the precise presentation of reality ... the desire among ordinary people is for the reinstatement of authority, the re-establishment of order in the world'.[24] Ross's emphasis on the adequacy of the representations available to the writer is echoed by Christine Brooke-Rose when she reminds us that 'it is often forgotten for instance that the *nouveau roman*, when it burst out in the fifties, first acquired the label *nouveau realisme*'.[25] Similarly, Michael Butor argues in 'The Novel as Research' that 'formal invention in the novel, far from being opposed to realism as short-sighted critics often assume, is the *sine qua non* of a greater realism.'[26]

   J. G. Ballard was unaffiliated with any group. But his 1970 collection of 'condensed novels', *The Atrocity Exhibition*, had much in common with the writing of authors such as Alan Burns, who was exploring collage (notably in 1969's *Babel*) and who was also influenced by William Burroughs. Ballard was one of those interviewed for *The Imagination on Trial*, where he commented: 'I thought the balance between reality and fiction had tilted by the mid-sixties so we were living inside an enormous novel' (p. 20). Commenting on *The Atrocity Exhibition*, he wrote, 'The modern mind is used to cutting, we're trained to accept not just cutting, but the tradition of modern sculpture, where mass is defined not by ten tons of basalt carved in a huge block but by a couple of apparently unrelated armatures' (p. 24). Alan Burns, talking about his writing in the early 1960s, expresses similar impulses towards the abstraction entailed by cut-ups: 'I was considering the question of connection and flirting with the notion of disconnection. ... Disconnection fascinated me partly from an immature wish to shock, go to an extreme, make a break, an iconoclastic need to disrupt or cock a snook at the body of traditional literature'.[27] This notion, articulated by Burns, a friend and ally of B.S. Johnson's, is key: for many of these writers disconnection was a formal principle as well as a mimetic mode. Johnson's 1969 novel *The Unfortunates* goes as far as any example of British fiction in replicating the aleatorical principles that were being embraced elsewhere – the book itself is dismembered, unbound, with individual chapters to be shuffled. William Burroughs and others were exploring cut-up techniques in America, and works by Marc Saporta (*Composition No. 1*, 1962), and Julio Cortázar (*Hopscotch*, 1963) similarly experimented with unbound formats for their anti-linear narratives. *Albert Angelo* (1964) contains collage elements – adverts and posters – and typographical layouts to represent the doubleness of consciousness. But disconnection for Johnson was a matter of content as well as technique. As he writes in *The Unfortunates*, 'The mind has fuses': our perception of events is itself nonlinear.[28] Johnson's work also discloses anxieties that rotate around displacement, evacuation, extinction, and his own continual marginalisation; his brand of experimentalism is not (or not just) a joyful exploration of artistic possibility but also a negative practice, an embrace of the self-annihilating aspects of writing.

   Johnson's formal experimentation was also strictly in the service of the truth. 'Telling stories is telling lies',[29] he declares in *Albert Angelo*, declining to perform such cheap party-tricks: 'fuck all this lying' (p. 163). Autobiographical truth and fiction cannot remain separate. The task, as he sees it, is to efface that sense of artificiality which suddenly and urgently reflected a deeper inauthenticity characterising contemporary reality. This principle, though, is also an articulation of the importance of contingency. Johnson's challenge to himself is to lay bare the causes of things, by a continual dredging up of formative experience: to trace the teleology of events backwards. In this sense Johnson's prose is taut with a metaleptic awareness of loss. In *The Unfortunates* this notion of loss is transferred to the reader, as inherent in the idea that every individual reading is unlikely to be replicated is a heightened sense of the peculiar contingency of each life, its refusal of other possibilities. Johnson's endless trawl (in his novel *Trawl*, and elsewhere) through his experience to 'research the causes of my isolation' continually attempts to pinpoint the order of things – the moment things went wrong, the possibility missed. Johnson's explicit hostility to traditional realism in favour of a representation of the way contingency and possibility become implicated in reality can be seen not as an outright rejection of realism but a complex and constructive set of responses to its perceived inadequacies.

Eva Figes, one of the key experimental writers of the postwar period, often expressed familiar dissatisfaction with seemingly dishonest, outdated narrative methods: 'I discovered that life was not continuous, that the novels of the past were portraying a false reality'.[30] She wrote that her mimetic urge is what led her to 'constant literary innovation', as 'the old modes seem hopelessly inadequate; they also seem excruciatingly boring, both to read and to emulate. ... What matters is that the writer should shock into awareness, startle, engage the attention: above all that he should not engage in the trade of reassurance'.[31] *Winter Journey* (1967) tracks the moment before the death of an elderly man where 'eternity splits into a second', and her work frequently expresses the need to represent history as means of ordering the past. Doris Lessing's *The Golden Notebook* (1961) is similarly preoccupied with the contrast between narrative organisation and the representation of experience: '[Anna Wulf] keeps four, and not one, because, as she recognises, she has to separate things off from each other, out of fear of chaos, or formlessness – of breakdown'.[32] In addition to Lessing, Figes, Brooke-Rose, and Quin, prominent women writers who produced experimental novels include Brigid Brophy, Anna Kavan, Maggie Ross, and Maureen Duffy.

And yet women writers also occupy an uneasy position in the critical reassessment of the period. In its marginalised role, and its status as a tributary of the mainstream, experimental literature is seen as both an easier for them to enter – the avant-garde is culturally less important – and yet it is also paradoxically resistant to such infiltration – the avant-garde is traditionally, as well as etymologically, seen as aggressive: hard, masculinist, and cold.[33] It is likewise inescapable that there were more experimentalist men than women, and those writers included in surveys of the era are, usually, mostly male. Gasiorek's observation that the stylistically experimental does not necessarily marry with a politically subversive content would seem pertinent here. As Brooke-Rose writes, 'It does seem to be, in other words, not only more difficult for a woman *experimental* writer to be accepted than for a woman writer ... but also more difficult for a *woman* experimental writer to be accepted than a *male* experimental writer'.[34] However, given the assumptions about the automatic centrality of writing by men, already-marginalised experimental writing has overall been more open to women writers and articulations of women's experiences. In addition to the contemporary emergence of influential theoretical work such as Hélène Cixous's exploration of the subversive potential of the disruptive *ecriture feminine*, Ellen Friedman and Miriam Fuchs suggest that 'radical forms – nonlinear, non-hierarchical, and decentering – are, in themselves, a way of writing the feminine'.[35]

As Giles Gordon tells us in the introduction to Ann Quin's first novel, *Berg* (1964), John Calder published few English novelists, so when her debut came out, it was similarly firmly allied with the avant-garde: 'Here was a working-class voice from England quite unlike any other'.[36] For Quin, an interest in the non-linear and decentred are coupled with a desire to explore the radical dissolution of subjectivity. *Berg*'s merging of content and form results in a novel in which the crisis of reality renders the characters' actions hazy and uncertain, and their ability to know anything at all becomes radically ambiguous. Her work's avant-garde refusal of linearity is absolute. As Philip Stevick argues: 'Linearity is abandoned, not, apparently, in pursuit of some "poetic" effect ... but rather because Quin, quite simply, does not see the world as narrator'.[37] Quin's writing is opaque and sometimes amorphous, concerned with the negation of all authority, and her perception of the world shocks the reader, as objects lose their definition and merge into each other with fluidity: 'Blue flowers lost their blueness in a room caught between two others, but gave back their colour in the glass. ... Grains, sand grains of varied length spread, took on the colour of what was in the room. Objects he touched, ran his finger along. Blue dust, pollen he rubbed off.'[38] Subjectivity is constantly threatened, dissolving into the material world around it. Quin's novels are all preoccupied with paradoxical images of being, where selfhood seems only fully realised in terms of its own displacement and marginalisation. She shared the era's preoccupation with language's ability to represent truth, and yet her work consistently and radically questions its possibility. More than any other writer, Quin's voice was perhaps more distinctively and explicitly avant-garde, despite her novels' sometimes beguiling thematic simplicity.

Although the ongoing critical reassessment of the experimental literature of the period has seen Christine Brooke-Rose emerge as an increasingly significant figure, she remains, like Johnson, resistant to any easy classification. The price of 'slip[ping] through all the labels' is 'to belong nowhere'[39]: this, she argues, happens to all experimental writers, but to women in particular. Brooke-Rose's ability to evade pigeonholing is partly due to her ambivalent relationship to Britain. She lived and worked in France for many years, and was linked to the Ouvroir de Littérature Potentialle group, sharing with them an interest in creativity under constraint and the use of devices such as embedded lipograms. As such, she stands alongside Rayner Heppenstall as one of the most important links between the British generation of avant-garde writers and the continent. Her major experimental novels (after an initial period of writing more conventionally realist novels, which she later disavowed) are *Out* (1964), *Such* (1966), *Thru* (1975), *Between* (1968), and *Amalgamemnon* (1984). The novels become increasingly concerned with language and its relationship to reality, as she commented: '*Verbivore* (and less directly all my novels) are about all our suppositions being simulations of one kind or another'.[40]

If Brooke-Rose shares the period's preoccupation with the crisis or rupture in artistic engagements with reality, she also extends this to scientific and theoretical discourses. In an essay called 'Dynamic Gradients', she discusses the relationship between the new science of uncertainty and the current state of experimental literature. No longer is there a possibility, she argues, of absolute truth or absolute falsity, merely a shifting register of probabilities. In 1987, looking back on the same period, she noted that 'all our systems and fictions ... right up to, I suppose, the Second World War, people still believed in the "truth"'. That position, for her, is 'absolutely untenable now'.[41] In 'Dynamic Gradients' she discusses Natalie Saurraute and her 'tropisms'. For Brooke-Rose, these tropisms present a new way of thinking about 'external stimuli such as objects, events, conversations, as they affect, in a diminishing gradient, the subconversations on the threshold of consciousness'. Saurraute is engaged with recording and amplifying 'the way words lose their usual efficacy in the face of the opaque.'[42] This stands as a good description of Brooke-Rose's own literary philosophy: the 'meaning-making means at our disposal (linguistic, economic, political, scientific)', she wrote, now appeared so inadequate 'simply to explain the world'.[43] Brooke-Rose's literary language embraces the possibilities of opacity rather than mourning the lost 'efficacy' of words. And one of her solutions was to explore the possibilities of negation. As Karen Lawrence has written, 'Obsolescence and extinction ... haunt her texts', and this heightened awareness of extinction was explicitly linked, as it was for so many writers of her generation, to the threat of a nuclear war: 'Never before has man been so squarely faced with the possible annihilation of mankind'.[44] For Brooke-Rose, the post-war period's global instability is precisely the cause of the growing chasm between language and the reality it seeks to describe. 'These essential differences [between our century and others] are deeply linked to the sense we have that the real has become unreal.' In her novels of the late 1960s this 'essential difference' is posthuman, as she explores the representational possibilities of the human body as a site of incoherence, and other forms of displacement and marginalisation. Brooke-Rose had good reason herself to feel marginalised and displaced as an experimental woman writer, and the critical reaction to her work was often baffled and dismissive.[45] Reviewing *Out*, Isobel English wrote that 'it belongs to a genre which one can't exactly stigmatise as well-established, but which is nonetheless fashionable ... there is some voguish ballast in the cargoes of enthusiasm that come from Paris via John Calder'.[46]

One of the defining characteristics of any avant-garde, according to Peter Bürger, is that it shocks: it has radical intent and effect.[47] As we have seen, though, it is easy to conflate formal and political radicalism. Arguing instead that there is no fixed association between literary form and political position, Andrzej Gasiorek suggests that any 'such linkage is contingent and arbitrary'.[48] Indeed, any distinction between a realism that has long been assumed to be allied with a vague sort of liberal humanism and a reactionary avant-garde is imprecise, just as a distinction between the socially-engaged writers of the 1950s and the solipsistic experimentalists is unfair as well as inaccurate. Quin, Burns, and B. S. Johnson, among others, write novels that are intensely engaged with contemporary class structure and working-class experience, and that are imbued with the realities of life in postwar Britain.

And yet if we widen the parameters of what counts as radical just a little, there is a sense in which this experimental writing was and remains challenging beyond aspects of form alone. As Julia Kristeva has written, 'For at least a century, the literary avant-garde ... has been introducing ruptures, blank spaces and holes into language. ... The fragmentation of language in a text calls into question the very posture of th[eir] mastery'.[49] That these writers so often shared thematic as well as formal concerns does, I think, say something about the avant-garde's response to the specific literary-historical conditions of late modernism. The revocation of the possibility of know-ledge seen in the work of Samuel Beckett, Ivy Compton-Burnett, and Henry

Green has its counterpart in the mimetic crisis articulated by experimental writers of the 1960s. Such avant-gardists assert their authority to experiment with form while simultaneously undermining that authority; the linearity and order central to realism is identical with a type of political power. As Friedman and Fuchs have written, 'Despite their textual disruptions, the works of [male experimentalists] often display a nostalgic yearning after and grieving for the comforting authority of linear narrative – its teleology and its Newtonian certainties. In contrast, contemporary women experimentalists, for the most part, declare themselves on the side of ruptured and unreliable narrative'.[50]

When tracing the aftermath of modernism, scholars have seen a resistance to coherence that is both bodily and historical. Late-modernist writers, in Tyrus Miller's account, 'represent a world in free fall, offering vertiginiously deranged commentary as word, body and thing fly apart with a ridiculous lack of grace'.[51] For the writers of the 1960s and 1970s avant-garde, radical incoherence was still pressing, but with an added emphasis on what Brian McHale calls a '*hemorrhage*', or a 'leak[ing] away': their self-effacement and destabilization of the writer's authority synchronised with a desire to give voice to marginalization, displacement, and negation.[52] It is possible, then, to see this generation as the reverse of the authoritative modernists, who metaphorically occupy so much space: instead, postwar innovators negate their own authority, render that same literary space white or silent, and through an attraction to meaninglessness throw into question language's ability to capture a fugitive notion of reality. Either like Johnson, in service of a mourning for truth that recognises its impossibility; or like Brooke-Rose's embrace of possibility; or Quin's understanding of the contingency of all perception – these negations perhaps let in previously repressed elements of narrative fiction. Such elements included female experience, the radical artificiality of reality, and other incoming cultures and voices, making for a more socially and philosophically engaged experimentalism than before.

Late-twentieth-century experimental fiction is currently being taken up with renewed enthusiasm by general readers as well as by scholars and students of this period. In turn, these writers also stand, collectively, as an important prefiguring of current debates about modernism's legacy with regards to contemporary writers such as Tom McCarthy, Eimear McBride, Will Self, and Zadie Smith. Postwar experimentalists, then, succeeded in developing modernism in the only way possible – paradoxically, by doing something different. That we can now allow for a more nuanced picture of the ongoing late-modernist and avant-garde project in this era means that we will in future be able to read these writers fairly: not as a fag end or a cul-de-sac, and not as a symptom of a simplistic binary opposition between realism and experimentalism, but as a generative cluster of movements in their own right. As Brooke-Rose wrote in 1964, 'It is legitimate to criticize these experimental writers in relation to what they are trying, implicitly or explicitly, to do. But let us first grasp what it is they are doing'.[53]

NOTES

1   B. S. Johnson, 'Experimental British Fiction', unpublished transcript, 20 August, 1967, p. 1. Hereafter cited parenthetically.
2   Lecia Rosenthal, *Mourning Modernism: Literature, Catastrophe, and the Politics of Consolation* (New York: Fordham, 2011), pp. 5–6.
3   Beckett to MacGreevy, June 1930, quoted in Knowlson, *Damned to Fame* (London: Bloomsbury, 1997), p. 121.
4   Henry Green, 'The Art of Fiction', in *Surviving: The Uncollected*, ed. Matthew Yorke, (London: Harvill, 1994), p. 247.
5   Israel Shenker, 'Moody Man of Letters: Interview with Samuel Beckett', 6 May 1956, section 2, p. 3.
6   David Lodge, 'The Novelist at the Crossroads', in *The Novel Today: Contemporary Writers on Modern Fiction*, ed. Malcolm Bradbury (Manchester: Manchester University Press, 1977), p. 88. Hereafter cited parenthetically.
7   John Wain, *Essays of Literature and Ideas* (London: Macmillan, 1963), pp. 49–50.
8   Malcolm Bradbury, ed., *The Novel Today: Contemporary Writers on Modern Fiction* (London: Fontana, 1990), p. 6.
9   David Lodge, *The Novelist at the Crossroads and Other Essays of Fiction and Criticism* (London: Routledge and Kegan Paul, 1984), p. 22.
10 Ian McEwan 'The State of Fiction: A Symposium', *New Review*, 5.1 (Summer 1978), p. 51.
11 In any case, as Susan Sontag points out, the distinction is simplistic: 'Every style embodies an epistemological decision, an interpretation of how and what we perceive. ... Every style is a means of insisting upon something'. Susan Sontag 'On Style,' *Against Interpretation* (New York: Noonday, 1966), p. 35.
12 B. S. Johnson, 'Holes, Syllabics and the Succussations of the Intercostal and Abdominal Muscles', in *Well Done God!*, eds. Jonathan Coe, Philip Tew, and Julia Jordan (London: Picador, 2013), p. 393.
13 Giles Gordon, 'Introduction' to Ann Quin, *Berg* (London: Calder and Boyars, 1964), p. vii.
14 Ibid., p. ix.
15 Thomas S. Davis, 'Late Modernism: British Literature at Midcentury', *Literature Compass* 9.4 (2012), p. 333.
16 B. S. Johnson, *Aren't You Rather Young to be Writing Your Memoirs?*, in *Well Done God!*, p. 29.
17 Giles Gordon, 'Introduction,' in *Beyond the Words: Eleven Writers in Search of a New Fiction*, ed. Giles Gordon (London: Hutchinson, 1975), p. 11.
18 Tyrus Miller, *Late Modernism: Politics, Fiction, and the Arts Between the World Wars* (Berkeley: University of California Press, 1999), p. 13.

JULIA JORDAN

19 Alan Burns and Charles Sugnet, eds., *The Imagination on Trial* (London: Allison & Busby, 1981), p. 164.
20 Andrzej Gasiorek, *Post-War British Fiction: Realism and After* (London: Edward Arnold, 1995), p. v.
21 Ibid., p. 19.
22 '"Experimental" is the dirtiest of words, invariably a synonym for "unsuccessful"' as Johnson writes in 'Holes, Syllabics...', in *Well Done God!*, p. 396.
23 Charles Sugnet, 'Introduction', in *The Imagination on Trial*, eds. Charles Sugnet and Alan Burns (London and New York: Allison and Busby, 1981), p. 4. Hereafter cited parenthetically.
24 Maggie Ross, 'Interview', in Giles Gordon, ed., *Beyond the Words*, p. 280.
25 Christine Brooke-Rose, 'Illiterations', in *Breaking the Sequence: Women's Experimental Fiction*, eds. Ellen G. Friedman and Miriam Fuchs (Princeton: Princeton University Press, 1989), p. 63.
26 Michael Butor, 'The Novel as Research', in *The Novel Today: Contemporary Writers on Modern Fiction*, ed. Malcolm Bradbury (Manchester: Manchester University Press, 1977), pp. 48–53, p. 50.
27 Alan Burns, 'Essay', in *Beyond the Words: Eleven Writers in Search of a New Fiction*, ed. Giles Gordon (London: Hutchinson, 1975), p. 64.
28 B.S. Johnson, *The Unfortunates* (London: Secker & Warburg, 1969), 'Just as', p. 5. Here I follow the convention of identifying the unbound chapters of the *Unfortunates* by their first two words.
29 B. S. Johnson, *Albert Angelo* (London: Constable, 1964), p. 167. Hereafter cited parenthetically.
30 Eva Figes, *The Imagination on Trial*, p. 33.
31 Eva Figes, 'Note', in *Beyond the Words*, p. 113.
32 Doris Lessing, 'Preface to *The Golden Notebook*', in *The Novel Today*, p. 169.
33 Rayner Heppenstall reminds us that the avant-garde is 'a detachment sent out in front to protect the main body of troops against surprise attack' (*The Fourfold Tradition* [London, Barrie: 1961], p. 135).
34 Brooke-Rose, 'Illiterations', p. 65.
35 Friedman and Fuchs, *Breaking the Sequence*, p. 3.
36 Gordon, 'Introduction', *Beyond the Words*, p. ix.
37 Philip Stevick, 'Voices in the Head: Style and Consciousness in the Fiction of Ann Quin', in *Breaking the Sequence*, p. 237.
38 Ann Quin, *Passages* (London: Calder & Boyars, 1969), p. 18.
39 Brooke-Rose, 'Illiterations', p. 67.
40 Brooke-Rose, 'Illicitations,' *Review of Contemporary Fiction* 9 (Autumn 1989), p. 108.
41 Quoted in Sarah Birch, *Christine Brooke-Rose and Contemporary Fiction* (Oxford: Clarendon Press, 1994), p. 5.
42 Brooke-Rose, 'Dynamic Gradients', *The London Magazine* 4.12 (March 1964), p. 92.
43 Brook-Rose, *A Rhetoric of the Unreal* (Cambridge: Cambridge University Press, 1981), p. 6.
44 Ibid., p. 8.
45 'I have been called "*nouveau roman* in English" and *nouveau nouveau*, I have been called Postmodern, I have been called Experimental, I have been included

in the SF Encyclopaedia, I automatically come under Women Writers (British, Contemporary), I sometimes interest the Feminists' (Brooke-Rose, *Stories, Theories, Things* [Cambridge: Cambridge University Press, 1991], p. 4).

46 Isobel English, 'Mistaken Mortals', *The Catholic Herald*, 7 December 1964.

47 Peter Bürger, *Theory of the Avant-Garde*, trans. Michael Shaw (Manchester: Manchester University Press, 1984).

48 Gasiorek, *Post-War British Fiction*, p. 4.

49 Julia Kristeva, 'Oscillation Between Power and Denial', trans. Marilyn A. August, in *New French Feminism*, eds. Elaine Marks and Isabelle de Courtivron (Amherst: University of Massachusetts Press, 1980), p. 165.

50 Friedman and Fuchs, *Breaking the Sequence*, p. 27.

51 Miller, *Late Modernism*, p. 19.

52 Brian McHale, *Postmodernist Fiction* (London: Methuen, 1987), p. 12.

53 Brooke-Rose, 'Dynamic Gradients', p. 96.

10

JOSEPH BROOKER

Reanimating Historical Fiction

Historical fiction carries a certain cognitive power. Its central characters' adventures help us to conceive the wider history of which they are part. Such a view is articulated in an illuminating essay by Perry Anderson, who sketches the history and theory of the historical novel. Anderson reminds us that Hungarian Marxist thinker Georg Lukács was among the most substantial commentators on the form. Lukács in turn viewed Sir Walter Scott as the genre's most significant founder. Anderson summarises Lukács' account as follows:

> The classical form of the historical novel is an epic depicting a transformation of popular life through a set of representative human types whose lives are reshaped by sweeping social forces. Famous historical figures will feature among the dramatis personae, but their roles in the tale will be oblique or marginal. Narratives will centre instead on middling characters, of no great distinction, whose function is to offer an individual focus for the dramatic collision of opposing extremes between whom they stand, or more often waver. What Scott's novels then stage is a tragic contest between declining and ascending forms of social life, in a vision of the past that honours the losers but upholds the historical necessity of the winners.[1]

According to this model, an authentically historical narrative suggests a parallel between individual and general, contingently local and socially typical. The form, Lukács writes, 'must disclose the social foundations of politics by portraying living human destinies, individual destinies which concentrate in their individual uniqueness the typical, representative features of these connexions'.[2] Fredric Jameson, a successor of Lukács in Marxist theory, has influentially talked of 'cognitive mapping' as a vocation for art, pedagogically locating its audiences in social space.[3] We might say that historical fiction, in a Lukácsian account, analogously allows its readers to locate themselves in historical time.

Much of Lukács's account remains suggestive even for the historical novel of the twenty-first century. But in Anderson's narrative, the form has known its vicissitudes since the age of *Waverley*. It fed into the main current of the nineteenth-century realist novel, reaching an apex along with that form in Tolstoy. With the rise of modernism, though, the historical novel is marginalised. Aside from the prescient play of Virginia Woolf's *Orlando* (1928), the form becomes regarded as middlebrow or even lowbrow. But a further turn is in store. Since the 1970s, Anderson proposes, the genre has staged a startling revival. The advanced historical novel of recent decades, though, is a different model from that known to its earlier writers and theorists:

> Now, virtually every rule of the classical canon, as spelled out by Lukács, is flouted or reversed. Among other traits, the historical novel reinvented for postmoderns may freely mix times, combining or interweaving past and present; parade the author within the narrative; take leading historical figures as central rather than marginal characters; propose counterfactuals; strew anachronisms; multiply alternative endings; traffic with apocalyptics. (p. 27)

This era of reanimation claims our attention now, as we consider a range of British writers who have diversely meditated on history through fiction.

Within British fiction, if one work announced the arrival of Anderson's new era it was John Fowles's *The French Lieutenant's Woman* (1969). Fowles's third novel tells a story of England in 1867, in which the male protagonist encounters the dilemma of whether to leave his fiancée for the disgraced woman of the title. The story's depiction of Victorian sexual mores thus already considers the period in ways not always evident at the time. But Fowles plays much more explicitly on the gap between nineteenth and twentieth centuries. At times his novel is a stylistic homage to novelists of the period described, most notably Thomas Hardy, who wrote of the West Country depicted by Fowles. At other moments, Fowles interjects anachronisms. His chapters bear epigraphs from Victorian thinkers, such as Marx and Darwin, who went uncited in actual Victorian fiction. He comments on events in the story with knowledge unavailable to the characters but available to the author a century on. A seemingly innocuous date in 1867, the narrator insists, 'is the point from which we can date the beginning of feminine emancipation'.[4] The effect is a remarkable double vision, split between diegesis and discourse. Fowles's Victorian world retains its own integrity, but his narration effects an anachronistic visitation into the past. In a particularly striking intervention, he professes his own ignorance about his character's motivations, then offers a meditation on authorial knowledge,

JOSEPH BROOKER

proposing that this should be diminished in an age less keen on divine omniscience: 'an age', indeed, 'of Alain Robbe-Grillet and Roland Barthes' (p. 85).

Fowles's subject matter apparently belongs to the Victorian novel, but he writes it from a historical standpoint already aware of the emergence of post-structuralism – as well as the existentialism that is his own primary philosophical emphasis. From this postwar perspective, Fowles intervenes to offer three different endings to his novel. They correspond to different outlooks that are themselves historically particular: the last two endings are more congenial to the standpoint of the 1960s than the first, conventionally Victorian, conclusion. Fowles's own essay on the novel blithely states that the historical novel is 'a genre in which I have very little interest'.[5] But in dramatically staging this confrontation between the Victorian era, the Victorian novel, and the strikingly different view from the 1960s, Fowles increased others' interest in the possibilities of historical fiction.

Fowles's book stands as benchmark and inspiration for the metafictional historical novel in Britain. It would be cited, alongside many other titles, when the critic Linda Hutcheon produced the major theorisation of this mode. In numerous critical works of the 1980s, Hutcheon identified 'historiographic metafiction' as combining referentiality with reflexivity, in a mode that was politically virtuous for its work in alerting us to the constructed and partial nature of our accounts of the world.[6] Hutcheon was in key with the theoretical climate in literary studies. This climate produced an increasingly congenial critical reception for novelists who, in Fowles's wake, turned to history in self-conscious mode.

Another writer of Fowles's generation was exceptionally creative in his treatment of history. William Golding's second novel, *The Inheritors* (1955), travelled back almost to prehistory in dramatising the triumph of early human beings over Neanderthals. Golding narrates most of the narrative from the Neanderthals' point of view, before switching late on to third-person narrative, then to the point of view of the 'new people'. The technical decision carries unusual force here, as point of view swings from one species to another: common enough in science fiction but a rare feat in historical fiction. In *The Spire* (1964), Golding narrates the construction of a medieval cathedral. The mental landscape here is not as far from the present as his Neanderthals', but far enough to challenge the modern reader, as the Dean's commitment to his god drives him into hallucinations. Golding turned to history sparingly – several of his other novels are set in the twentieth century – but with particular intentions and striking effect. His most extended venture into history was the late 'sea trilogy' of *Rites of Passage* (1980), *Close Quarters* (1987), and *Fire Down Below* (1989). The novels venture into the realm of the seafaring yarn of the early nineteenth century, popularised by C. S. Forester and Patrick O'Brian's novel sequences. Yet they feature relatively little of the derring-do associated with that genre. On the last page of *Rites of Passage*, Golding's hero, Edmund Talbot, declares: 'Why – it has become, perhaps, some kind of sea-story but a sea-story with never a tempest, no shipwreck, no sinking, no rescue at sea, no sight nor sound of an enemy, no thundering broadsides, heroism, prizes, gallant defences and heroic attacks!'[7] Golding here tacitly admits that this naval novel has been less a conventional military adventure and more an investigation of other issues.

In its treatment of language and narration, *Rites of Passage* is strikingly reflexive. The novel's text purports to be Talbot's journal, written for his godfather to read. This allows it to make regular reference to the act of writing. Its sections are numbered, but these headings become increasingly unstable. Thus: 'I have placed the number "2" at the beginning of this entry though I do not know how much I shall set down today' (p. 11). An entry headed '*(x)*' commences with Talbot admitting: 'I *think* it is the seventh – or the fifth – or the eighth perhaps – let "X" do its algebraic duty and represent the unknown quantity' (p. 46). The textual apparatus becomes stranger still, with one entry headed '(?)' (p. 72), and another '*(Z)*': 'Zed, you see, zed, I do not know what the day is' (p. 95). We are in the hands of an amateur writer, whose text regularly points up the uncertainty of its own record of time, place, and event. Talbot's journal also meditates upon the issues of genre and representation it raises. 'Your lordship may detect in the fore-going a tendency to *fine writing*', Talbot suggests after concluding a long paragraph, 'a not unsuccessful attempt, I flatter myself' (p. 67). Elsewhere he compares his own writing to that of Defoe and Sterne, recognising that his factual journal is inflected by the forms of what is for him relatively recent fiction. The journal, the form in which we read the story, is also an object within the world of the novel. On the final page Talbot will finish writing the journal, then resolve to 'lock it, wrap it and sew it unhandily in sailcloth and thrust it away in the locked drawer' (p. 278). The journal is not only the frame through which we read of events; it is also an object that might influence characters' behaviour. In Talbot's own words, 'I must keep all locked away. This journal has become deadly as a loaded gun' (p. 184). Talbot's journal comes to incorporate a long letter from the Reverend Colley, whom Talbot has represented contemptuously and who has finally been persecuted to death by the crew. Colley's letter shows that he blamed himself for each situation, and idolised Talbot even as the latter tormented him. Golding's reflexivity is thus able to raise ethical issues: an action that Hutcheon would soon be arguing was characteristic of historiographic metafiction.

Golding famously won the 1980 Booker Prize, in what was depicted as a close race with Anthony Burgess – who in *Earthly Powers* had penned his own wry, epic retrospect on the century's chaos. In an indication of the growing prominence of the theme, the following year's Booker saw another stand-off between two novels concerned with modern history. D. M. Thomas's *The White Hotel* (1981), a novel that fictionalizes Freud as well as the Holocaust, was pipped for the prize by Salman Rushdie's *Midnight's Children*. In Rushdie's book an alternative version of India's postwar history is narrated by Saleem Sinai, who was born at the same instant as the nation. The novel makes a strong comparison with another key novel of the era, by Rushdie's friend and comrade in magic realism Angela Carter. In her *Nights at the Circus* (1984), set in 1899, the American journalist Walser follows the inexplicably winged woman Fevvers on her picaresque journey to Russia with an American travelling circus. The two novels share notable resemblances, though they relate differently to the paradigms of historical fiction. Rushdie's novel would not pass the test of the Historical Novel Society, which proposes that historical fiction should be set at least fifty years prior to the present. Indeed, in being partially inspired by the India that Rushdie had personally known, *Midnight's Children* fails that definition's main point: that the author should be writing of an era beyond his direct experience.[8] And yet the novel demands consideration here, for it has been a central one, as much as Fowles's, in subsequent discussions of fiction and history.

Both Carter and Rushdie are obsessed with the act of storytelling. Rushdie's Saleem warns on his first page of the lengthy yarn he is about to spin: 'an excess of intertwined lives events miracles places rumours, so dense a commingling of the improbable the mundane'![9] This mode has numerous ancestors, from Sterne to Dickens, but one more proximate precursor worth naming is Thomas Pynchon's *Gravity's Rainbow* (1973). Pynchon's epic of the Second World War was written only a quarter-century or so after the events it reconfigures. But the advent, in that quick span, of the Beat Generation and 1960s counter-culture meant that Pynchon's book looked back as though on a radically different epoch, remaking the conjuncture of D-Day in the mood of Altamont. Something of Pynchon's irrepressible urge to narrate, digress, and embellish recent history would be an important component in the metafictional historical novel.

In this discursive mode, the concept of history is centrally at stake. Carter's narrator, like Fowles's, seems aware of how the new century will turn out.

When the circus arrives in St Petersburg, Carter observes that the local peas-
ants 'do not know what we know about their city':

> They lived on, without knowledge or surmise, in this city that is on the point
> of becoming legend but not yet, not quite yet; the city, this Sleeping Beauty of a
> city, stirs and murmurs, longing yet fearing the rough and bloody kiss that will
> awaken her, tugging at her moorings in the past, striving, yearning to burst
> through the present into the violence of that authentic history to which this
> narrative – as must by now be obvious! – does not belong.[10]

Like Fowles, Carter plays upon the dramatic irony afforded by history. She
knows, as her fictional Russia does not, that revolution is due within two
decades. The imminent movement of real history is asserted, even as the
novel's membership of that history is emphatically rejected. But in referring
to this distinction, Carter seems to wish to remain on terms with the real.
In a sly return to the theme, she finally implies that a Marxist character has
encountered Lenin in the British Museum, and that her whole journey has
helped lay the path to the revolution (p. 346). The mixture here – of history
and fantasy, a desire both to refer to political events and to rewrite them – is
typical of fictional history in the new epoch limned by Perry Anderson.

Lukács's historical novel bridged private life and public history. Rushdie's
narrator does the same, but with deliberately flagrant directness. A letter
from the new nation's prime minister informs him that his life 'will be, in a
sense, the mirror of our own' (p. 122). Almost every major historical event
becomes improbably twinned with the latest twist in the life of Saleem,
who actually claims to have been the reluctant cause of numerous political catastrophes. Explaining that 'I was linked to history both literally and
metaphorically, both actively and passively' (p. 238), he systematically combines these four elements into the potential 'modes of connection' between
himself and the nation. This is the novel's most gleefully reflexive moment.
Rushdie's *combinatoire* of formulations seems like a parody of Lukács himself. He subsequently uses them to comment on the action (pp. 290, 299,
329, 351). Here, as in Carter, the novel of history temporarily becomes a
locus of critical theory.

Rushdie is insistently but ambiguously preoccupied with the possibility
of historical truth. Saleem declares that 'reality is a question of perspective; the further you get from the past, the more concrete and plausible
it seems – but as you approach the present, it inevitably seems more and
more incredible' (p. 165), and later repeats that 'we are too close to what-is-
happening, perspective is impossible ... only subjective judgments are possible' (p. 435). The novel hankers for historical truth, allying itself with
a hidden counter-history (p. 421); but it is too dominated by doubts and

fictions to present this as definitive. 'Aircraft, real or fictional, dropped actual or mythical bombs', Saleem recalls in recounting a war: 'It is, accordingly, either a matter of fact or a figment of a diseased imagination' that three of them happened to hit buildings containing members of his family (p. 341). The first sentence here seems sarcastically to insist on the reality of war's destructiveness. Yet the second sentence takes us into fiction. Those family members never existed, so what Saleem describes is not a 'matter of fact' but, indeed, the figment of someone's imagination. As a novel, *Midnight's Children* cannot authoritatively announce historical truth. Instead, it uses its fictional license to work around what is known, often by means of the magical and fantastic. The novel of history here incorporates those modes least congenial to the historian.

Carter and Rushdie were exemplary for other novelists' sallies at history. Jeanette Winterson is a notable example. Her first novel, *Oranges Are Not The Only Fruit* (1985), is a fictionalized autobiography spliced with fairy tale. Yet at its centre is a miniature essay on the nature of history. Though employing plentiful metaphor and anecdote, this brief chapter also talks at us very directly:

> Everyone who tells a story tells it differently, just to remind us that everybody sees it differently. Some people say there are true things to be found, some people say all kinds of things can be proved. I don't believe them. The only thing for certain is how complicated it all is, like string full of knots. ... People like to separate storytelling which is not fact from history which is fact. They do this so that they know what to believe and what not to believe. This is very curious.[11]

The scepticism voiced here was growing increasingly familiar in fictional discussions of history.

Winterson's third novel, *The Passion* (1987), is as close as she comes to a historical novel proper.[12] The era of Napoleon's European wars (a favourite setting for the genre, at least since Tolstoy) is dramatised, in properly Lukácsian fashion, through the experiences of marginal characters: Henri, Napoleon's cook, and Villanelle, a Venetian casino worker. While major events in the novel's background correspond to the historical record, Winterson's central story grows akin to fable. As we read of boatmen with webbed feet (p. 129), a lookout with a telescopic eye (pp. 21–23), and a woman whose heart is stored in a jar (pp. 120–1), what seems a historical novel also partakes of the possibilities of fairy tale. Hence the novel's leitmotif, repeated by both main characters after narrating something unlikely: 'I'm telling you stories. Trust me' (pp. 5, 13, 160). The phrase summarises a whole strain of literary endeavour in this period: at once emphasizing, even delighting in, the act of narration and placing in question its veracity, while leaving us no firm ground on which doubt could end. This mood flourished in fictions about history. The world of recorded, researchable fact was precisely the zone in which novelists most consistently contested the status of fact, exploring the dizzyingly provisional discourses of narrative art.

The theme was also taken up by writers of less fantastic sensibility. In Julian Barnes's *Flaubert's Parrot* (1984), the retired doctor Geoffrey Braithwaite meditates on his literary idol, Gustave Flaubert. The novel belongs to a mode identified by Suzanne Keen: the 'romance of the archive', in which the role of the researcher is highlighted. (A. S. Byatt's *Possession: A Romance* [1990], which centres on contemporary academics uncovering the truth about nineteenth-century poets, is the ultimate instance of this mode.)[13] Barnes suggests a certain relativism in the sheer multiplicity of discourses available. *Flaubert's Parrot* splices genres of writing, including three differing chronologies of Flaubert's life (themselves arranged to tell three different stories), a dispute with an imagined foe of Flaubert ('The Case Against'), the voice of Flaubert's lover Louise Colet, an A–Z of Flaubert, and an examination paper. Numerous ways of seeing are available, each of them rooted in recorded fact. A similar gesture is implicit in Barnes's *A History of the World in 10½ Chapters* (1989). This series of related stories ranges from Biblical times to late medieval France to the dawn of the Victorian era, as well as contemporary settings. The book's internal heterogeneity posits human history as itself rangy and varied, though also honeycombed with odd connections and echoes.

Barnes addresses history as explicitly as any of his contemporaries. This meditation from Braithwaite is characteristically direct:

> How do we seize the past? Can we ever do so? When I was a medical student some pranksters at an end-of-term dance released into the hall a piglet which had been smeared with grease. It squirmed between legs, evaded capture, squealed a lot. People fell over trying to grasp it, and were made to look ridiculous in the process. The past often seems to behave like that piglet.[14]

Braithwaite multiplies other images for the past. It is a riot-wrecked city in which 'lost, disordered, fearful, we follow what signs there remain; we read the street names, but cannot be confident where we are' (p. 60). 'We can study files for decades', Braithwaite admits, 'but every so often we are tempted to throw up our hands and declare that history is merely another literary genre: the past is autobiographical fiction pretending to be a parliamentary report' (p. 90). In *A History of the World*, Barnes, like Winterson, is still more direct:

> History isn't what happened. History is just what historians tell us. ... And we, the readers of history, the sufferers from history, we scan the pattern for

hopeful conclusions, for the way ahead. ... The history of the world? Just voices echoing in the dark; images that burn for a few centuries then fade; stories, old stories that sometimes seem to overlap; strange links, impertinent connections.[15]

It is a paradox that novels of this period speak so authoritatively about the loss of epistemological authority.

Graham Swift's *Waterland* (1983) is comparable to *Midnight's Children* as a work that hardly qualifies as a 'historical novel', yet which rapidly became central to discussions of history and the novel. Swift's narrator Tom Crick is, emblematically, a history teacher in a London school. He tells the history of the English fens, the landscape of his own family background, while also detailing the early-1980s present in which his job is assailed by gloomy pupils and government cuts. Like Barnes's Braithwaite, Crick readily swings into miniature essays on matters of fact. Swift, too, splices facts into his fiction, elegantly allowing them to combine in a continuous, recursive speculation on the nature of knowledge. This takes the form of Crick's wandering address to his class of schoolchildren. He offers them a scattered series of definitions of history: 'this cumbersome but precious bag of clues'; 'that impossible thing: the attempt to give an account, with incomplete knowledge, of actions themselves undertaken with incomplete knowledge'; 'a lucky dip of meanings'; 'a settling for roles'.[16] All of these stress the limits of history: the necessary incompleteness of human knowledge, the randomness of meaning, the role of performance. Indeed, Crick also notes history's proximity to histrionics, defining it afresh as 'the fabrication, the diversion, the reality-obscuring drama' (p. 34). Human beings, Crick avers, seek causality: man is 'the animal that asks Why' (p. 92). History is thus hard-wired to humanity. But it is less solid than it seems. From the start, Crick emphasises the role of narrative, which is equally native to humanity, 'the story-telling animal' (p. 53). His family told stories to 'outwit reality' (p. 15). Crick repeatedly deploys the fairy-tale opening 'Once upon a time', claims that he 'grew up in a fairy-tale place' (p. 1), and refers to real lives as 'those most unbelievable yet haunting of fairy tales' (p. 6). Seeking explanations in history, he has discovered 'more mysteries, more fantasticalities', and concluded that 'history is a yarn' (p. 53).

Yet these novelists are not ecstatic about the relativisation of history into narrative. Progress does not exist, Tom Crick declares, but we can aspire to 'the reclamation of land': a fenland metaphor for the slow recovery of historical fact. This 'dull yet valuable business' should retain its modesty, and not be mistaken for 'the building of empires' (p. 291). History, Crick opines, can at least teach mistakes, against those who claim to know 'how to do it' (p. 203). Julian Barnes, too, for all the wry scepticism fostered by his work, maintains a commitment to what he dares to call 'objective truth': 'we must believe that it is 99 per cent obtainable; or if we can't believe this we must believe that 43 per cent objective truth is better than 41 per cent' (*History of the World*, pp. 245–6).

Historiographic metafiction was closely accompanied by another tendency in the late twentieth century. This is revisionism: the attempt to reconsider historical consensus and offer critique, or to include unaccustomed voices and agents in the historical account. Kazuo Ishiguro's *The Remains of the Day* (1989) undertakes such a project by distinctive narrative means. The novel's narrator, Mr Stevens, a butler from the fictional Darlington Hall, speaks to us from 1956. But his narrative constantly reaches back in turn to the 1920s and 1930s, the great years of Stevens's employment under his former master, Lord Darlington. There are thus, effectively, three times in question: the interwar period, the postwar, and also tacitly the late 1980s, when Ishiguro writes and publishes the novel. Nineteen fifty-six was the year of the Suez Crisis, in which an ill-starred military adventure into the Middle East saw the demonstration of Britain's diminished global power, in the face of the ascendant United States. While Suez remains unmentioned, the geopolitical dimension is at least implicitly signalled by the arrival of an American businessman, John Farraday, as new owner of Darlington Hall. The book's title thus takes on some public import: the remains of the Empire, of British power, or of one version of England itself are the ground in which Ishiguro digs. History is explored partly through narrative voice: Ishiguro delicately fashions the voice of his somewhat unreliable narrator, seeding it with historical traces of class identity and anxiety.

As Ishiguro wrote the novel, the ideological role of the stately home and English countryside was under fresh scrutiny. Patrick Wright had argued that 'heritage' was doing dubious, conservative ideological work in the Thatcher decade. The popularity of what Andrew Higson dubbed the 'heritage film' – generally adaptations of classic English novels from the Merchant-Ivory production company – granted a bigger screen to such spectacles.[17] It is in this climate that Ishiguro's novel subtly intervenes. Most contentiously, it reimagines the relations between the Nazis and the upper classes of inter-war England, suggesting a widespread entanglement with fascism that has been sidelined from the national past. Ishiguro troubles the clear distinction between righteous Britons and their political others. Thus, Lord Darlington orders the expulsion of two Jewish servants from the house, a decision in which Stevens – only following orders – naturally acquiesces. Meanwhile, Lord Darlington and his associates make the case against democracy as such, as an outdated and inefficient system: 'Look at Germany and Italy,

Stevens. See what strong leadership can do if it's allowed to act. None of this universal suffrage nonsense there'.[18] The novel's presentation of these positions is the more probing in that they come not from a Nazi thug but from an English gentleman. Ishiguro's multi-layered fictional reconstruction bids us question whether a convenient forgetfulness has enabled Britain's status as constant bulwark against totalitarianism.

In its revision of geopolitical conflict, the politics behind such conflict, and the private psychology tied up in these public matters, *The Remains of the Day* shares a space of concerns with Pat Barker's *Regeneration Trilogy* (1991–95). Barker's volumes return to the moment of the First World War and consider it through shell shock or post-traumatic stress. In her sophisticated treatment of trauma and its effects on the self, language, and narrative, Barker is bringing later psychological frames to bear on the earlier conflict, though the era of military shell-shock was a significant stage in the development of ideas of trauma. Barker encourages readers to think about realities of the 1910s that were occluded by the narratives of the time. These, notably, include the bisexual experiences of the major character Billy Prior in the second volume *The Eye in the Door* (1993). With different methods, both Barker and Ishiguro can be found to write fictions that criticise earlier episodes in English history from a progressive late-twentieth-century standpoint. Both writers, in these novels, can be reckoned revisionists in their treatment of pivotal points in the nation's modern history.

An element of such revision can also be seen in Ian McEwan's *Atonement* (2001). Without questioning any overall consensus about the Second World War, McEwan's treatment of the 1940 Dunkirk evacuation reminds us of its surreal horror – an element less often mentioned amid recollections of this triumph for national solidarity. McEwan's novel concludes by insisting that what we have just read is a fiction within a fiction. The narrator, Bryony Tallis, has sought to reunite in art the lovers that her childish malice sundered in reality. The reader may hesitate between embracing the consolation of a happy ending, and the knowledge of its unreality – within, of course, a novel in which every character is ultimately unreal anyway. (The exception is Cyril Connolly, whom McEwan deftly ventriloquizes in a letter to Bryony about her post-Woolfian fiction.) Approaching twentieth-century history from a series of points of view that complicate and undermine each other in turn, McEwan's novel arrestingly asks about art's capacity to make reparation for historical wrongs.

In the twenty-first century, Sarah Waters has become one of Britain's most successful historical novelists: in public popularity (assisted by television adaptations), in critical acclaim, and in scholarly interest. Waters's first three novels, *Tipping the Velvet* (1998), *Affinity* (1999), and *Fingersmith*

(2002), all reimagine the Victorian period. They also recast the Victorian novel, whether in the picaresque series of escapades in Waters's debut, or the more complex narrative web of her subsequent novels. Waters's formal prose often appears to be a pastiche of a nineteenth-century narrator. But this period pastiche is the setting for Waters's most consistent radical gesture, telling the stories of lesbians in nineteenth-century England. An old rumour holds that Queen Victoria refused to credit the existence of lesbianism. In this sense Waters's fiction inserts a hitherto unknown experience into history, or imaginatively brings it to visibility. The gesture applies also to our conception of the Victorian novel. The story of Nancy ('Nan') King in *Tipping the Velvet*, journeying from humble Whitstable to the bustle of London's theatres, might resemble a tale from Dickens. But without Waters to inspire us, we would not think to imagine Dickens's story of a young woman discovering her forbidden sexuality. Actual sexual experience, too, is present in Waters's writing in a way impermissible to the canon of Victorian fiction. In fact, Nan's first experience of intimacy with a woman, the vaudevillian Kitty Butler, carries a sense of wonder that distinguishes it from the garrulously ingenuous narrative that has preceded it.[19]

Waters has since published historical novels set in the twentieth century. *The Night Watch* (2005) and *The Paying Guests* (2014) reprise her imaginative exploration of queer historiography, in the 1940s and 1920s, respectively. It becomes apparent that, while Waters has been undertaking an unusually consistent literary project concerning sexual identity, she is also drawn to the differing periods she writes about, with their peculiar idioms and their shifting nuances of social class. Waters stands out among British historical novelists for her bold exploration of sexuality, but she has also come to experiment with narrative: notably in *The Night Watch*, whose challenging structure works backwards from 1947 into the Second World War. Another reason for Waters's success is that her work plays not just with period but with genre: from the picaresque of her debut to crime fiction in *Fingersmith* (set at a time when crime fiction was only incipient) and the ghost story in *The Little Stranger* (2005). Waters's fiction arises from a dialogue not just with the historical past, but also with the history of fiction itself.

If William Golding has a literary successor, it might be Jim Crace. Like Golding, Crace has published an array of strikingly distinctive novels, veering between present and past settings according to his own intellectual concerns. As a historical novelist, Crace has notably focused on distant temporal settings that are challengingly alien to the reader – a gesture that recalls the even further reach into the primitive past made by Golding's *The Inheritors*.

In *Quarantine* (1997) he returns to the time of the New Testament, focusing on Jesus's period of fasting in the desert. A story that has been important to much of Western culture is here rewritten. The story of Crace's Jesus is surrounded by those of other characters, some of whom have their own reasons for fasting at the same time. Crace varies the story – his Jesus does not survive the fast – while inserting delicate echoes; thus, the Biblical characters Mary and Martha are refigured here, in a different context, as Miri and Marta. In returning to the founding era of a world religion, Crace echoes the move controversially made in parts of Rushdie's *The Satanic Verses* (1988), though in a more muted and naturalistic key and with a greater sense of the physical hardship of the distant past.

In his earlier novel, *The Gift of Stones* (1988), Crace reconstructs the twilight of the Stone Age. An unnamed village on the coast is kept economically viable by the skill of its stonemasons. Near the novel's end, the killing of a woman, Doe, with a bronze arrowhead is taken as significant less for Doe's death, more for the arrival of a new crafted material that will render the people with the 'gift of stones' historically obsolete. In dramatising this epochal shift of productive forces, Crace can be said to fulfil the Lukácsian commitment evoked earlier: he depicts 'a tragic contest between declining and ascending forms of social life, in a vision of the past that honours the losers but upholds the historical necessity of the winners'.[20] Here, too, as in that Lukácsian account, history is revealed via the experiences of marginal figures. The whole novel, we come to learn, is narrated by a girl whose surrogate father is the book's prime protagonist. This unnamed father has lost an arm in youth: unable to contribute to the working of stone, he has thus become literally marginalised by the village, wandering away in search of new experiences. But he realises that he possesses a talent for oral narrative, and compensates for his physical unproductivity with this gift of stories.

The girl's narrative thus frequently opens directly on to that of the protagonist, who in turn embellishes and teases his audience with multiple narrative possibilities. The novel's embedded acts of storytelling move between fantasy and the closest thing we have, within this fiction, to fact. The villagers like the protagonist's lies, but are sometimes repelled when he tells the truth. Near the novel's end, truth grows more difficult to determine. We are told several versions in turn of how Doe's killing took place. As one version branches off from another, the uncertainty of which narrative branch to rely on might even recall Fowles's extravagant proliferation of endings in *The French Lieutenant's Woman*. Crace's novel has developed a parallel between storytelling and stonecraft. Accordingly, the narrator talks of an existing story of the murder as 'a rough and ready core': 'The craftsman in me wants to strike it softly here and there, to give it shape and symmetry, to hone and burnish it'.[21] These reflections on storytelling make the novel close to the metafictional mode we surveyed earlier. One thing that distinguishes Crace from those writers is his fascination with the distant past and its physical austerity. *The Gift of Stones*, in which a goose egg or a red pebble represent precious luxuries, confronts us with an ancient world whose repetitive hardship is part of its alterity to the contemporary reader. Indeed, language, too, is rationed in Crace's world, as is indicated by the sparseness of proper names for his characters. Crace's interest in history has continued to yield such scenes. *Harvest* (2013) depicts another remote English village: though the novel is set centuries later than *The Gift of Stones*, the villagers are hardly more cosmopolitan or comfortable than their Stone Age precursors. While staging historical change in Lukácsian fashion, Crace is distinct in his insistence on the harsh strangeness and poverty of the past.

The most celebrated writer of historical fiction in Britain this century is Hilary Mantel. Mantel had crafted fiction from historical research before, with ambitious fact-based novels set in the eighteenth century. But it is her more recent trilogy of Tudor times that has made her pre-eminent in the field.[22] The court of Henry VIII is among the most frequently treated settings in historical fiction. Shortly before Mantel, for instance, Philippa Gregory had published her popular *Tudor Court* sextet of novels, each book focusing on royal or noble women of the era. Mantel's trilogy centres on Thomas Cromwell, who climbs from modest origins to be the right-hand man first of Cardinal Wolsey then of Henry VIII himself. Mantel typically writes from Cromwell's point of view, always in the present tense but not in the first person: rather the pronoun 'he' becomes peculiarly attached to him, sometimes extended to 'he, Cromwell' for an awkward clarity's sake.

One of Mantel's themes is the landscape of social class in which Cromwell is able to rise from Putney blacksmith's son to Lord Chancellor and Master Secretary. Cromwell's experiences as a soldier and merchant in the Low Countries and Italy give him a range of cosmopolitan expertise that, coupled with his dogged cunning, allows him to outflank his more ponderous and parochial rivals in the English aristocracy. In focusing unabashedly on high politics and famous names, Mantel actually strays from Lukács' prescriptions. But her work does limn the origins of a great 'transformation of popular life', in Anderson's phrase: the shift from Catholicism to the Protestant Church of England. This development notoriously sprang from the whims and passions of Henry VIII. Mantel indeed treats at painstaking length the legal trials and political dealings through which Henry attempts to divorce his first wife. But she also shows England's religious life already changing of its own accord, under new, heretical influences to which Cromwell himself is discreetly sympathetic. The downfall of Sir Thomas More, with which *Wolf Hall* (2009) concludes, is emblematic of the shift.

Perhaps Mantel's most distinctive stroke is simply to centre on the inner life of the pragmatic Cromwell, rather than the more glamorous royal persons. In a sense, he stands as a 'modern' beside his 'feudal' contemporaries, and is thus ahead of every other player in the game. Mantel gives vivid novelistic life to the case first influentially made by Geoffrey Elton, that Cromwell's continental nous had made him the true architect of the modern bureaucratic British state.[23] Unlike Barker or Waters, Mantel cannot be primarily considered a revisionist. She has revitalized a quite traditional form (and a very traditional subject) of historical fiction through the depth of her historical knowledge, her patient structuring of a multi-volume narrative – and, not least, her way with words. Mantel's narrative is massive, yet composed of thousands of little touches, economically rendering light, shade, place and weather as Cromwell schemes and bargains his way through them.

If Mantel has a rival in this regard it is David Mitchell, whose fifth novel *The Thousand Autumns of Jacob de Zoet* (2010) portrays eighteenth-century Japan through a proliferation of prose observations virtually transferrable to haiku form. Near the novel's end, indeed, Mitchell unleashes a page-long prose poem: 'Gulls fly through clouds of steam from laundries' vats; over kites unthreading corpses of cats; over scholars glimpsing truth in fragile patterns; over bath-house adulterers; heartbroken slatterns; fishwives dismembering lobsters and crabs; their husbands gutting mackerel on slabs; woodcutters' sons sharpening axes; candle-makers, rolling waxes'.[24] For a moment, this crescendo allows Mitchell to luxuriate in poetic play. The effect is startling, and uncharacteristic of almost all the other fiction we have considered here. (Winterson, with her neo-modernist attraction to poetic prose, might be an exception.) But in a sense, it is also in keeping with the rest of Mitchell's novel, in which historical verisimilitude has coexisted with a delicate attention to stylistic grace. We might say that Mitchell eschews the metafictional historical novel for its poetic counterpart. Though highly conscious of their own narrative art, neither he nor Mantel are overwhelmingly concerned to discuss the nature of history in their fiction, as so many writers scanned here have been. The 1980s and 1990s were the high tide of historiographic metafiction. It is hazardous to generalize about so capacious a field. But it might be that the energies of the historical novel have lately moved from the explicit to the implicit; that the formal pendulum has swung from loud authorial intervention to more seamless fictional diegeses. In these novels' worlds, social changes (like those surrounding the rise of Protestantism in Mantel) and cultural conflicts (like the encounter between Japan and Europe in Mitchell) continue to be exemplified and played out.

Historical fiction can make us think and learn about specific eras of the past – even those that have (like Mantel's Tudors and Waters's Victorians) already been extensively imagined elsewhere. It can also bring us to think about the ways in which we know the past, especially the ways that narrative shapes our conception of history. Lastly, it might also remind us that even fictions of the present take place not in a neutral no-time but in a time that is always becoming historical. This is one response to Jameson's injunction to 'grasp the present as history'.[25] 'Historical fiction', as a specific genre, necessarily has defining limits. But it can also encourage us to reflect on how all fictions are historical, sooner or later.

NOTES

1 Perry Anderson, 'From Progress to Catastrophe', *London Review of Books* 33.15 (28 July 2011), p. 24. Hereafter cited parenthetically.
2 Georg Lukács, *The Historical Novel*, trans. Hannah and Stanley Mitchell (Harmondsworth: Penguin, 1969), p. 158.
3 Fredric Jameson, 'Cognitive Mapping', in *The Jameson Reader*, eds. Michael Hardt and Kathi Weeks (Oxford: Blackwell, 2000), pp. 277–87.
4 John Fowles, *The French Lieutenant's Woman* (London: Panther, 1972), p. 95. Hereafter cited parenthetically.
5 John Fowles, 'Notes on an Unfinished Novel', in *The Novel Today*, ed. Malcolm Bradbury (Glasgow: Fontana, 1990), p. 147.
6 See Linda Hutcheon, *A Poetics of Postmodernism: History, Theory, Fiction* (London: Routledge, 1988), especially chapter 11.
7 William Golding, *Rites of Passage* (London: Faber, 1980), pp. 277–8. Hereafter cited parenthetically.
8 See http://historicalnovelsociety.org/guides/defining-the-genre/.
9 Salman Rushdie, *Midnight's Children* (London: Jonathan Cape, 1981), p. 9. Hereafter cited parenthetically.
10 Angela Carter, *Nights at the Circus* (London: Vintage, 2006), p. 111. Hereafter cited parenthetically.
11 Jeanette Winterson *Oranges Are Not the Only Fruit* (London: Vintage, 1991), p. 91.
12 Jeanette Winterson, *The Passion* (London: Bloomsbury, 1987). Hereafter cited parenthetically.
13 See Suzanne Keen, *Romances of the Archive in Contemporary British Fiction* (Toronto: University of Toronto Press, 2002).
14 Julian Barnes, *Flaubert's Parrot* (London: Jonathan Cape, 1984), p. 14. Hereafter cited parenthetically.
15 Julian Barnes, *A History of the World in 10½ Chapters* (London: Jonathan Cape, 1989), p. 242. Hereafter cited parenthetically.
16 Graham Swift, *Waterland* (London: William Heinemann, 1983), pp. 92, 94, 122, 143. Hereafter cited parenthetically.

17 See Patrick Wright, *On Living in an Old Country* (London: Verso, 1985); and Andrew Higson, *English Heritage, English Cinema* (Oxford: Oxford University Press, 2003).

18 Kazuo Ishiguro, *The Remains of the Day* (London: Faber, 1989), pp. 147, 198–9.

19 Sarah Waters, *Tipping the Velvet* (London: Virago, 1998), pp. 102–6.

20 Anderson, 'From Progress to Catastrophe', p. 24.

21 Jim Crace, *The Gift of Stones* (London: Secker and Warburg, 1988), p. 153.

22 See Hilary Mantel, *Wolf Hall* (London: Fourth Estate, 2009), and *Bring Up the Bodies* (London: Fourth Estate, 2012). The third novel, *The Mirror and the Light*, was unpublished at the time of writing and scheduled for 2015.

23 See Geoffrey Elton, *The Tudor Revolution in Government* (Cambridge: Cambridge University Press, 1953). Robert Eaglestone (Royal Holloway, University of London) was the first to point this out to me.

24 David Mitchell, *The Thousand Autumns of Jacob de Zoet* (London: Sceptre, 2010), p. 441.

25 Fredric Jameson, *The Ideologies of Theory: Essays 1981–1986. Volume 2: The Syntax of History* (Minneapolis: University of Minnesota Press, 1988), p. 113.

II

MICHAEL LEMAHIEU

The Novel of Ideas

Although it represents an ambitious and accomplished genre of post-1945 British fiction, the novel of ideas remains stubbornly difficult to define and consistently subject to denigration. The *Dictionary of Literary Terms and Literary Theory* expresses this slippery sense of disapproval: 'A vague category of fiction in which conversation, intellectual discussion and debate predominate, and in which plot, narrative, emotional conflict and psychological depth in characterization are deliberately limited'.[1] The very features that have come to identify the novel – plot, narrative, conflict, depth, character – are those that, this definition would have it, are 'deliberately limited' in the novel of ideas. When it succeeds, therefore, the novel of ideas succeeds inasmuch as it is not quite a novel; in this sense, 'novel of ideas' appears to be a contradiction in terms.[2]

Yet even as novels of ideas are not quite novels, all novels are in some sense novels of ideas. To withhold the designation, to exclude certain works from the category, particularly those considered great ones, would be to imply they are somehow intellectually deficient. The proposition that, because they are not considered novelists of ideas, one will not find ideas in the work of Austen or Dickens, Angela Carter or Salman Rushdie, immediately rings false. In this sense, Mary McCarthy views the term not as contradictory but tautologous: 'So intrinsic to the novelistic medium were ideas and other forms of commentary, all tending to "set" the narration in a general scheme, that it would have been impossible in former days to speak of "the novel of ideas." It would have seemed to be a tautology'.[3] The critical and historical context out of which the term emerges helps to explain its definitional tension and disapproving connotations. When McCarthy speaks of 'former days,' she refers to the nineteenth century of Balzac, Dostoevsky, Melville, and George Eliot. Although these novelists are now often implicitly associated with the novel of ideas, McCarthy rightly notes that such a use of the term is anachronistic. But it is also correct.[4] Novels and ideas were once cut from the same cloth.

So how do they come to be opposed? The concept of the novel of ideas emerges out of and against a modernist aesthetic ideology, *l'art pour l'art*, which in its most radical form excludes the possibility of a novel of ideas: an autonomous art insulated from outside influences or external sources of value is its own 'idea,' as it were; art, and the novel as art form, need not look elsewhere, whether to science, politics, religion, or philosophy. While such period designations and ideological descriptions are always a bit rough and ready – their influence and usefulness outstripping their precision and accuracy – neither are they unfounded. In the Anglo-American tradition, the figure that looms largest in the elevation of the art novel and the denigration of the ideas novel is Henry James, with his 'mind so fine that no idea could violate it'.[5] Whether or not T. S. Eliot meant this description of the master's mind as a compliment or a criticism – surely both – the assumptions that underwrite it endure, a lasting legacy of modernism's aesthetic ideology, as McCarthy notes of Eliot's remark:

> Implicit in it is the snubbing notion, radical at the time but by now canon doctrine, of the novel as a fine art and of the novelist as an intelligence superior to mere intellect. In this patronizing view, the intellect's crude apparatus was capable only of formulating concepts, which then underwent the process of diffusion, so that by dint of repetition they fell within anybody's reach. The final, cruel fate of an idea was to turn into an *ideé reçue*. The power of the novelist insofar as he was a supreme intelligence was to free himself from the work-load of commentary and simply, awesomely, to show: his creation was beyond paraphrase or reduction. (pp. 3–4)

James's insistence that novelists show and not tell, echoed in Conrad's attempt to make his readers 'see,' and promulgated in the twentieth century, as Mark McGurl demonstrates, in the rise of university creative writing programs, runs directly counter to the novel of ideas.[6] Or again, in McCarthy's phrase: 'If you are going to voice explicit ideas in a novel, evidently this requires a spokesman' (p. 29).

A common criticism that results from this requirement, as seen in the primer definition cited above, holds that because its primary concern emanates from the conceptual realm, the novel of ideas necessarily subordinates plot and character: action is sacrificed to discussion between persons who function as personifications of concepts or mouthpieces for ideas. When Arnold Baffin criticises Bradley Pearson in Iris Murdoch's *The Black Prince* (1973) for sounding 'as if you were quoting something all the time', the barb reads as if the author were giving voice to the imagined frustrations of her readers.[7] The demands of realism, J. M. Coetzee's narrator suggests in *Elizabeth Costello* (2003), require ideas to be embodied in situations:

Realism has never been comfortable with ideas. It could not be otherwise: realism is premised on the idea that ideas have no autonomous existence, can exist only in things. So when it needs to debate ideas, as here, realism
is driven to invent situations – walks in the countryside, conversations – in
which characters give voice to contending ideas and thereby in a certain sense
embody them.[8]

No matter how movingly, brilliantly, or convincingly achieved – those alpine
exchanges between Naphta and Settembrini in Mann's *The Magic Mountain*
(1924), for example – such devices always risk appearing crude, forced, con-
trived. They tell more than they show. Indeed, James's critical pronouncements reflect his influential conception of the novel, famously explicated in
'The Art of Fiction':

Only a short time ago it might have been supposed that the English novel was
not what the French call *discutable*. It had no air of having a theory, a conviction, a consciousness of itself behind it – of being the expression of an artistic
faith, the result of choice and comparison. I do not say it was necessarily the
worse for that: it would take much more courage than I possess to intimate
that the form of the novel as Dickens and Thackeray (for instance) saw it had
any taint of incompleteness.[9]

Theories, convictions, and self-consciousness: James suggests these are not
necessary components of a novel – their absence in no way creates a sense
of incompleteness. While James goes on later in the essay to discuss the
'idea' which gives rise to a novel, he means this term in the sense of 'subject
matter' and insists it is beyond reproach: 'We must grant the artist his subject, his idea, his *donnée*: our criticism is applied only to what he makes of
it' (p. 14). And, extending this same logic, James insists that 'questions of
art are questions (in the widest sense) of execution; questions of morality
are quite another affair' (p. 20). James's aesthetic pronouncements exerted
a significant influence in twentieth-century fiction. By 1940, the American
critic Philip Rahv, for example, would lament what he found to be a 'unique
indifference ... to ideas generally, to theories of value' in American fiction.[10]
The concept of the novel of ideas emerges as a negative counterpart to the
modernist, Jamesian aesthetic: the novel of ideas defined against the novel as
art. In *Point Counter Point* (1928), Aldous Huxley opines that the 'real, the
congenital novelists' – Dickens, Thackeray, and James presumably qualify –
do not write novels of ideas. Huxley, a seminal influence on the development
of the novel of ideas after 1945, defines himself against this tradition: 'I
never pretended to be a congenital novelist'.[11]

It follows, then, that the novel of ideas emerges on its own terms after
the end of modernism. And although we are well past the time when

postmodernism was understood to be a straightforward rejection of modernism – the latter was always too conflicted for any rejection to be straightforward – the proliferation of the novel of ideas since 1945 can be seen from such a perspective: freed from the shackles of modernist aesthetic ideology, saddled with the weight of a second world war, and faced with rapidly changing scientific discoveries and technological developments, the form begins to flourish. 'The "novel of ideas"', Timothy Bewes suggests, 'is the product of a highly reflective age', and thereby 'a characteristic form of postmodernity'.[12]

Even more than most genre terms, the novel of ideas tends to be a hybrid designation. A deliberate novel of ideas sometimes reads as a dressed-up political polemic, position paper, or expository essay: what McCarthy calls 'a missionary novel' or 'tract' (p. 25). Something of this more limited meaning is captured by the French *roman à thèse*, a form that traffics in the pedantic tone of didacticism.[13] Even novels of ideas that succeed are often praised in partial terms. In a review of Dave Eggers's novel *The Circle* (2013), Margaret Atwood writes: 'The outpouring of ideas is central to *The Circle*, as it is in part a novel of ideas. What sort of ideas? Ideas about the social construction and deconstruction of privacy, and about the increasing corporate ownership of privacy, and about the effects such ownership may have on the nature of Western democracy'. Despite the scale and scope of the ideas Atwood enumerates, she lauds Eggers's novel of ideas by qualifying the description of it as such: a good novel is never more than a novel of ideas 'in part'.[14]

Their protean quality means that novels of ideas take many different forms. One prominent tradition in postwar British literature that displays affinities with the novel of ideas, and one in which the presence of Huxley looms large, is dystopian fiction. These 'new maps of hell', as Kingsley Amis famously referred to them, take as governing conceits ideas such as human nature, social control, the common good, and the rights of women.[15] George Orwell's *Nineteen Eighty-Four* (1949), William Golding's *Lord of the Flies* (1954), and Anthony Burgess's *A Clockwork Orange* (1962) are landmark works in this tradition, one represented in the succeeding generation by works such as Atwood's *The Handmaid's Tale* (1985) and Kazuo Ishiguro's *Never Let Me Go* (2005). Like works of dystopian, speculative, or science fiction, fantasy literature also often foregrounds ideas as organizing tropes. Philip Pullman's *His Dark Materials* trilogy – *The Golden Compass* (1995), *The Subtle Knife* (1997), and *The Amber Spyglass* (2000) – while marketed as young adult fiction, nevertheless dramatizes, on both a narrative and a structural level, concepts such as dark matter, possible worlds, and secular humanism.

In its affinities with science fiction, the novel of ideas reflects larger cultural trends and political preoccupations, but it also opposes other aspects of the zeitgeist. Or, at least novelists of ideas consider themselves in opposition to mass culture, as Huxley indicates in *Point Counter Point*:

> Novel of ideas. The character of each personage must be implied, as far as possible, in the ideas of which he is the mouthpiece. In so far as theories are rationalizations of sentiments, instincts, dispositions of the soul, this is feasible. The chief defect of the novel of ideas is that you must write about people who have ideas to express – which excludes all but about .01 per cent. of the human race. (p. 294)

The lack of ideas in contemporary culture, Huxley suggests, is the 'great defect of the novel of ideas' and what necessarily renders it 'a made-up affair': 'Necessarily; for people who can reel off neatly formulated notions aren't quite real; they're slightly monstrous' (p. 295). Writing over four decades later in the 1971 Preface to *The Golden Notebook*, Doris Lessing lodges a similar complaint: 'But there is no doubt that to attempt a novel of ideas is to give oneself a handicap: the parochialism of our culture is intense'.[16]

Notwithstanding the occupational hazard represented by cultural philistinism, philosophical fiction also flourishes in the contemporary period. Whether it is the lives of animals or the minds of others, the meaning of life or the right to die, the origins of the species or the death of the universe, these novels of ideas are animated by an organizing concept or question. Before turning to fiction, Iris Murdoch, about whom more below, was a lecturer of philosophy at Oxford. Over the course of a career spanning four decades, she wrote more than two dozen novels and half a dozen works of philosophy. She was an acquaintance of Sartre, the subject of her first published work, and a student of Wittgenstein, a not infrequent presence in her works ('Ought I to read Wittgenstein?' (p. 233), Julian asks Bradley in *The Black Prince*). More recently, Jennie Erdal's *The Missing Shade of Blue* (2012) takes its title and premise from Hume's famous thought experiment, a challenge to his robust empiricism, in which he asks if a person who has seen every shade of blue but one might not imagine that missing shade – 'raise up the idea' of it, as Hume puts it – without any direct sensory experience of it. Two of the most accomplished recent works whose very titles announce their conceptual kinship to the novel of ideas are Zadie Smith's *On Beauty* (2005) and Hari Kunzru's *Gods Without Men* (2011).

Works written in the wake of, and clearly indebted to, the theories and discoveries of quantum physics comprise another identifiable strand in the postwar novel of ideas, what Dennis Bohnenkamp describes as 'physics fiction'.[17] Anna McGrail's *Mrs. Einstein* (1998) and H. R. McGregor's *Schrodinger's Baby* (1999) allude to two of the century's more famous scientists in their titles and draw on aspects of relativity theory and quantum mechanics in their narratives. In Michael Frayn's play *Copenhagen* (1998) – an example of the drama of ideas – the actors portraying Niels Bohr and Werner Heisenberg circle on stage in patterns that mimic the movement of electrons around the nucleus of an atom. Nicholas Mosley employs a similar device in *Hopeful Monsters* (1990), the culmination of his ambitious Catastrophe Practice series. The movements of and communication between the two main characters in the novel, Max Ackerman and Eleanor Anders, enact Schrodinger's concept of quantum entanglement or action-at-a-distance.[18] Mosley – son of Sir Oswald Mosley, leader of the Blackshirts – charts the lives of the two characters, who alternately narrate the novel, from 1920s Weimar Germany through the Spanish Civil War and World War II: Marxism, fascism, and the splitting of the atom told from a Cold War perspective. Establishing its philosophical bona fides with references to Nietzsche, Heidegger, and Wittgenstein, the novel develops a plot and structure that draws on the vocabularies of quantum mechanics and Lamarckian biology. The inheritance of acquired traits is long discredited as a biological phenomenon, but Mosley finds in the idea a way to reflect on cultural transmission and inheritance: the novel, Neil Levi suggests, is less a *Bildungsroman* than 'the story of how what Max and Eleanor have learned can be transmitted to later generations'.[19] Mosley's is one of the most accomplished novels of ideas published in the postwar period and deserving of increased scholarly attention.

III

At one point in the *Hopeful Monsters*, Eleanor asks about 'the connection between philosophy and physics'.[20] The question is indicative of a larger shift in the post-1945 novel of ideas, a move from Heidegger to Heisenberg, so to speak, that is exemplified in the difference between Iris Murdoch's philosophical novels of ideas to Ian McEwan's scientific ones. Both Murdoch and McEwan, however, deal in broad strokes with very old questions and debates: faith versus reason, religion versus science, logic versus emotion. And both writers make a case, as much by showing as by telling, for the ongoing importance of literature in the realm of ideas.

Although Murdoch professed 'absolute horror' at the thought of import-ing 'philosophical ideas' into literature, her novels of ideas – works such as *Under the Net* (1954), *The Bell* (1958), *The Unicorn* (1963), and *The Black Prince* – more than those of any other postwar British writer, engage the shared concerns of literature and philosophy.[21] A. S. Byatt states that 'there is a sense in which all Iris Murdoch's novels contain Platonic dia-logues'; Martha Nussbaum remarks that Murdoch's 'novels have a rich vein of philosophy running through them; many focus on philosophical issues that are also central to her theoretical work'.[22] And, indeed, other differ-ences notwithstanding, Murdoch considers both literature and philosophy 'truth-revealing activities'.[23]

Although influenced by both Sartre and Wittgenstein, Murdoch explicitly employs a moral vocabulary that puts her work at odds with postmodern literature and with the predominant philosophies of her time, existentialism and logical positivism: 'it is interesting that by dissimilar paths the existen-tialists and the logical positivists have reached positions which are in some ways strikingly alike'.[24] Each of these philosophies, Murdoch suggests, puts forward an impoverished conception of morality: the existentialists through an excess of subjectivism and the positivists through an excess of objectiv-ism. Hence, in *The Black Prince*, Bradley Pearson articulates the problem in a way that reflects Murdoch's views:

> There is thus an eternal discrepancy between the self-knowledge which we gain by observing ourselves objectively and the self-awareness which we have of ourselves subjectively: a discrepancy which probably makes it impossible for us ever to arrive at the truth. Our self-knowledge is too abstract, our self-awareness is too intimate and swoony and dazed. Perhaps some kind of integrity of the imagination, a sort of moral genius, could verify the scene, pro-ducing minute sensibility and control of the movement as a function of some much larger consciousness. Can there be a *natural*, as it were Shakespearean felicity in the moral life? (pp. 181–2)

Noteworthy in this passage, and typical of Murdoch's work, is the use of value-laden terms that take on simultaneous moral and aesthetic aspects: 'integrity', 'sensibility', and 'felicity'. Typical, too, is the suggestion that the imagination provides one possible path to overcoming the discrepancy between abstract self-knowledge and swoony self-regard. Murdoch empha-sizes how language can both enable and fail the literary artist and the moral agent: 'There are situations which are obscure and people who are incom-prehensible, and the moral agent, as well as the artist, may find himself unable to describe something which in some sense he apprehends. Language has limitations and there are moments when, if it is to serve us, it has to be used creatively, and that effort may fail'.[25] Situations wherein apprehension exceeds description call for literature's creative uses of language to take over from philosophy's propositional form. But, Murdoch cautions, that effort is always subject to failure.

In Murdoch's first novel, *Under the Net*, these concerns about language, morality, and subjectivity converge on the problem of other minds. In the opening paragraphs, Jake Donoghue introduces his companion Finn as someone who has 'very little inner life' when compared with Jake's own 'complex and highly differentiated one'.[26] Finn's unannounced departure at the end of the novel forces Jake to realize that he has 'conceived things' as he has pleased and 'not as they were' (p. 247). His other pivotal revelation occurs when Anna Quentin, longstanding object of his affection, reveals that she has for many years loved Hugo Belfounder, Jake's sometime friend:

> I had no longer any picture of Anna. She faded like a sorcerer's apparition; and yet somehow her presence remained to me, more substantial than ever before. It seemed as if, for the first time, Anna really existed now as a separate being and not as part of myself. To experience this was extremely painful. Yet as I tried to keep my eyes fixed upon where she was I felt towards her a sense of initiative which was perhaps after all one of the guises of love. Anna was something that had to be learned afresh. When does one ever know a human being? Perhaps only after one has realized the impossibility of knowledge and renounced the desire for it and finally ceased to feel the need of it. But then what one achieves is no longer knowledge, it is simply a kind of co-existence; and this too is one of the guises of love. (p. 238)

Murdoch's use of 'initiative' in this passage exemplifies her approach to articulating a moral vision that extends beyond particular judgments. In her essay 'The Darkness of Practical Reason', she differentiates between 'disciplined scientific or scholarly beliefs' and those in which 'the active imagination and will play a part,' as with one's dispositions towards others: 'The formulation of beliefs about other people often proceeds and must proceed imaginatively and under a direct pressure of will. We have to attend to people, we may have to have faith in them, and here justice and realism may demand the inhibition of certain pictures, the promotion of others'.[27] Anna's revelation to Jake demands that he revise his 'picture' of her – and in fact to make do without any picture whatsoever – which in turn disposes him less toward knowledge and more toward acknowledgment, in Stanley Cavell's sense of that term.[28] In this way, the virtue of not knowing allows other virtues to emerge: through a sense of initiative as learning rather than a claim to knowledge as mastery, Jake begins to recognize the various 'guises of love'. Murdoch's naturalised theory of ethics sees concepts such as 'love' or 'faith' or 'goodness' as perceptible features of the world of human interactions: 'Human good is something which lies in the foreground of life and not in its background'.[29] These features of the world find expression in her novels of ideas, which enact her aesthetic philosophy: 'Art and morals are … one'. Unlike the logical positivists, however, Murdoch's linking of ethical and aesthetic values in not eliminative but substantive: 'Their essence is the same. The essence of both is love. Love is the perception of individuals. Love is the extremely difficult realisation that something other than oneself is real. Love, and so art and morals, is the discovery of reality'.[30]

The foremost practitioner today of the British novel of ideas, Ian McEwan defies received wisdom with works that combine intellectual aspirations with narrative suspense. Whether treating psychopathology, neuroscience, global warming, or what his latest novel, *The Children Act* (2014), describes as 'the turbulent realm of religious and philosophical ideas,' his novels resemble less Platonic dialogues than genre fiction[31]:

> Though [McEwan] is animated by ideas, he would never plop two characters on a sofa and have them expound rival philosophies. The opening to *Enduring Love* offers a crisp illustration of game theory: when a balloon becomes untethered, each of the five men holding a rope is forced to make a decision without knowing what the others will do. But most readers enjoy it as a thrilling set piece.[32]

This coupling of concept and cliffhanger displays all the genre hybridity endemic to the novel of ideas. Judith Seaboyer classifies nearly all of McEwan's works as novels of ideas, but additional genre terms supplement the description of each: *The Comfort of Strangers* is 'darkly gothic'; *The Child in Time* is 'speculative'; and *The Innocent* (1989) a 'gothic-realist' 'espionage thriller'. On top of this proliferation, she describes McEwan's novels of ideas as 'contemporary realism', which is often opposed to the novel of ideas.[33]

McEwan is an accomplished stylist whose prose displays traits particularly well suited for his signature combination of ideas and suspense. Enlivening adjectives couple with abstract nouns in order to lend life to ideational content. The first two chapters of *Enduring Love* (1997) feature numerous examples: 'comforting geometry' (p. 3), 'moving bodies' (p. 3), 'human variety' (p. 5), 'mammalian conflict' (p. 15), 'ruthless gravity' (p. 17). This vivifying effect on the abstract works in both directions; adjectives drawn from physics, mathematics, and biochemistry modify nouns that burn or exalt, throb or traffic: 'nuclear furnace' (p. 3), 'mathematical grace' (p. 3), 'neuronal pulse' (p. 14), 'biochemical exchanges' (p. 25).[34] As it does for

Michel Houellebecq in *Les Particules Élémentaires* (1998), the word 'element' provides McEwan with raw material: 'elemental gas' (p. 3) and 'necessary element' (p. 25). This tactic can fall flat when adjective and noun balance symmetrically, neither term tipping its partner: 'logarithmic complexity' (p. 14). And McEwan at times risks a formulaic quality by recycling ideas across multiple works: *Enduring Love* refers to 'that preverbal language of instant thought linguists call mentalese' (p. 180), and *Saturday* (2005) to 'the pre-verbal language that linguists call mentalese'.[35] But such moments are rare in McEwan's prose, which reveals and revels in the texture – the drama – in the unfolding of ideas.

McEwan often draws his ideas, particularly in his more recent works, from science; like his American counterpart Richard Powers, he represents and ultimately questions what C. P. Snow first called in 1956 the 'two cultures' of science and literature. The proliferation of the contemporary novel of ideas after 1945 reflects a cultural anxiety that science has become the sole source of ideas, that literature, once the site of invention, is now capable only of reporting discoveries from other realms. The protagonist of *Enduring Love*, Joe Rose, is a successful science journalist who stands in as a figure for this authorial anxiety. In 'a piece on narrative in science', Rose writes about 'the nineteenth-century culture of the amateur that nourished the anecdotal scientist' (p. 51), a phenomenon that spurred and was spurred by the great novels of the time: 'The dominant artistic form was the novel, great sprawling narratives that not only charted private fates but made whole societies in mirror image and addressed the public issues of the day' (pp. 51–2). With the advent of modernity, however, science and literature each moved into their own distinct spheres:

> Science became more difficult, and it became professionalized. It moved into the universities; parsonical narratives gave way to hard-edged theories that could survive intact without experimental support and that had their own formal aesthetic. At the same time, in literature and other arts, a newfangled modernism celebrated formal, structural qualities, inner coherence, and self-reference. A priesthood guarded the temples of this difficult art against the trespasses of the common man. (p. 52)

McEwan places his contemporary novel of ideas in opposition to the modernist tradition of art for art's sake and indirectly claims affiliation with the nineteenth-century novel.

McEwan's celebrations of science, which are often set in the well-appointed homes of his successful professionals (journalists, writers, surgeons, scientists, and judges), find their counterpart in his criticisms of religion. *Enduring Love*, like McEwan's entire oeuvre, is unsympathetic in its portrayal of religious belief. McEwan has been outspoken in his views: his late friend Christopher Hitchens once remarked that he approaches his atheism with 'the zeal of a convert'; two critics label him 'the New Atheist novelist *par excellence*,' a writer who displays 'his readiness to proselytize on behalf of this new, secular belief system'.[36] Here McEwan differs from Murdoch, whose writings are, if not religious per se, committed to a quasi-mystical idea of goodness that is consonant with religious thinking and belief. McEwan's portrayal of religious belief, however, does parallel Murdoch's criticisms of an excessive self-regard. The fictional case study appended to *Enduring Love* posits 'a close relationship ... between some pathological aspects of love and the tenets of the church for religious believers' (p. 257). A similar thought occurs to Henry Perowne in *Saturday*:

> The primitive thinking of the supernaturally inclined amounts to what his psychiatric colleagues call a problem, or an idea, of reference. An excess of the subjective, the ordering of the world in line with your needs, an inability to contemplate your own unimportance. In Henry's view such reasoning belongs on a spectrum at whose far end, rearing like an abandoned temple, lies psychosis. (p. 17)

McEwan's treatment of religion leads Bewes to consider *Enduring Love* philosophically dishonest – an aesthetic flaw more than a moral one in this context – inasmuch as what initially appears to be a good faith exploration of the competing claims between science, religion, and literature 'concludes with an overwhelming endorsement of Joe's scientific rationalism against both Jed's religious fanaticism and Clarissa's sympathetic literary sensitivity'.[37] But while McEwan is unsparing in his criticisms of religion, he does not, as did the logical positivists, conflate religious beliefs and aesthetic values.

In McEwan's staging of the two cultures' debate as faith versus reason, literature plays an ambiguous role as the *tertium quid* – now resembling revealed religion, now secular humanism. *Enduring Love* and *Saturday* each represent the nineteenth century as a premodern, antediluvian exemplar of harmony between literature and science: the former's touchstone is Keats's 'beauty is truth, truth beauty'; the latter's, Darwin's 'there is grandeur in this view of life'. That McEwan turns alternately to a Romantic poet and an evolutionary biologist to play this role is itself a testament to his view of a time preceding the two cultures divide. The two novels also share a number of structural and narrative parallels. Both begin with the observation of an accident involving aircraft (one real, one perceived); both end with the protagonist's wife held captive at knifepoint; and both move from one of these set pieces to the other by means of meditations on science, perception, evolution, and neurochemistry. In addition, both propagate a gendered logic in which a female character is associated with poetry (one a poetry scholar, the other a poet) in order to provide thematic counterpoint, questioning the validity of the respective masculine protagonist's scientific worldview by pointing to its incompleteness. Throughout *Enduring Love*, Clarissa Mellon, the Keats scholar, indicates that Joe may be as delusional as Jed, but for different reasons. Joe's exclusive reliance on logic – his faith in reason, as it were – results in his blindness to ethical, emotional, and subjective factors. He is not unlike Murdoch's Jake Donoghue inasmuch as he singularly desires to prove his point but lacks initiative vis-à-vis other people. Joe's rationalism is proven correct but not right: his victory over Parry concludes not with his triumphant return to the domestic happiness with which the novel begins but instead with the dissolution of his relationship with Clarissa. When the case study in the appendix indicates in passing that 'R[ose] and M[ellon] were reconciled and later successfully adopted a child' (p. 259), the implication is that Joe has learned the limitations of his own philosophy, but the larger point remains clear: scientific rationality can explain the external world much more effectively than it can account for the people who inhabit it. McEwan leaves the reader with something of the sense that Wittgenstein expresses at the conclusion of the *Tractatus*: 'We feel that even when all *possible* scientific questions have been answered, the problems of life remain completely untouched'.[38] Unlike in Wittgenstein and Murdoch, McEwan's work does not leave open the possibility of a mystical supplement to this feeling of incompleteness, but neither does he follow the logical positivists in their ideal of a complete description of a unified science. In McEwan's novels, the ideas of science and the problems of life inform and inflect each other.

Postwar British writers have thus put the persistently elusive genre of the novel of ideas to incredibly productive use. These works represent both a break from and, in other respects, an extension of the Jamesian aesthetic, which, as McCarthy defines it, is shorn of ideas – no theories, no concepts – to the point that, absent the discourses of politics, religion, or philosophy, she concludes, 'the Jamesian people are reduced to a single theme: each other' (p. 10). If such is what the art novel reduces to – and McCarthy exaggerates for effect – then it might be that which the ideas novel aspires to: replete with ideas, the protagonists of these novels work towards each other. It is no coincidence that novels such as Murdoch's *Under the Net* and McEwan's *Atonement* resolve around the attempt, and often the failure, to know other minds, what *Atonement* describes as 'the failure to grasp the simple truth that other people are as real as you'.[39]

Such failures are part and parcel of the effort to represent ideas by means of the particular details, samples, and slices of the world that novelists invent and represent: what Murdoch refers to as reality's 'unutterable particularity'.[40] And such are the cross-purposes, McCarthy suggests, that characterise from the outset the effort to write any novel, but especially a novel of ideas: the novelist must 'save the particulars' and sacrifice 'the perfection of the design': 'An idea cannot have loose ends, but a novel, I almost think, needs them' (p. 117). To succeed in writing a novel is to fail to represent an idea, as Briony similarly concludes in *Atonement*: 'It was always an impossible task, and that was precisely the point' (p. 351). Herein lies both the constant suspicion and the continued appeal of the novel of ideas: the productive, dialectical tension between embodying ideas in persons and things and of abstracting ideas out of them. That is the drama and conflict at the heart of the novel of ideas. But such failures might be better understood as transformations: 'If a so-called "novel of ideas" is bad art its ideas if any would have been better expressed elsewhere', Murdoch writes, 'If it is good art the ideas are … transformed'.[41] Novels of ideas do not simply report, describe, or communicate ideas; they do not leave them intact but instead alter, transform, and examine them. As Arnold puts it to Bradley in *The Black Prince*: 'Every book is the wreck of a perfect idea' (p. 164).

NOTES

1 J. A. Cuddon, ed., *Dictionary of Literary Terms and Literary Theory* (London: Penguin, 1999), p. 602.
2 Novelists who write novels of ideas, Martin Puchner notes, face a 'long-standing prejudice' against the form; critics interested in the novel of ideas, Adam Kelly suggests, confront the apparent 'uselessness of the category "novelist of ideas"' (Puchner, *The Drama of Ideas: Platonic Provocations in Theater and Philosophy* [Oxford: Oxford University Press, 2010], p. 177; Kelly, 'Development through Dialogue: David Foster Wallace and the Novel of Ideas', *Studies in the Novel* 44.3 [Fall 2012], p. 280).
3 Mary McCarthy, *Ideas and the Novel* (New York: Harcourt Brace Jovanovich, 1980), p. 18. Hereafter cited parenthetically.
4 'So powerful is George Eliot's writing and presence in our retrospect of the nineteenth-century British novel that she seems to guarantee a whole tradition: that of ideas realized in fiction'. Gillian Beer, 'George Eliot and the Novel of Ideas', in *The Columbia History of the British Novel*, ed. John Richetti (New York: Columbia, 1994), p. 429.
5 T. S. Eliot, 'In Memory of Henry James', *The Complete Prose of T. S. Eliot: The Critical Edition, vol. 1*, eds. Jewel Spears Brooker and Ronald Schurchard (Baltimore: Johns Hopkins University Press, 2014), p. 650. Leon Sachs, writing about James's contemporary, the French novelist Paul Bourget, observes: 'Critics and scholars since the late nineteenth century have treated Bourget as a literary

"heretic", an enemy of *l'art pour l'art*, a practitioner of that moralizing and oppressively artless genre: *litterature à thèse* or thesis literature'. 'Literature of Ideas and Paul Bourget's Republican Pedagogy', *French Forum* 33.1–2 (Winter/Spring 2008), p. 53.

6 Mark McGurl, *The Program Era: Postwar Fiction and the Rise of Creative Writing* (Cambridge, MA: Harvard University Press, 2009).

7 Iris Murdoch, *The Black Prince* (1973; New York: Penguin, 2003), p. 42. Hereafter cited parenthetically.

8 J. M. Coetzee, *Elizabeth Costello* (New York: Viking, 2003), p. 9.

9 Henry James, *The Art of Fiction and Other Essays* (New York: Oxford University Press, 1948), p. 3. Hereafter cited parenthetically.

10 Philip Rahv, 'The Cult of Experience in American Writing', *Literature in America*, ed. Philip Rahv (New York: Meridian, 1957), p. 360.

11 Aldous Huxley, *Point Counter Point* (New York: Grosset & Dunlap, 1928), p. 295. Hereafter cited parenthetically. See also Frederick J. Hoffman, 'Aldous Huxley and the Novel of Ideas', *College English*, 8.3 (1946): pp. 129–37; Charles G. Hoffmann, 'The Change in Huxley's Approach to the Novel of Ideas', *Personalist* 42 (1961): pp. 85–90; Jerome Meckier, 'Aldous Huxley and the Congenital Novelists: New Ideas about the Novel of Ideas', *Southern Review: Literary and Interdisciplinary Essays* 13.3 (1980): pp. 203–21.

12 Timothy Bewes, 'What is Philosophical Honesty in Postmodern Literature?', *New Literary History* 31.3 (Summer 2000), p. 432.

13 Susan Rubin Suleiman's observation about the *roman à these* holds true for the novel of ideas: while 'highly problematical in its own right', the term has 'the advantage of being an accepted, if ill-understood and unanalyzed, term in literary theory and criticism'. Suleiman, *Authoritative Fictions: The Ideological Novel as a Literary Genre* (New York: Columbia University Press, 1983), p. 2.

14 Margaret Atwood, 'When Privacy is Theft', Review of *The Circle*, by Dave Eggers. *New York Review of Books* 60.18 (November 21, 2013), p. 6.

15 Kingsley Amis, *New Maps of Hell: A Survey of Science Fiction* (New York: Harcourt, Brace, 1960).

16 Doris Lessing, 'Introduction: 1971', *The Golden Notebook* (New York: Perennial Classics, 1999), p. xix.

17 Denis Bohnenkamp, 'Post-Einsteinian Physics and Literature: Toward a New Poetics'. *Mosaic* 22 (1989): pp. 19–30.

18 Sean Kinch, 'Quantum Mechanics as Critical Model: Reading Nicholas Mosley's *Hopeful Monsters*', *Critique* 47.3 (Spring 2006): pp. 289–308.

19 Neil Levi, 'The Persistence of the Old Regime: Late Modernist Form in the Postmodern Period', in *Modernism and Theory: A Critical Debate*, ed. Stephen Ross (London: Routledge, 2009), p. 124.

20 Nicholas Mosley, *Hopeful Monsters* (London: Dalkey Archive, 1990), p. 102.

21 Iris Murdoch, 'Literature and Philosophy', in *Existentialists and Mystics: Writings on Philosophy and Literature*, ed. Peter Conradi (New York: Penguin, 1997), p. 19.

22 A. S. Byatt, 'Introduction', in Iris Murdoch, *The Bell* (London: Penguin, 1999), p. viii; Martha Nussbaum 'Introduction', in Iris Murdoch, *The Black Prince* (New York: Penguin Classics, 2003), p. x.

23 Murdoch, 'Literature and Philosophy', p. 11.

24 Murdoch, 'The Novelist as Metaphysician', *Existentialists and Mystics*, p. 105.
25 Murdoch, 'Vision and Choice in Morality', *Existentialists and Mystics*, p. 90.
26 Murdoch, *Under the Net* (New York: Penguin, 1982), p. 9. Hereafter cited parenthetically.
27 Murdoch, 'The Darkness of Practical Reason', *Existentialists and Mystics*, p. 199.
28 Cf. Stanley Cavell, *The Claims of Reason: Wittgenstein, Skepticism, Morality, and Tragedy* (Oxford: Oxford University Press, 1979).
29 Murdoch, 'Existentialists and Mystics', *Existentialists and Mystics*, p. 231.
30 Murdoch, 'The Sublime and the Good', *Existentialists and Mystics*, p. 215.
31 Ian McEwan, *The Children Act* (New York: Doubleday, 2014), p. 126.
32 Daniel Zalewski, 'Ian McEwan's Art of Unease', *The New Yorker*, 23 February 2009. Retrieved from http://www.newyorker.com/magazine/2009/02/23/the-background-hum.
33 Judith Seaboyer, 'Ian McEwan: Contemporary Realism and the Novel of Ideas', in *The Contemporary British Novel Since 1980*, eds. James Acheson and Sarah C. E. Ross (New York: Palgrave Macmillan, 2005), pp. 27, 28, 27.
34 Ian McEwan, *Enduring Love* (New York: Anchor, 1997). Hereafter cited parenthetically.
35 Ian McEwan, *Saturday* (New York: Anchor, 2005), p. 81. Hereafter cited parenthetically.
36 Arthur Bradley and Andrew Tate, *The New Atheist Novel: Fiction, Philosophy, and Polemic after 9/11* (London: Continuum, 2010), 17. Zalewski quotes Hitchens in 'The Background Hum'.
37 Bewes, 'What Is Philosophical Honesty in Postmodern Literature?', p. 430.
38 Ludwig Wittgenstein, *Tractatus Logico-Philosophicus*, trans. D. F. Pears and B. F. McGuinness (London: Routledge, 1961), p. 73.
39 Ian McEwan, *Atonement* (New York: Anchor, 2001), p. 38.
40 Murdoch, 'The Sublime and the Good', p. 215.
41 Murdoch, 'Literature and Philosophy', p. 19.

12

NICKY MARSH

Finance, Fiction, and the Genre of a World Economy

Observing the curious mixture of financiers, politicians, and celebrities that attended the World Economic Forum in Davos led a journalist to describe it as an 'action packed thriller' with a 'plot that runs thus: a bunch of rich white men gather in an Alpine hamlet. There's a schlubby bald Chicagoan, a Parisian banker in a suit lush enough to eat, and the obligatory Belarusian with a PhD in physics and a dentist keen on gold crowns'.[1] Against this idiosyncratic backdrop, he fantasises, the 'real action is slowly revealed. The businessmen summon prime ministers and presidents to secret meetings in tiny rooms, where they order the lives of the billions consigned to the plains below – and so make themselves even richer'.[2] To describe finance using the generic terms of the literary thriller has become familiar. The report of the Senate Subcommittee into the wide-scale fraud at Credit Suisse, for example, detailing hidden remote-control elevators in Zurich airport and the secretion of balance sheets in the pages of sports magazines, read like 'a thriller' according to *The New York Times*, suggesting a familiar combination of intrigue, power, and concealment.[3]

This chapter explores the ways in which the thriller offers a generic paradigm through which the peculiar spatial and temporal logics of finance can be understood. The thriller functions in this analogy in two ways. Firstly, it speaks to the secretive and ad hoc operation of the offshore, meetings and dealings in the post-national territories of Davos or Zurich. This is a world, Randy Martin has suggested, in which political decisions are 'no longer rationalized by the administration as inevitable acts and natural consequences of progress but taken as discretionary activities advanced by states and markets', in which the 'investor who knows no country' has replaced 'the consumer-citizen of the nation state'.[4] Secondly, it places us inside the pre-emptive temporality of finance. This is the logic of futures and derivatives that 'colonise the future', in Anthony Giddens phrase, in order to bring it profitably into the present.[5] Hence, what Peter Middleton described as the 'subjunctive' qualities of popular fiction, as it 'unfolds in the shadow of its own end', structurally both enact and contain the uncertainties of financial risk analysis.[6] The 'magic' agency that literary critic Michael Denning attributes to the thriller suggests its capacities to both control and produce new modalities of time and space.

Yet, as Denning's language also suggests, the agency possessed by the protagonist of the thriller is an exorbitant one, this is a fantasy of wish-fulfilment that can 'cut through the opacities' of the contemporary. The futurist offshore agency produced by the thriller is nearly impossible to achieve: the omniscience of the individual who can see everything, and can control the present and the future on that basis, is necessarily quixotic or dangerous. The thriller's dramatic scale can make the agency that it produces seem implausible, in other words, as the ability to see everything and to prevent the apocalypse is the preserve of the hero and thus the thriller can threaten the very thing it promises to enable.

This chapter uses this ambivalence, the magical agency of the protagonist who can manipulate the changing relationship between states and markets and can reach into the future in order to control the present, to explore the increasingly central role that finance has played in postwar British fiction. It opens with Ian Fleming's 1959 *Goldfinger*, arguing that the eponymous protagonist's offshore status models the threats to national autonomy that finance would come to represent. The slick prescience of Fleming's ability to deflect this threat is contrasted against the state of the nation novels that appeared in the following decades, novels that struggled to represent an increasingly powerful but also threateningly unknown world economy. Writers as different from one another as Muriel Spark, J. G Ballard, Margaret Drabble, Ian McEwan, and Martin Amis, critically or parodically engaged with the certainties of the thriller, seeking not to directly represent or narrate the particular glamour of finance but rather to detail its grotesque effects. Yet in the late nineties, as the financial offshore became a paradoxically celebrated aspect of Cool Britannia, then the financial thriller emerged in less critical ways. The final section examines how this impulse was itself exhausted by the crisis of 2007. It offers a brief survey of the fiction that has emerged since, paying particular attention to the role that thrillers played in producing a now damning critique of the hubris of financial futurism.

The history of the postwar thriller is the history of the professional for whom the ideological battles of the Cold War, fought on behalf of the nation, have been superseded by the pragmatic battles with, and on behalf of, the corporation. The 'shift from political and military espionage to corporate espionage' that John Scaggs identifies is elaborated upon by Michael Denning when he describes the genre's concern with a 'deeper, more critical tale where the real enemy is the organisation itself, the organisation that never keeps faith, the organisation that betrays its own men'.[7] Jerry Palmer similarly suggests that the corporate professional has emerged as the archetype for the late twentieth-century thriller as it seeks to resolve 'the contradiction between individuality and sociality' to the 'benefit of individuality.'[8]

The history of the postwar capitalist state that this shift suggests, threatened not by communism but by the capitalism from which it was formed, is also apparent in its economic history. The very concept of the nationally bounded economy, against which the world economy might be positioned, is both a relatively recent and a relatively short-lived phenomena. Economic and cultural historians such as Tim Mitchell and Jed Esty suggest that this national economy was a product of the Keynesian turn of the late forties that 'established a tighter discursive and statistical net around national economies', rendering them 'dynamic objects susceptible to state intervention'.[9] Although these ideological principles were formed in the postwar financial agreement, it was not until the late fifties, according to economist Susan Strange, that it could begin to function, freed from the particular exigencies of war's aftermath. This was an 'open, liberal world market economy' in which nation states were granted some degree of autonomy by the fixed exchange rates agreed at Bretton Woods.[10]

Yet this vision of the national economy came to fruition just as the seeds of its decline had already been sewn. Although its origins remain appropriately opaque, 1958 is frequently identified as the moment in which the offshore financial market first appeared. It was the year in which postwar restrictions on sterling convertibility were lifted and the U.S dollars stored in London created a market that existed 'totally beyond the reach of U.S. regulation'.[11] This rapidly growing 'Eurodollar' market facilitated the speculative currency trading that the postwar agreement had been designed to inhibit and has been represented as the first 'truly borderless' market.[12] Hence, as Jerry Coakely and Laurence Harris have noted, the postwar undermining of British economic sovereignty was the result not of 'a plot from abroad – the Gnomes of Zurich or the IMF furthering U.S. capital's hegemony' but from the 'operations of the City of London pursuing its interests'.[13] The offshore's power derived from its apparent invisibility: its participants evaded tax, regulation, and scrutiny and were given 'complete anonymity'.[14] The investigative journalist Anthony Sampson describes the 'conspiracy of silence' that concealed the offshore, citing a financial journalist who 'stumbled' on the 'existence' of this market 'by sheer accident in October 1959' but whose enquiries were halted by the bankers who 'emphatically asked' him 'not to write about the new practice'.[15]

The irony of a national economy that was undermined before it was even able to properly operate, that remains only ever an unrealised ideal although the threat to it cannot be seen, can be read against one of the most paradigmatic thrillers of the postwar period: Ian Fleming's 1959 *Goldfinger*. In this novel, Bond is deployed by Colonel Smithers, the chief researcher for the Bank of England (whose department is described as 'nothing more or less than a spy system'), to defend the economy:

> Gold and gold-backed currencies are the foundation of our international credit. We can only tell what the true strength of the pound is, and other countries can only know it, by knowing the exact amount of the valuta we have behind our currency ... we are asking you to bring Goldfinger to book, Mr Bond, and get that gold back. You know about the currency crisis and the high interest rate? Of course. Well England needs that gold, badly – and the quicker the better.[16]

Goldfinger's threat to the autonomy of the nation is closely identified with his offshore status, a status that represents both a resistance to national identification and an allegiance to the principles of speculative capitalism that Keynesianism notions of the national economy were so precisely turned against. He may be the chief treasurer for the communist SMERSH but he is also a UK citizen naturalised to Nassau in the Bahamas (with bank accounts in Zurich and Panama): the richest man in England who has never paid taxes there. The repugnance that Goldfinger engenders is more closely tied to his relationship with gold than to his political sympathies and his lack of national affiliation and his love of destructive accumulation are entwined. Fleming's curious play with Goldfinger's ethnicity, as he simultaneously suggests and disavows his Jewishness, can be read through his offshore status. Goldfinger's love of gold parallels the antisemitic displacement of capitalism's irrational antagonisms, its 'powerful bursts of feeling', onto the figure of the Jew in ways so effectively described by Jonathan Freedland.[17] Hence, Freedland's description of the figure of the Jew 'as a malign embodiment of the possibility of gentile pleasure at their own success in a capitalist economy – a twisted alibi for the pleasures that such an economy brings along with it' corresponds to Fleming's depiction of Goldfinger's monstrousness, an attraction to gold that both replaces the nation and is disturbingly sensuous. Goldfinger's crime is a hyperbolic version of the thriftiness that Keynesian principles of expenditure and flow sought to destroy. He is the constipated hoarder (when Bond furtively searches Goldfinger's home he finds 'precious little except that Goldfinger suffered from constipation and a dirty mind') who disrupts Keynes's emphasis on the necessity of money's circulation (p. 120).

It doesn't seem entirely unlikely that Fleming was unaware of the emergence of this new market and its implications for Britain in a post-Suez world. Fleming came from a banking family and he had been both a banker and a stockbroker before entering the world of military espionage. Although a notoriously poor financier, 'lacking staying power and bored by the minutiae of money making',[18] accounts of him from the late fifties suggest that he remained interested in '"very speculative securities"' and gave other bankers 'the impression that he had received underground information about some very unorthodox investment – a silver mine in Bulgaria, something of that sort'.[19] This interest in the secret workings of finance was revived when he returned to the Bank of England to complete research for *Goldfinger* and was commissioned to write a non-fictional book on diamond smuggling.[20] When the Bond novels were first anthologised in the early sixties, the titles of the collections, *Gilt-Edged Bonds* and *More Gilt-Edged Bonds*, played quite obviously on Fleming's identity as both banker and writer.

Fleming's apparent awareness of the emergence of the offshore market seemed to be unique in British fiction of the period. Although concerns about Britain's dwindling political and economic influence abounded they were more often filtered through the changes taking place in class and industrial relations. Alan Sillitoe's 1958 *Saturday Night and Sunday Morning*, for example, is explicit about the liberation of demand that followed Keynesian expansion and the subsequent creation of a working-class consumer culture. The antihero Arthur Seaton's adoration of his sumptuous wardrobe – the 'rows of suits, trousers, sports jackets, shirts all suspended in colourful drapes and designs' – almost rivals the tears of ecstasy that Daisy Buchanan so tellingly sheds over Gatsby's scattered shirts in Fitzgerald's classic 1925 novel. Yet whereas Gatsby's shirts have been paid for by the invisible sources of finance capital (Gatsby makes his dubious money from selling among other things bonds), Seaton's emphatically have not: his wardrobe represents 'a couple of hundred quids worth, a fabulous wardrobe. Of which he was proud because it had cost him so much labour'.[21] The novel gestures to the role of this labour in shoring up Britain's imperial ambitions in the post-imperial, cold-war climate of the Suez crisis. It is valuable not simply because it affords Seaton the clothes for the 'bingiest glad-time' of a Saturday night, but also because of its role in maintaining the value of sterling itself in the face of recurring currency crises (p. 9). He watches his factory send 'crated bicycles each year from the Despatch Department ... boosting post-war (or perhaps pre-war, Arthur thought, because these days a war could start tomorrow) export trade and trying to sling a pontoon over a turbulent unbridgeable river called the Sterling Balance' (p. 27).

It was not until the early seventies, when the ending of the Bretton Woods agreement and the subsequent oil crisis brought the offshore cultures of speculative finance to the fore, that the power of the world economy really began to concern British novelists. One of the earliest novels to articulate this concern was Muriel Spark's 1976 *The Takeover*. The novel gestures to the power of the offshore world economy but struggles to produce a language that can comprehend it. Instead it is concerned with the crisis of epistemology that it heralds, and Spark's critique of the moral emptiness at the heart of her central characters often parallels an account of the emptiness of this new money. The characters are blind to the fact that they are living through 'the beginning of something new in their world'. Although they talk 'of recession and inflation, of losses on the stock-market, failures in business', while 'band[ying] the phrases of newspaper economists' such as 'hedges against inflation' and the 'mood of the stock-market', it did not occur to them that a 'complete mutation not merely to be defined as a collapse of the capitalist system or a global recession, but such a sea-change in the nature of reality as could not have been envisaged by Karl Marx or Sigmund Freud. Such a mutation that what were assets were to be liabilities'.[22]

The dematerialisation and flight of money are explored in the novel through the question of ownership. The material evidence and reproducibility of wealth – of homes, art, jewellery – become paradoxical. Characters do not own the homes they have bought, those who forge art seek recompense for the loss of the originals, jewel thieves are ushered into grand homes as tourists. The central protagonist is the vain Maggie Radcliffe, and the theft of her wealth by those paid to manage it can only occur because she had already participated in its theft: allowing her money to be secreted away in the offshore, a space that is appropriately imagined as both invisible and omniscient. She spends much of the novel following it 'from Switzerland to the Dutch Antilles and the Bahamas' tracing the 'financial network' orchestrated by her accountant whose 'favourite word was "global". He produced an appealing global plan for Maggie's fortune, so intricate that it might have been decided primordially by the angels as a mathematical blueprint to guide God in the creation of the world' (p. 100). Spark draws on the tropes of the thriller to produce a jarringly conclusive ending: Maggie tracks down her accountant and circumvents the powerlessness of the law in this new world order by arranging for him to be kidnapped until he agrees to 'make everything over to me in Switzerland'. Spark is emphatic and literal about this rematerialisation; the novel ends with Maggie visiting the accountant, who is 'right here in a cave in this cliff, well guarded. ... I simply had to go and gloat' (p. 189). The critical consensus on the limitations of this novel are interesting in what it suggests about the impossibility of encompassing the scale of the world economy in this moment. Spark was repeatedly critiqued for her use of an overblown metaphysical language of financial omniscience. In her review in *The New York Times*, Margaret Drabble, for example, suggests that the dialogue of the novel reads 'more like a parody of Spark than Spark herself'. Though Spark is well positioned to write of 'the kind of colorless, odorless, tasteless, unspendable money that passes in hieroglyphics through computers from one part of the globe to another', such a 'theme is, not surprisingly, too large for the book' and, tellingly, the 'omniscience that sat so easily on her in her earlier novels has been shaken'.[23] This sense that the novel form cannot capture the 'scale' of finance also recurs through its academic reception. Rodney Stenning Edgecombe suggests that 'the "corrective" metaphysical framework that governed and shaped the early work with such purposefulness has now been dismantled', and Rod Mengham similarly suggests that this is a novel that 'attempts to establish its control over material that does not comfortably fit into the scale of a novel'.[24]

By the 1980s, fiction had become increasingly attentive to the violent divisions that Spark's novel grasps at: divisions that cultural geographers Angus Cameron and Ronen Palan have suggested occurred between the offshore financial realm, the newly privatised former public realm, and the 'anti-economy' of the deindustrialised working class, who were problematically excluded from economic participation.[25] Indeed, the formal impossibility of imagining the co-existence of the offshore, the private, and the anti-economy can be read into many of the grotesque perversions that characterised the state-of-the-nation novels that appeared in the decade. Novels as different from one another as Ian McEwan's *The Child in Time* (1987), Margaret Drabble's *The Radiant Way* (1987), Salman Rushdie's *Satanic Verses* (1988), J. G Ballard's *Running Wild* (1988), and Ian Sinclair's *Downriver* (1991) all register the divided triad of the global economy through metaphors of violence. The power of these critiques lies in their resistance to simply representing finance as a knowable entity. They avoid the resolutions of the thriller, apparent in the unlikely conclusions offered by both Fleming and Spark, by instead registering offshore finance as an absence whose violent effects are unreal, evident only in the other economies it produces.

Hence, finance is a brooding backdrop; the protagonists who represent it appear in ways that are as fleeting as they are devastating. In *Running Wild*, for example, finance is present in the bodies of the fathers, merchant bankers, stockbrokers, and CEOs, who have been murdered by their own children. The first of these is found in his chauffeured car, still assuming, after being fatally shot by his own son, that 'he would be driven to his office in the City'.[26] In *The Child in Time*, financialisation is represented by the Machiavellian figure of Charles Darke, the entrepreneur turned Conservative politician who makes his millions whilst in his youth and goes on to advocate the benefits of licensed begging for introducing 'men, women and children' to the 'pitfalls and strenuous satisfactions of self-sufficiency long familiar to the business community'.[27] Darke's eventual regression into childhood is represented as both sexually perverse and destructive, his childish suicide suggests a loss of responsibility that parallels the callousness of his politics. A similar combination of excess and self-destruction is touched upon by Drabble and Rushdie. The party that opens both the novel and the decade in *The Radiant Way* is attended by 'the investor about to hang himself in the expectation of plenty'[28], and the slight but memorable Hal Vance in *The Satanic Verses* is the self-made man who is represented as interested only in pornography and a fundamentalist conviction about Thatcherite neo-liberalism.

Yet these protagonists are distant from the violence of financialisation: it is in the diminishment of the public realm and the emergence of the under-class that its effect re-emerges. The mass parricide in *Running Wild* is Ballard's metaphor for the distortion of the social that the privatised gated community of Pangbourne village, 'built in the 1980s in areas of deregulated farmland' and lacking any 'connections, social, historical or civic, with Pangbourne itself', represents (p. 13). McEwan's condemnation of the violence and absurdity of the privatised state is apparent from its first wry sentence: 'Subsidising public transport had long been associated in the minds of both Government and the majority of its public with the denial of individual liberty' (p. 7). The destruction of the social is evident in Drabble's novel through the lurking figure of the 'Harrow Road Murderer', whose final victim is found by his ex-social worker, ridden with guilt because she feels complicit with the state's abandonment of him; in Rushdie's novel the callous and contradictory state is represented through the goat-like demeanour Saladin assumes when he is denied legitimate access to it.

It is, appropriately enough, Martin Amis's *Money* (1984) that most powerfully draws out the violence that the co-existence of these disparate narrative spaces of the economy has created. The novel opens with a reference to the moment money 'went wrong' in the early seventies, and uses the language of the apocalypse in an attempt to re-render the extraordinary character of what has been accepted as the ordinary. Amis's antihero, John Self, sits uncomfortably between money's different economies. For much of the novel he is both one of the 'white moneymen' and also 'one of the unemployed. What do we do all day? We sit on stoops and pause in loose knots on the stained pavements'.[29] From his vantage point, in the 'gap between things', he watches 'primitive' financiers 'driving around with their

money in their Torpedoes and Boomerangs. ... They don't do anything; it's
their currencies that do things', whilst also observing the violent effects of
money on the urban poor, money that 'is so near you can almost touch it,
but it is all on the other side' (p. 153).

Self is unemployed because he has left his advertising company, without understanding the offshore sources of its profitability, in order to make
Hollywood movies. The financiers who fund him, but who are actually the
men who seek to destroy him, are the Iago-like Fielding Goodney and the
mercurially cool Ossie Twain. Twain, as his name suggests, is Self's more
successful other and sexual rival. He works

> in money, in pure money. His job has nothing to do with anything except
> money, the stuff itself. ... Equipped with only a telephone, he buys money with
> money, sells money for money. He works in the vents and cracks of curren-
> cies, buying and selling on the margin, riding the daily tides of exchange. For
> these services he is rewarded with money. Lots of it. It is beautiful and so is he.
> (pp. 119–20)

Fielding Goodney, who tricks Self into both producing and paying for his
own expensive failures, has a voice that is 'full of passionate connoisseurship,
with many parallels and precedents, Italian banking, liquidity preference,
composition fallacy' (p. 23). Goodney is the 'absolutely unexplained' 'confidence trick' that Amis has described as a 'good analogy for money'.[30] He initially tortures Self over the phone and the literal violence that he then inflicts
upon him corresponds with the grotesque perversity of money: Goodney
punctures Self's back with a stiletto heel but Self is never sure who he is,
leaving him both bewildered and emasculated.

Amis's fantasy of self-destruction, the peculiar and paradoxical destructiveness of finance, appeared prophetic in the mid-nineties when Barings
Bank collapsed, apparently at the hands of a working-class man, who, like
Amis's Self, had been given inappropriate access to the money economy.
And, as in the eighties, evidence that the financial sector was incapable
of self-governance was ignored and further powers were seceded to it by
the New Labour government. The ascendancy of the financial sector that
ensued was apparent in popular genre fiction: the figure of the financier fully
re-emerged from its malevolent shadows.

The popular novels that emerged in Britain from the mid-nineties onwards
reclaimed the thriller paradigm that had been suggested by Fleming a
half-century earlier: texts written by bankers-turned-novelists about bankers who became spies, by writers such as Michael Ridpath, Paul Kilduff,
and Linda Davies, made it into the best-selling list. The formerly mysterious
and abstracted workings of high finance were central to these narratives

and reviews of the emerging genre read it through the Barings crisis and celebrated its ability to make finance visible. The *Financial Times* noted that 'if the public can lap up the kind of hardware details beloved by Tom Clancy, surely they can learn to love the world of Eurobonds and leveraged buy-outs?'[31], and *The Independent* that writers 'shrewdly twigged that, in the post–Cold War world, the mysteries of casino capitalism exert the same allure of mingled risk and thrill that tales of espionage once had. For agents, read dealers; for secret services, frontier-hopping finance firms. ... The book trade has seen the future for hi-tech thrillers, and it deals rather than spies'.[32] *The Guardian* celebrated the appearance of 'unreal places like "offshore"' and suggested that 'Nick Leeson's greatest service will be neither to banking nor even to the clarification of German extradition law, but rather to fiction. ... It could be that we will finally see the end of the financial-based novel that tries desperately to conceal its subject matter'.[33]

These novels treat the implications of the complexities of the financial system in ambivalent ways. On the one hand, their apocalyptic scenarios of mass destruction revel in the always-present destructive potential of the market. Novels such as James Harland's *The Month of the Leopard* (2002), David Schofield's *The Pegasus Forum* (2001), and Paul Kilduff's *The Frontrunner* (2002) all provide scenarios in which a rogue trader is able to single-handedly bring about global apocalypse by doing little more than punching a series of numbers into a laptop. In each, the trader represents the physical individualisation of capitalism and is thus both capitalism's end and its salvation. The eponymous 'Leopard Trust' is so-named because 'it is no use asking why a giant cat hunts its prey. It does it because it is what it was built for. And so for ourselves. It is no use asking why the fund destroys its opponents in the market. It does it because that was what it was built for'.[34] Similarly, the conspiracy in *The Pegasus Forum* is motivated by the desire to 'expose the largely unworthy, fraudulent and shallow basis of our financial system' by using legal means that do not dilute the 'spirit of the law with equivocations or trickery. Our very justification lies in the fact that we are using the system to hang itself'.[35]

These plans rest upon the hubristic perversion of money's auto-generative capacities: the ability of capital to recreate itself without recourse to either production or territory provides the energy for money's unstoppable destruction as well as its infinite wealth. Yet the fantasy of self-destruction that these novels revel in is consistently vanquished by a parallel profession-alism. Their heroes are bankers who are committed to the moral codes of the professional but are redeemed by their distance from its corrupting eco-nomic excesses. In *The Pegasus Forum*, for example, the plot is unravelled by a cyberpunk with 'the most technically advanced and brilliant civilian mind' who doesn't adhere to the 'financial effort/risk-reward equation'.[36] The hero of *The Devil's Banker* is a cerebral 'quant jock' who is the 'new kind of soldier. You know, brains instead of brawn' fighting 'a bureaucrat's game'.[37] Hence, these novels propose the near and inevitable possibility of economic crash only to reveal that professionalism has already protected us from it and, as Paul Crosthwaite has put it, the destructive 'subversive impulses' that pervade the market are distilled into 'the depiction of a small cadre of villainous conspirators, who can be safely dismissed as aberrant deviations from the norm'.[38]

The thriller's production of a recurring alibi for finance, the protagonist who defuses the threat of financial crisis that he also represents, became impossible to sustain in the aftermath of the 2007–8 financial crisis. Although the figure of the financier became a renewed source of fascination, appearing in novels including Sebastian Faulk's *Week in December* (2009), Amanda Craig's *Hearts and Minds* (2009), Alex Preston's *This Bleeding City* (2010), Justin Cartwright's *Other People's Money* (2011), Marina Lewycka's *Various Pets Alive and Dead* (2012), John Lanchester's *Capital* (2012), and Mark Lawson's *The Deaths* (2013), these novels were often concerned with understanding the human figure of the banker rather than the processes of finance. As the banker-turned-novelist Alex Preston suggested, they referred back to the realist traditions of the nineteenth-century novel, that of Anthony Trollope in particular, producing a cast 'drawn from across the social spectrum', and taking an 'essentially tribal approach to London, showing the isolation of the urban condition', while counteracting it 'structurally by using the intersection and (often romantic) coming together of the various strands to give London life a comforting coherence'. Hence, for Preston, these novels highlight a certain tension: alongside the familiar generic properties of financial writing – the 'racy thriller-ish subplot that hurries the narrative along' – they offer themselves as 'beacons against the alienating multiplicity of city life'.[39]

Preston's language is telling in terms of the role that these determinedly realist narratives play in the wider history of financial fictions. The 'comforting coherence' that they offer is often redemptive, as it salves the social divisions – the violence of the private and the anti-economy – that rendered the eighties novel so grotesque. The alienating loss of the social depicted by Drabble, McEwan, Ballard, and Rushdie's novels is replaced by a communal fantasy of connection, as characters are saved by their mutual, if often invisible and unknown, interdependencies.

Sebastian Faulks's *Week in December* most clearly exemplifies the tension between the thriller of financial fiction and the redemptive 'beacon' of the realist fiction that emerged after the crisis. The narrative's cross-section of London includes a comparison between the actions of the innocent putative terrorist and the actions of the non-innocent hedge-fund manager. The characters are paired because of the ways in which they resist the novel's centrifugal drive in favour of a course of action that will actively destroy it. The parallel, inevitably, breaks apart in the conclusion. Hassan as-Rashid, the son of the chutney magnate, drops his unexploded device harmlessly into the Thames, whereas Veal ploughs on with his 'bombproof' deal, knowing that it will precipitate a financial crisis that will reap him billions whilst 'millions around the globe would lose their jobs; other millions would go without food'.[40] The end of the novel may echo with the triumphalist omniscience of Tom Wolfe's *Bonfire of the Vanities*: 'I have mastered this world. ... To me there is no mystery, no nuance, and no complication', but the statement is without consequences. Wolfe's sensitivity to finance's complicity in the distortion of the social, evident in his critically parodic tone and in Sherman McCoy's hubristic downfall, are both absent from Faulks's novel. Instead, we are left with the impression that the changes occurring in Veal's home life, the recuperation of his symbolically insane son, may offer him an alternative to his own madness.

The post-crash novel that resisted social coherence in favour of social destruction was the one that returned most decisively to the thriller form. Robert Harris's 2011 novel *The Fear Index* is relatively unique amongst post-crash fiction because its personification of finance speaks to its gothically spectral powers. The novel is set in the offshore world of Geneva, and its central protagonist is a British computer scientist, Alex Hoffman (the name is telling: Hoffman was the name of the author who wrote the story of the 'The Sandman' from which Freud derived this theory of the uncanny), who has perfected Artificial Intelligence. Hoffman uses this technology to profit from the so-called Fear Index, the Chicago VIX index that predicts market volatility and thus profits from political or environmental disturbance. The novel literalises this destructive logic, Hoffman's computer takes over his life and attempts to kill him before seeking to bring about a global apocalypse that will maximize its profits even as it brings the world to an end. Hoffman's technology is explicitly compared to Frankenstein's monster from the novel's opening; it is a gothic double that makes the very divisions between the monster and the human both necessary and impossible. The metaphor is extended throughout the novel. Hoffman lacks the family that provides redemptive paternity in other post-crash novels. His child is a monster without life: dying before it was born, with a head that 'was disproportionately large for its body, its spindly legs drawn up and tucked beneath it. Viewed from the side it had depth, but as one shifted one's perspective

... it seemed to dwindle and disappear entirely.' Alex follows the fate of his child: he prevents an apocalyptic disaster but is consumed in the ensuing fire, a 'fiery outline of a man' who falls 'like Icarus'.[41]

The literary thriller remains a vital form for charting the role that the emergence of the global financial economy has played in postwar British life – enacting its peculiar distortions of space and time, both the secretive post-national space of the offshore and the exuberant futurist time of speculation. Yet how authors have used this resource has changed dramatically, and it is too simple to assign either a critical or celebratory role to the form. For writers such as Harris, the genre encapsulates the violent logic of finance, whereas for others, especially those closest to the industry, the parallels suggest a verisimilitude that captures the heroic self-identity of the financier with a rather ambivalent irony. It is, perhaps, those novelists who negotiate the assumptions of the genre more tangentially – Spark, Amis, Ballard, even Faulks – who allow us to see its value and its limitations in this context. For these writers, the parallels between the thriller and the financial world are suggestive because they speak of the peculiar powers that finance has gained in the postwar period, but they are also limited because the logic is too narrowly tautological: it is the difficult, fraying social relations of those that exist beyond it, this still-growing political and cultural power, that literature needs to be able to continue to articulate.

NOTES

1 Aditya Chakrabortty, 'An Action Packed Thriller is about to Unfold in Davos, Switzerland', *The Guardian*, 11 January 2013. Retrieved from http://www .theguardian.com/commentisfree/2013/jan/21/davos-switzerland-rich-plotting-richer.
2 Ibid.
3 Sydney Ember, 'Credit Suisse Under Scrutiny', *New York Times*, 27 February 2014. Retrieved from http://dealbook.nytimes.com/2014/02/27/morning-agenda-credit-suisse-under-scrutiny.
4 Randy Martin, *American War and the Financial Logic of Risk Management* (New York: Duke University Press, 2007), pp. 5, 30.
5 Anthony Giddens, *Modernity and Self-Identity: Self and Society in the Late Modern Age* (Stanford: Stanford University Press, 1991), p. 117.
6 Peter Middleton, 'How Novels Can Contribute to Our Understanding of Climate Change', in *History at the End of the World?*, eds. Mark Levene, Rob Johnson, and Penny Roberts (Penrith: Humanities-EBooks, 2010), p. 220.
7 Michal Denning, *Cover Stories: Narrative and Ideology in the British Spy Thriller* (London: Routledge, 1987), p. 140.
8 Jerry Palmer, *Thrillers: Genesis and Structure of a Popular Genre* (London: Palgrave Macmillan, 1979), p. 204.

9 Esty suggests that before Keynes's *The General Theory* economists had 'analyzed the behaviour of individuals and firms within a given market' and had 'thought of the national income (or debt) in terms more or less dictated by the metaphor of nation-as-household. Keynes vigorously disputed the terms of this metaphor, pointing out that a simple extension of household virtues (including thrift) to social aggregates led to bad theory and bad policy.' Jed Esty, *A Shrinking Island: Modernism and National Culture in England* (Princeton: Princeton University Press, 2004), p. 173.

10 Susan Strange, 'From Bretton-Woods to Casino Capitalism', in *Money, Power, Space*, eds. Nigel Thrift, Stuart Corbridge, and Ron Martin (Oxford: Blackwell, 1994), p. 55.

11 Gregory J. Millman, *Around the World on a Trillion Dollars a Day* (London: Bantam Press, 1995), p. 84.

12 Tony Golding, *The City: Inside the Great Expectation Machine* (London: Pearson Education, 2001), p. 19.

13 Jerry Coakley and Laurence Harris, *The City of Capital: London's Role as a Financial Centre* (Oxford: Blackwell, 1983), p. 27.

14 Golding, *The City*, p. 19

15 Anthony Sampson, *The Money Lenders: Bankers in a Dangerous World* (London: Hodder and Stoughton, 1981), p. 111.

16 Ian Fleming, *Goldfinger* (London: Penguin, 1959), p. 56. Hereafter cited parenthetically. As Alissa Karl has argued of the film, it is Britishness itself that is under threat here and that 'Goldfinger's peculiar personage suggests that delimiting Britain is a matter of running a tight economic ship, and of prosecuting boundaries for financial and economic transactions.' ('Goldfinger's Gold Standard Negotiating the Economic Nation in Mid-Twentieth Century Britain', *International Journal of Cultural Studies* 11 [2008], pp. 177–192).

17 Jonathan Freedland, *The Temple of Culture: Assimilation and Anti-Semitism in Literary Anglo-America* (Oxford: Oxford University Press, 2000), p. 66.

18 Andrew Lycett, *Ian Fleming* (London: Phoenix, 1995), p. 70.

19 Ibid., p. 72

20 John Pearson, *The Life of Ian Fleming* (London: Arium Press, 2003), p. 361.

21 Alan Sillitoe, *Saturday Night and Sunday Morning* (London: W. H. Allen, 1958), p. 169. Hereafter cited parenthetically.

22 Muriel Spark, *The Takeover* (London: Penguin, 1973), p. 91. Hereafter cited parenthetically.

23 Margaret Drabble, 'Muriel Spark: A Glittering, Knowing Novel about the Decline of the West', *The New York Times*, 3 October 1976. Retrieved from http://www.nytimes.com/books/97/05/11/reviews/spark-takeover.html.

24 Rodney Stenning Edgecombe, *Vocation and Identity in the Fiction of Muriel Spark* (Missouri: University of Missouri Press, 1990), p. 113; and Rod Mengham, '1973: The End of History: Cultural Change According to Muriel Spark', in *An Introduction to Contemporary Fiction*, ed. Rod Mengham (London: Polity, 1999), p. 133.

25 Ibid., p. 17.

26 J. G. Ballard, *Running Wild* (New York: Farrar, Straus and Giroux, 1988), p. 9. Hereafter cited parenthetically.

27 Ian McEwan, *The Child in Time* (London: Jonathan Cape, 1987), p. 39. Hereafter cited parenthetically.

28 Margaret Drabble, *The Radiant Way* (London: Penguin, 1987), p. 36.

29 Martin Amis, *Money* (London: Penguin, 1984), pp. 154, 153. Hereafter cited parenthetically.

30 Cited in Nicolas Tredell, *The Fiction of Martin Amis* (London: Palgrave, 2000), p. 62.

31 Philip Coggan, 'Finance Loses the Plot: Thrillers', *The Financial Times*, 9 May 1998, p. 6.

32 'Books: Hypewatch', *The Independent*, 21 March 1998, p. 15.

33 Dan Atkinson, 'We're in the Money: Fictional Currency of the Week: Financial Thrillers', *The Guardian, Features*, 31 March 1995.

34 James Harland, *The Month of the Leopard* (London: Simon and Schuster, 2001), p. 138.

35 David Schofield, *The Pegasus Forum* (London: Simon and Schuster, 2001), p. 29.

36 Ibid., p. 47.

37 Christopher Reich, *The Devil's Banker* (London: Headline Publishing, 2003), pp. 20, 110.

38 Paul Crosthwaite, 'Blood on the Trading Floor: Waste, Sacrifice, and Death in Financial Crises', *Angelaki* 15.2 (2010), pp. 3–18.

39 Alex Preston, 'The Way We Live Now? Follow the Money Trail Back to Anthony Trollope', *The Observer*, Sunday, 12 February 2012. Retrieved from http://www.theguardian.com/books/2012/feb/12/trollope-state-nation-london-novel.

40 Sebastian Faulks, *Week in December* (London: Hutchinson, 2009), p. 390.

41 Robert Harris, *The Fear Index* (London: Random House, 2011), pp. 34, 314.

13

MATTHEW HART

Globalism and Historical Romance

A phrase such as 'novel of globalization' reeks of the present. Although nothing in it directly denotes temporal concepts of the now, that expression unmistakably evokes the possibility of fiction that, rather than just being written in a globalised age, takes on the task of describing that world. For Peter Osborne, the 'fiction of the contemporary is primarily a global or a planetary fiction', by which he means that the idea of transnational linkage is now the major 'socio-spatial form' through which we understand the present as historical – as something we can see or represent as a moment unto itself.[1] Any inquiry into art's contemporaneity, Osborne insists, must ask how it is shaped by social relations among globally distributed spaces.

But what of novels that impute a long history to globalization, rather than seeing it as the mark of the present? In recent years, writers such as Amitav Ghosh, Timothy Mo, and Eleanor Catton have authored novels that attribute an extended historical arc to political, economic, and cultural globalisation. In this chapter, I focus on Salman Rushdie and David Mitchell – novelists from different generations, and with distinct styles and sensibilities, whose work is nevertheless joined by how they address the question of globalization from the standpoint of historical romance. By 'globalisation' I mean more than the simple fact of international or transnational relation. (What era has not been 'global' in that sense?) I mean, instead, the proposition that there exists, now and in the past, a political-economic system in which events occurring in one part of the world have effects for every part of that system. This picture of globalisation as a seamless grid or network is more ideological than actual, describing less some actual system of planetary interconnection than, in Gayatri Spivak's words, the discursive 'imposition of the same system of exchange everywhere'.[2] Rather than engaging a concrete set of historical practices, this chapter therefore addresses what Manfred B. Stenger calls 'globalism': a 'hegemonic system of ideas that makes normative claims about a set of social processes called "globalization"' and that, by representing those processes as an historical fait accompli, limits 'public discussion on the meaning and character of globalization'.[3] The chapter therefore describes how Rushdie and Mitchell imaginatively extend the history of globalisation in space and time; its central argument, however, concerns the way their novels, formally as much as thematically, justify that extension in universal language. In so doing, they identify the history of globalisation with the possibility of thinking historically at all.

Consider, first, the manifest content of Rushdie's *The Enchantress of Florence* (2008) and Mitchell's *The Thousand Autumns of Jacob de Zoet* (2010). These novels, set, respectively, in the Renaissance and the Napoleonic eras, share a thematic interest in the historical coevality of Europe and Asia. This theme is most clearly articulated in the scrupulous care with which they research and depict the complex particularity of, respectively, the cultures of Mughal India and Edo-period Japan – and in the scathing manner with which they deal with European characters blind to such subtleties. As such, these novels imply that the contemporary 'rise' of Asian economies signals a welcome shift from a world system unnaturally dominated by Euro-America to a multi-polar arrangement more nearly balanced between East and West, if not North and South. For all that, however, the globalist aspect of Mitchell's and Rushdie's fiction is most clearly legible not in their plots, settings, or themes but at the level of novelistic style – for instance, in the nesting-doll structure of Mitchell's *Cloud Atlas* (2004) and in Rushdie's affirmation of storytelling as a kind of secular magic.

The proposition that narrative aesthetics acts as a vehicle for globalist thinking is best exemplified by a signature aspect of Mitchell's fiction, which imagines at a formal level what it might mean to live within a 'linked set of emerging global conditions'.[4] Mitchell's novels feature metaleptic networks of narrative association in which the same characters appear across discrete parts of multi-section novels and, increasingly, across different novels altogether. Thus, a minor figure in *Ghostwritten*, a writer named Luisa Rey who calls into a late-night radio show, not only recalls that novel's epigraph from Thornton Wilder's *The Bridge of San Luis Rey* (1927) but also reappears as the protagonist of 'Half Lives: The First Luisa Rey Mystery' in *Cloud Atlas* and as a magazine editor in *The Bone Clocks* (2014). One could cite many such examples – indeed, Kathryn Schulz lists twenty-three recurring characters across Mitchell's six novels.[5] It is for this reason that Pieter Vermeulen has suggested that the metaleptic structure of *Ghostwritten* 'not only *portrays* how processes of globalization connect very different lives with each other in a way that does not require a central agency' but also 'embodies that mode of decentered relatedness in its formal organization'.[6] As Mitchell's multinational and multiracial cast reappears across an expanding range of space-times, the formal allegory Vermeulen identifies in *Ghostwritten* expands from a property of one novel into a basic component of what Mitchell calls the 'Über-book' that is his whole oeuvre.[7] That Mitchell would now describe his corpus as a single great book feels like a natural extension of his often-quoted dictum that, for him, 'structure need not just be a frame on which you hang narrative, but a kind of plot in its own right, running parallel to the narrative-plot'.[8] In the wake of *The Bone Clocks*, we can see how structural principles of decentred relatedness operate for Mitchell not just as 'a kind of plot' but as a kind of authorial firmware – something akin to an aesthetic ground plan – for a narrative secondary world that is at once generically diverse and structurally systematic.

What we have here, then, is a novelistic oeuvre that is itself a formal allegory for a networked world. There is a difference, however, between such an oeuvre and making historiographical conjectures about that world's origins or nature. Salman Rushdie's *The Enchantress of Florence* contains none of the structural interlacing that characterises *Ghostwritten* or *Cloud Atlas* but it is, Rushdie claims, his most-heavily researched book.[9] This is something it certainly advertises, concluding with a bibliography of more than ninety texts relevant to its two late-fifteenth-century settings: Nicolo Machiavelli's Florence and the city of Fatehpur Sikri, built by the third Mughal Emperor, Akbar the Great. 'Oh that's not the show-off bibliography', Rushdie said at the time of the book's release. 'There's one that's about four times as long'.[10]

The historical character of *Enchantress* is not, however, just an expression of its author's commitment to research; nor is it only about floating a luminous contemporary detail atop a skein of illusion, seducing us to believe in a time 'before the real and unreal were segregated forever'.[11] *Enchantress* implies that modernity does not only belong to the Atlantic world. The novel begins with the visit to Fatehpur Sikri of a mysterious traveller from Florence. Using papers stolen from an English ambassador, he takes the name Mogor dell'Amore (Mughal of Love), wins an audience with Akbar, and eventually claims to be the son of Akbar's long-lost great-aunt, the legendary princess Qara Köz. The story that ensues is, of course, more complicated and fantastical than even this. What is important here is that *Enchantress* begins with the arrival, in a great Asian capital, of the unknown offspring of a Mughal enchantress and an Italian merchant – Ago Vespucci, fictional cousin of the real-life Amerigo and Machiavelli's best friend. In the romantic entanglements of his characters, as in his imaginative juxtaposition of Florence and Fatehpur Sikri, Rushdie enjambs two, historically coincident, moments of renaissance. The implicit argument is that there is no separating India and Italy – at least not according to a zero-sum calculus in which one culture's modernity determines the other's backwardness.

The novel's first section does much to advance this notion. For instance, an early scene sees an English ambassador, Lord Hauksbank of That Ilk, speak to Mogor about how, being from centre of the *Rinascimento*, he will 'know of the majesty of that highest of sovereigns, the individual human self' (*EF* p. 17). Skip forward one chapter, and we encounter Akbar, his empire at peace but his mind troubled, musing on 'the disturbing possibilities of the first person singular – the "I"' (*EF* p. 30). Europe's great discovery – the individual subject, bearer of conscience and reason and (eventually) rights – appears to be the property, too, of Islamic India.

In this way, *Enchantress* participates in the historiographical discourse that Sanjay Krishnan names 'global anti-Eurocentrism'.[12] This body of thought contests the West's traditional sense of its pre-eminence in narratives about how we became 'global' but does not undermine the sense that we do indeed live – then, as much as now – within the horizon of a single system that transcends any particular perspective on it. '*The curse of the human race*', thinks Akbar towards the end of Rushdie's book, 'is not that we are so different from one another, but that we are so alike' (*EF* p. 311; emphasis in original). The thesis that human history has a universal character, and that this historical universality might have a social and ethical expression, is one that has detained Rushdie repeatedly over the last two decades. As he asked in a 1999 newspaper column, 'Are there other universals besides international conglomerates and the interests of super-powers?' (*SAL* p. 268).[13] His answer to this question is an emphatic 'yes'.

I will return to that column later, exploring how it relates to the unspoken problem of Rushdie's and Mitchell's recent fictions – the way that, in their novels, the globalised world system is simultaneously their manifest subject and something the nature of which is left unsaid. It is the novels' overt subject because what Rushdie calls the 'new, permeable post-frontier' of globalisation is represented as both the peculiar condition of the present and the truth of human history in general (*SAL* p. 365). It is unspoken because, if the permeability of frontiers and the fact of human interconnection indeed lies behind all human endeavour, then globalisation is less a thing to be seen than a condition of seeing or thinking in general.

Mitchell's writing shows a similar mix of anti-orientalism and universalising globalism. Critics have already described Mitchell as an author whose work engages overtly with questions of globalisation.[14] At the level of setting, his novels flit all over the planet – only Africa and Antarctica are, among the continents and including outer space, not yet central to his imaginative geography. Mitchell's plots also regularly involve the tropes and technologies of transnational exchange. This might mean, as in the fourth section of *The Bone Clocks*, the way the movements of the international literary festival circuit provides a structure and occasion for the picaresque adventures of the novelist Crispin Hershey. It might also mean, as in the apocalyptic future settings of the middle two novellas of *Cloud Atlas*, imagining the systemic division of world political economy into spheres of murderous over-consumption and ecologically disastrous resource extraction.

Like Rushdie's *Enchantress*, Mitchell's settings and plots emphasise the coevality of Asia and the West, with the difference that Mitchell is more interested in Asia-Pacific than the Indian subcontinent.[15] Japan provides the setting for *number9dream* (2001) and *Jacob de Zoet*, as well the first two parts of *Ghostwritten* (1999). That novel also includes chapters set in China, Hong Kong, and Mongolia, while important parts of *Cloud Atlas* and *The Bone Clocks* take place in or otherwise draw on Korea, China, Oceania, and Hawai'i.[16] All these novels combine a sense of historical depth with imaginative geographies in which East Asia and the Pacific occupy privileged positions. This is something one can illustrate by making an obvious point about *Jacob de Zoet*. Beginning on the Dutch East India Company trading outpost of Dejima in the late eighteenth century, it tells the story of what to many readers will be an obscure moment from an obscure chapter of mercantilism; for all that obscurity, however, it reminds us that the developmental history of Japan is not merely a narrative about waves of Western influence. Its story of how two isolated and artificially separated national groups came to know and influence one another is an imaginative riposte to stereotypes of East Asian states as unchanging miniature worlds, impervious to and uninvolved in the current of modernity. '*I am Adam Smith's translator*', thinks a young Japanese scholar, Uzaemon Ogawa, '*I don't believe in omens*'.[17] The world systems theorist Giovanni Arrighi called his study of Asia's economic renaissance *Adam Smith in Beijing* (2007); here, we witness Adam Smith's eighteenth-century arrival in Nagasaki, translated into Japanese out of a Dutch edition bought in Jakarta.

We will return to Adam Smith and omens in a moment. For now, let us briefly note that, around the same time as Rushdie was editorialising on the subject of globalisation and Mitchell was waiting for *Ghostwritten* to go on sale, the academy gave birth to several new economic histories consistent with the way these novels position Asian cultures and states as coeval with Europe. One of the better-known examples is Andre Gunder Frank's *ReORIENT: Global Economy in the Asian Age* (1998). Frank is justly exercised about the false universalism of Eurocentric historiography. This does not lead him, however, to criticise globalist thinking as such. Instead, he describes a 'world economic perspective' in which 'Eurocentric social theory' is 'turned on its head' and Asia is restored to the centre of things.[18] 'The Western interpretation of its own 'Rise of the West', Frank writes,

> has suffered from a case of 'misplaced concreteness'. ... 'Development' was not so much 'of the West' as it was of and in the world economy. 'Leadership' of the world system ... has been temporarily 'centered' in one sector and region (or a few), only to shift again to one or more others. This happened in the nineteenth century, and it appears to be happening again at the beginning of the twenty-first, as the 'center' of the world economy seems to be shifting back to the 'East'.[19]

About similar passages in Frank's book and others, Krishnan remarks that the 'substitution of historical protagonists only confirms how firmly the [globalist] mode of evaluation remains in place'.[20] There is no 'Western capitalism' or 'Western modernity' here – at least, not in the sense that there exists some proprietary or necessary relationship between the adjectival and nominative parts of those phrases. There is only a world system with a somewhat mobile centre, a spatio-temporal empire of the same.

This aspect of Frank's analysis has its counterpart in *Enchantress*, which is set before the onset of what Kenneth Pomeranz, in another signature work of the new economic world history, called the 'great divergence' between Europe and Asia: the shift after 1800 or thereabouts to a 'Europe-centered world system'.[21] Set between the 1490s and the abandonment of Fatehpur Sikri in 1585, *Enchantress* predates the era of European imperialism in Asia and the final eclipse of Mughal sovereignty after 1857. By setting its historical allegory so early, *Enchantress* sidesteps the argument that globalisation represents just the newest variant of imperialism. The empires that matter in *Enchantress* are Mongol, Timurid, Mughal, and Ottoman; they are Islamic and territorially contiguous, not Christian and maritime; and they are decentred tributary empires, not projects of settler colonialism. In this same spirit, Amerigo Vespucci's voyages across the Atlantic feature in *Enchantress* – but only as a promise yet to be fulfilled. Europe's colonisation of the New World thereby becomes not the first chapter in the history of modernity but a sign of Europe's comparative under-development relative to the great Asian empires of the fifteenth and sixteenth centuries.

Mitchell's fiction approaches the question of historical coevality in a different manner but to similar effect. His most celebrated novel, *Cloud Atlas*, wraps three stories set in the twentieth-century West within past and future tales set in a vast Asia-Pacific region. The novel begins and ends with a nineteenth-century maritime tale set en route from the Chatham Islands to California; at its centre lie two post-apocalyptic narratives, one taking place in a future Korea, the other on Hawai'i. We are shown, over and again, how events in Asia-Pacific evoke the same problems of predacity and unsustainable development more usually associated with the novel's North American and European settings. This does not mean, however, that the Korea or Hawai'i sections symbolise the apotheosis of an historical logic that begins in the West. This is because the book's 'nesting doll' structure, underpinned by its theme of metempsychosis or reincarnation, militate against any sense that history has a linear direction or single destination.[22] At one point in future Korea, a quasi-messianic clone, Somni-451, declares that 'time is the speed at which the past decays'; but, in a novel in which characters are resurrected, the past can never wholly decay.[23] *Cloud Atlas* therefore generates multiple metaphors for how we might figure time's passing: 'Time, no arrow, no boomerang, but a concertina. Bedsores' (*CA* p. 354). At one point a scientist, hurtling towards a violent death he has not imagined, even sketches in his notebook the proposition that time owns a similar structure to the novel in which he appears as a character: 'an infinite matryoshka doll of painted moments, each "shell" (the present) encased inside a nest of "shells" (previous presents) I call the actual past but which we *perceive* as the virtual past' (*CA* p. 393; emphasis in original). By breaking all but one of its narrative shells in half, moving forwards into a speculative future only to reverse course and end in the epoch in which it began, *Cloud Atlas* does more than imply that modernity might have an Asian origin. Its narrative structure suggests that all beginnings and ends are matters of perspective, virtual pasts and futures that afford no culture or region the privilege of priority.

Does this mean, then, that Rushdie and Mitchell are novelists of so-called alternative modernities?[24] It does not. Justin Neuman has argued that *Enchantress of Florence* depicts a singular modernity in which Florence and Fatehpur Sikri are joined by their common expression of 'nonsecular atheism'. In this worldview, gods are not real but magic is epitomised in the transformative wonders of storytelling.[25] *Enchantress* therefore contains an imaginative history in which Islam is exemplified not by the frightened singularities of *The Satanic Verses*' exiled Imam ('The Imam is a massive stillness, an immobility. He is living stone') but by Akbar's famous tolerance and syncretism.[26] Akbar's historical example allows Rushdie to imagine a form of belief committed to the proposition that 'difference existed' – a faithless faith that might allow a believer to wonder, as Akbar does, whether 'discord, disagreement, irreverence, iconoclasm, impudence, even insolence might be the wellsprings of the good' (*EF* p. 310). In the history of the Mughal Empire, Rushdie locates an answer to his own post-9/11 challenge to 'the world of Islam' to 'take on board the secularist-humanist principles on which the modern is based' (*SAL* p. 341).[27] What's more, he locates that answer not in some future reformation movement, but in the century that Martin Luther posted his Ninety-Five Theses on the door of Wittenberg's Castle Church.

The implication is that, far from representing the anti-modern side of an historic clash of civilizations, the 'world of Islam' contains the seeds of its own secularisation; it is just another pole in a single, if uneven, global system. Without a second step, however, *Enchantress'* anti-Orientalist globalism would be compromised by the fact, ruminated upon in its final chapter, that Akbar's pluralism did not long survive his death: 'In the future, it was harshness, not civilization, that would rule' (*EF* p. 347). This is why Rushdie's celebration of Akbar's liberalism has to be matched by the re-enchantment of the supposedly secular West. When the narrative gets to Florence we read a second story about the growth of the 'sovereign individual', this time emerging not out of Akbar's philosophic meditations but from the Medicis' violent realpolitik (*EF* p. 238). This story is followed, however, by the Florentine Republic's subsequent re-enchantment by Qara Köz, whose charismatic presence mists the air 'with a benevolent haze which filled the thoughts of Florentines with images of parental, filial, carnal, and divine love' (*EF* p. 278). Such moments are common in Rushdie's novels – recall, for instance, the way that *The Satanic Verses'* Gibreel Farishta transforms rainy London into a subtropical city. Still, the point is not just that the West is capable of magical transformation; it is that, as Rushdie sees it, the very DNA of secular modernity is anything but routine or routinising. When he argues, for instance, in favour of Darwinian evolutionary theory, Rushdie has recourse to one of his favourite metaphors of secular magic: Frank Baum's land of Oz and the unreal, but never quite ersatz, magic of its presiding wizard: 'If the over-abundant new knowledge of the modern age is, let's say, a tornado, then Oz is the extraordinary, Technicolor new world in which it has landed us, the world from which – life not being a movie – there is no way home' (*SAL* p. 282). This is what Rushdie's character Shalimar the clown learns in the novel to which he gives his name: 'The universe was everything at once, science and sorcery, what was occult and what was known'.[28]

Back now to omens, Adam Smith, and a similar elision of the occult and the known. Some reviewers hailed *The Thousand Autumns of Jacob de Zoet* as a stylistic shift on Mitchell's part – from genre-bending experimentalism to earnest historical fiction.[29] It is true that *Jacob de Zoet* lacks the structural complexity of *Ghostwritten*; it is also fair to say that much of it more closely resembles an historical novel by Hilary Mantel than a generic confabulation such as *Cloud Atlas*. Yet this contrast is easily overstated. At the centre of *Jacob de Zoet* lies not historical realism but gothic romance – a melodramatic interstitial tale in which Uzaemon, our Japanese translator of *The Wealth of Nations*, leads a band of masterless samurai on a doomed attempt to rescue a scarred beauty, Orito Aibagawa, from a mountain fastness. Locked in a walled shrine, Orito (a midwife who, like Uzaemon, symbolizes Japanese rationalism and openness to the West) is the prisoner of Abbot Enomoto, a feudal landowner who believes that he can achieve immortality by harvesting the souls of babies. The narrative resulting from this generic mash-up is not, as Dave Eggers described it, 'a straight-up, linear, third-person historical novel'.[30] *Jacob de Zoet* possesses a hybrid generic status in which historical realism is haunted by a hallucinatory tale reminiscent of the interpolated dream visions that punctuate the main narrative of Haruki Murakami's *The Wind-Up Bird Chronicle* (1994–5).

Nor is this just a matter of genre. While the Abbot is defeated by the novel's close, he is hardly an obscurantist; after all, he values Orito precisely because her European-derived obstetric skill benefits the nuns who provide him with sacrifices. He dies insisting 'the creeds *work*. ... Oil of souls *works!*' (*JZ* 460; emphasis in original). And nobody contradicts him. *Jacob de Zoet* cannot be read as a teleological tale about the victory of enlightenment over unreason, a stage on Japan's road to modernity. As with Rushdie's enchantment of the Italian renaissance, *Jacob de Zoet* maintains a minimal ontological difference between illusion and reality, secular facts and occult mysteries, but tends otherwise to erase the border between such oppositions – just as it obliterates distinctions between stereotyped versions of Eastern backwardness or Western historical priority. Both novels split the difference between antitheses, insisting that the truth lies, not on either side of those binaries, but in the fact of their constant collapsing and fusing into one another. 'How does newness enter the world?', Rushdie asked, notoriously, in *Satanic Verses*; 'Of what fusions, translations, conjoinings is it made?' (*SV* p. 8). The answer is all of them – and one.

To return to Krishnan's terms, these are novels that, for all their brilliant complexity, affirm the epistemological power of the 'unilinear character of the global'.[31] This is the condition in which the very idea of a universal system or experience loses the status of an empirically testable claim: the hypothesis, for example, that there are (or are not) similar values that link Tuscany and Uttar Pradesh or underwrite historical realism and occult romance. Such propositions lose their empirical status because they are no longer claims about the present or the past but about 'the condition of correct or adequate representation' of the world.[32] This is one of the reasons why, for Rushdie, a particularist ideology such as cultural nationalism always represents a 'trap' – a way of not-seeing, of failing to understand how the things we try to keep separate always and inevitably merge (*SAL* p. 151).

There is a tension, however, in maintaining this globalist double perspective. Consider Rushdie's newspaper column – quoted from earlier – that contests the thesis that globalisation is just another word for creeping cultural homogenisation on an American model. The key part of the argument begins with a trope familiar to Rushdie's regular readers:

> Is not mélange, adulteration, impurity, pick 'n' mix at the heart of the idea of the modern, and hasn't it been that way for most of this all-shook-up century? Doesn't the idea of pure cultures … lead us inexorably toward apartheid, toward ethnic cleansing, toward the gas chamber? Or, to put it another way: are there other universals besides international conglomerates and the interests of super-powers? And if by chance there were a universal value that might, for the sake of argument, be called freedom, whose enemies – tyranny, bigotry, intolerance, fanaticism – were the enemies of us all; and if this 'freedom' were discovered to exist in greater quantities in the countries of the West than anywhere else on earth; and if in the world as it actually exists, rather than in some unattainable Utopia, the authority of the United States were the best current guarantor of that 'freedom'; then might it not follow that to oppose the spread of American culture would be to take up arms against the wrong foe? (*SAL* pp. 268–9)

Setting aside the political implications of this passage, note how Rushdie's argument about globalisation becomes, via an association between the contingencies of American power and the twentieth century's 'pick 'n' mix' culture, a defence of universal liberal values. That is, his argument presumes the equivalence of the contingent historical fact of globalisation and the moral truths enshrined in a word such as 'freedom'. Because they are universal, the liberal values advanced by Rushdie necessarily exceed any particular space or time: his conception of 'freedom', appears to mean the same, in basic terms, to fourteenth-century Mughals as to contemporary Americans, to men in Hay-on-Wye as to women in Afghanistan. Because they are universal, no state (not even the United States) can live up to such ideas at all times – that is why, elsewhere in the essay, Rushdie is careful to reference U.S. foreign policy errors in Sudan and Iraq (*SAL* p. 269). Nevertheless, Rushdie not only associates the language of liberal universalism with U.S. power but identifies both with the 'idea of the modern' (*SAL* p. 268). Globalisation is figured here as the geopolitical instantiation of universal liberal and cosmopolitan values. It names a political-economic system in which cultural mélange is the ethical sprit of all the world's pasts and futures. Thinking globally is less a matter of keeping 'our eyes on the prize', as Rushdie has it, than of being able to think at all (*SAL* p. 269).

For all this, Rushdie is not naïve about the prospects for freedom on a 'pick 'n' mix' model. He may believe that 'in our deepest natures, we are frontier-crossing beings', but he also knows that 'at the frontier our liberty is stripped away' (*SAL* pp. 350, 354). This is the subject, among other things, of *Shalimar the Clown* (2005), in which the Indo-Pakistani conflict over Kashmir is mapped onto a broader geopolitical story. The key character here is Max Ophuls, a Jewish Alsacienne who escapes from World War II, marries a great Kashmiri beauty, and becomes one of 'the architects of the postwar world' (*SC* p. 7). Max helps systematise and expand U.S. power during the Cold War and sets the groundwork for the expansion of neoliberal capitalism afterwards. But he is also that system's victim. He helps bring into being the illusion that capitalism and liberal democracy might spread everywhere and go on forever – and when he starts to really believe in this fantasy, a clown cuts his throat.

This irony is built into *Shalimar*'s first chapter, one of two sections set in the final decade of the twentieth century that together bookend a story that takes us from WWII to the years just after the Cold War. Chapter one begins with Max's 1990 birthday visit to his impossibly lovely daughter, India, and ends with his murder. Along the way, India recalls Max's lectures about the nature of liberty: 'Do not enter the labyrinth as a supplicant. Come with meat and a sword. ... Freedom is not a tea party, India. Freedom is a war' (*SC* p. 17). In keeping with his aphoristic manner, Max is repeatedly described as a world-historical figure, a man out of Machiavelli's *The Prince*: 'Max, the Resistance hero, the philosopher prince, the billionaire power-broker, the maker of the world!' (*SC* p. 27). The novel's first chapter even looks forward to the moment in which we learn of young Max's appointment to the 1944 Bretton Woods Conference, birthplace of the key economic institutions of postwar globalisation: the International Monetary Fund and the International Bank for Reconstruction and Development, later renamed the World Bank.

Still, among these tributes and foreshadowings, chapter one also makes clear that Max has stumbled. India becomes newly aware that her father is an old man, prone to statements such as ' "my time is being swept away" ' (*SC* p. 19). The bigger problem is that, like a Francis Fukuyama with actual government experience, Max has surrendered 'to the utopian fallacy, to the myth of the perfectibility of man' and to the possibility of a 'world without walls, a frontierless newfound land of infinite possibility' (*SC* p. 20). In this respect, India knows better than her father. She remembers Max's own lesson about the temporality of violence: the collision that made the

Himalayas, when the landmass that became India smashed into the giant plate of Asia, '*is still happening*' (*SC* p. 20; emphasis in original).

One cannot, then, accuse Rushdie of ignoring the violence and unevenness of the global order his 1999 essay defends, even if he asserts that 'globalization isn't itself the problem; the inequitable distribution of global resources is' (*SAL* p. 269).[33] His novels dramatise how 'the new permeability of the frontier' creates disruptive new points of contact between people, only some of whom share his cosmopolitan values (*SAL* p. 366). But none of this affects his commitment to the global as both the signature fact of our present age and the condition of properly historical thought.

This is, again, an aspect of the Max Ophuls story. As a young economist, Max predicted the economic rise of Brazil, India, and China. He also coins the notion of 'South-South collaboration ... a theoretical model of how Third World economies might flourish by learning to bypass the U.S. dollar' (*SC* p. 178). At the end of his life, Max sees these academic interventions as his enduring success. Although he has spent decades as an agent of American power, Max cherishes the hope that nations such as India 'would be the world's new powerhouses, the counter-weights to the emerging hegemony of which he had always, as an internationalist, disapproved' (*SC* p. 20). And from the perspective of an economic historian such as Frank or Pomeranz, Max is correct. This is not just because of the prominence, in news reports and balance sheets over recent years, of the so-called BRIC axis (Brazil, Russia, India, China) of developing economies from outside the traditional capitalist core – the fact of which Max's prophecy is clearly supposed to evoke.[34] It is because, for historians such as Pomeranz and Arrighi, the 'great divergence' between Europe and Asia was far from inevitable; in fact, it represented an anomalous 'rupture' within the normal historic patterns of world economic development.[35] It is in this sense, and despite being written first, that a novel such as *Shalimar* brings up to date the historical narrative that *Enchantress* begins. In its focus on the transition between the Cold War and what comes after, it signals the re-emergence of the multi-polar global age that obtained in the age of Akbar the Great. Taken together, the two novels bookend Rushdie's fictional long history of the global.

Rushdie's often-controversial political attitudes emerge directly from his anti-Orientalist globalism. It is harder to say the same about Mitchell, who is less outspoken as a public intellectual and whose novels, while they protest problems such as environmental depredation and corporate greed, lack the polemical qualities central to Rushdie's. In fact, the reception of Mitchell's latest novel, *The Bone Clocks*, suggests that the globalist tension between historical contingency and ethical universalism affects his fiction in a precisely opposite way – that is, not through the production of political controversy but through a kind of generalised vagueness. In his account of *The Bone Clocks*, Brian Finney describes Mitchell as 'the preeminent novelist of globalism, not because his books take readers across the world, but because he creates characters that are simultaneously unique and yet interchangeable, just as his locations are specific yet share features … that are indistinguishable'.[36] Finney means this as a compliment, but his praise weirdly evokes James Wood's critique of *The Bone Clocks* for the way it builds to a fantastic conclusion in which the quiddities of human character and action become negligible. There is something increasingly troubling about Mitchell's brand of novelist maximalism, in which characters, locations, genres, and even basic ontological assumptions are interchangeable. 'Both the book's exuberant impossibilities and its restlessly proliferating realities have a way of refocussing one's suspicions of his earlier work', Wood complains about *The Bone Clocks*: 'Mitchell has plenty to tell, but does he have much to say?'[37] It is a fair question. It is not that Mitchell's novels lack any point of resistance or awareness of incommensurable difference, just that those sticking points tend to the bromidic: it is better to be kind than predatory; sustainable worlds are better than those that eat themselves; our capacity to love is valuable because we are fickle and unfaithful, not despite those vulnerabilities. These are unimpeachable but unexacting themes. As Mitchell's narrative universe expands inexorably (he has apparently planned his next five volumes), the principles of interconnection and exchangeability that unite his oeuvre tend to produce an emptiness only just buoyed up by his remarkable talents as a stylist and storyteller.

Wood's complaint about *The Bone Clocks* depends on a somewhat schematic opposition between the 'theological allegory' of the epic and the 'secular novel'.[38] In concluding this chapter, it is therefore worth considering how these globalist fictions are neither creative imitations of academic history nor epic perversions of some novelistic secular mission. They are, instead, versions of romance – a term I use in the sense developed by John A. McClure, who describes an imaginative prose genre caught between the idea of a world system and the desire that such a world might sustain pockets of disorder in which to experience 'wanderings and disorientations', quests and conquests.[39] For McClure, this ambivalence means that romance is basically, if imperfectly, hostile to a phenomenon such as globalisation, with its implicit systematisation of the variety of human experience. This is the contradiction that Rushdie's and Mitchell's globalist style attempts to resolve. If evolutionary biology is a species of sorcery – if the surprise common to gothic history and science fiction is that we are basically similar and always were – then there is no need to fear that the reduction of a heterogeneous planet to a unitary globe signifies the end of mystery, anarchy, or desire. Even though the novels analysed in this chapter are committed to the unitary logic of the global, they nevertheless celebrate the power of fantasy and the moral authority of the iconoclast. This theme is given great emphasis in *Shalimar*'s conclusion. Although that novel imagines and mourns the gradual collapse of Kashmiri people's belief in their secular paradise, it ends with India Ophuls's successful defense of her home against Shalimar, who has escaped from prison in order to complete his revenge. India is every bit the fairy-tale princess-turned-warrior, able to slay the bogeyman who murdered her parents. Romance survives, if only in one corner of the world. The novel's final lines drive home the point, alluding to India's recent decision to adopt the name given to her by her dead mother: 'There was no second chance. There was no India. There was only Kashmira, and Shalimar the clown' (*SC* p. 398). If Kashmir cannot survive geopolitical strife, then at least Kashmira can.

Rushdie spoke many years ago about the 'connection of history and story. .... The Italian word *storia* means both things; the Urdu word *qissa* means a tale and it means history'. The millennial turn, he suggested, ought to be grasped as 'a time for synthesis' between the story of the tale and the story of history proper.[40] For all that, the encounter between historical fact and novelistic 'luxury' is not a meeting between equals: in these novels, the transformative power of fiction holds the whip hand. The key synthesis of the globalist novel does not lie in the way it erases – in a manner familiar from decades of magical realist writing – the distinction between historical fact and literary fiction. It inheres in the attempt to find aesthetic common ground between the nonsecular magic of novelistic style and the levelling notion of a world system. Because the imaginative geography of such novels encompasses the whole world, and centuries of human history, they open up to a dazzling array of characters, idioms, and shaggy dog stories. They make room for a novel of globalisation that includes Dutch merchants as well as sentient clones, runaway princesses as well as fugitive clowns. The result is a globalist style that is open to anything except the proposition that there might be limits to such openness. When writing the long history of globalisation means writing the history of everything, are we still thinking historically at all?

NOTES

1 Peter Osborne, *Anywhere or Not at All: Philosophy of Contemporary Art* (London: Verso, 2013), p. 26.
2 Gayatri Spivak, *Death of a Disciple* (New York: Columbia University Press, 2003), p. 72.
3 Manfred B. Steger, 'Globalization and Ideology', in *The Blackwell Companion to Globalization*, ed. George Ritzer (Oxford: Blackwell Publishing, 2007), p. 369.

4 Rita Barnard, 'Fictions of the Global', *NOVEL: A Forum on Fiction* 42.2 (2009), p. 211.

5 Kathryn Schulz, 'Boundaries Are Conventions. And *The Bone Clocks* Author David Mitchell Transcends Them All', *New York Magazine*, 21 August 2014. Retrieved from http://www.vulture.com/2014/08/david-mitchell-interview-bone-clocks-cloud-atlas.html. Accessed 14 January 2015. One might quibble with these numbers – not just because, as Schulz admits, her table is 'surely incomplete' (it omits, e.g., Timothy Cavendish's cameo in *The Bone Clocks*) but because it doesn't account for the trope of reincarnation in *Cloud Atlas*, in which Cavendish is indubitably himself *and* the reincarnation of Luisa Rey and the novel's other four protagonists. Should Cavendish and Rey be counted as two characters, then, or one?

6 Pieter Vermeulen, 'David Mitchell's *Ghostwritten* and the "Novel of Globalization": Biopower and the Secret History of the Novel', *Critique: Studies in Contemporary Fiction* 53.4 (2012): 383.

7 Schulz, 'Boundaries Are Conventions'.

8 David Mitchell, 'Playing with Structure'. This essay, originally a creative writing tutorial on the BBC website, is now available via the Internet Archive Wayback Machine. Retrieved from http://web.archive.org/web/20080301101136/http://www.bbc.co.uk/dna/getwriting/module15p. Accessed 25 February 2015.

9 Naresh Fernandes, 'Salman Rushdie on *The Enchantress of Florence*', *Time Out London*, 21 April 2008. Retrieved from http://www.timeout.com/london/books/salman-rushdie-on-a-the-enchantress-of-florencea. Accessed 16 July 2013.

10 Andrew Anthony, 'The Bookers' Favourite', *The Observer*, 5 April 2008. Retrieved from www.guardian.co.uk/books/2008/apr/06/classics.salmanrushdie. Accessed 3 April 2013.

11 Salman Rushdie, *The Enchantress of Florence* (New York: Random House, 2008), 324. Hereafter cited parenthetically as *EF*.

12 Sanjay Krishnan, *Reading the Global: Troubling Perspectives on Britain's Empire in Asia* (New York: Columbia University Press, 2007), pp. 6–11.

13 Salman Rushdie, *Step Across this Line: Collected Nonfiction 1992–2002* (New York: The Modern Library, 2003), p. 268. Hereafter cited parenthetically as *SAL*.

14 See, e.g., Peter Childs and James Green, 'The Novel in Nine Parts', in *David Mitchell: Critical Essays,* ed. Sarah Dillon (Canterbury: Glyphi Limited, 2011), pp. 25–27; Berthold Schoene, *The Cosmopolitan Novel* (Edinburgh: Edinburgh UP, 2009), pp. 97–126.

15 This difference is attributable to biography. Just as Rushdie has ancestral ties to the subcontinent, so did Mitchell live for eight years in Japan – the country where he met his wife, Keiko Yoshida, with whom he translated Naoki Higashida's memoir, *The Reason I Jump* (2013).

16 Only *Black Swan Green* (2006), with its English regional setting, is the exception here. Still, given its connections at the level of character to *Cloud Atlas* and *The Bone Clocks*, it clearly forms part of Mitchell's wider narrative world.

17 David Mitchell, *The Thousand Autumns of Jacob de Zoet* (New York: Random House, 2010), p. 291; emphasis in original. Hereafter cited parenthetically as *JZ*.

18 Andre Gunder Frank, *ReORIENT: Global Economy in the Asian Age* (Berkeley: University of California Press, 1998), p. 51.

19 Frank, *ReORIENT*, p. 7.

20 Krishnan, *Reading the Global*, p. 8.

21 Kenneth W. Pomeranz, *The Great Divergence: China, Europe, and the Making of the Modern World Economy* (Princeton: Princeton UP, 2000), p. 4.

22 To explain: *Cloud Atlas* comprises six novellas linked by theme, by the way the protagonist of each story somehow knows or discovers the narrative of the previous section, and by the implication (materialised in a shared birthmark) that the six protagonists represent the reincarnation of a single person. The first five sections are interrupted at mid-point; only the sixth or middle section is unbroken. After the sixth novella, the interrupted chapters conclude in reverse order, such that the novel ends with the completion of its first part.

23 David Mitchell, *Cloud Atlas* (New York: Random House, 2004), p. 235. Hereafter cited parenthetically as *CA*.

24 For this concept, see Dilip Parameshwar Gaonkar, ed., *Alternative Modernities* (Durham: Duke University Press, 2001).

25 Justin Neuman, 'The Fictive Origins of Secular Humanism', *Criticism* 50.4 (2008), p. 682.

26 Salman Rushdie, *The Satanic Verses* (New York: Random House, 2008), p. 214. Hereafter cited parenthetically as *SV*.

27 Rushdie has addressed the co-presence, within the history of Islam, of puritanical and syncretic strains: 'For every Akbar there's an Aurangzeb. ... To use an absurd "Star Wars" comparison, Akbar is Obi Wan Kenobi and Aurangzeb is Darth Vader'. Still, he emphasises that *Enchantress* is set when 'Indian Islam developed its much more open, multiple, pluralistic philosophy which embraced and was affected by the other older belief systems of India' (Fernandes).

28 Salman Rushdie, *Shalimar the Clown* (New York: Random House, 2006), p. 51. Hereafter cited parenthetically as *SC*.

29 See, e.g., Ron Charles, 'Book Review of "The Thousand Autumns of Jacob de Zoet", a Novel by David Mitchell', *Washington Post*, 30 June 2010. Retrieved from http://www.washingtonpost.com/wp-dyn/content/article/2010/06/29/AR2010062904512.html. Accessed 27 February 2015.

30 Dave Eggers, 'Empire of Desire', *New York Times*, 4 July 2010, BR1. Any sense that *Jacob de Zoet* diverges from the main track of Mitchell's fiction is weakened further by the way that its occult *divertissement* expands in *The Bone Clocks*, where it provides the backbone for the novel's entire plotline about a war between two sets of immortals, one benignly reincarnated, the other vampiric and predatory.

31 Krishnan, *Reading the Global*, p. 5.

32 Krishnan, *Reading the Global*, p. 13.

33 Rushdie repeats a version of this line in his Tanner Lectures, attributing it to Amartya Sen: 'The problem is not globalization. The problem is a fair distribution of resources in a globalized world' (*SAL* 356). The obvious objection here is that economic globalisation depends structurally on the unequal distribution of resources – e.g., in multinational corporations' well-known exploitation of wage differentials between nations. Moreover, neoliberal globalisation exacerbates such inequalities, the reason being that the economic liberalisation policies pursued by institutions such as the IMF tend to reduce minimum wages and weaken employment laws and protections. For a non-polemical account of

these problems, see United Nations Department of Economic and Social Affairs, *The Inequality Predicament: Report on the World Situation* (New York: United Nations, 2005), pp. 105–12.

34 Of the BRIC group of nations, only Russia is missing from Max's early prediction. This absence is explained by the Cold War context of Max's academic research, in which nobody much counted on the capitalist future of the Soviet Union. Since 2010, South Africa has been included in the bloc, leading to the use of the modified acronym, BRICS.

35 Pomeranz, *The Great Divergence*, p. 8.

36 Brian Finney, 'Adding to the Übernovel: Why David Mitchell Does What He Does', *Los Angeles Review of Books* (28 September 2014). Retrieved from http://lareviewofbooks.org/review/adding-ubernovel-david-mitchell. Accessed 28 February 2015.

37 James Wood, 'Soul Cycle: David Mitchell's *The Bone Clocks*', The New Yorker (8 September 2014). Retrieved from http://www.newyorker.com/magazine/2014/09/08/soul-cycle. Accessed 1 February 2015.

38 Wood, 'Soul Cycle'.

39 John A. McClure, *Late Imperial Romance* (London: Verso, 1994), p. 3.

40 Salman Rushdie, Interview with David Brooks (1984), in *Conversations with Salman Rushdie*, ed. Michael R. Reder (Jackson: University Press of Mississippi, 2000), p. 69.

14

WEIHSIN GUI

Transnational Forms in British Fiction

'The form found me' is Bernardine Evaristo's almost apologetic response when asked why she wrote two of her novels in verse. Rather than pitting rhythmic poetry against narrative prose, underlying Evaristo's combination is an understanding that 'accessible writing need not be simplistic or any less sophisticated than more obscure, denser work ... there are depths, references and allusions to plummet'.[1] Writing shortly after 9/11, Martin Amis defends the novel as an imaginative counterpoint to terror and fanaticism: they create 'worlds' that 'aspire to pattern and shape and moral point' and should be seen as 'a rational undertaking; it is reason at play, perhaps, but it is still reason'.[2] For both Evaristo and Amis, fictional form has a tangible, almost tactile, presence extending beyond an individual writer's style or a particular novel's genre. Form may be a creature of reason but it also seems to have a mind of its own, playing with and shaping words into patterns of deep meaning and pointed reason within imaginary worlds close enough but not entirely conforming to ours.

The very term 'form' is highly ambiguous yet seemingly indispensable; it 'suggests in itself something of the very multi-dimensionality, the unsettled busyness, of the artwork'.[3] In Raymond Williams's social theory of literature, form extends beyond genre, because 'the problem of form is a problem of the relations between social (collective) modes and individual projects', with these relations being 'necessarily variable'.[4] Genre may thus be understood as a set of relations between varying conventions and types existing within and across different texts, whereas form sets up a variable relationship between a text, which may be a mixture of different genres, and the social and material world. Form deploys genres such as the epic or satire to provoke 'the activation of specific relations' between human subjects and between humans and 'things' of the non-human world (p. 190). By 'concentrat[ing] on language or form' as a setting to work of the text in relation to the world, one arrives at 'an intense and irreplaceable experience in which these fundamental elements of human experience are directly stimulated, reinforced, or extended' (p. 156).

Williams further elaborates on form through the idea of *stance*, 'a mode of basic (social) organization which determines a particular kind of presentation' such as 'the telling of a story' or 'the presentation of an action through characters' (p. 183). Stance is both a mode of fictional organization and a kind of rhetorical address, a crucial component of argumentative (as distinct from narrative or dramatic) writing. Indeed, the term 'form' when used in martial arts sometimes names a particular set or combination of defensive or attacking techniques; this illustrates how form connects the different stances, movements, and flourishes of literary genres and writerly styles into firm yet fluid responses to the actions of one's sparring partner or opponent, a relational, dynamic, and 'constantly interactive' process (p. 187). Form is tangible through the 'formative moment[s]' that bring about 'precise material articulations' (p. 191) between a literary text's 'expressive significance' and the global moment within which a text is written and read (p. 167). The idea of a global moment 'connote[s] a spatial and temporal conjunction' because 'a moment is both a rotational force' – hence the word "momentum" – 'as well as an instant in time', and is distinguished from common understandings of globalisation as transnational financial, cultural, and demographic flows taking place since the 1970s. In keeping with the tangible, forceful understanding of form developed earlier, this chapter focuses on the encounters between fiction's formative moments and the 'sweeping force field of narratives of cultural and economic globalization' that make up the post-1945 world order.[5]

Other critics have delineated contemporary British fiction in terms of tensions between realism and other seemingly experimental modes of writing,[6] a profound amalgamation of postcolonialism, feminism, and postmodernism, and post-imperial representations of historical myth, urban life, and multicultural hybridity in contemporary Britain.[7] This chapter takes a different tack by treating the genres, theories, themes, and topoi discussed in the body of criticism above as well as in other essays in this collection as constitutive elements of a literary text's formative moments and movements. Taken together, Evaristo, Amis, and Williams encourage us not so much to read for form but rather to *perform* reading and enact interpretation, a process of plummeting that falls into the depths of fiction, that measures how fiction's play of references and allusions patterns and shapes the worlds it inhabits and imagines, that articulates the expressive significance of the text along, against, or athwart the momentum of the global moment.

What follows is an examination of several British authors and their fiction through two forms: post-imperial recognition and historical remapping. These forms articulate existing genres with the socio-political situation of the authors and texts rather than treating genres as transcendent categories or socio-political issues as thematic foci. So, rather than asking how a particular author or novel does or does not fit well with a specific genre, or to what extent a specific social topic or political question is thematised in a fictional work, we might ask: How does the play of a certain genre with other genres and elements, both within and without the text, enable a kind of reading and interpretation that constitutes a formative moment? The writers and their fiction grouped under each of these formal terms are intended to be contrapuntally illustrative, rather than categorically exclusive or exhaustive. Any given text considered under one form might shade into another; my intent is to offer contrasting ways in which these forms play out, and they might also play out differently in the work of many other contemporary British writers not discussed here.

Post-Imperial Recognition

As critics such as Gayatri Chakravorty Spivak and Simon Gikandi point out, it is impossible to understand arts and letters during the heyday of British imperialism without acknowledging the shaping presence of its colonies. With the gradual end of empire after World War II, British writers who were overseas and writers from the (post)colonies who had journeyed to Britain responded by recognising the shifting order of things, not only identifying the profound changes taking place in the power relationships between coloniser and colonised but also realising these changes through the style and subject of their prose. In line with Spivak's tracing of empire's civilising project as 'a tangent that escapes the closed circle of the *narrative* conclusion' in *Jane Eyre*, one may track a formative moment of post-imperial recognition that sweeps back against the shrinking boundaries of Empire's decline.[8]

Anthony Burgess, better known for *A Clockwork Orange*, wrote an early trilogy of novels from 1954 to 1957 while he worked as an English teacher for the British colonial service in Malaya. Published together as *A Long Day Wanes*, they depict a country on the cusp of national independence and in the throes of a politico-military action against communist insurgents. Narrated in a third-person voice of wry detachment, the novels combine realistic details of everyday life in colonial Malaya with the travails of Victor Crabbe, a thirty-five year-old Englishman, who as the trilogy progresses rises from fresh-faced history teacher to school headmaster to regional education officer handing the reins over to his nationalist Malay successor. The rise of Crabbe's career is matched by the ebb in his personal life: while Crabbe craves a fresh start in the 'warmth of Malaya' with his second wife Fenella, their marriage collapses.[9] Crabbe then discovers from another British colonial officer that his first, deceased wife, whose memory he cherishes dearly, had an affair. Stung in his heart by his dead wife's infidelity and stung in his foot by a scorpion, the wounded Crabbe falls and drowns ignobly in a river.

With its colourful descriptions and multitudinous cast, Burgess's trilogy demonstrates an ethnographic impulse that gets stronger even as the British Empire grows weaker: 'Here a little work in the paddy-fields suffices to maintain a heliotropic, pullulating subsistence. ... The towns echo with trishaw-bells, the horns of smooth, smug American cars, radios blaring sentimental pentatonic Chinese tunes, the morning hawking and spitting of the *towkays*, the call of the East' (p. 29). The flood of sensory impressions culminates in a vulgar 'hawking and spitting' of local shop owners, undermining the romantic notion encapsulated in the clichéd 'call of the East'. This foreshadows the fate of Victor Crabbe, who holds a similarly romantic ideal. Filled with 'love' for Malaya and 'feel[ing] protective towards it', Crabbe regards his pedagogical presence in Malaya as 'prefigured and ordained by history' (pp. 54, 49). Paradoxically, because of such grand historical notions of *noblesse oblige*, Crabbe 'has no stake in this country' emerging out of a British colony, and thus believes he 'can really help' prepare the different peoples of Malaya for national independence (p. 375).

But Crabbe's bathetic and watery demise signals that Burgess's trilogy is also satirising stories of colonial exploits and tales of imperial exhaustion. Instead of exotic adventure or tropical horror, 'the romantic dream [Crabbe] had entertained ... was no longer appropriate' because 'the whole East was awake, building dams and canals, power-houses and car factories, forming committees, drawing up constitutions' (p. 295). While recognising that he and his compatriots have outstayed their welcome as 'a sort of Malayan unity' takes shape in his classroom and in society at large against 'British injustice' (pp. 33, 46), Crabbe also identifies important cultural attributes and aesthetic practices among the people of Malaya he fears will diminish with the coming of a new, technocratic national government. He is delighted that a young composer has written music expressing 'a national image' of Malaya, 'a genuine synthesis of Malayan elements' (p. 366) and encourages him to get his symphony recorded. An attractive Chinese girl singing a 'pure simple melodic line' convinces Crabbe that Malayans are 'civilized' and that 'this was perhaps the only country in the world for any man who cared about history' (p. 422). Crabbe's fears that Malaya's 'incredible, head-reeling collocation of cultures' will suffer from the 'cold, purely legal unification provided by the State' apparatus of the new nation is echoed by

Burgess himself (pp. 433, 398). While paying lip service to the pomp and circumstance of British colonialism with 'deliberate self-mockery', Burgess nonetheless admits that 'this colonial order [is] itself a kind of work of art', even musing that 'the literary talent and the colonizing talent are cognate in that they both forge an image of unity in a world split like an abscess'.[10] Both Burgess the author and Crabbe the protagonist are engaged in a kind of salvage ethnography, trying to recognise, identify, and describe local cultural traditions and artistic practices with an anthropologist's eye and a colonialist's pen by the fading light of an imperial sunset.

Contemporaneous with *A Long Day Wanes*, Lee Kok Liang's semi-autobiographical *London Does Not Belong To Me* reverses Burgess's ethnographic gaze with its first-person narrator sojourning in the imperial metropolis. Written in the 1950s but unpublished until 2003, the novel's narrator, a student from a tropical colonial country, spends his last days in London before returning home, socialising with a group of white expatriates from Australia, Ireland, and France as well as a gay and disaffected Englishman who is disgusted by the state of Britain. The narrator is smitten by an Australian woman named Cordelia, who disappears mysteriously shortly after they meet. He then begins a rocky romance with her friend Beatrice, another Australian, hoping that she will lead him to Cordelia, but to no avail. Frustrated and displaced, the narrator finally bids farewell to London at the train station where Tristram, the gay Englishman, gives him a copy of Norman Collins's *London Belongs to Me* as a souvenir, hence the ironic title of Lee's own book.

Lee paints a portrait of London that undermines its cultural and political position as the civilising centre of the British empire. The narrator notes as the novel begins that 'London was full of rooms' where he 'lived the life of a troglodyte, learning the tribal customs of feints and apologies'.[11] Lee's London is a claustrophobic and enervating underworld that is crepuscular on the surface, for 'the darkness had settled over the houses and streets, washing the air with a dampness peculiar to London. ... The roof-tops had the appearance of a vast pincushion with all those TV antennae sticking up in the dull sky' (p. 106). The narrator finally concludes that 'London life was so abrasive' that 'the human mind locked up in its loneliness ground away emotions' until 'self-interest was the genuine touchstone of everyone's action' (p. 229). The cold, technocratic grip of modernity that Crabbe feared would rob Malaya of its cultural vitality has already taken hold of London itself.

The novel is replete with relationships that lack reciprocation as characters converse and copulate with each other yet remain estranged and aloof, such as the narrator's torrid romance with Cordelia. Cordelia is 'a secret toy which [he] hid from the whole world' (p. 112), while she wishes she could make him 'younger and younger until [he] became a baby', for 'only then could she feel satisfied' (p. 237). The narrator recognises the colonialist and racist discrimination he faces as someone who is 'small, taut, dark' and 'absolutely passive' (pp. 69, 15), and eventually recognises the impossibility of being treated as an equal on the Empire's terms. Even the most progressive organisation in the novel, the 'League of the Coloured People', is led by the self-loathing Tristram, whose affected 'mannerisms' during their deliberations make them 'so comical that [the narrator] could have laughed' in derision (pp. 143, 144).

But what makes *London Does Not Belong to Me* more than a story of anti-colonial resistance is the narrator's movement away from defining himself in opposition to England and empire toward a recognition of other avenues of self-formation. While at the start the English language seems like 'a loose string of beads' (p. 26), the narrator realises that this linguistic 'unfamiliarity and strangeness' causes him to 'be slow, manoeuvring for words' (p. 99). This slowness confers an unlikely advantage: it 'gave [him] time to absorb the shocks' of social interaction and racial discrimination and also 'time to devise a roundabout way of expressing [himself]' (p. 99). The narrator's verbal resilience contrasts with the equally circular elocution of Tristram, the Englishman, whose language 'go[es] around in a circle' while 'building a brittle shell where all his precious ideas remain hidden' (p. 131). Lee's narrator concludes the novel by becoming 'a tangent that escapes the closed circle' of London and all that it represents,[12] as he sits on a train that 'moved swiftly' and soundlessly away from the seat of empire (p. 287). The narrator no longer needs to respond to Tristram's evasive eloquence by striving for directness and clarity; instead, he recognises that self-expression can come through literature written with 'curved words like stones' (p. 136).

Britain's national self-expression hinges upon a legacy of colonialism and slavery interrogated by David Dabydeen, whose fiction tracks the outward and inward movement of colonial culture and attitudes across the Atlantic. Dabydeen's *Disappearance* (1993) is narrated by a nameless Afro-Guyanese engineer supervising the reinforcement of a sea wall for a coastal English village threatened by marine erosion. He is hosted by Mrs Rutherford, a middle-aged woman who once visited Africa and decorates her house with 'three ancient masks' that both fascinate and disgust the narrator.[13] The narrator was trained in Guyana by Professor Fenwick, a 'true Englishman' (p. 76), hence he refuses to be interpellated as an ex-colonial subject: 'I was no African ... I was a black West-Indian of African ancestry, but I was an engineer, trained in the science and technology of Great

Britain' (p. 14). As the novel progresses, however, colonial history surfaces as the narrator remembers growing up and working in Guyana and Mrs Rutherford recounts her time showering 'white benevolence' upon Africans when teaching local children (p. 73).

Gradually, readers become aware, even if he himself does not, that the narrator was trained not wisely but too well by Professor Fenwick. His passion for marine engineering has overtones of colonialism and slavery: he must 'shackle [the sea] with modern tools' and 'enslave it to [his] will and make it work for [him]' (p. 23); he commands 'hundreds of bare-backed coolies ... with a pharaoh's authority' when supervising Guyanese engineering projects (p. 29). If Britannia did indeed rule the waves in days of imperial glory, the narrator's presence is the ironic culmination of empire's civilising mission. While Mrs Rutherford's African masks are exhibits of primitive savagery, the village as a community depends on the Afro-Guyanese narrator to rescue it from the encroaching waves through an expensive feat of engineering that will cost 'a sum equal to the total industrial revenue' of the narrator's home country (p. 27). This astronomical expense may be due to Professor Fenwick, who engineered a 'dirty little secret' scheme to defraud the village council (p. 147). Disgusted, the narrator concludes that 'the Empire had ended and what was left was palsied decay, like the state of the cliff' upon which the village stands (p. 119). The country has 'drift[ed] into a deliberate unconsciousness' with 'any awakening being a jolt of patriotic sentiment' such as a nostalgia for heritage rather than a sober recognition of the past (p. 157).

The specular aspect of recognition is foregrounded in *A Harlot's Progress* (1999), a novel inspired by the appearance of a black boy in William Hogarth's eponymous engravings of a prostitute's life. This little boy, now an old man named Mungo, is interviewed by Mr Pringle of the Abolition Society, who wants Mungo's story to conform to the accepted genre of a slave narrative, 'a sober testimony that will appeal to the Christian charity of an enlightened citizenry' and 'bring great dividends' for the Abolition Society.[14] To achieve this, Pringle must transform Mungo from 'a ruined archive' by 'endowing' the black man with 'the gift of mind and eloquence' (p. 3).

But Mungo departs from the slave narrative's structure of suffering and uplift by dwelling on visually striking images that illustrate the contradictory strands of civilisation and slavery constituting British culture. Recounting his sexual abuse by the slaver Captain Thistlewood, Mungo describes himself as 'the still point from which a perfect arc could be drawn' (p. 108), because 'the Negro trade demands a precision, nay, a patriotism worthy of Newton's computations that have given England such a reputation for genius' (p. 111). Encountering musical notation for the first time, Mungo thinks of each round note as a 'bubble ... padlocked in its own line', which describes his own perpetual state of enslavement, 'padlocked and meeting death' and 'sing[ing]' his tale to Mr Pringle (p. 182). Dressed up as an exotic page to Lady Montague, Mungo is 'remodelled into a fantastic land creature, part Indian (his turban), part English coxcomb (his suit), part Chinese (his slippers)' (p. 207), and his occasional outbursts of violence fill the Lady 'not with fear but with perverse pleasure' (p. 22). From Mungo's point of view, slavery is no mere side effect but rather an integral part of Britain's scientific, artistic, and domestic life.

The visual representations of Mungo as an abject yet fantastic and threatening figure culminate in William Hogarth's prints, where he 'will forever be associated with the indecencies of merchants and whores' and seen as 'a pimp, pickpocket, purveyor of filth' (p. 273). Dabydeen's novel, therefore, attempts to re-cognise – to see and think again from other perspectives – the figure of the Negro as, in Mungo's words, 'ordinary man and woman, deserving of the ordinary human feeling that yet creates and recreates glimpses of new worlds' (p. 273). Mungo's circuitous story, told in fits and starts, is a formal counterpoint to the series of paintings and images depicting his progression from recalcitrant slave to ruined archive.

Historical Remapping

British fiction's post-imperial recognition offers not only a retelling of the relations between empire and colony but also a remapping of those historical connections and of Britain's own national and cultural past. Undoubtedly, the rise of the English heritage industry and a nostalgic British nationalism during Margaret Thatcher's tenure as prime minister created a milieu for the selective recollection and proud showcasing of Britain's history. The centripetal pull of the patriotic past, however, is matched by the centrifugal thrust of fictional narrative, in which the terrains of lived experience, scientific knowledge, and cultural tradition are mapped anew through oblique lines of transnational thought and movement. Fiction performs different kinds of historical remapping, as the very contours of the past are redrawn into a series of intersecting and conflicting stories rather than a convergent and triumphant tale of progress.

Bernardine Evaristo's semi-autobiographical *Lara* (expanded in 2009) maps anew both a family history and the lineaments of fiction. Evaristo's transformation of the genealogical novel through unrhymed couplets of free verse offers greater expressive latitude and descriptive plenitude. For example, Lara da Costa's Nigerian father, Taiwo, condenses the ambivalent relationship between Britain and its colonies during and after World War II in a few short lines: 'To a city burnt out from doodlebug/and Luftwaffe, they doffed cap, donned greatcoat,//dreams of prosperity, milk and gold, they were sold./Now the emperor's disowned sons/congregate in Commonwealth dance halls'.[15] Similarly, the novel telegraphs in spare but telling details the different reactions of Lara's grandparents when they discover their daughter Ellen is in love with a black man: 'Leslie cleared his throat, the throttle of a car starting./Taiwo looked curiously at this blank page in the story.//'I don't care where you're from, just look after my Ellen'./Peggy snapped a Digestive, Ellen restrained a giggle' (p. 74). These scenes, like many others, might have been drawn out over paragraphs, but Evaristo's versification brings a fluid intensity to Lara's narration, sketching out the conflicts in pithy and eloquent lines.

The lines of Lara's extended family tree illustrated at the beginning of the book suggest that the novel is also remapping a standard white-versus-black racial binary. *Lara* moves across time and space, from the nineteenth to the twentieth centuries and from England and Ireland to Nigeria and Brazil. We learn that Lara's maternal ancestors are of 'half-German' and 'half-Irish' stock rather than purebred English (p. 80); her father is descended from emancipated African slaves from Brazil who, upon migrating to Nigeria, identified themselves as 'prosperous, ambitious' Brazilians and set up their own enclave in Lagos (p. 180). Lara thus takes after her father, Taiwo, who in his youth 'dreamt of exploring the world these immigrants' to the port city of Lagos 'left to memory: Lebanon, Libya, China, India' (p. 168), for she, too, becomes a world traveller, searching for 'an image, a story' that can 'speak' her multivalent identity (p. 123). She provincialises Britain as an 'island, the 'Great' Tippexed out of it/tiny amid massive floating continents, the African one/an embryo within' her being (p. 188). This versified novel of family history and self-discovery thus traverses a familiar terrain of black British fiction but resists both a monopatriotic nationalism and a politics of racial essentialism.

Evaristo's *Soul Tourists* (2005) unfolds a similar travel narrative through the journey of Stanley Williams and Jessie O'Donnell out of Britain, across various European countries, and finally into the Middle East. Stanley is mourning his Jamaican father Clasford, whose death makes him realise that his London life is but 'pure emptiness' and his accountant job has him 'trapped in a steel and glass temple'.[16] On a whim he starts a romance and a road trip with the tempestuous Jessie, who resembles 'everyone's idea of a soul diva' and is driving as far as she can to Australia to find her estranged son (p. 32). The novel, written in a mixture of free verse and prose, unfolds the affection and tensions between Stanley and Jessie, who hold different views on what it means to be black in Britain: Stanley, schooled by his authoritarian father, inherits 'the immigrant mentality' of 'always work[ing] to the best of his ability' to assimilate (p. 45); Jessie, graduating from life's 'University of H K, Hard Knocks' (p. 81) identifies herself as 'a Yorkshire woman, and reet proud of it' rather than with a pan-African or Black Power identity (p. 198).

This romance-cum-travelogue, however, takes a historiographic twist as Stanley begins encountering ghosts of black personages from different time periods and countries such as Lucy the Dark Lady of Shakespeare's sonnets, Hannibal, Mary Jane Seacole, and Alexander Pushkin. Hearing their stories, Stanley realises that 'the journey ... with all its characters and happenings, had not only freed him from the bondage of his early years but also opened up the history of his country and continent to him' (p. 239). *Soul Tourists* remaps Europe's past by recounting the lives of important black men and women who have been marginalised or effaced from official histories of civilisation and progress. Furthermore, Stanley and Jessie's failed romance, described as being 'divided into segments of browns, the geometry of dis-membered planes' (p. 59), is a reminder that there is no one single or mono-lithic black identity, as the black presence is dispersed and variable across European time and space.

Our understanding of temporality and spatiality is challenged by Rebecca Stott's novels, which interweave elements of the romance, mystery, and ghost story with historical realism and scientific history. The narrator of *Ghostwalk* (2007), Lydia Brooke, agrees to ghost write an unfinished biog-raphy of Isaac Newton by a recently deceased Cambridge University his-torian, Elizabeth Vogelsang, who was also the mother of her former lover, Cameron Brown, a neuroscientist who has invented a new drug to treat men-tal illness. Elizabeth's notes reveal that Newton was part of a secretive net-work of alchemists and that his success was largely due to Ezekiel Foxcroft, a fellow Cambridge mathematician and alchemist. Foxcroft killed various people to assure Newton's ascendance and reputation as 'a national saint', whereas the former's own writings make him appear more like 'a character from a revenge tragedy'.[17] Foxcroft's ghost, restless and unappeased, begins haunting Lydia. As her research progresses and the novel unfolds, the seven-teenth and the twenty-first centuries gradually bleed into each other, 'not [with] a simple causal relationship but something as delicate as a web' or 'like a palimpsest – time layered upon time so that one buried layer leaks into the one above' (p. 12).

The remapping of the present through the past is further compounded when Cameron, whose new medicine can be weaponised as a nerve gas for the war on terror, turns out to be the leader of the Syndicate, a clandestine association of scientists and pharmaceutical businesses trying to obliterate opposing animal rights' groups by orchestrating increasingly violent attacks on their own people and then framing the activists. The novel draws parallels between Newton's older practice of alchemy and the Syndicate's modern scientific research: in the past 'all scientists were alchemists to some degree ... they all depended on networks' rather than 'work[ing] in isolation'; in the present, 'you need sponsorship to pay for the labs and equipment' and 'the sponsors have their own agendas' (p. 97). The convoluted relationships between Lydia's past and present, and between her research and romance, are explicated through quantum physics rather than linear causality: 'Moments in time become entangled in the same way that photons become entangled' (p. 195). The development of scientific knowledge, like that of a nation's history or a work of fiction, depends upon narrative twists and turns as well as compromises and contracts with external forces. Lydia's ghost writing, which requires 'making a new prism, a new way to see our world' (p. 89), parallels the novel's remapping of the conflicts and contingencies involved in any invocation of the past; bygones are rarely benign, nor is heritage always halcyon.

A similar set of entanglements appears in *The Coral Thief* (2009), in which medical student Daniel Connor arrives in Paris from Edinburgh in 1815 to study under the renowned French scientist Georges Cuvier, whose taxonomical work 'of fixed and vertical hierarchies' is opposed to Jean-Baptiste Lamarck's biological transformism and, later, Charles Darwin's theory of evolution.[18] The novel juxtaposes Daniel's entry into Parisian life with Napoleon's expulsion from France and exile to St. Helena, underscoring how Napoleon's imperial conquests allowed many scientific and cultural artefacts from around the world to be brought to Paris for viewing and research. Cuvier's declaration that scientific 'enlightenment must transcend national borders' has sinister connotations, for enlightenment is entangled with empire building and zoological taxonomies mirror rigid social structures (p. 251). Daniel's initial work involves dogsbodying for Cuvier; if he excels in such mundane tasks, Cuvier will deploy Daniel to spy on 'other natural philosophers in the British and Dutch colonies' for the sake of Cuvier's research and 'the reputation and honor of France' (pp. 188–9).

However, Daniel becomes romantically entangled with Lucienne Bernard, a transformist natural philosopher and leader of a band of master thieves, who enlists Daniel in their final heist: stealing a fabled diamond from Cuvier's collection. Lucienne's hold on Daniel is both amorous and scientific: he could no longer 'separate Cuvier's taxonomic questions from Lucienne's speculative ones. ... The facts would not stay as facts; they kept transforming into difficult questions about divergence and variation' (p. 113). Daniel's worldview gradually evolves to match Lucienne's, for whom 'nature is a great tangle ... like a garden in which everything lives on everything else' (p. 228). After successfully assisting Lucienne, Daniel 'had taken a step into the undergrowth, where branchings and forkings chanced along a different axis' (p. 275). Leaving France, Daniel practices medicine in London and 'challenges the old orthodoxies buried deep in the parlors and church halls of provincial England' by making 'small incremental changes' that 'might add up to something meaningful' (p. 276). *The Coral Thief* shows that evolution was already theorised by a range of established and itinerant scholars long before Darwin's *Origin of Species*. It interrogates two premises of the heritage industry: first, that solitary geniuses or individual nations are solely responsible for their own rise to scientific or geopolitical eminence; second, that a linear progression from past glory to present grandeur can be reconstructed from the preservation of storied artefacts and architecture. Instead, remapping historical knowledge shows how 'slow' and incremental it is, like 'a net or a web or a branching tree' (p. 278).

Tan Twang Eng's novels are a fine example of how British fiction branches out in a global moment: although Tan has never lived or worked in Britain, he sees Booker-Prize-winning author Kazuo Ishiguro as 'the gold standard' and inspiration for his own writing.[19] Tan adapts Ishiguro's idea that his celebrated novel *The Remains of the Day* (1989) is generically '*more English than English*' for his own resplendently exotic *The Gift of Rain* (2007).[20] The narrator-protagonist, Philip Hutton, of mixed British and Chinese parentage and growing up in British colonial Malaya during World War II, is 'too foreign for the Chinese, and too Oriental for the Europeans';[21] he befriends and becomes a student of a Japanese aikido master, Endo-san, who turns out to be a spy for the invading Japanese army and makes Philip his accomplice. Secretly saving as many people as he can from the Japanese military, Philip survives World War II but is both lionised and vilified by the local community, which views him either as a saviour or a turncoat. Having killed Endo-san at his request so he would not be tried for war crimes, Philip spends his twilight years alone in independent Malaysia.

The Gift of Rain focuses on an especially traumatic period in Malaysia's history that is formative of the country's decolonising struggle and postcolonial identity. However, the novel deflects the desires of readers hankering after historically realistic war stories with its lush, meditative passages, such as Philip's prefatory remarks about his youth: 'The one impression that remains now is of rain ... smearing the landscape into a Chinese brush painting. Sometimes it rained so often I wondered why the colors around me never faded' (p. 1). This introspective, occasionally ornate, style suggests that the novel is performing at a textual level what Endo-san describes in aikido terminology: 'You do not meet the force of the strike head-on ... you redirect the force and unbalance your opponent' (p. 52). Rather than offer a veritable facsimile of colonial Malaya and postcolonial Malaysia, Tan's novel remaps cultural history and reconfigures national identity with its emphasis on Philip Hutton's duality. As Philip's grandfather advises him, 'You are of two worlds. ... You have the ability to bring all of life's disparate elements into a cohesive whole' (p. 234). *The Gift of Rain* offers Philip Hutton's biracial hybridity as an alternative form or stance for the nation instead of the belligerent struggles against the Japanese military and British colonial regimes.

Instead of aikido, Japanese gardening is the central metaphor in Tan's second novel, *The Garden of Evening Mists* (2012), which focuses on the relationship between a Straits Chinese Malaysian woman, Teoh Yun Ling, and Nakamura Aritomo, once the gardener for the Japanese emperor and now living in self-imposed exile in Malaya's Cameron Highlands. Yun Ling, formerly imprisoned by the Japanese during World War II, retires from her post as a federal judge and returns to the highlands to restore Aritomo's garden and write her memoirs. The novel has hints of a sensational war story, as Aritomo is suspected to have links with Japan's 'Golden Lily' operation to loot the 'royal collections and national treasuries' of countries conquered during World War II for the imperial family and hide these treasures in the Malayan countryside from the victorious Allied troops.[22] But this aspect of the plot never resolves as the novel moves back and forth between present-day Malaysia and colonial Malaya during the years of the communist insurgency (1948–60) when Yun Ling was apprenticed to Aritomo, who eventually disappears while walking alone in the highlands.

Just as Aritomo uses the principle of borrowed scenery or *shakkei*, 'taking in elements and views from outside a garden and making them integral to his creation' (p. 34), so, too, the novel borrows the historical events of World War II and the Malayan Emergency to map out the affiliative ties between the diverse communities in Malaya that cannot be reduced to any narrow ethnic nationalism or racial superiority. Aritomo, as skilled in woodblock printing as he is in gardening, produces an illustration of 'what initially appear to be the veins of tealeaf' that 'transform into a detailed drawing' of the highlands, 'with Majuba House mazed into the lines' (p. 21). He gifts this to Magnus Pretorious, a Dutch Boer who owns Majuba House and a tea plantation in the highlands and who holds weekly parties attended by people from the different communities in Malaya. All of Aritomo's woodblock prints are 'views of Malaya' rather than those of Japan, indicating that he, together with Magnus and Yun Ling, has become part of Malaya's landscape and history (p. 115); Yun Ling's restoration of his garden 'will also be a living memory' of their friendship in a country where the Japanese are historically associated with cruelty and death (p. 347).

Although, as Aritomo says, 'every aspect of gardening is a form of deception' (p. 150), such deception can lead to truth and realisation, for the 'objects' in his garden 'signal to the traveller that he is entering another layer of his journey' and that he should 'stop and gather his thoughts' (p. 94). Herein lies a conceptualisation of literary form that relates back to Evaristo's and Amis's statements about form as both a seeking force and a rational undertaking with which this chapter began. The post-imperial recognition and historical remapping of the novels discussed here are not simply a by-product of Britain's postcolonial situation. In ways that not only represent but also possibly try to resolve what Raymond Williams called 'a problem of the relations between social (collective) modes and individual projects' (p. 187), these fictions imaginatively contribute to the sweep and salience of a global moment in which histories, communities, and narrative genres combine.

NOTES

1 Bernadine Evaristo, 'Q&A with Bernardine Evaristo'. Interview with Karen McCarthy. *Valparaiso Poetry Review* 4.2(2003).. Retrieved from: http://www.valpo.edu/vpr/evaristointerview.html (3 July 2014)
2 Amis, Martin. 'The Voice of the Lonely Crowd'. *The Guardian*, 31 May 2002. Retrieved from: http://www.theguardian.com/books/2002/jun/01/philosophy.society (3 July 2014)
3 Angela Leighton, *On Form: Poetry, Aestheticism, and the Legacy of a Word* (Oxford: Oxford University Press, 2007), p. 3.
4 Raymond Williams, *Marxism and Literature* (Oxford: Oxford University Press, 1977), p. 187. Hereafter cited parenthetically.
5 Weihsin Gui, *National Consciousness and Literary Cosmopolitics: Postcolonial Literature in a Global Moment* (Columbus: Ohio State University Press, 2013), p. 2.
6 See Andrej Gąsiorek, *Post-War British Fiction: Realism and After* (London: Edward Arnold, 1995).
7 See the thematic organisation of critical perspectives in collections from Richard Lane, Rod Mengham, and Philip Tew, eds, *Contemporary British Fiction* (Cambridge: Polity Press, 2003); and from James Acheson and Sara C. E. Ross, eds., *The Contemporary British Novel Since 1980* (Edinburgh: Edinburgh University Press, 2005).
8 Gayatri Chakravorty Spivak, 'Three Women's Texts and a Critique of Imperialism', *Critical Inquiry* 12 (1985), p. 249. See also Simon Gikandi, *Maps of Englishness: Writing Identity in the Culture of Colonialism* (New York: Columbia University Press, 1996).
9 Anthony Burgess, *The Long Day Wanes: A Malayan Trilogy* (New York: Norton, 1964), p. 36. Hereafter cited parenthetically.

10 Burgess, 'Conflict and Confluence', *Urgent Copy: Literary Studies* (London: Jonathan Cape, 1968), p. 271.

11 Kok Liang Lee, *London Does Not Belong to Me* (Petaling Jaya: Maya Press, 2003), p. 9. Hereafter cited parenthetically.

12 Spivak, 'Three Women's Texts', p. 249

13 David Dabydeen, *Disappearance* (Leeds: Peepal Tree, 2005), p. 15. Hereafter cited parenthetically.

14 Dabydeen, *A Harlot's Progress* (London: Vintage, 2000), pp. 34, 3. Hereafter cited parenthetically.

15 Bernardine Evaristo, *Lara* (London: Bloodaxe Books, 2000), p. 22. Hereafter cited parenthetically.

16 Evaristo, *Soul Tourists* (London: Hamish Hamilton, 2005), pp. 11, 46. Hereafter cited parenthetically.

17 Rebecca Stott, *Ghostwalk* (New York: Spiegal and Grau, 2008), pp. 98, 135. Hereafter cited parenthetically.

18 Stott, *The Coral Thief* (New York: Spiegal and Grau, 2010), p. 54. Hereafter cited parenthetically.

19 Michelle Li Peng Tam, 'Labour of Love', *The Star Online* 14 September 2012. Web. Accessed 6 October 2014.

20 Allan Vorda and Kim Herzinger, 'Stuck on the Margins: An Interview with Kazuo Ishiguro', in *Face to Face: Interviews with Contemporary Novelists*, ed. Allan Vorda (Houston: Rice University Press, 1993), p. 14.

21 Twan Eng Tan, *The Gift of Rain* (New York: Weinstein Books, 2008), p. 96. Hereafter cited parenthetically.

22 Tan, *The Garden of Evening Mists* (Newcastle upon Tyne: Myrmidon Books, 2012), p. 315. Hereafter cited parenthetically.

FURTHER READING

General Studies and Surveys

Acheson, James, and Sara C. E. Ross, eds. *The Contemporary British Novel since 1980*. Edinburgh: Edinburgh University Press, 2005.

Bentley, Nick. *Contemporary British Fiction*. Edinburgh: Edinburgh University Press, 2008.

Boxall, Peter. *Twenty-First-Century Fiction: A Critical Introduction*. Cambridge: Cambridge University Press, 2013.

Bradbury, Malcolm. *The Novel Today*, second ed. London: Fontana, 1990.

The Modern British Novel, 1878–2001, revised ed. London: Penguin, 2001.

Brannigan, John. *Orwell to the Present: Literature in England 1945–2000*. Basingstoke: Palgrave Macmillan, 2003.

Caserio, Robert L., ed. *The Cambridge Companion to the Twentieth-Century English Novel*. Cambridge: Cambridge University Press, 2009.

Childs, Peter. *Contemporary Novelists: British Fiction Since 1970*. Basingstoke and New York: Palgrave Macmillan, 2005.

Connor, Steven. *The English Novel in History, 1950–95*. London: Routledge, 1996.

Eaglestone, Robert. *Contemporary Fiction: A Very Short Introduction*. Oxford: Oxford University Press, 2013.

English, James F., ed. *A Concise Companion to Contemporary British Fiction*. Oxford: Blackwell, 2006.

Head, Dominic. *The Cambridge Introduction to Modern British Fiction, 1950–2000*. Cambridge: Cambridge University Press, 2002.

The State of the Novel: Britain and Beyond. Oxford: Wiley-Blackwell, 2008.

James, David, ed. *The Legacies of Modernism: Historicising Postwar and Contemporary Fiction*. Cambridge: Cambridge University Press, 2012.

King, Bruce. *The Oxford English Literary History, Vol. XIII: 1948–2000: The Internationalization of the English Novel*. Oxford: Oxford University Press, 2004.

Lane, Richard J., Rod Mengham, and Phillip Tew, eds. *Contemporary British Fiction*. Cambridge, UK: Polity, 2003.

Leader, Zachary, ed. *On Modern British Fiction*. Oxford: Oxford University Press, 2002.

Matz, Jesse. *The Modern Novel: A Short Introduction*. Oxford: Blackwell, 2004.

McIlvanney, Liam, and Ray Ryan, eds. *The Good of the Novel.* London: Faber and Faber, 2011.
Mengham, Rod, ed. *An Introduction to Contemporary Fiction: International Writing in English Since 1970.* Cambridge, UK: Polity Press, 1999.
Mengham, Rod, and Phillip Tew, eds. *British Fiction Today.* London: Continuum, 2006.
Parrinder, Patrick, Andrew Nash, and Nicola Wilson, eds. *New Directions in the History of the Novel.* Basingstoke: Palgrave Macmillan, 2014.
Shaffer, Brian W., ed. *A Companion to the British and Irish Novel, 1945–2000.* Oxford: Blackwell, 2005.
Squires, Claire. *Marketing Literature: The Making of Contemporary Writing in Britain.* Basingstoke: Palgrave Macmillan, 2007.
Stevenson, Randall. *The Oxford English Literary History, Vol. XII: 1960–2000: The Last of England?* Oxford: Oxford University Press, 2004.
Taylor, D. J. *After the War: The Novel and English Society since 1945.* London: Chatto and Windus, 1993.
Tew, Philip. *The Contemporary British Novel.* London: Continuum, 2004.
Waugh, Patricia. *Harvest of the Sixties: English Literature and Its Background, 1960–1990.* Oxford: Oxford University Press, 1995.

Interviews

Chambers, Claire. *British Muslim Fictions: Interviews with Contemporary Writers.* Basingstoke: Palgrave Macmillan, 2012.
Guignery, Vanessa. *Novelists in the New Millennium: Conversations with Writers.* Basingstoke: Palgrave Macmillan, 2012.
Monteith, Sharon, Jenny Newman, and Pat Wheeler, eds. *Contemporary British and Irish Fiction: An Introduction Through Interviews.* London: Hodder Arnold, 2004.
Nasta, Susheila, ed. *Writing Across Worlds: Contemporary Writers Talk.* London: Routledge, 2004.
Tew, Philip, Fiona Tolan, and Leigh Wilson, eds. *Writers Talk: Conversations with Contemporary Novelists.* London: Continuum, 2008.

See also the range of British authors included in the *Literary Conversations Series* from University Press of Mississippi (general editor: Peggy Whitman Prenshaw), and the interviews conducted for volumes on individual novelists in the *Contemporary Critical Perspectives* series from Bloomsbury (general editors: Jeannette Baxter, Sebastian Groes, and Sean Matthews).

Postmodernism in British Writing

Baker, Stephen. *The Fiction of Postmodernity.* Edinburgh: Edinburgh University Press, 2000.
Connor, Steven, ed. *The Cambridge Companion to Postmodernsim.* Cambridge: Cambridge University Press, 2004.

d'Haen, Theo, and Johannes Bertens, eds. *British Postmodern Fiction*. Amsterdam: Rodopi, 2003.

Gasiorek, Andrzej. 'Postmodernisms of English Fiction', in *The Cambridge Companion to the Twentieth-Century English Novel*, ed. Robert L. Caserio. Cambridge: Cambridge University Press, 2009. 192–209.

Lee, Alison. *Realism and Power: Postmodern British Fiction*. London: Routledge, 1989.

Nicol, Bran. *The Cambridge Introduction to Postmodern Fiction*. Cambridge: Cambridge University Press, 2009.

Platt, Len, and Sara Upstone, eds. *Postmodern Literature and Race*. New York: Cambridge University Press, 2015.

Stevenson, Randall. 'Postmodernism and Contemporary Fiction in Britain', in *Postmodernism and Contemporary Fiction*, ed. Edmund J. Smyth. London: Batsford, 1991. 19–35.

Waugh, Patricia. *Feminine Fictions: Revisiting the Postmodern*. London: Routledge, 1989.

Metafiction: The Theory and Practice of Self-Conscious Fiction. London: Routledge, 1984.

Wells, Lynn. *Allegories of Telling: Self-Referential Narrative in Contemporary British Fiction*. Amsterdam: Rodopi, 2003.

Literary Experimentation: Aesthetics, Ethics, and Politics

Boxall, Peter. *Since Beckett: Contemporary Writing in the Wake of Modernism*. London: Continuum, 2009.

Bray, Joe, Alison Gibbons, and Brian McHale, eds. *The Routledge Companion to Experimental Literature*. New York: Routledge, 2014.

Detloff, Madelyn. *The Persistence of Modernism: Loss and Mourning in the Twentieth Century*. Cambridge: Cambridge University Press, 2009.

Gasiorek, Andrzej. *Postwar British Fiction: Realism and After*. London: Arnold, 1995.

Gasiorek, Andrzej, and David James, eds. *Postmillennial Commitments*, special issue of *Contemporary Literature*, 53.4 (Winter 2012): 609–905.

Hale, Dorothy J. *Social Formalism: The Novel in Theory from Henry James to the Present*. Stanford: Stanford University Press, 1998.

James, David. *Modernist Futures: Innovation and Inheritance in the Contemporary Novel*. Cambridge: Cambridge University Press, 2012.

'"Style is Morality"? Aesthetics and Politics in the Amis Era', *Textual Practice*, 26.1 (February 2012): 11–25.

James, David, and Urmila Seshagiri. 'Metamodernism: Narratives of Revolution and Continuity', *PMLA*, 129.1 (January 2014): 87–100.

Jordan, Julia. *Chance and the Modern British Novel: From Henry Green to Iris Murdoch*. London: Continuum, 2010.

Jordan, Julia, and Martin Ryle, eds. *B. S. Johnson and Postwar Literature: Possibilities of the Avant-Garde*. Basingstoke: Palgrave Macmillan, 2014.

MacKay, Marina, and Lyndsey Stonebridge, eds. *British Fiction after Modernism*. Basingstoke: Palgrave Macmillan, 2007.

Marcus, Laura. 'The Legacies of Modernism', in *The Cambridge Companion to the Modernist Novel*, ed. Morag Shiach. Cambridge: Cambridge University Press, 2007, 82–97.

Marx, John. *Geopolitics and the Anglophone Novel, 1890–2011*. Cambridge: Cambridge University Press, 2012.

Seshagiri, Urmila. 'Making it New: Persephone Books and the Modernist Project', *Modern Fiction Studies* 59.2 (Summer 2013): 241–87.

Su, John J. *Imagination and the Contemporary Novel*. Cambridge: Cambridge University Press, 2011.

Waddell, Nathan, and Alice Reeve-Tucker, eds. *Utopianism, Modernism, and Literature in the Twentieth Century*. Basingstoke: Palgrave Macmillan, 2013.

Walkowitz, Rebecca L. *Born Translated: The Contemporary Novel in an Age of World Literature*. New York: Columbia University Press, 2015.

Nationhood, Cosmopolitanism, and Postcoloniality

Ahmed, Rehana. *Writing British Muslims: Religion, Class and Multiculturalism*. Manchester: Manchester University Press, 2015.

Arana, R. Victoria, and Lauri Ramey, eds. *Black British Writing*. Basingstoke: Palgrave Macmillan, 2004.

Baucom, Ian. *Out of Place: Englishness, Empire, and the Locations of Identity*. Princeton: Princeton University Press, 1999.

Bell, Ian A., ed. *Peripheral Visions: Images of Nationhood in Contemporary British Fiction*. Cardiff: University of Wales Press, 1995.

Boehmer, Elleke. *Colonial and Postcolonial Literature: Migrant Metaphors*. Oxford: Oxford University Press, 1995.

Bohata, Kirsti. *Postcolonialism Revisited: Writing Wales in English*. Cardiff: University of Wales Press, 2004.

Clingman, Stephen. *The Grammar of Identity: Transnational Fiction and the Nature of the Boundary*. Oxford: Oxford University Press, 2009.

Craig, Cairns. *The Modern Scottish Novel: Narrative and the National Imagination*. Edinburgh: Edinburgh University Press, 1999.

Finney, Brian. *English Fiction Since 1984: Narrating a Nation*. Basingstoke: Palgrave Macmillan, 2006.

Fraser, Robert. *Lifting the Sentence: A Poetics of Postcolonial Fiction*. Manchester: Manchester University Press, 2000.

Gikandi, Simon. *Maps of Englishness: Writing Identity in the Culture of Colonialism*. New York: Columbia University Press, 1996.

Gilmour, Rachael, and Bill Schwarz, eds. *End of Empire and the English Novel Since 1945*. Manchester: Manchester University Press, 2011.

Gilroy, Paul. *There Ain't No Black in the Union Jack: The Cultural Politics of Race and Nation*. London: Hutchinson, 1987.

Gui, Weihsin. *National Consciousness and Literary Cosmopolitics: Postcolonial Literature in a Global Moment*. Columbus: Ohio State University Press, 2013.

Gunning, Dave. *Race and Antiracism in Black British and British Asian Literature*. Liverpool: Liverpool University Press, 2010.

Hart, Matthew, and Jim Hansen, eds. *Contemporary Literature and the State*, special issue of *Contemporary Literature* 49.4 (Winter 2008): 491–718.

Kalliney, Peter J. *Commonwealth of Letters: British Literary Culture and the Emergence of Postcolonial Aesthetics.* New York: Oxford University Press, 2013.
Lassner, Phyllis. *Colonial Strangers: Women Writing the End of the British Empire.* New Brunswick: Rutgers University Press, 2004.
Lazarus, Neil. *The Postcolonial Unconscious.* Cambridge: Cambridge University Press, 2011.
Lee, Robert A., ed. *Other Britain, Other British: Contemporary Multicultural Fiction.* London: Pluto, 1995.
McCulloch, Fiona. *Cosmopolitanism in Contemporary British Fiction: Imagined Identities.* Basingstoke: Palgrave Macmillan, 2012.
McLeod, John. *Postcolonial London: Rewriting the Metropolis.* London: Routledge, 2003.
Nasta, Susheila. *Home Truths: Fictions of the South Asian Diaspora in Britain.* Basingstoke: Palgrave Macmillan, 2001.
Parrinder, Patrick. *Nation and Novel: The English Novel from Its Origins to the Present Day.* Oxford: Oxford University Press, 2006.
Phillips, Caryl. *A New World Order: Selected Essays.* London: Vintage, 2002.
Colour Me English. London: Harvill Secker, 2011.
Procter, James. *Dwelling Places: Postwar Black British Writing.* Manchester: Manchester University Press, 2003.
Robbins, Bruce. *Feeling Global: Internationalism in Distress.* New York: New York University Press, 1999.
Sauerberg, Lars Ole. *Intercultural Voices in Contemporary British Literature.* Basingstoke: Palgrave Macmillan, 2001.
Upstone, Sara. *British Asian Fiction: Twenty-First-Century Voices.* Manchester: Manchester University Press, 2010.
Walkowitz, Rebecca L. *Cosmopolitan Style: Modernism Beyond the Nation.* New York: Columbia University Press, 2006.
'The Post-Consensus Novel: Minority Culture, Multiculturalism and Transnational Comparison', in *The Cambridge Companion to the Twentieth-Century English Novel*, ed. Robert L. Caserio. Cambridge: Cambridge University Press, 2009. 223–37.
Wallace, Gavin, and Randall Stevenson, eds. *The Scottish Novel Since the Seventies: New Visions, Old Dreams.* Edinburgh: Edinburgh University Press, 1993.

Gender and Sexuality

Anderson, Linda, ed. *Plotting Change: Contemporary Women's Fiction.* London: Hodder Arnold, 1990.
Armitt, Lucie. *Contemporary Women's Fiction and the Fantastic.* Basingstoke: Macmillan, 2000.
Barrett, Michèle. *Imagination in Theory: Essays on Writing and Culture.* Cambridge: Polity, 1998.
DuPlessis, Rachel Blau. *Writing Beyond the Ending: Narrative Strategies of Twentieth-Century Women Writers.* Bloomington: Indiana University Press, 1985.
Carroll, Rachel. *Rereading Heterosexuality: Feminism, Queer Theory and Contemporary Fiction.* Edinburgh: Edinburgh University Press, 2012.

Duncker, Patricia. *Sisters and Strangers: An Introduction to Contemporary Feminist Fiction*. Oxford: Blackwell, 1992.
Friedman, Susan Stanford. *Mappings: Feminism and the Cultural Geographies of Encounter*. Princeton: Princeton University Press, 1998.
Harrias, Andrea L. *Other Sexes: Rewriting Difference from Woolf to Winterson*. New York: State University of New York Press, 2000.
Jeffrey-Poulter, S. *Peers, Queers and Commons: The Struggle for Gay Law Reform from 1950 to the Present*. London: Routledge, 1991.
Knights, Ben. *Writing Masculinities in Twentieth Century Fiction*. New York: St Martin's Press, 1999.
Lea, Daniel, and Berthold Schoene, eds. *Posting the Male: Masculinities in Post-War and Contemporary British Literature*. Amsterdam; New York: Rodopi, 2003.
Palmer, Paulina. *Lesbian Gothic: Transgressive Fictions*. London: Continuum, 1999.
Smith, Patricia. *Lesbian Panic: Homoeroticism in Modern British Women's Fiction*. New York: Columbia University Press, 1997.
Wallace, Diana. *The Woman's Historical Novel: British Women Writers, 1900–2000*. Basingstoke: Palgrave Macmillan, 2005.
Werlock, Abby H. P., ed. *British Women Writing Fiction*. Tuscaloosa: University of Alabama Press, 2000.

History, Memory, and Temporality

Boccardi, Mariadele. *The Contemporary British Historical Novel: Representation, Nation, Empire*. Basingstoke: Palgrave Macmillan, 2009.
Boxall, Peter. 'Late: Fictional Time in the Twenty-First Century', *Contemporary Literature* 53.4 (Winter 2012): 681–712.
Crosthwaite, Paul. *Trauma, Postmodernism, and the Aftermath of World War II*. Basingstoke: Palgrave Macmillan, 2009.
Currie, Mark. *About Time: Narrative, Fiction and the Philosophy of Time*. Edinburgh: Edinburgh University Press, 2010.
  The Unexpected: Narrative Temporality and the Philosophy of Surprise. Edinburgh: Edinburgh University Press, 2013.
Eaglestone, Robert. *The Holocaust and the Postmodern*. Oxford: Oxford University Press, 2004.
Higdon, David Leon. *Shadows of the Past in Contemporary British Fiction*. London: Macmillan, 1984.
Holmes, Frederick. *The Historical Imagination: Postmodernism and the Treatment of the Past in Contemporary British Fiction*. Victoria: University of Victoria Press, 1997.
Keen, Suzanne. *Romances of the Archive in Contemporary British Fiction*. Toronto: University of Toronto Press, 2001.
Middleton, Peter, and Tim Woods. *Literatures of Memory: History, Time and Space in Postwar Writing*. Manchester: Manchester University Press, 2000.
Onega, Susana, and Jean-Michel P. Ganteau, eds. *Ethics and Trauma in Contemporary British Fiction*. Amsterdam: Rodopi, 2011.
  eds. *Trauma and Romance in Contemporary Literature*. London: Routledge, 2013.

Robinson, Alan. *Narrating the Past: Historiography, Memory and the Contemporary Novel*. Basingstoke: Macmillan, 2011.

Su, John J. *Ethics and Nostalgia in the Contemporary Novel*. Cambridge: Cambridge University Press, 2005.

Literary Geographies and the Environmental Imagination

Alexander, Neal, and James Moran, eds. *Regional Modernisms*. Edinburgh: Edinburgh University Press, 2013.

Ball, John Clement. *Imagining London: Postcolonial Fiction and the Transnational Metropolis*. Toronto: University of Toronto Press, 2004.

Bottalico, Michele, Maria Teresa Chialant, and Eleonora Rao, eds. *Literary Landscapes, Landscapes in Literature*. Rome: Carocci, 2007.

Bracke, Astrid. *Ecocriticism and the Contemporary British Novel*. Radboud: University Nijmegen Press, 2012.

Buell, Lawrence. *The Future of Environmental Criticism: Environmental Crisis and Literary Imagination*. Oxford: Blackwell, 2005.

Bulson, Eric. *Novels, Maps, Modernity: The Spatial Imagination, 1850–2000*. London: Routledge, 2009.

Burden, Robert, and Stephan Kohl, eds. *Landscape and Englishness*. Amsterdam: Rodopi, 2006.

Champion, A. G., and A. R. Townsend. *Contemporary Britain: A Geographical Perspective*. London: Edward Arnold, 1990.

Colombino, Laura. *Spatial Politics in Contemporary London Literature: Writing Architecture and the Body*. London: Routledge, 2013.

De Lange, Attie, Gail Fincham, Jeremy Hawthorn, and Jakob Lothe, eds. *Literary Landscapes: From Modernism to Postcolonialism*. New York: Palgrave Macmillan, 2008.

Guignery, Vanessa, ed. *Re-Mapping London: Visions of the Metropolis in the Contemporary Novel in English*. Paris: Éditions Publibook Université, 2008.

Head, Dominic. 'The Politics of Nostalgia in the Rural English Novel', in *Literary Politics: The Politics of Literature and the Literature of Politics*, eds. Deborah Philips and Katy Shaw. London: Palgrave Macmillan, 2013. 117–36

Heise, Ursula K. *Sense of Place and Sense of Planet: The Environmental Imagination of the Global*. New York: Oxford University Press, 2008.

James, David. *Contemporary British Fiction and the Artistry of Space: Style, Landscape, Perception*. London: Continuum, 2008.

Kalliney, Peter. *Cities of Affluence and Anger: A Literary Geography of Modern Englishness*. Charlottesville: University of Virginia Press, 2006.

Upstone, Sara. *Spatial Politics in the Postcolonial Novel*. Aldershot: Ashgate, 2009.

INDEX

The Cambridge Companions to...

AUTHORS

Edward Albee edited by Stephen J. Bottoms

Margaret Atwood edited by Coral Ann Howells

W. H. Auden edited by Stan Smith

Jane Austen edited by Edward Copeland and Juliet McMaster (second edition)

Beckett edited by John Pilling

Bede edited by Scott DeGregorio

Aphra Behn edited by Derek Hughes and Janet Todd

Walter Benjamin edited by David S. Ferris

William Blake edited by Morris Eaves

Jorge Luis Borges edited by Edwin Williamson

Brecht edited by Peter Thomson and Glendyr Sacks (second edition)

The Brontës edited by Heather Glen

Bunyan edited by Anne Dunan-Page

Frances Burney edited by Peter Sabor

Byron edited by Drummond Bone

Albert Camus edited by Edward J. Hughes

Willa Cather edited by Marilee Lindemann

Cervantes edited by Anthony J. Cascardi

Chaucer edited by Piero Boitani and Jill Mann (second edition)

Chekhov edited by Vera Gottlieb and Paul Allain

Kate Chopin edited by Janet Beer

Caryl Churchill edited by Elaine Aston and Elin Diamond

Cicero edited by Catherine Steel

Coleridge edited by Lucy Newlyn

Wilkie Collins edited by Jenny Bourne Taylor

Joseph Conrad edited by J. H. Stape

H. D. edited by Nephie J. Christodoulides and Polina Mackay

Dante edited by Rachel Jacoff (second edition)

Daniel Defoe edited by John Richetti

Don DeLillo edited by John N. Duvall

Charles Dickens edited by John O. Jordan

Emily Dickinson edited by Wendy Martin

John Donne edited by Achsah Guibbory

Dostoevskii edited by W. J. Leatherbarrow

Theodore Dreiser edited by Leonard Cassuto and Claire Virginia Eby

John Dryden edited by Steven N. Zwicker

W. E. B. Du Bois edited by Shamoon Zamir

George Eliot edited by George Levine

T. S. Eliot edited by A. David Moody

Ralph Ellison edited by Ross Posnock

Ralph Waldo Emerson edited by Joel Porte and Saundra Morris

William Faulkner edited by Philip M. Weinstein

Henry Fielding edited by Claude Rawson

F. Scott Fitzgerald edited by Ruth Prigozy

Flaubert edited by Timothy Unwin

E. M. Forster edited by David Bradshaw

Benjamin Franklin edited by Carla Mulford

Brian Friel edited by Anthony Roche

Robert Frost edited by Robert Faggen

Gabriel García Márquez edited by Philip Swanson

Elizabeth Gaskell edited by Jill L. Matus

Goethe edited by Lesley Sharpe

Günter Grass edited by Stuart Taberner

Thomas Hardy edited by Dale Kramer

David Hare edited by Richard Boon

Nathaniel Hawthorne edited by Richard Millington

Seamus Heaney edited by Bernard O'Donoghue

Ernest Hemingway edited by Scott Donaldson

Homer edited by Robert Fowler

Horace edited by Stephen Harrison

Ted Hughes edited by Terry Gifford

Ibsen edited by James McFarlane

Henry James edited by Jonathan Freedman

Samuel Johnson edited by Greg Clingham

Ben Jonson edited by Richard Harp and Stanley Stewart

James Joyce edited by Derek Attridge (second edition)

Kafka edited by Julian Preece

Keats edited by Susan J. Wolfson

Rudyard Kipling edited by Howard J. Booth

Lacan edited by Jean-Michel Rabaté

D. H. Lawrence edited by Anne Fernihough

Primo Levi edited by Robert Gordon